REINVENTING
Richard Nixon

CultureAmerica

Karal Ann Marling
Erika Doss
Series Editors

REINVENTING
Richard Nixon

A Cultural History of an American Obsession

DANIEL FRICK

UNIVERSITY PRESS OF KANSAS

Published by the
University Press of
Kansas (Lawrence,
Kansas 66045), which
was organized by the
Kansas Board of Regents
and is operated and
funded by Emporia State
University, Fort Hays
State University, Kansas
State University, Pittsburg
State University, the
University of Kansas, and
Wichita State University

Library of Congress Cataloging-in-Publication Data

Frick, Daniel E.
   Reinventing Richard Nixon : a cultural history of an
American obsession / Daniel Frick.
      p.   cm. — (CultureAmerica)
   Includes bibliographical references and index.
   ISBN 978-0-7006-1599-5 (cloth : alk. paper)
   1. Nixon, Richard M. (Richard Milhous),
1913–1994—Public opinion. 2. Presidents—United
States—Biography. 3. National characteristics,
American. 4. Culture conflict—United States.
5. Political culture—United States—History—20th
century. 6. Public opinion—United States—History—
20th century. 7. Popular culture—United States—
History—20th century. 8. United States—Politics and
government—1969–1974. 9. United States—Politics
and government—1945–1989. I. Title.
   E856.F75 2008
   973.924—dc22   2008020141

British Library Cataloguing-in-Publication Data is
available.

Printed in the United States of America
10 9 8 7 6 5 4 3 2 1

For Tamara, Eleanor, and Evelyn

CONTENTS

ABBREVIATIONS USED IN THE TEXT

RN   Nixon, *RN: Memoirs of Richard Nixon*

SC   Nixon, *Six Crises*

Best   Gore Vidal, *The Best Man*

Services *Services for Richard Nixon, 37th President of the United States, Wednesday, April 27th, 1994*

ACKNOWLEDGMENTS

I've spent more than twenty years reinventing Richard Nixon. My brother, David Frick, started it all back in the mid-1980s when he wondered aloud whether there was a dissertation topic to be found in Richard Nixon's appearance in Philip Roth's *Our Gang* and Robert Coover's *The Public Burning*. His musing was the first in a long series of debts I have incurred while working on this project.

From the beginning, I have benefited from generous institutional support. In 1987, as I was starting my research, the American Studies Program at Indiana University granted me an Associate Instructorship, an award that permitted me to teach my first course on Nixon as a cultural icon. More recently, Franklin and Marshall College's Committee on Grants provided me with funds to support a 2002 research trip to the Richard Nixon Library and Birthplace in Yorba Linda, California, and in 2005 to help offset the costs of obtaining copyright permissions for the images I planned to use in this book. That same year, the committee also permitted me to work with an exceptional student, Justin B. Hopkins, as part of the Hackman Summer Scholars Program. Doing his research on copyright law, Justin also helped me in identifying the holders of the rights to nearly every one of the cartoons and graphics that appear in this book. He proved an indefatigable detective, tracking down leads in cases where the trail seemed to have gone cold years ago. Kent Trachte, the dean of the college at Franklin and Marshall, supplemented the research and travel funds available to me, ensuring that I did not have to choose between working on this project and keeping current in my professional development as director of the college's Writing Center. And finally, in 2007, as this project was reaching completion—and just at the moment I most needed help—Dean Trachte and Franklin and Marshall College provost Ann Steiner granted me the time to concentrate on moving the book through the production process quickly, and Provost Steiner underwrote my purchasing the reprint rights for all the remaining images. I am proud to be a part of Franklin and Marshall College, a fine liberal arts institution that values and supports the research of its teacher/scholars.

During my research, I benefited from the help of many excellent librarians and archivists. Particularly, I wish to acknowledge Stephen E. Greene of the Nixon Presidential Materials staff of the National Archives and Records Administration for his orientation to the Nixon audiovisual collection. During my June 2003 research visit to the Nixon Library, Susan Naulty, the archivist at that time, and her assistant Beverly Lindy proved to be cheerful and invaluable guides to the library's collections of editorial cartoons. Meanwhile, back home, Mary Shelly, Franklin and Marshall College's ever-resourceful interlibrary loan librarian, always found a way to get me the books, articles, and microfilm I needed. Librarians Scott Vine, Christopher Raab, and Michael Lear worked hard to help me create digitized versions of several of the images that appear in chapter 5.

Especially important to me have been the numerous people who have read portions of the manuscript and offered me constructive criticism. Special thanks goes to my dissertation committee, Patrick Brantlinger, James Justus, and Christoph Lohman, and particularly to my director, Paul John Eakin, who pushed me to think more deeply about this topic. His prodding "so what?" questions put their indelible mark on my dissertation, and on this work as well. While at Indiana University, I received helpful readers' comments from David Nordloh and David Smith. At various stages of the revision process, Tamara Goeglein, John Parsley, Jonathan Strout, and Michael Deeter read chapters-in-progress and offered highly constructive criticism. Ruth Frick, Robert Battistini, Kerry Sherin Wright, and Ellen Barley also shared their perceptive advice. As director of Franklin and Marshall's Writing Center, I have the honor of working with the best students the college has to offer. My thanks to all of them, but especially to Amanda Blewitt, Joan Brumbaugh, Pam Eisenberg, Laura Michaels, Lauren Neal, and Audrey Stokes for their commentary.

Generous friends and colleagues encouraged me to keep working and stay focused. I have been extremely lucky to know Joel Martin and Alison Kibler. Without their incisive readers' comments and unflagging moral support, I never would have finished this book. In addition, Joel and Lisa Martin always proved gracious hosts during my research trips to the Nixon Library. David Schuyler deserves particular mention. At a time when I had stopped working on this project, David refused to let me give up, making sure that, during her spring 2001 visit to Franklin and Marshall, Karal Ann Marling and I would have a chance to talk about all things Nixon (and Disney too!). Soon after that meeting, I was writing again.

Through the review process at the University Press of Kansas, I am indebted to many insightful readers—particularly Melvin Small, Karal Ann Marling, and Erika Doss. Thank you for your enthusiastic support and spot-on editorial advice. Special appreciation and praise are due to my editors: first, to Nancy Scott Jackson, who supported me through the long, and slow, revision process, and, then, to Kalyani Fernando and Jennifer Dropkin, who have been great guides in helping me bring this book to publication.

Through it all, I have had the encouragement of a tremendously supportive family. First, to Arlene "Cookie" Faust, who is as dear as family, my thanks for your assisting me with the faxes, overnight letters, phone calls, and disbursement vouchers that marked the book's production process. My brothers-in-law, Tom Goeglein, Tim Goeglein, and Ted Goeglein, have all helped me along the way, from offering legal advice, to a spare bedroom to call home while on research trips to Washington, D.C., to timely help in wrapping up the last few outstanding copyright permissions. To my in-laws, Stanley and Shirley Goeglein, to my sister, Susan, and to my parents, Ivan and Ruth Frick, thank you for your love and support through the years. Finally, to my own family, my daughters, Eleanor and Evelyn, and my wife, Tamara Goeglein, I acknowledge my greatest debts. For your understanding when Richard Nixon occupied my thoughts a little too much, for your enthusiastic cheerleading of this book, and, above all, for the laughter and joy of our life together, reminding me of what is most important, I am forever grateful.

RICHARD NIXON AND THE MANY FACES OF A REPRESENTATIVE AMERICAN

In death, Richard Nixon seemed ready, at last, to fulfill a twenty-five-year-old promise. "Bring Us Together Again," a pledge taken from a campaign placard Nixon saw during a 1968 whistle-stop train tour through northwest Ohio, was supposed to become the guiding principle for the Nixon administration—or so the new president-elect told the nation the morning after the election. But little healing took place in the years that followed. After five and a half tumultuous years, which included the secret bombing and subsequent invasion of Cambodia, the killing of college students at Kent State University and Jackson State College, the burglary of Daniel Ellsberg's psychiatrist's office by White House operatives, the bugging of the Democratic National Headquarters, the firing of special prosecutor Archibald Cox, and the erasure of eighteen and one-half minutes from one of his secret tapes, Nixon left the White House with the nation just as divided as it had been—if not more so. In fact, the only thing that seemed to unite people in August 1974 was the desire to be rid of Richard Nixon once and for all. The Gallup Poll, taken in the week before the resignation, found that 66 percent of respondents disapproved of the job Nixon was doing as president (46 percent of them strongly), and 65 percent favored his impeachment.[1]

But, on Wednesday, April 27, 1994, during a somber ninety-minute state funeral, the atmosphere was different. Amazingly enough, Nixon appeared to have finally brought the United States together. In part, the possibility of national healing was because a state funeral honoring the only president to ever resign from office was happening at all. The response to Nixon's death would have been entirely different had he died—as he nearly had—following surgery for phlebitis in the fall of 1974. For Richard Nixon, then, living long was the best revenge. Enough time had passed that the unimaginable had become the possible. What is more, over twenty years had passed since the last funeral for an ex-president,

Lyndon Johnson's in January 1973. As an unprecedented story for an entire generation of reporters, Nixon's ceremony garnered fascinated attention—even though South Africa's first biracial election was a competing news item.[2] That the service immediately followed the major networks' national news broadcasts in the eastern and central time zones ensured a sizable audience. Even more significant, the saturation coverage of the ceremony created the aura of an entire nation tuned in to the events at Yorba Linda. Television news existed in a new, vastly expanded, world since LBJ's death. Nixon's funeral was carried live on no less than six national television networks: ABC, CBS, and NBC were joined by PBS, CNN, and C-SPAN.

While these factors guaranteed that Nixon's service would be a major news story, the dramatic structures of this state funeral made certain that the nation would see a tale of reconciliation. The platform on which the ceremony took place was constructed in the Richard Nixon Library and Birthplace's parking lot, directly in front of the small, wood-frame house in which he was born. The image of the flag-draped casket set before the building that Nixon's father had constructed suggested a return to origins, a life brought full circle. ABC News commentators characterized Nixon's birthplace as "the California equivalent of a log cabin."[3] These images of humble beginnings combined with numerous markers of a singularly accomplished life: a military honor guard, an air force flyover, a twenty-one-gun salute, a flag-draped casket, the strains of "Hail to the Chief" and the National Anthem, and the presence of President and Mrs. Clinton and all the living former presidents and first ladies. Acting as his generation's national religious leader, the Reverend Dr. Billy Graham officiated at the service, while an army band and navy chorus led the mourners in "The Battle Hymn of the Republic" and "America, the Beautiful," those inspirational hymns glorifying the nation's self-anointed righteousness and sacred purpose. Through this familiar blend of the patriotic and the evangelical, the imprimatur of the nation's civil religion was bestowed upon Nixon once again.

The ceremony itself balanced the rhetoric of unabashed celebration with that of political forgiveness and spiritual healing. On its simplest, and most blatantly political, level, the funeral did more than just honor a virtuous man; read as symbolic text, it also commemorated a Horatio Alger–style life that embodied all that was good about the United States. Predicting that "the second half of the twentieth century will be known as the age of Nixon," Senator Robert Dole, tuning up for his 1996 run for the

Republican presidential nomination, proclaimed that the former president was "one of us." Thus, in celebrating Richard Nixon, Dole sought to vindicate a particular vision of the United States. Nixon's experiences served as the proof-text for a set of national values: pioneer spirit ("He was a boy who heard the train whistle in the night and dreamed of all the distant places that lay at the end of the track"); work ethic ("He was the grocer's son who got ahead by working harder and longer than everyone else"); self-reliance ("He was a student who met expenses by doing research at the law library for 35 cents an hour while sharing a run-down farmhouse without water or electricity"); motherhood ("He was the husband and father who said that the best memorial to his wife was her children"); tenacity ("a great patriot who never gave up and who never gave in"); and ceaseless striving ("'You must never be satisfied with success,' he told us, 'and you should never be discouraged by failure'"). In sum, Dole's Nixon stood as an archetypal American hero, a mix of Daniel Boone, Benjamin Franklin, Dale Carnegie, and Ward Cleaver. In celebrating this exemplar of private character and public probity, Dole gave voice to the Silent Majority, those who had trusted in Richard Nixon with the same intensity that they believed in "working hard, worshiping God, loving their families, and saluting the flag."[4]

From Henry Kissinger, Nixon's national security advisor turned secretary of state, came a vision of Nixon as peacemaker and the United States as a redeemer nation bringing the light of freedom and democracy to the world. Claiming that Nixon's first term fell at a historic transition point in international relations, Kissinger credited his president for moving American behavior in foreign policy from rule by domination to leadership by example. Having inherited a world of dangerous uncertainty—war in Southeast Asia, angry silence in relations with the People's Republic of China, diplomatic stalemate with the Soviet Union, and smoldering Muslim resentment against U.S. pro-Israel policies in the Middle East, Nixon accomplished breakthroughs on all fronts, creating the foundation for a freer, safer world. For those who saw Nixon as a mere practitioner of realpolitik, Kissinger insisted that his boss's achievements were "as much moral as [they were] political." Embracing America's obligation, as "the greatest free nation in the world," to be a leader in world affairs, Nixon envisioned a utopian result from his country's exercise of power: "A new international order that would reduce lingering enmities, strengthen historic friendships and give new hope to mankind, a vision where dreams and possibilities conjoined" (*Services*, 4, 5).

Had the Nixon funeral contained only this kind of preaching to the converted, the ceremony could only have been expected to exacerbate old divisions. Whatever evocative power the funeral service might have had must have come from its enactment of a ritual of political forgiveness between longtime warring camps. Nixon himself could not have selected a more perfect candidate to fulfill this task than Democratic president Bill Clinton. First of all, as a Vietnam-era college student who had avoided the draft and protested the war, he effectively symbolized the irresponsibility and lack of patriotism that Nixon had claimed epitomized too many in the baby boom generation. And, second, Watergate had been pivotal in opening Clinton's political career. He had returned to Arkansas to run for Congress against an otherwise popular Republican incumbent who had continued to support the president during the Watergate scandal. Had Nixon not been forced out of office before the general election campaign even got started, Clinton might very well have won.[5] So, when, in his eulogy, President Clinton affirmed that Nixon had made mistakes and that these were part of his record, no one could miss the unspoken reference to Watergate. Only someone well-schooled in the catechism of anti-Nixonism could credibly offer the absolution that followed: "Today is a day for his family, his friends and his nation to remember President Nixon's life in totality. To them, let us say: may the day of judging President Nixon on anything less than his entire life and career come to a close" (*Services*, 14). As an attempt to face the past and move on, this moment was the political high point of the ceremony: offering to Nixon's memory a pardon more genuine and complete than the merely legal one that Ford had granted.

Bringing about true healing, however, required that the ceremony itself move beyond politics to a higher spiritual plane. Clearly, this charge belonged to the Reverend Dr. Billy Graham. Understood in this light, the opening text for his funeral sermon seemed especially appropriate. Choosing 2 Samuel 3:38, "Do you not know that a prince and a great man has fallen this day in Israel," Graham, attributing these words to David on hearing of the death of Saul, "a bitter enemy," urged us to recognize Nixon as an exceptional leader.[6] Those who knew the biblical story, though, could find something even more thought-provoking in Graham's typology of Nixon as Saul. Reading the noted Hebrew Bible scholar Ernest Wright's characterization of the first king of the Israelites evokes an unsettling case of reverse déjà vu: "Saul had some fine political successes, but he seems to have possessed a certain instability of character."[7] By conjuring up this tragic figure of a man who could have been a great king had it not been for "an evil spirit from the Lord [that] tormented him,"[8] Graham reminded us of Richard Nixon's presidential accomplishments while calling us to mourn that he had succumbed to his demons. At the same time, Graham insisted, the nation must cease to condemn Nixon, because "in the end the only thing that really counts is not how others see us here, but how God sees us" (*Services*, 18). Pronouncing that he believed Nixon was now in heaven, Graham attempted to complete the process of spiritual healing by forever taking the power to judge the former president out of the secular realm and by aspiring to inter not just Nixon's physical remains but also the uneasy spirit of his political legacy that had haunted recent American experience. Ironically, Nixon biographer Stephen E. Ambrose, working as a commentator for ABC News, did as much as anyone to suggest that the funeral service had achieved this goal. As the casket was being carried off for the committal, he surrendered to the ceremony's barrage of mythic symbols, running up the verbal equivalent of a white flag: "Every American over 30 years old is astonished at this *outpouring* of affection and emotion for Richard Nixon. Thinking back to the summer of 1974, I just don't understand how this happened and no one could have predicted it—except one person. And I think he saw it . . . and [he] devoted himself to this moment, to making this moment happen. And he did it. . . . . To everyone's amazement, except his, he's our *beloved* elder statesman." Taken in totality, the funeral suggested that the problem of Richard Nixon had been solved, that he was, well, history.

Powerful symbols and forgiving words notwithstanding, the impression of national reconciliation that the ceremony fostered was illusory. Four years later, the novelist Philip Roth included a biting demythologization of the Nixon funeral in *I Married a Communist*, a story of the destructive McCarthy era. At the end of the penultimate chapter, eighty-seven-year-old Murray Ringgold, whose brother Ira, a radio celebrity whose career had been ruined by accusations that he was a communist spy, watches the "barely endurable" Nixon funeral with the revulsed fascination of a rubber-necking motorist passing a gory four-car pileup. Deriding the use of patriotic songs and evocative symbolic gestures—such as an interracial team of servicemen pallbearers for the flag-draped casket—as "designed to shut down people's thinking and produce a trance state," Murray saves his most venomous commentary for the eulogizers and the eulogized himself. Sneering at the politicians who spoke that day, Murray marvels at their ability for "uttering all the well-known, unreal, sham-ridden cant about everything but the dead man's real passions." Ringgold saves special contempt, however, for Henry Kissinger, who inappropriately borrowed a line from *Hamlet*—"He was a man, take him for all and all, I shall never look upon his like again"—seemingly unaware of the ambiguous, conflicted nature of Hamlet's reference to his father. What's more, Murray insists that the "court Jew" ignored the more relevant analogy to Nixon, that of the "usurping murderer" Claudius: "Who there at Yorba Linda dares to call out, 'Hey Doctor—quote *this:* "Foul deeds will rise / Though all the earth o'whelm them, to men's eyes"'?" And though Murray claims to have found Nixon's funeral "sensationally hilarious" in its verbal and moral contortions, in "the indignities to which they descended to dignify that glaringly impure soul," his searing, judgmental anger surges through as he remembers his late brother's fate at the hands of Nixon's allies: "Had Ira been alive to hear them, he would have gone nuts all over again at the world getting everything wrong."[9]

These contradictory versions of Nixon's funeral suggest a special position for this controversial politician in the national public consciousness. As its central goal, *Reinventing Richard Nixon: A Cultural History of an American Obsession* seeks to explore and explain this singular standing. This book deals with representations of Nixon in popular culture, images that inspire some and appall others, yet which seem to fascinate us all—even to the point of obsession. Most important, such reinventions of Nixon resonate with certain foundational national myths, stories that impart cultural values that have driven the United States from its earliest days. In their eulogies, for example, Bob Dole and Henry Kissinger molded Nixon's life into cohesive stories that lionized industry, selflessness, love of family and country, and dedication to a national mission—all models for behavior epitomizing what is best about the United States. For the faithful, Richard Nixon, as a representative American, symbolizes the nation's hopes and dreams. But, for many others, as Roth's alternate version of the Yorba Linda funeral makes clear, Nixon functions as an emblem of those myths' emptiness and hypocrisy. Throughout this book, therefore, we encounter a contentious debate, not just about the man but about the nature of the United States. Does, as the myth of the self-made man would have it, America provide unlimited opportunity for self-expression and fulfillment? Or does the nation's glorification of individualism maim, and even ultimately defeat, the self and destroy our larger social community? Is America a city on a hill, a shining exemplar with a mission to establish freedom in the world? Or, instead, is the United States a self-interested, perhaps even an imperialistic, dominating power, seeking an empire? This book studies these mythic representations of Nixon, understanding them as expressions of competing versions of what America is and should be. In so doing, *Reinventing Richard Nixon* navigates the tempestuous last sixty years of U.S. history, a period when the question of national identity has become particularly problematic. Observing Nixon's representations in popular culture permits us to see the ideological orthodoxies of the post–World War II Cold War consensus during the late 1940s, 1950s, and early 1960s; to observe their critique, fueled by the counterculture and opposition to the Vietnam War, begin to take hold in the late 1960s and early 1970s; and, finally, to witness their resurgence in the 1980s, continuing through to the present, thanks to the efforts of the New Right. Put another way, our reinventions of Richard Nixon map out the terrain of what we have come to know as the culture wars.

In saying that Nixon was a representative American, Bob Dole was absolutely correct. Arguably, no living politician can match the captivating force that Nixon exerted—and continues to exert—on the culture of the United States. As early as 1967, when the thought of a Nixon presidency seemed only the pipe dream of a few true believers, the political columnist Meg Greenfield labeled those who had turned twenty-one in time to vote in 1952 as the Nixon generation: "We are too young to remember a time when Richard Nixon was not on the political scene, and too old reasonably to expect that we shall live to see one."[10] Despite his exit from the White House in disgrace, his capacity to fascinate us was undiminished. The famous *Newsweek* cover story from May 1986 that pronounced "He's Back" got it wrong. Richard Nixon never left. In fact, no other recent politician has so thoroughly saturated America's public culture: from the media of mass culture—film, television, popular music, editorial and strip cartoons, and popular fiction—to literary fiction, poetry, drama, and opera, he surfaces as a character again and again.[11] Of all the photographs in the National Archives, none has been more requested than the one of Nixon shaking hands with Elvis Presley during the King of Rock and Roll's 1970 visit to the White House. Novelty shops offered plastic Nixon "Inflatable Houseguests," showerhead attachments, and Halloween masks. Billy Joel mentions Nixon's name twice in his 1989 number one hit single "We Didn't Start the Fire," a song that tells U.S. history from 1949 through 1989 in a stream of consciousness series of cultural references. And if we take the word "Watergate" as synonymous with Nixon, then he is mentioned three times—more than any other figure in the song.[12] Arbiters of

American culture as diverse as *Time* magazine and Trivial Pursuit confirm his special status. The Baby Boomer Edition of this popular board
game contains more Nixon-related questions and answers than are given
to any other political figure. In fact, Nixon wins in a landslide, besting
his nearest political rival, JFK, by more than a two-to-one margin.[13] In
late November 1994, *Time* ran an advertisement that consisted of a photo
of a brooding Nixon, out for a stroll in a suit and dress shoes, with arms
crossed and eyes studying the ground. His head and torso are enclosed in
a rectangular frame with the magazine's familiar logo across the top. The
ad's headline boasts: "We covered every moment of his political career.
Except, of course, for 18 minutes. Understanding comes with TIME." In
this sales pitch, Nixon becomes the gold standard for judging journalistic
excellence.

So Bob Dole did not have it wrong when he pronounced post–World
War II America as the "age of Nixon."[14] His error came in offering a single
mythic story about the man and insisting that it was the only one possible.
As a nation, we have *never* told the same stories about Richard Nixon. For
some, he was the crusading anticommunist, the man who defended freedom by rooting out subversives in government. On Monday, December
6, 1948, his picture appeared on the front page of the *New York Times* for
the first time. That summer, Whittaker Chambers, a former communist
agent turned informer, had gone before the House Committee on Un-
American Activities to accuse Alger Hiss, a former State Department official, of being a communist. When Hiss sued for libel, Chambers produced
the "Pumpkin Papers," the sensationalistic name given to a microfilmed
stash of pirated government documents from the 1930s. At the time this
bombshell was released to the public, Nixon was on a Caribbean cruise,
and as a Coast Guard amphibious aircraft returned him to the mainland,
press photographers captured the youthful congressman bolting off the
plane. The urgency of the situation is captured in the attitude of Nixon's
body (he looks like a sprinter pushing off the starting block) and in his face
(the mouth set in grim determination, the eyes focused directly ahead).
The headlines also spoke of emergency, telling readers that Richard Nixon
was so needed in Washington that he was "Taken Off Ship, [and] Flown to
Capital." Today, in the post–Cold War era, the apocalyptic importance that
was attached to the Hiss case has to be reconstructed. In his best-selling
1952 memoir *Witness*, Whittaker Chambers himself explained the perspective of those who admired Nixon's actions during this episode: "The
world, the whole world, is sick unto death and . . . this Case has turned

The President meets the King. The most requested photograph from the National Archives memorialized a White House visit so resonant in the national cultural mythology that it has spawned a movie, a novel, and truckloads of commemorative souvenirs. Oliver Atkins Richard Nixon White House Photographs, Special Collections and Archives, George Mason University Libraries.

a finger of fierce light into the suddenly opened and reeking body of our time."[15] For those persuaded by such attitudes, the effect of the photo and headline in the *Times* was to make Nixon appear as a white knight on a crusade to rescue and redeem the country.

But for equally important groups of people, Nixon stood for something darker in the national life. In one of his most famous *Washington Post* editorial cartoons, drawn in 1954 at the high tide of the McCarthy era, Herbert Block (Herblock) fashioned Richard Nixon as a creature of the sewer: a mud-slinging master of the low road emerging from an open manhole. The tags on his suitcase and the filth smeared on his stubbly cheeks show his familiarity with this route. As Nixon climbs out, he receives the welcome of a mass of chubby, round-headed white men in business suits, not one of whom—with the exception of the one who calls out "Here He Comes Now"—has an expression betraying any hint of individuality or

Novelty shops have found numerous ways to market Nixon's iconic face.
Items from the author's personal collection. Photo by John Herr Photography.

intelligence. The specter of these dimwits tells us all we need to know about Block's opinion of those who follow "Tricky Dick."

This radical duality in the responses to Richard Nixon exposes Dole's celebration of the former president as "one of us" for what it was—a battle cry. In Dole's hands, Nixon functioned as a vehicle for promoting the rightness of the conservative vision of the United States, as a place where individuals, without government help or interference, can make of themselves anything they desire. If this goal were its sole agenda, then the eulogy would not be at all troubling. But a narrative of Nixon's life that can inspire one to exclaim "How American!" over and over also implies the opposing label of "un-American" for those who do not share the same

"Here He Comes Now"

"Here He Comes Now," a 1954 Herblock cartoon, copyright by The Herb Block Foundation. *Reprinted with permission. All rights reserved.*

feelings for the man. Dole's eulogy appropriates true patriotism to Nixon's faithful defenders, denying political, even moral, legitimacy to those who question the premises of its mythic narrative. For many liberals, Dole's sentiments closed another—though far less seemly—symbolic circle in Nixon's life. Given that Nixon first gained political office by engaging in red-baiting, his opponents could hear in Dole's words a return-to-origins story that seemed more fitting than the cotton-candy one about the ex-president's homecoming to the house his father built. Here, in the compulsion to pass judgment on others' loyalty, was the essence of the man they had loathed.

We have grown used to thinking, reading, and debating about the uneasy state of contemporary U.S. culture. Evidence of conflict surfaces in nearly all aspects of public life. In education, defenders of curriculums based on the traditional works of Western civilization face off against those who promote opening the canon to multicultural influences.[16] Supporters of creationism demand that this biblical view on the origins of life be taught in public school districts as an alternative to evolution. Conservative talk show hosts, even entire TV networks, challenge what they see as the liberal and secular bias of the mass media.[17] African Americans battle each other over the meaning of their lives as a minority in the United States, arguing over whether affirmative action is necessary to combat institutionalized, entrenched racism or whether it is a debilitating drain on individual initiative.[18] An evangelical Christian kills an abortion clinic physician, claiming his action saved the lives of untold unborn babies and, thus, was justifiable homicide. The city of San Francisco and the state of Massachusetts offer civil marriage ceremonies to gay couples, while President Bush and many of his supporters threaten an amendment to the Constitution barring same-sex unions. The cultural climate is so thick with competing grievances that people from all shades of the ideological spectrum have taken to metaphors of warfare to describe the condition of contemporary life in the United States.[19]

As Nixon's career suggests, however, this kind of struggle within the mainstream culture is nothing new—the recent high-pitched rhetoric notwithstanding. In fact, no public figure better illustrates the ongoing divisiveness of the nation's post–World War II experience than Nixon. Take, for example, a 1972 cartoon from the *Chicago Daily News*, with its annotations by an irate reader, which the artist John Fischetti published in *Zinga, Zinga, Za!*, a 1973 collection of his work. Personified as a smiling Richard Nixon, the "Secret Plan to End the War" appears full-bodied and real in 1968, the year in which Nixon ran for president and promised that he would bring the Vietnam War to an honorable end, without commenting specifically on how he might accomplish what Lyndon Johnson could not. In each succeeding year of Nixon's first term, though, the familiar caricature fades slowly away, until, in 1972, another election year, there is nothing left but the ghostly, mocking grin of the Cheshire Cat. The American people, the cartoonist implied, had been taken in by a smiling, insubstantial fraud who claimed to be a peacemaker. Notice, however, that, for the angry annotator, what Fischetti portrayed as foggy inexactitudes form a well-defined policy. Where the artist intended for Nixon's body to disappear, his critic, with each succeeding frame, fills in details, working to give the impression of a reemerging physical presence. The heading 1969 becomes January 1969, not an imprecise twelve-month span, and 1972 is limited to May 1972. The 550,000 troops sent to Vietnam by Democratic presidents have shrunk, three years later, to 69,000 soldiers. What is becoming invisible in this version is not Nixon's plan for peace but the war itself. "It looks to me like he is ending the war," this anonymous citizen insists. Involved in this interpretative disagreement are competing sets of assumptions about Richard Nixon's honesty, the status of the war, and the American condition in 1972. But what is most remarkable about the dialogic interchange in this cartoon is how it makes visible the contest between two entirely different story lines battling for dominance over one another.

But why are we, as a nation, so particularly preoccupied with Richard Nixon? And why are we obsessed with continually reinventing him? Describing the efforts of rival groups in Great Britain to claim William Shakespeare, the Renaissance literature scholar Louis A. Montrose saw nothing less than "a struggle to shape and reshape national identity and collective consciousness."[20] The same can be said for the United States in its struggle over Richard Nixon. Michael Schudson recognized part of this truth in his 1992 study *Watergate in American Memory: How We Remember, Forget, and Reconstruct the Past.* Identifying competing public stories about Watergate and its significance—some posit the episode as a constitutional crisis, while others see it as a scandal; some understand it as purely routine politics, while others cast it as an aberration—Schudson explored the ways in which these different narratives struggled for dominance in the nation's collective memory, or, as he defined it, "the ways in which group, institutional, and cultural recollections of the past shape people's actions in the present." And although Schudson staunchly held to the idea that

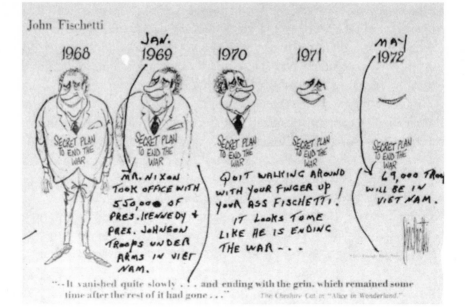

The battle between conflicting versions of the president becomes visible in this 1972 John Fischetti cartoon, annotated in angry rebuttal by an anonymous reader. Reproduced with permission of the Fischetti Estate. All rights reserved.

Watergate was a serious constitutional crisis, he realized that "the place of Watergate in our memory lies not with one interpretation or another exclusively but with the play of leading interpretations against one another."[21] David Greenberg's fascinating 2003 book, *Nixon's Shadow: The History of an Image*, extends this type of analysis to Nixon's entire career, categorizing his representations in primarily journalistic, historical, and biographical writing as a story of evolving and overlapping images: from the "populist everyman" to Tricky Dick; from the evil conspirator against American freedoms to the tragic victim of the liberals and the media; from paranoid madman to wise elder statesman; from the last Liberal to the nation's preeminent comeback artist. For Greenberg, "these debates about Nixon's image and meaning disclose the diversity of political viewpoints in postwar America; collectively, they also limn a growing concern in the years after World War II with images in politics."[22] So if, as I argue, Richard Nixon functions as a representative symbol for certain national mythic stories, he does not do so as some singular emblem expressing the essence of a unitary culture. Rather, Richard Nixon serves as a field of play upon which contradictory symbolic representations of the man and the nation he represents contend with one another.

At stake in the construction of conflicting narratives about Richard Nixon is control over the first draft of recent U.S. history, a competition that explains the tangle of emotions that invariably threaten to erupt in any discussion of Nixon and his career. In a very real sense, the power to dominate the national debate over the man and post–World War II America— the Cold War, the civil rights movement, Vietnam, and Watergate—is still up for grabs. All can agree, for instance, that Nixon resigned on August 9, 1974, but this point on a timeline is not, by itself, history. History must explain, and an explanation of Nixon's resignation can only come from telling a story about it. And the shape of the narrative frame into which the details of Richard Nixon's life will be placed is far from certain. Does Watergate show us that America's constitutional system can function even when a corrupt president tries to block it? Or does Nixon's resignation suggest that the electoral process can be circumvented by a cynical political minority and a biased news media? As the critic Stanley Fish tells us, "What is at stake in a disagreement is the right to specify what the facts can hereafter be said to be."[23] This assertion is what it means to say that history gets written—and rewritten—by the winners of cultural conflict. The disconcerting possibility for the participants in the dispute over Nixon is that their interpretation of his significance to contemporary America may not ever be taken as the truth. This matter is of great consequence, because from the ability to define the past comes control of the stories we use to understand the world in the present. And these narratives lead us to take certain actions that, in turn, help shape the future. Imagine the measures that a nation takes if it believes that it has the most to fear from a powerful executive branch, compared to those that it takes if convinced that its enemies are the liberals and the media. The outcome of the continuing battle over Richard Nixon, therefore, could not be more crucial.

The chapters that follow will explore the many faces of Richard Nixon in the continual reinventions of him as a cultural icon. Focusing on Nixon's first two autobiographies, on campaign biographies and political memorabilia produced during election years from 1946 through 1972, and on drawings by admiring editorial cartoonists, chapters 1 and 2 examine the relationship between Nixon and the two main mythic stories of post– World War II America's ideological orthodoxy: the myths of the self-made man and of national mission. These chapters show how many people,

Nixon partisans as well as Nixon himself, used the man's life and career to exemplify the notion that success in the United States transcends socioeconomic barriers and the conviction that America has been ordained by God to be both an example of and a missionary for freedom, democracy, and equality. Yet, even in the act of doing so, many Nixon partisans betray anxiety—incipient and contained at first, but, during Watergate and after the resignation, growing more insistently pronounced—that paradise has been lost, that the nation is falling away from its calling.

The next two chapters study representations of Nixon created to critique the orthodox ideology's shallowness and corruption. Chapter 3 looks at plays, poems, feature and documentary films, and episodes of classic television situation comedies from the 1970s, 1980s, and 1990s—as well as the creations of editorial cartoonists and other graphic artists. Taken together, these works raise serious reservations about almost every aspect of the myth of success—from questioning whether the American dream really is attainable to wondering about the spiritual costs of pursuing and obtaining it. Knowing a cultural myth is destructive, however, does not automatically liberate one from its unhealthy influence. The reinvented Richard Nixons featured in chapter 4 outline the tyrannical and injurious power of America's myth of national mission and the feebleness of almost all efforts to oppose it. While some of these works can, at times, be sympathetic, for many more Nixon provokes only anger. Chapter 5 takes a look at reinventions of Richard Nixon born out of the artists' rage at their inability to stop the man and what he represents. In frustration, the creators of these works often turn to what seems their only outlet: demonizing the man. Although understandable, especially when observed coming from minority cultures, this tendency to demonize Nixon and the myths he represents leaves the cultural left with no constructive alternate mythology to offer.

Because no culture can function without stories to tell about itself, the neoconservative movement has had considerable success in reasserting the orthodox myths. Chapter 6 looks at those reinventions of Nixon beginning in the late 1980s (with particular emphasis on the museum at the Richard Nixon Library and Birthplace) to demonstrate the power—and danger—of the principle that a worn-out story may be better than none at all. And, finally, chapter 7 shows that, in the immediate aftermath of the former president's death to the present, we have found little consensus about Richard Nixon and what he represents. In the years since 1994, the competing reinventions of the man fought on—during the Bill Clinton impeachment struggle, in a string of surprisingly sensitive and forgiving portrayals in fiction, film, and theater, and in the unflagging efforts of both Nixon critics and loyalists, who remain interested in their own vindication rather than forgiveness.

Richard Nixon's state funeral tried to do more than lay his physical remains to rest; it attempted to bury the sources of our divisions over the nation's thirty-seventh president as well. Even Ambrose, whose biographical study is, at times, harshly critical of Nixon, found himself so carried away by what he saw as the ceremony's celebration of the nation's form of government that he blurted out during ABC's broadcast: "This is a great day for democracy!" (*State Funeral*, ABC). Of course, Ambrose and the other participants could be forgiven for such excesses. Long ago, in a burlesque of etiquette manuals, Mark Twain warned that funerals make the perfect place for cover-ups: "Listen, with as intense an expression of attention as you can command, to the official statement of the character and history of the person in whose honor the entertainment is given; and if these statistics should seem to fail to tally with the facts, in places, do not nudge your neighbor, or press your foot upon his toes, or manifest, by any other sign, your awareness that taffy is being distributed."[24] So, despite the rhetoric of forgiveness and healing, nothing was really resolved that overcast afternoon in Yorba Linda. Richard Nixon still haunts us in all the conflicting stories that we tell about him. Nor can we ever put him to final rest. Because when we fight about Nixon, we are fighting about the meaning of America. And that is a struggle that never ends.

CHAPTER ONE

"RAGGED DICK" NIXON, AMERICAN MISSIONARY

For Richard Nixon, nothing succeeded better than failure. By the last years of his life, this message had become a truism. In April 1990, an editorial cartoon in the *Portland Oregonian* pictured six *Time* magazine covers, beginning with the youthful politician and ending with the elder statesman, all bearing the identical triumphant caption, "Nixon's back!" But this latter-day conventional wisdom was not so indisputable in 1962 when Nixon published *Six Crises*. In this first of his ten books, three of which were autobiographies, Richard Nixon borrowed the narrative structure of familiar cultural myths to create his own legend of a loser who single-handedly transforms defeat into victory. True, there had been previous attempts to establish Nixon as a representative of the sustaining values of U.S. public culture, most notably in political books, editorial cartoons, and campaign paraphernalia from 1946 through 1960. All the same, none of these matched the impact of *Six Crises*, which joined their separate themes into the mythic leitmotif that would resound throughout the remainder of Nixon's life. To begin to understand Richard Nixon's uses as a cultural symbol, therefore, we should start with this book written in the aftermath of his failed 1960 campaign for president.

Solicited by Doubleday in April 1961 and delivered to the press by the end of the year, *Six Crises* was published on March 29, 1962.[1] A book that touched a large audience, the memoir debuted on the *New York Times Book Review*'s best-seller list on April 8 at number fourteen and appeared every week until August 19, rising as high as number four. Widely reviewed in newspapers and magazines, it drew a diverse range of notices: from the favorable one in the *San Francisco Chronicle*, predicting "something of a crisis" for Nixon-haters, looking to the book for "justification for [their] mistrust and uncharitableness," to the dismissive one in the *National Review*, which groused aloud about "whether this fat autobiography was put together by a person, or a cagey committee." Quite often, *Six Crises* received judgments that were more estimations of the man than they were of his book. For instance, the *Christian Century* found Nixon to be "sensitive and intelligent rather than cynical," although, at the same time, "a man marked by shallow piety and opportunism." And Tom Wicker, reviewing for the *New York Times Book Review*, saw *Six Crises* as a continuation of Nixon's tragic unwillingness to "make himself known to a public that has given him so many chances." Still, despite the less-than-unanimous critical response, the book managed to sell over 250,000 copies, generating over $200,000 in royalties for its author.[2]

Six Crises tells the story of Nixon's life by relating the events during which his character was most tested and, consequently, most revealed to the American public. The first crisis—the Hiss case of 1948—began when Whittaker Chambers, *Time* magazine editor and an admitted ex-communist agent, appeared before the House Committee on Un-American Activities (HUAC) and accused Alger Hiss, a highly placed member of the Roosevelt and Truman State Department, of being a communist. Nixon convinced reluctant HUAC members to pursue the case, supported Chambers's assertions, and gained a national following. Nixon's second test, the Fund scandal, came during a one-week period in which he nearly lost his place as Eisenhower's running mate on the 1952 Republican ticket due to accusations concerning an $18,000 political fund. Nixon saved his career by making a televised appeal known to his supporters as the Fund speech—his detractors disparagingly tagged it the Checkers speech (for its famous moment when he referred to his daughters' puppy). The third chapter centers on the difficulties Nixon faced in keeping the government running without appearing to be power-hungry during Eisenhower's 1955 coronary, his ileitis attack in 1956, and his 1957 stroke. The fourth crisis, his 1958 trip to South America, was a goodwill tour marred by communist-led riots. During a brief stay in Caracas, Venezuela, Nixon and his wife were spat upon at the airport and nearly killed by a rock-throwing mob during their motorcade to the American Embassy. The fifth episode, the July 1959 "kitchen debate" with Khrushchev, pitted Soviet rockets against American washers and dryers, as Nixon, the official host of the U.S. Exhibition held in Moscow's Sokolniki Park, defended the American way of life against the Soviet premier's scornfully dismissive attacks.

To the degree that its title suggests parity between the episodes, however, *Six Crises* is misnamed. The literary critic Georges Gusdorf has argued that political autobiographies most frequently must be understood as "the final chance to win back what has been lost."[3] And Nixon's first memoir is all about the sixth crisis—the 1960 election. Both the longest chapter and the only one Nixon wrote by himself, this final section unifies the separate events into a single, cohesive narrative.[4] The book begins with Nixon's observation that the Hiss case made him enough friends to win the 1960 Republican nomination, but it also created enough enemies for him to lose the general election. Linking this earliest crisis of his public life with the results of an election twelve years later alerts Nixon's audience to interpret the entire book in light of his defeat in that campaign. Read in its totality, the memoir functions as an extended proof—using five highlighted moments from his career as evidence—of the claim that Nixon deserved to win in 1960. Each chapter studies Nixon's successful resolution of a political problem—with the story's moral condensed into a chapter-opening epigram. The Hiss case, for example, teaches that "the ability to be cool, confident, and decisive in crisis is not an inherited characteristic but is the direct result of how well the individual has prepared himself for the battle." As its lesson, the Fund episode establishes that "going through the necessary soul-searching of deciding whether to fight a battle, or to run away from it, is far more difficult than the battle itself."[5] By the end of the book, Nixon presents the very presidential-looking portrait of a man who has learned from, and triumphed over, adversity.

To cement its argument that Nixon was the better man in 1960, *Six Crises* draws on the authority of two potent cultural myths. The first, the myth of the self-made man, encourages the belief that all things are possible with determination, perseverance, and hard work. The second, the myth of American mission, proclaims that the United States has been divinely chosen to be an example to the world and to bring about God's will on Earth. By claiming to embody the nation's most sacred stories about itself, Nixon dons a presumably impenetrable mantle of God and country to deflect the blame for his defeat. Yet this self-absolution creates a new, more troubling, question: by rejecting one so in tune with these sustaining mythic narratives, has the nation lost faith and fallen into decline?

A dogged insistence that class functions differently in the United States has long held a central place in the national self-image. Rejecting the idea of rigidly fixed castes, Americans have favored instead a vision of mobility across a relatively fluid social structure. Rank in this system is a reward not of birth but of ambition and accomplishment, perhaps even one's godliness and virtue. Cotton Mather urged his fellow Puritans toward not just spiritual but also material success. In his 1701 tract *A Christian at*

His Calling, Mather branded anyone who did not work for the benefit of himself as well as his community as "unrighteous," derelict to one's duty to self, loved ones, neighbors, and nation. "Young man, work hard while you are young; you'll reap the effects of it when you are old. Yea, how can you ordinarily enjoy any rest at night if you have not been well at work in the day?"[6] In the aphorisms peppered through each year's edition of *Poor Richard's Almanac*, in essays like "The Way to Wealth," or in his iconic self-representation as the archetypal rags-to-riches story in his autobiography, Benjamin Franklin popularized and refined Mather's philosophy, serving as a "Johnny Appleseed of the idea of success[,] . . . cast[ing] his seeds across the meadows of the American mind."[7] Fertilized throughout the nineteenth century by popular texts like the McGuffey readers (which sold more than 120,000,000 copies between 1836 and 1890), Horatio Alger's series of novels, and the 1899 tract *A Message to Garcia* (which reached an estimated distribution of 40,000,000 copies), the American myth of success preached that "the hero is the man who does the thing—does his work."[8] In the twentieth century, *Forbes Magazine*, launched in 1916, spouted updated *Poor Richard*–like slogans, such as "ASPIRE—then perspire" and "PUT the I CAN in Amer-i-can." Meanwhile Dale Carnegie's *How to Win Friends and Influence People* (published in 1936 and hailed as the top-selling nonfiction book of the twentieth century), Napoleon Hill's 1937 book *Think and Grow Rich* (with conservative sales estimates of 1,200,000 copies), and Norman Vincent Peale's *The Power of Positive Thinking* (published in 1952 and a best seller for more than three years) convinced scores of Americans that no challenge was insurmountable—if you just put your mind to it.[9] No wonder that Richard Huber calls the national success mythology "a force which drove men on to build America."[10]

Appearing in 1962, Nixon's *Six Crises* came at the tailfin end of a period of intoxicating optimism about the nation's present and future. It was the time of "the proud decades," a time of "grand expectations," nothing less than an "American high," as the titles of three historical studies of the period proclaim.[11] For the cultural critic Thomas Hine, the ten years between 1954 and 1964 were the "Populuxe" era, a time defined by houses, cars, televisions, and other accoutrements of the good life—the things once deemed luxury items—becoming more affordable for more Americans than ever before. "There was so much wealth," Hine notes, "it did not need to be shared. Each householder was able to have his own little Versailles along a cul-de-sac."[12] Richard Nixon's entrance onto the national stage coincided with what seemed to be the fulfillment of these hopes of a material Shangri-la. From 1948 to 1956, the percentage of families that owned cars rose from 54 percent to 73 percent, while television ownership increased by 79 percent. In 1946, only half of the American homes wired for electricity had electric washing machines. Ten years later, 86.8 percent did.[13] Living in what seemed to be a "fairy tale of health, wealth, and happiness," Americans came to expect not just that their hard work would continue to be rewarded, but that their children's lives and achievements would outdo their own.[14] Such confidence manifested itself in the baby boom, an unprecedented increase in the birthrate, and an explosion in the housing market—by 1960, one-quarter of all Americans had moved to the suburbs.[15] Having survived the Great Depression and World War II, adult Americans in 1962 might be forgiven for seeing themselves as a "God-graced generation," reaping the benefits of their virtue and diligent labor.[16] According to William L. O'Neill, Americans during this period held to the faith that anyone willing and able to work would succeed: "In the land of opportunity there was no excuse for failure except being handicapped." American ingenuity and determination could transcend any limits; it was a time of "deep faith in America's possibilities."[17]

By 1962, when Nixon's first autobiography appeared, the practice of this national faith had become formulaic. Two of the most influential odes to success at that time—Carnegie's *How To Win Friends and Influence People* and Peale's *The Power of Positive Thinking*—shared a conviction that success was a matter of attitude. A person secured allies, gained a powerful reputation, and developed a confident manner by following a prescribed set of exercises—conveniently printed at the end of each section of these books. Both systems banished failure by making it simply unthinkable. In its six-phase program for managing crises, the epigrammatic lessons that begin each chapter, Nixon's book shares these success manuals' love of both systematic procedures and the instructional maxim. Yet this common form masks significant disagreement about content. In practice, Carnegie and Peale offer a soothing psychological approach—almost as if one could think oneself to success. By contrast, Richard Nixon operated within an older tradition, holding to the sterner precept that achievement comes from the development of a moral character. In his autobiography, Benjamin Franklin listed thirteen cardinal virtues, such as industry, frugality, and temperance.[18] He described keeping a weekly ledger book in which he made a mark for every failure to attain the traits on which he had concentrated. When his page was free of blots, he moved on to the next virtue, until they were all mastered. Franklin had a sense of humor about this scheme, admitting its impossibility while still affirming its usefulness, but those who followed him were less able to mix irony with seriousness of purpose. In over 130 books, which sold an estimated 16 to 17 million copies between 1868 and 1910, Horatio Alger preached self-reliance to the Gilded Age by portraying street urchins who aspired to middle-class respectability.[19] In the first of Alger's novels, Ragged Dick, an orphaned shoeshine boy, accidentally runs into Mr. Whitney, himself a self-made man, who inspires Dick to seek a better life: "You know in this free country poverty in early life is no bar to a man's advancement." The novel ends with Dick having built a modest bank account, joined a Sunday school class, learned to read and write, and, finally, obtained a clerk's position in a counting room. Alger concludes with the promise that Ragged Dick has transformed himself into Richard Hunter, a young gentleman "on the way to fame and fortune."[20]

From the beginning of his career, Nixon and his supporters understood his life in terms of this character-based tradition. In 1946, when Nixon made his first run for Congress, he didn't spend his money on flashy, but essentially useless, political buttons. The sole campaign item was a thimble: "NIXON for CONGRESS: Put the Needle in the P.A.C." This functional article, useful after the campaign was over, suggested the candidate's solidarity with frugal homemakers who made and mended their families' clothes. On August 13, 1952, just after Nixon's nomination to be the Republican vice presidential candidate, the *San Pedro (CA) News-Pilot* published a cartoon titled "An American Epic," which showed a book called *The Nixon Story* being pulled off a shelf labeled "Books on Success."[21] One button from the 1960 campaign actually spells out Nixon's connection to the Franklin and Alger gospel of success. In printing "Dick Nixon," the letters of the first name are presented as an acronym for four laudable qualities: Dependability, Integrity, Capability, and Knowledge. The graphics tell the story at a glance; the virtues of his character spell out Nixon's identity. A poster from the first presidential campaign takes this same idea to its logical extreme by publishing his job history. Nixon deserves to be president, we are told, because of "Fourteen Years of Training and Accomplishment" in national and international politics and in both the legislative and executive branches of government. If the presidency is a meritocracy, then let the best résumé win.

Six Crises fills out the shorthand versions of the story that these campaign items tell by presenting a man who from humble beginnings rose to prominence, though only to moderate financial wealth, by means of

This thimble from Nixon's 1946 congressional campaign, which reads "Nixon for Congress, Put the Needle in the P.A.C.," represented Nixon as a family values candidate. At the same time, it insinuated that Nixon's opponent was a puppet of the communist-controlled CIO-PAC, if not a communist himself. Item from author's personal collection. Photo by John Herr Photography.

honest, hard work. That is to say, Nixon portrays himself as "Ragged Dick" Nixon to propose that he deserved to succeed in 1960. Unlike the typical Horatio Alger hero, Nixon was not destitute at the opening of his first crisis, but he was poor in influence and power—a disadvantage for a politician as severe as financial poverty. When, in August 1948, Whittaker Chambers, a *Time* magazine editor and an admitted ex-communist agent, appeared before HUAC and accused Alger Hiss, who had been a highly regarded member of the Roosevelt and Truman State Department, of being a communist, Nixon convinced reluctant committee members to pursue the case. Taking Chambers's side against Alger Hiss put Nixon, the freshman congressman, in a precarious position: "I was opposing the President of the United States and the majority of press corps opinion, which is so important to the career of anyone in elective office" (*SC*, 11). Further complicating his situation, the vast majority of the American public, not to mention HUAC members, believed Hiss. Like Benjamin Franklin writing in the *Autobiography* of his arrival in Philadelphia, wandering its streets eating one loaf of bread while carrying two others pinned beneath his arms, Nixon wants to be seen as starting out totally alone.

In painting such a picture, *Six Crises* borrows a rhetorical strategy that Nicholas von Hoffman identifies as typical of the conservative movement

This button from the 1960 presidential campaign presents the candidate's qualifications as a series of Ben Franklin–esque virtues. Item from the author's personal collection. Photo by the author.

in the second half of the twentieth century—"the presumption that institutional power is arrayed against the narrative's hero."[22] Ralph de Toledano's *Nixon*, first published in 1956 and revised for the 1960 campaign, indulges this tendency even more freely than does *Six Crises*. A correspondent for *Newsweek* during the Hiss case and a frequent contributor to anticommunist journals like *American Mercury*, de Toledano looks to the Hiss case as a defining moment for both man and nation. In characteristically overwrought prose, he conjures up the shadowy menace of Nixon's opponents: "In an office in New York a mimeograph machine was turning out copies of the letters which Hiss' friends had written to him. The letters, sent where they could do Hiss the most good, were a formidable display."[23] The explicitly named list of letter writers that follows—including such prominent figures as the dean of Stanford Law School and the U.S. representative on the UN Trusteeship Council—only heightens the presumed malignity hiding behind the framing story's passive constructions. Who was operating that mimeo machine and mailing the letters? Who waits at unnamed locations, ready to use the letters for Hiss's benefit? In de Toledano's rendition of the case, Nixon battles against an insidious, anonymous, powerful evil.

And he makes his stand as a solitary warrior. As *Six Crises* insists, the result of this critical national security investigation depended entirely on Nixon's efforts. After Alger Hiss, a dapper, well-spoken former New Deal bureaucrat, denied the accusations brought against him by the mumbling, disheveled Whittaker Chambers, only Nixon demonstrates the will to pursue the charge that Hiss had been a member of the Communist Party. The rest of HUAC—and nearly all of the press—wanted to see the matter dropped. But Nixon observed what others missed: Hiss never denied knowing Whittaker Chambers, only a man by that name. Studying the recorded testimony in lonely late-night sessions until he knew the details of the case better than anyone else, Nixon devised a test that would demonstrate that Hiss knew Chambers in the 1930s. A tireless worker, Nixon cut short a long-delayed Caribbean cruise with Pat, returning to Washington when news leaked of the "Pumpkin Papers," the microfilm containing evidence that Hiss had participated in Chambers's espionage ring. "Ragged Dick" Nixon had won the day. Ceaseless persistence had lifted him out of obscurity, onto the front page of the *New York Times*, into the Senate, and eventually into the vice presidency.

In fact, *Six Crises* establishes diligence as the hallmark of Nixon's life. A biographical passage that opens the memoir's final chapter claims: "I won my share of scholarships, and of speaking and debating prizes in school not because I was smarter but because I worked longer and harder than some of my more gifted colleagues" (*SC*, 295). Throughout his crises, Nixon embraces a commitment to the work ethic so complete that he repeatedly drives himself nearly to the point of collapse. For instance, while clocking up to twenty-hour days during the Hiss case, Nixon suffered from quick temper, irritability, loss of appetite, and insomnia, what he calls "the inevitable symptoms of tension" (*SC*, 40). Even so, he stoutly defends his refusal to rest, as he explains in the chapter on the Fund episode: "It has been my experience that once the final period of intense preparation for battle begins, it is not wise to break it" (*SC*, 105). With such behavior, Nixon seems to flout the advice of Norman Vincent Peale, who counseled that "there is no virtue in overtrying or overpressing."[24] Instead, Nixon insists on his unflaggingly zealous industry, making a virtue out of what, in other people, his good friend Dr. Peale might have labeled a workaholic vice.

Here too, Nixon perfects a preexisting representation of himself. Unquestionably, the most common feature of the early campaign biographies is their celebration of Nixon's work ethic. Even Earl Mazo's *Nixon: A Political and Personal Portrait* (1959), the most balanced of these books, glorifies Nixon's remarkable perseverance. Written by a reporter for the *New York Herald Tribune* known for his highly critical coverage of HUAC prior to the Hiss case, Mazo's *Nixon*, arguably the most influential and popular of the pre-presidency biographies, competed for fifteen weeks on the *New York Times Book Review*'s best-seller list, debuting at number eleven on July 19, 1959, and rising as high as number six.[25] Noting that work in the family store and his participation in extracurricular activities at school did not keep Nixon from being an honor student, Mazo rhapsodizes: "What with jobs, school and studies, sixteen-hour workdays were commonplace . . . before he was sixteen years old." At that young age, he already possessed incredible staying power, what a law school acquaintance would later immortalize as an "iron-butt."[26]

In the world of Franklin and Alger, however, disciplined striving should be about attaining virtue, not necessarily wealth or power. And Nixon's narrative of his second crisis, the Fund episode, in its rejection of financial wealth as a goal in itself, heralds his lineage as a child of this orthodox success mythology. On September 18, 1952, the *New York Post*, a staunchly Democratic paper, printed a banner headline that accused Nixon of living a luxurious life funded by clandestine donations from wealthy businessmen. Having promised to run a crusade against the Truman administration's corruption, Dwight Eisenhower responded that, to remain as his running mate, Nixon had to be as "clean as a hound's tooth." Forced on the defensive, Nixon went on television to explain the workings of the fund and protest his innocence, blunting accusations of secret wealth by baring a financial history of multiple mortgages, Oldsmobile car payments, and outstanding loans from his parents. With the disclosure of this precariously balanced ledger book, Nixon suggested to his audience that he shared their everyday penny-pinching concerns: no new-model car in his driveway, no mink coats filling his wife's wardrobe. And—appearances be damned—the doting father defended his children's right to keep their puppy, Checkers, even if the cocker spaniel was a gift from a political supporter. Heralding his honest labor to make a good life for his family, Nixon spoke directly to the hearts—and pocketbooks—of average Americans.

Nixon's critics scoffed, but we must not pass too quickly over that word "honest." In the orthodox myth of success, honesty is the essential element. The McGuffey Readers, the primer for generations of U.S. schoolchildren, taught that "while 'strict honesty is not always the shortest way to success' it is 'the surest, the happiest and the best.'"[27] Nixon, clearly, mastered his lessons, declaiming during the Fund speech, "Pat and I have the satisfaction that every dime we have got is honestly ours" (*SC*, 115). His extensive financial confessions, both in the details and in the act of disclosure itself, proved his fidelity to the public trust. Nor were these claims a momentary expediency. During the 1960 presidential campaign, Nixon further showcased his middle-class honesty. Even more aggressive in its message, the "Not for Sale/Elect Nixon" button hinted broadly that Nixon's opponent believed that the White House, like any other piece of real estate, could be bought. By contrast, if Nixon took up residence at 1600 Pennsylvania Avenue, he would have earned it, sent there by people's votes.

Perhaps because Nixon spent his first moments as a national political candidate deflecting charges of corruption, the campaign biographies switch into rhetorical overdrive when defending his honesty. In discussing the Hiss case, de Toledano tells the story of a young Richard Nixon and his mother, Hannah, observing a woman shoplifting in their store. Rather than turn her over to the police, a course favored by Nixon's father, Richard advises his mother to follow her conscience and deal with the woman in private. Years later, when Hannah helps her son decide whether to proceed with the HUAC investigation of Alger Hiss, she repeats his advice: "Don't give in. Do what you think is right."[28] The conflation of the two episodes gives an unmistakable message: In pursuing Hiss, Richard Nixon is pursuing truth, not ambition. Hungarian refugee Bela Kornitzer, whose 1960 book *The Real Nixon* benefited from exclusive interviews with the candidate's mother, goes even further back into Nixon's childhood, to the time of the Teapot Dome scandals. As the daily newspapers revealed more and more corruption in the Harding administration, the young boy absorbed it all quietly—until one day he blurted out: "Mother, I would like to become a lawyer—an honest lawyer, who can't be bought by crooks."[29] Mazo manages to avoid such blatant hagiography, but he does report Nixon's contention that public service actually detracted from his potential earning power. Comparing Nixon's net worth in 1946 to that in 1959, Mazo, in a revival of the Fund speech, reprises all the familiar categories— mortgages, life insurance policies, and Oldsmobiles—and quotes Nixon's insistence that "we live actually on the basis that we spend everything that we get in."[30]

Notably, these stories betray a hyperconscious expectation that they will be challenged. In his dramatic rendition of Nixon agonizing over the Hiss case, de Toledano's syntax divulges his real anxiety: "Though his political opponents have zealously labored to question Nixon's moral nature, it is a strongly operative facet of his inner self."[31] Before de Toledano can affirm Nixon's morality, he must address the doubts. At times, these prickly apologetics erupt into lamentations tinged with wounded righteousness. Kornitzer recites a series of false accusations that the Nixons were purchasing

Nixon lost few opportunities to remind voters in 1960 that he was running against a millionaire's son. Item from the author's personal collection. Photo by the author.

luxurious homes and squirreling away great wealth, noting savagely that "it is perhaps one of Nixon's misfortunes that, while not one accusation impugning his personal honesty has been proved, the suspicion of some sort of wrongdoing lingers on."[32]

There's good reason for such defensiveness. Try as he might, Nixon cannot escape the skeptics. In fact, *Six Crises* itself gives the critics evidence for questioning his honesty by failing to deliver on its promise of complete candor. On the simplest level, the book distorts through omission. By selecting neither the 1946 nor the 1950 elections as crises, Nixon erases from his life two of his most controversial moments: his tarring of Jerry Voorhis as a puppet of the communist-dominated CIO-PAC and of Helen Gahagan Douglas as the "pink lady." In his *Autobiography*, Benjamin Franklin imagined his life as a text—the writing of his story served as a way to amend and correct the errata of his life. By contrast, Nixon dreams of making his text into his life: what he doesn't write about didn't happen.

Beyond these omissions, *Six Crises* engages in some sins of commission as well, twisting the facts to fit the stories it does tell. For instance, Nixon firmly maintains that the entire Alger Hiss episode was so unexpected that he nearly skipped Chambers's testimony in order to answer his mail. Even though he dutifully attended the hearing, the allegation that Alger and Donald Hiss were communists lacked impact because "this was the first time I had ever heard [of the Hiss brothers]" (*SC*, 4). Yet it seems unlikely that Nixon considered playing hooky, since Father John Cronin, the Catholic church's leading investigator of communists in government and the labor movement, had, in 1947, provided Nixon with copies of reports expressing suspicions that Alger Hiss had been a communist spy. Several sources, even some extremely sympathetic to Nixon, cite Father Cronin's assertions—made during the 1950s, 1960s, and 1970s—that he had told Nixon about Hiss prior to August 1948.[33] Irwin F. Gellman challenges these stories, claiming that in 1990 the priest had "repudiated his earlier position" and that Nixon critics use the Cronin story as a smokescreen to avoid having to concede that Nixon was correct about Hiss.[34] But this debate is somewhat misdirected. First of all, since the publication of *Perjury*, Allen Weinstein's definitive study of the case, most Nixon scholars recognize that Hiss was a communist agent. Furthermore, one can accept this strange reversal of Cronin's often-repeated story and can concede the possibility that Nixon might not have encountered Hiss's name in Cronin's documents, but doing so does not make Nixon's self-portrait as a lonely pursuer of truth any less false. For even the 1990 interview, which Nixon defenders use as proof that Father Cronin had not mentioned Hiss prior to August 1948, goes on to reveal a great deal of secret help available to the congressman. "From [the time of Hiss's public denial] on," Cronin told author Jonathan Aitken, "I worked with Nixon a lot and gave him everything I had on Hiss. He needed that help. He was very unsure of himself at the beginning." Whatever this statement suggests about what Nixon knew about Hiss before the HUAC hearings, it explicitly claims that Cronin's information, which included material leaked by an FBI agent involved in the case, was of tremendous importance. Yet Father Cronin's name never once appears, and the outside help Nixon received goes unmentioned, in *Six Crises*. Similarly, Robert Stripling, the primary investigator for HUAC, who at some critical moments filled a lead role in the pursuit of Hiss, gets relegated to secondary status. In fact, Nixon's rendering of the case upset Stripling enough for him to flatly declare that "*Six Crises* is pure bullshit!"[35] Being right about Alger Hiss, an extremely significant, and in 1962 still hotly disputed, claim, was not enough for Richard Nixon's telling of the story. He needed to be seen as having prosecuted the case practically single-handedly.

If in the Hiss case chapter Nixon keeps mum about his hidden advantages, his deceptions in the chapter on the Fund come from his attempts to exploit advantages he did not really possess. To be fair, Nixon's fund—neither secret nor illegal—existed to supplement the office expense allowance allotted to each senator. Revealingly, however, his defense did not rest on this legitimate point. Instead, he claimed to be protecting the public's hard-earned money. As he told an audience at a Marysville, California, whistle-stop train rally, he had refused to charge "the American taxpayer with the expenses of my office, which were in excess of the amounts which were allowed under law" (SC, 83). But he had saved the public nothing; had he charged the public with his office expenses, he would have broken the law. His pose of extraordinary virtue is nothing more than following the rules. Given his position during the 1952 campaign, one might forgive Nixon's desire to gain any rhetorical benefit possible. Yet he repeats this specious argument in 1962 rather than concentrate on his genuine defenses. And the pattern continues. At other places during the chapter, he deceives—and sometimes for appallingly trivial benefits. In a transparent sop to certain ethnic voters during the closing moments of the Fund speech, Nixon praises his wife's fortitude because "her name was Patricia Ryan and she was born on St. Patrick's Day, and you know the Irish never quit" (SC, 117). But Pat Nixon was born Thelma Catherine Ryan and, though she celebrated her birthday on St. Patrick's Day, she was born on March 16.[36]

Merely cataloging these falsifications, however, misses the larger point. As the literary critic Jean Starobinski argues, "No matter how doubtful the facts related, the text will at least present an 'authentic' image of the man who 'held the pen.'"[37] In short, truth can be found even in the lies we tell. Nixon's insistence on his total veracity is significant—*especially* in light of its inappropriateness. If *Six Crises* is about the 1960 election, then Nixon hints that in the things that really matter, like the presidency itself, he possesses an unimpeachable integrity. Appearing before a machinists' union convention, Nixon compares his behavior to Kennedy's abundant "pie in the sky" promises: "If I were solely concerned about votes . . . I would say that I was 100 per cent for everything that . . . [you] are for. . . . It might win votes, but . . . it would not be good for the labor movement . . . and it would not be good for America for a President of the United States to make that kind of statement" (SC, 332). His regard for the office caused him to stand on principle, abandoning pragmatic politics. Similarly, Nixon personally avoided the religion issue in 1960 and forbade those campaigning for him to use it. Disassociating himself from all anti-Catholic comments made by his supporters, Nixon squelched an article by Billy Graham set to appear in *Life* magazine in which the evangelist endorsed Nixon "unqualifiedly and enthusiastically, largely on grounds of [his] experience in world affairs and foreign policy" (*SC*, 365). Despite Graham's exclusion of religion as a criterion in rendering his judgment, Nixon would not permit even the appearance of impropriety in his handling of Kennedy's Catholicism. More than just a convenience, Nixon's insistence on his honesty in *Six Crises* reveals an essential element of his self-image.

Many people in the United States can claim to be self-made, but few deserve to be president. Consequently, Nixon does not rest his case solely on his exemplary character. He also fits his life inside the plot line of another one of mainstream America's favorite stories: the myth of national mission, that is, the expectation that God intends the United States to play a messianic role in world history.[38] U.S. cultural historian Sacvan Bercovitch identifies the persistent belief in "the redemptive meaning of America" as a conception offering "one of the most powerful unifying elements of the [dominant] culture."[39] All believers in America's divine role held that God meant their country to be an example to other nations, nothing less than a new promised land. John Winthrop's sermon aboard the *Arbella* before the Puritans had even set foot in New England speaks in purposefully symbolic terms: "For we must consider that we shall be as a City upon a Hill, the eyes of all people are upon us."[40] In December 1862, Abraham Lincoln insisted that the world would watch and judge his administration and Congress by its efforts to preserve a nation of redemptive promise: "We shall nobly save, or meanly lose, the last best hope of earth."[41] Despite a strong contrary current of isolationism, the majority of disciples of the myth of American mission also preached that the nation could complete God's work on Earth only by carrying the light of the New World example out to redeem the old one from darkness. In 1850, Herman Melville concluded a chapter in *White-Jacket* with a passage insisting that America's manifest destiny required it to expand across the continent while doing God's work on earth:

> We Americans are the peculiar, chosen people—the Israel of our time; we bear the ark of liberties of the world. . . . God has predestinated, mankind expects, great things from our race; and great things we feel in our souls. The rest of the nations must soon be in our rear. . . . Long enough have we been skeptics with regard to ourselves, and doubted whether, indeed, the political Messiah had come. But he has come in *us*, if we would but give utterance to his promptings.[42]

Woodrow Wilson, one of Richard Nixon's favorite presidents, enthusiastically embraced Melville's messianic vision for the United States. Following the cataclysm of World War I, he tried to make the Senate accept the League of Nations and the Treaty of Versailles as "the moral obligation that rests upon us . . . to see [the peace process] through to the end and make good [American soldiers'] redemption of the world."[43] Flushed with the Allies' victory in World War II, *Time* magazine editor Henry Luce famously proclaimed the beginning of the "American century," earnestly insisting that "America must be the elder brother of the nations in the brotherhood of man."[44] And in the events that followed—the Marshall Plan's reconstruction of a war-devastated Europe, the Truman Doctrine's promise to provide military aid to any nation fighting the communists, the subjugation of Eastern Europe by the Soviet Union, and the ensuing Cold War, Americans, a people who viewed "foreign policies in a highly moralistic way," acted with a passion and sense of righteousness born out of unshakable belief in "the rightness of their political institutions and the meaning of their history."[45]

From the mid-1950s through the early 1960s, the early years of Nixon's national career, public opinion showed widespread support for the myth of mission. Asked by Gallup pollsters in January 1956 whether they favored Wilson's view that *all* nations—even those dominated by the Soviet Union—should be given the right of self-determination, 61 percent approved of the idea. Large numbers of people also supported using teachers to promote goodwill between the United States and other nations, spending federal money to send them overseas to live, study, and write during their summer vacations. Finally, in 1962, the newly formed Peace Corps enjoyed overwhelming public confidence in its mission, with 74 percent favoring the group's activities, compared to only 9 percent who disapproved.[46]

In *Six Crises*, Nixon taps into this mythic tradition to bolster his implicit argument that he had earned the presidency. Throughout the early chapters of the memoir, he is mainly concerned with the protection of America's exemplary nature. For Nixon, the Hiss case reveals the nation's involvement in a cosmic battle between totalitarianism and liberty, what Whittaker Chambers called "the two irreconcilable faiths" of the twentieth century (*SC*, 61). Preaching his central homily, Nixon exhorts the United States not to forget its sustaining principles: "Our fundamental belief that every nation has a right to be independent, that individual freedom and human rights are grounded in religious faith and because they come from God cannot be taken away by men, must be instilled in the new generation" (*SC*, 68). In short, the gravest crisis of the Hiss case is the possibility that the United States will abdicate its responsibility to be a city on a hill.

Once again, *Six Crises* develops themes already introduced in the literature on Nixon. Visions of imminent apocalypse dominate *Witness*, Whittaker Chambers's account of the Alger Hiss case—a book that, like *Six Crises* and Mazo's *Nixon*, spent considerable time on the best-seller list.[47] From its Shakespearean epigraph ("If thou art privy to thy country's fate, which, happily, foreknowing may avoid, O speak—") to its concluding paragraph, prophesying either awesome redemption or awful oblivion ("when the witness that was laid on us shall have lost its meaning because our whole world will have borne a more terrible witness or it will no longer exist"), Chambers decries a world so sick that only America can save it.[48] And, for his supporters, only Nixon can save America. Borrowing Chambers's religiously charged term, de Toledano describes Nixon as a witness to the "root evil which sought power not as an end but as a means to remake man in its totally materialistic image."[49]

But what Nixon has observed made him vulnerable to America's enemies. "No one can consistently take strong positions in public life on the issue of Communism, and particularly subversion at home," he told Bela Kornitzer, "without expecting to pay the penalty for the rest of his life."[50] Without detectable irony, *Six Crises* asserts that the social, political, and intellectual elites of the United States are in league with the enemy and that they cannot forgive Nixon for defending his country. The Hiss case manifested a fundamental tragedy: "Our national ideals no longer inspire the loyal devotions needed for their defense" (*SC*, 68). If Alger Hiss, to all appearances one of the most intelligent and dedicated public servants of his day, was a traitor, then the United States must be tottering on the edge of spiritual bankruptcy. Chambers fills *Witness* with examples of how the Communist Party recruited from the best families and schools in the country, winning over "the most literate, intellectually eager and energetic young men."[51] Stewing class resentments bubble to the top in the writings of these Cold War conservatives. Bemoaning the spiritual degeneracy of the ruling class, de Toledano reminds us that "Park Avenue, Wall Street, and the Washington cocktail circuit echoed with [Hiss's] praises."[52] In opposition to these decadent elites, Nixon in the Hiss case becomes the champion of those who hail "from the wrong side of the railroad tracks."[53] Before the 1968 campaign introduced the rhetoric of the forgotten American, here was Richard Nixon as the perfect embodiment and defender of traditional, but endangered, national values.

With this link established, any attack on Nixon, by extension, puts the nation in peril. In this way, the accusation that he enriched himself from a secret fund built by contributions from California business interests threatens to provoke "a [national] crisis of unbelievably massive proportions" (*SC*, 96). Nixon accomplishes this transformation of a strictly personal catastrophe into one of potentially global consequence by linking his destiny to Eisenhower's. Nixon bares his personal financial history willingly because, he claims, "I think my country is in danger. And I think the only man who can save America . . . is the man that's running for President, on my ticket, Dwight Eisenhower" (*SC*, 116). To this belief, Nixon adds the premise that if he had resigned or had been dumped from the ticket Eisenhower's candidacy would have been destroyed. Because only the general was capable of ending the Korean War and communist infiltration of the federal government, Nixon can characterize self-interested actions in wholly altruistic terms: "What I did would affect the future of my country and the cause of peace and freedom for the world" (*SC*, 96). This fear that Eisenhower would lose the 1952 election if Nixon were removed from the ticket existed largely in the imaginations of the vice presidential candidate and his immediate supporters—their concern being akin to, in Garry Wills's memorable phrasing, "worrying that the Milky Way might go out." All the same, that a proposition is improbable will not stop people from embracing it. Without any commentary, Mazo prints Nixon's remark that his efforts in the Fund crisis came from not wanting to "carry [the] responsibility [for Ike's defeat] for the balance of my life."[54]

Having rescued the United States from the calamity of President Adlai Stevenson, Nixon, on becoming vice president, could turn to promoting America's divinely appointed world mission. So, in the middle chapters of *Six Crises*, he switches his primary focus to representing himself as an effective missionary for the nation's redemptive calling. The third crisis—the chapter is titled "The Heart Attack" but actually covers Eisenhower's 1955 heart attack, his ileitis attack in 1956, and his stroke the following year—ostensibly shows how Nixon's hard work and sound judgment kept the government functioning smoothly during the absence of its elected leader. But the real story rests in how, through Nixon's behavior, the health of the country itself would be evaluated: "Every word, every action of mine would be more important now than anything I had ever said or done before because of their effect upon the people of the United States, our allies, and our potential enemies" (*SC*, 133). Throughout the sections dealing with his 1958 South American and 1959 Soviet Union trips, Nixon begs to be understood as the bearer of freedom's flame, as an interpreter of his country's values to the inhabitants of the world's captive nations. During his visit to Catholic University in Lima, Peru, Nixon reports stumbling upon a school-wide election: "The students wanted me to speak immediately. But I said, 'Nothing must interfere with a free election,' and sat on the stage with the student officers for about five minutes while they completed the counting of the ballots" (*SC*, 203). This transparently didactic story gets infinitely more interesting when we learn that Tad Szulc, a Spanish-speaking *New York Times* reporter who covered the Catholic University visit, claims that Nixon invented the student election episode.[55] From Nixon's point of view, the Catholic University visit *should* have happened the way he tells it because his South American journey was about providing instruction in the integrity of democratic processes. While on his visits to factories in the Soviet Union in 1959, Nixon often observed that people were prevented from applauding him. His reprimand of his hosts demonstrates the power of free speech: "The next time I see one of your policemen trying to keep a crowd from indicating its friendship for the United States, I am going to blast the whole bunch of you publicly in a way you'll never forget" (*SC*, 277). The threat of exposure halted the Soviet government's intimidation of its citizens during the remainder of Nixon's stay. For a few brief days, at least, those Soviet citizens in the vice president's presence tasted the freedoms of an open society.

Fulfilling the nation's destiny requires more than preaching virtue; the American missionary must actively oppose evil in the rest of the world. Thus, in the stories of his confrontations with the communists, Nixon details his exposure of their corruption. After a communist-led mob in Lima, Peru, bars his exit from San Marcos University by pelting his entourage with rocks, Nixon, refusing to turn his back on the horde, lashes out: "You are afraid of the truth! You are the worst kind of cowards" (*SC*, 202). Later he lectured the Peruvian people that this act "had unmasked the ugly face of Communism as it really was" (*SC*, 206). During the same South American trip, Nixon braved a twelve-minute attack by a rock-throwing, steel-pipe brandishing mob of communist agitators in Caracas, Venezuela, barely escaping with his life. Officials at the American embassy wanted to hide the battered car so that the delegation of Venezuelan officials coming to meet the vice president would not be "embarrassed," but Nixon refused on the grounds that "it's time that they see some graphic evidence of what

Communism really is" (*SC*, 222). When accused by *Pravda* of attempting to bribe Moscow citizens for whom he had only wanted to buy tickets to the first American exhibition staged in the Soviet Union, Nixon gambled future American access to the Soviet media by relating the truth on Russian television. "It was the first time in recent Soviet history that anyone had publicly challenged the veracity of *Pravda*," he exults, "[and] it stimulated quite a bit of debate among the Russian people about the accuracy of the news they were receiving" (*SC*, 279–280). Through these courageous, honest acts in South America and the Soviet Union, Nixon, now a recognized national leader, reminds people of America's global mission. The startling ferocity of the violence directed against him in Caracas, and his calm response to it, awakened concern for conditions in South America; it provided, he claims, "a much-needed shock treatment which jolted us out of dangerous complacency" (*SC*, 229). Likewise, Nixon insists that his quiet but firm opposition to Khrushchev's bombastic rhetoric and posturing during the kitchen debate instructed his fellow Americans to match the Soviets' sense of destiny with, as he phrases it, "our spiritual and moral heritage, our dedication to individual liberties, our belief in the right of all people to choose the kind of economic, social, and political system they want" (*SC*, 290). To fight the battle on these terms guarantees victory, Nixon assures his countrymen, because "it is freedom rather than Communism that is the wave of the future" (*SC*, 291).

The rendering in *Six Crises* of Richard Nixon as a disciple of the myth of American mission finds precursors as deeply rooted as those for Nixon as a Horatio Alger–like hero. On May 16, 1958, upon Nixon's return from South America, the *Washington Star* published a Jim Berryman cartoon that showed Nixon riding in a car, with the Capitol dome in the background, waving to a crowd singing his praises. Though Eisenhower rides with him, Nixon towers above the president, at this moment dominating even the hero of World War II. The next year, in July 1959, Carl Hubenthal, editorial cartoonist for the *Los Angeles Herald-Examiner*, drew a muscular, strong-jawed Nixon, as a traveling salesman for "Peace and Friendship with [the] U.S.," pounding on the door of the Kremlin, ready to bring the goods of freedom to those imprisoned inside. That same month, in another Hubenthal cartoon, Nixon, having scaled a huge vise labeled "Cold War Pressure," vigorously turns the wheel to provide some relief to a trapped and frightened world.[56] In the 1960 election, the Republican campaign team exploited this world-savior image. As the button bearing the legend "Man of Steel, Richard M. Nixon" implies, under his seemingly ordinary Clark Kentish exterior beats the heart of America's self-made superman—faster than a perjurious communist spy, more powerful than a rock-throwing Venezuelan mob, able to leap bombastic Soviet premiers with a single rhetorical flourish—all while battling for "truth, justice, and the American way." The campaign biographies also heralded Nixon's wizardry in international diplomacy. Contemporary readers must continually remind themselves that détente and his elder statesman role as the sage of Saddle River are years in the future. Earl Mazo dedicated fifty uninterrupted pages to Nixon's overseas journeys, depicting a dispassionately strategic Nixon, aware of the symbolic import of his actions, even in life-threatening situations. Ralph de Toledano insisted that the Soviets "frankly hoped that the frenzy of the mobs [in South America] would get so out of hand that a serious, and perhaps successful, attempt on Nixon's life would be sparked."[57] While de Toledano never accounts for how a well-known American anticommunist reporter would be made privy to the secret desires of the Kremlin, nevertheless his Nixon faces death, ready to martyr himself for the redeemer nation.

Steeped in a meritocratic faith, *Six Crises* skillfully develops Nixon as a personification of the myth of divine mission, leading its readers to expect his ultimate success. For this reason, the ramifications of Nixon's defeat in 1960 go beyond mere disappointed expectations; unrewarded virtue excites anxieties of incipient decadence in the United States. To be sure, many of Nixon's political allies find the rhetoric of national decline quite congenial. In *Witness*, Whittaker Chambers relates how, during a break in his testimony before a New York City grand jury in the late 1940s, a middle-aged man thanked him for what he was doing but added despairingly that "nothing can save the American people." In the early 1950s, Senator Joe McCarthy rallied his loyal troops by denouncing "twenty years of treason"—exactly the number of years that the Democrats had held the White House. Bela Kornitzer concludes his biography of Nixon by applying this melancholy conviction of laboring in a lost cause to the 1960 presidential election, worrying that "it is questionable whether the Horatio Alger image still fires the popular imagination. . . . Today it is the poor little rich boy, the millionaire's son, with whom the striving and seeking public yearns to identify itself. Does this new hero-image then mean the end of the traditional American dream, the toppling of the torch from the Statue of Liberty?"

The Self-Made Superman. No one
seeing this button from the 1960
campaign could help but make
the association between Richard
Nixon and U.S. pop culture's
preeminent superhero and
defender of "truth, justice, and
the American way." Item from
the collection of Ted Hake, Hake's
Americana and Collectibles.
Photo by Justin B. Hopkins.

In more scholarly, but no less passionate, rhetoric, Milton Friedman
also warned against the spiritual mutilation that Kennedy's victory in
1960 represented for the United States. In the Preface to *Capitalism and
Freedom*, published the same year as *Six Crises*, Friedman lambastes the
philosophy behind Kennedy's famous "ask not" passage from the inaugural address, declaring: "Neither half of the statement expresses a relation
between the citizen and his government that is worthy of the ideals of
free men in a free society." That same year, Ayn Rand inveighed against
the Kennedy administration's domestic policy as a betrayal of America's
founding values: "There can be no compromise between freedom and
government controls; to accept 'just a few controls' is to surrender the
principle of inalienable individual rights and to substitute for it the principle of the government's unlimited, arbitrary power, thus delivering
oneself into gradual enslavement."[58] Finally, as Nixon was settling in to
write his autobiography, the Kennedy administration launched the poorly
planned, badly executed Bay of Pigs invasion in an attempt to overthrow
Fidel Castro's communist government in Cuba. This humiliating failure
led to Republican charges that Kennedy "had been lax in dealing with
Cuba, America's 'back yard.'"[59]

As Nixon looked back on the 1960 campaign in *Six Crises*, he could not
resist joining with the anxious chorus bemoaning America's decline. He
fumes, for example, that a discerning electorate should have seen through

Kennedy. Re-creating his thoughts during one of the debates, Nixon hears his opponent's emotionally powerful platitudes and realizes that much of the public will not ask the practical questions: "How does he propose to do all these things? How much is it going to cost?" (SC, 338). That these penetrating questions were not asked is, to Nixon's post-election eyes, a sign that modern America is increasingly made up of "unsophisticated voters" (SC, 338) who prefer "simpler and more dramatic" (SC, 336) political rhetoric. Forget the five o'clock shadow and the sweaty upper lip, his poor showing in the debates is actually attributable to this fundamental misreading of public intelligence, treating the voters as responsible citizens, capable of comprehending a complex and low-key approach to the issues: "I had concentrated too much on substance and not enough on appearance" (SC, 340). Put bluntly, Nixon wants to attribute part of his defeat to the absence of the informed, conscientious citizenry that democracy needs to exist.

Despite the temptation of, and comfort offered by, such a conclusion, Nixon only flirts with these apocalyptic visions. Unable to follow where such unrelieved pessimism would lead, he shies away from faulting the people as a whole for his defeat. Instead, Nixon finds an escape hatch for his countrymen, and, in so doing, *Six Crises* transforms defeat into victory and a reaffirmation that the nation still has faith in him and, therefore, in its values. The first step toward such a momentous conclusion is an extremely mundane one: bad luck lost the 1960 election. By the end, as Nixon relates the story, his comedy of errors had assumed Shakespearean proportions. Henry Cabot Lodge, the vice presidential candidate, promised, without clearing his statement with Nixon first, the appointment of a black man to the cabinet. Seeming to play on religious bigotry, Nixon's close friend, the Reverend Dr. Norman Vincent Peale, voiced fears that Kennedy would be a captive of the pope. Just as the campaign got started, Nixon bumped his knee against a car door, developed an infection, and was hospitalized for two weeks. In scheduling the debates, his campaign saved the discussion of international relations—the area in which Nixon had the greatest expertise—for the later sessions, betting that the audience would grow as the debates continued. But twenty million more people watched the first debate than any of the other three. To make matters worse, the first debate occurred shortly after Nixon's hospital stay: he was ten pounds underweight and his clothes fit him loosely. To compound these problems, he refused to wear makeup and so appeared on camera as pasty-faced and poorly shaven.

But, according to Nixon, unlucky fate alone did not vanquish him; a biased national news media deserved much of the blame as well. Falling hard for the Kennedy charm, the press was seduced by the Democrats' "victory blitz" strategy, a full-scale public relations effort attempting to condition the press to expect a Democratic landslide. A late October NBC television special prematurely pronounced a Kennedy victory as a foregone conclusion—and so did the opinion columns of leading newspaper pundits like Rowland Evans, Joe Alsop, and James Reston and the mass-circulation weekly news magazines *Time*, *Newsweek*, and *U.S. News and World Report*. Election night reporting only deepened this irresponsible pattern of "political reporters . . . predict[ing] with their hearts rather than with their heads" (*SC*, 360). On election night, CBS television declared Kennedy the winner at 9 PM EST—before the polls had closed in the western United States and with only 8 percent of the vote counted nationally. Uninterested in the voices of actual people, the media relied on its computers, which predicted an overwhelming Kennedy victory, just as the actual vote total, popular and electoral, continued to narrow.[60]

Although this kind of biased reporting undoubtedly affected such a close race, nevertheless Nixon places primary responsibility for the result on vote fraud. With the precision of an IRS agent auditing a suspect ledger book, Nixon itemizes the cheating. To take just two of his examples, he reports that in "Fannin County, Texas (which went 3 to 1 for Kennedy): there were 4895 voters on the official 'poll tax list' but 6138 votes were counted" (*SC*, 412). Similarly, in a Chicago precinct "that voted for Kennedy by 451 to 67, the initial registration of a husband and wife was challenged on grounds of 'false address.' On election day, both voted. On recanvass, it was found that there were no such persons at the address listed" (*SC*, 412). With many more recorded cases of deception in an election that was decided by a margin of only 113,000 popular and 84 electoral votes, Nixon makes the case that he did not really lose the presidency. He lays out, state by state, how the slightest alterations in voting patterns would have changed the outcome: "A shift, for example, of 4000 votes each in Illinois and Missouri, and of a total of 3000 to 5000 votes in any two such states as New Mexico, Nevada, or Hawaii, would have changed the electoral results" (*SC*, 411–412). More than anything else, voting irregularities made the difference—a line of reasoning that allows Nixon to conclude that the American people are not corrupt—although, in so doing, he had to show that ruthless politicians can steal an election.

Such tortuous logic permits Nixon to turn the seemingly irreversible setback of losing a presidential election into a triumph. For only by absolving the American people from responsibility for his defeat can he begin processing the abundant evidence of their continued admiration for him. When told of her father's defeat, daughter Julie philosophized: "Well, maybe we didn't win the election, but we won in the hearts of the people" (*SC*, 393). The following days and weeks, as Nixon recounts them, confirm her pronouncement. As Nixon left his Los Angeles hotel headquarters to return to Washington, his supporters crowded the hallways: "People cheered, slapped us on the back, shook our hands as if we had won the election rather than lost" (*SC*, 399). Back in Washington, D.C., Nixon received a deluge of letters and telegrams, more than he had received at any other time in his public life. Near the end of *Six Crises*, Nixon relates an incident from the 1960 Christmas season: "Several people recognized us [as the Nixon family entered a Broadway theater] and started to applaud. Before we could find our seats, the entire audience rose and joined in. . . . As we rode back to our hotel from the theater, Tricia said to us: 'You see—the people still like you'" (*SC*, 414–415). Using this evidence of continued respect, Nixon contends that, although denied the presidency, he achieved a more authentic form of success. And, because his hard work still garnered spiritual rewards, the traditional success myth remains relevant. The Gallup Poll's annual "Most Admired Man" survey gives some evidence that Nixon's optimism was more than just wishful thinking. Asked at the end of 1961, as *Six Crises* was being completed for its spring 1962 publication, Gallup respondents ranked Nixon as America's eighth most admired man in the world—one place higher than he had been in 1959 when he was the sitting vice president.[61]

Seen in this light, *Six Crises* constitutes the debut of the full-blown Nixon mythology. Through the writing of his memoir, the losing candidate in a presidential election single-handedly re-creates himself as the true winner ready to contemplate a return to public life. Unwilling to openly articulate his new political goals, Nixon uses a February 1961 letter from Whittaker Chambers, urging him to run for governor of California in 1962: "[The defeat in 1960] does not change the nature of your journey. . . . Service is your life. You must serve. You must, therefore, have a base from which to serve" (*SC*, 425). By the end of his first autobiography, Nixon has exorcised his self-doubts and sees the potential for greater success beckoning to him. To mark this personal victory, the memoir concludes with a celebratory cadenza, hitting notes so resonant that Nixon offered encores in his two other autobiographies and Pete Wilson referred to it during his funeral tribute: "For me, the evening of my life has not yet come. But for the boy who, forty years ago, used to lie in bed in Yorba Linda, California, and dream of traveling to far-off places when he heard the train whistle in the night, I can say even now that the day has indeed been splendid" (*SC*, 426).

From another perspective, however, Nixon's inspiring conclusion complacently vindicates an exaggerated faith in individualism. Attentive readings of Franklin's *Autobiography* and Horatio Alger's novels indicate that, in actuality, the self-made man gets by with a good deal of outside help. Franklin would have failed in his first printing business—indeed, might have been jailed for debt—had not "two true Friends" approached him, separately and of their own will, "offering each of them to advance [him] all the Money that should be necessary."[62] Ragged Dick makes the connection that permits him to abandon his career as shoeshine boy simply by being in the right place at the right time—he saves the young son of his future boss from drowning. In this regard, *Six Crises* has more in common with the Westerns that dominated film during the 1950s and television during the early 1960s. Like those cowboy and sheriff heroes, Nixon, in *Six Crises*, acts alone. Other actors fade into the background as our solitary hero catches Hiss, defuses the Fund scandal, guides the government through Ike's illnesses, braves the hostile South American crowd, tests wits with Khrushchev, and runs for president. The same year that *Six Crises* was published, one of television's most outlandish tributes to the American dream, *The Beverly Hillbillies*, premiered and immediately leapt into the top ten.[63] In the story of Jed Clampett, the poor backwoodsman who discovers vast oil deposits while out hunting for game to feed his family, Americans reassured themselves that anyone who keeps shooting will hit the target someday.

Six Crises buys unreservedly into this big promise and refuses to recognize *any* limitations to the traditional myth of success. Yet its narrow focus on the life of one very successful man working in the highest circles of government cultivates an extremely rarified environment, a securely gated community locking out much of the history of the times. Younger readers of *Six Crises* might never guess that Michael Harrington's *The Other America* appeared the same year as Nixon's autobiography. Certainly, Harrington's insistence on making visible "the invisible land" of poverty where nearly fifty million Americans lived in physical and spiritual neglect challenges the nation's bland, unspoken "assumption that the basic grinding economic problems had been solved."[64] Seven years before *Six Crises* was published, African Americans in Montgomery, Alabama, staged a yearlong protest to win the right to sit in the front rows of public buses. Five years later, and in the midst of a presidential election year, black college students in various southern cities led sit-ins to win the right to eat at department store lunch counters. Even as Nixon was writing *Six Crises*, the Freedom Riders, a group of college-age students, were being attacked and beaten by mobs for attempting to integrate interstate buses and their station facilities. In defending his decision not to intervene on behalf of Dr. Martin Luther King Jr., who was jailed in the latter days of the 1960 campaign, Nixon protests "that well-informed Washington observers knew that I had been one of the most consistent and effective proponents of civil rights legislation in the [Eisenhower] Administration" (*SC*, 363). Strangely, though, this passage is one of only a few that deals with race in the entire book.

Similarly, the reader of *Six Crises* would have no clue of an emerging women's movement. Prepublication excerpts of Betty Friedan's *The Feminine Mystique* appeared in *Mademoiselle* in 1962, introducing readers to "the problem that has no name," the conviction that "something is very wrong with the way American women are trying to live their lives today."[65] For confirmation of her thesis, Friedan might have looked no further than the opening pages of *Six Crises*. The book's extraordinarily tone-deaf dedication—"To Pat, she *also ran*" (*SC*, vii, emphasis mine)—reveals a husband whose best attempt at expressing appreciation to his wife is to employ language most commonly used to denote a loser. Pat Nixon, when she appears in the book at all, offers encouragement to her husband from the sidelines, sitting next to him, but mostly off camera, during the Fund speech, distracting reporters at the entrance to their home while he sneaks out the back door to escape press scrutiny during the hours following the announcement of Eisenhower's heart attack. On the public stage of *Six Crises*, women play only bit parts—and minorities are kept almost entirely backstage.

Just as damaging as its unquestioning faith in the limitless power of individual initiative, *Six Crises*, through its blind adherence to the myth of national mission, promotes a Manichean worldview. The world splits into two opposing camps, with the United States representing absolute good and its enemies embodying unmitigated evil. In practice, this philosophy has led to unquestioning support for authoritarian right-wing military governments simply because they opposed the communists. In 1953, Nixon's first year as vice president, the CIA helped overthrow the nationalist and anticolonial Mosaddeq government in Iran, reinstating the brutal reign of the shah. The next year, the CIA overthrew the government of Guatemala after it had tried to nationalize the United Fruit Company. And by the time *Six Crises* hit the best-seller lists, U.S. involvement in Vietnam was slowly moving from flirtation with disaster to full-blown folly. Assured of the complete depravity of its foe, the U.S. government blinded itself to the irony of promoting democracy through morally questionable means in support of unsavory allies. By so doing, the nation set its course toward a war in which thousands of lives would be sacrificed on the altar of the myth of national mission.

Finally, churning underneath the surface of the seemingly complacent optimism of *Six Crises* is a festering, resentful anger that prefigures the mentality that created the Watergate scandal. Despite his claims to have accepted its outcome, Nixon remained bitter that the 1960 election rewarded corruption instead of integrity. Forced by his regard for the nation's reputation to forgo a challenge of the election returns, Nixon explained in *Six Crises:* "I could think of no worse example for nations abroad, who for the first time were trying to put free electoral procedures into effect, than that of the United States wrangling over the results of our presidential election, and even suggesting that the presidency itself could be stolen by thievery at the ballot box" (*SC*, 413). Yet his advertising of this heroic gesture less than two years after the fact, if it doesn't nullify some of the good it did, certainly taints its nobility. Apparently, virtue was not enough to satisfy "Ragged Dick" Nixon. Only the presidency itself could do that. But, convinced that he had been cheated once already, he would approach the prize feeling that he had moral carte blanche to take it by any means necessary. This principle, the sad lesson Nixon took from *Six Crises*, would lead directly to the Richard Nixon of Watergate.

CHAPTER TWO

JEREMIAH AT SAN CLEMENTE

RICHARD NIXON AND THE DECLINE

OF THE AMERICAN REPUBLIC

By 1972, Richard Nixon believed that the past granted him moral license. Determined to never be taken advantage of again, Nixon embraced a no-holds-barred attitude, epitomized by the transcript of the "smoking gun" Oval Office tape of June 20, 1972. In agreeing to use CIA pressure to call off the FBI's investigation of Watergate, Nixon urged his White House chief of staff, H. R. Haldeman, to "'play it tough,' because that was the way the Democrats always played it 'and that's the way we are going to play it.'"[1] The release of this conversation in early August 1974 completed the most precipitous fall in American presidential history. A mere two years separated Nixon's resignation from his visit to the People's Republic of China, the beginning of détente with the Soviet Union, and his landslide reelection victory. Given the totality of his disgrace, Nixon, rightly, feared for his legacy. When, in the days before the resignation, Henry Kissinger tried to console Nixon with the thought that history would rank him as a great president, Nixon responded, "That depends, Henry, on who writes the history" (*RN*, 1084). Certain of the assessment his presidency deserved, Nixon determined not to bow to the judgment of the political analysts, journalists, and academicians with the power to create the accounts of his tenure in office. In typically self-reliant fashion, Nixon resolved to write his story himself.

To that end, Nixon turned to familiar forums in which he had had previous success: television and autobiography. Taped in March 1977, *The Nixon Interviews with David Frost* aired on a network of independent television stations, presenting four different programs in May and one in September of that year. The May 4 debut attracted perhaps as many as fifty million viewers—a record audience for a news interview. The subsequent programs did not draw quite as well but garnered sizable audiences and generated front-page news. Providing immediately needed cash ($540,000 was the final payment), these sessions afforded Nixon a dress rehearsal for an even more significant event: the publication of his second autobiography, *RN: The Memoirs of Richard Nixon*.[2] Despite some difficulties in finding a publisher and bumper stickers and T-shirts advertising a "Don't Buy Books by Crooks" boycott attempt, the book arrived in bookstores on May 15, 1978. Even with an unusually hefty retail price ($19.95), Nixon's memoirs belied early predictions of failure by debuting on the *New York Times Book Review*'s best-seller list at number four, on June 4, 1978, sharing the spotlight during its eleven-week run with other nonfiction titles such as *The Complete Book of Running*, *My Mother, My Self*, the self-help book *Pulling Your Own Strings*, and former Nixon treasury secretary William Simon's paean to the free enterprise system, *A Time for Truth*, as well as with the novels *The World According to Garp*, the feminist classic *The Women's Room*, and James Michener's *Chesapeake*.[3] With these two much-publicized events, his television interviews and the publication of his memoirs, Nixon began his last campaign: the fight for his personal and political rehabilitation.

In the earliest phase of this final comeback attempt, Nixon sought self-redemption by ascribing his fate to an incipient decay in the nation's moral fiber. Donning the robes of a hellfire and brimstone preacher, he transformed the story of his public shame into one about America's betrayal of its ideals. Yet even as his televised interviews with David Frost and his second book of memoirs chronicled America's fall from grace, Nixon exhorted the nation to reclaim its promise. Stripped of his role as a leader and exiled from Washington, D.C., Nixon fashioned himself in the unlikely role of a Jeremiah at San Clemente.

Those who doubted Nixon's ability to bounce back from Watergate ignored history. In winning the presidency in 1968, Richard Nixon had already achieved the seemingly impossible. After the excruciating defeat to Kennedy in 1960 came the humiliation of losing the California governor's race in 1962. In the aftermath of his self-declared "last press conference" and his bitter promise that the media wouldn't have him "to kick around any more," Richard Nixon had become little more than a political punch line. In a 1963 television appearance, he had to force a good-natured chuckle at Jack Paar's joke that his daughter, hearing that the former vice president would be a guest, had worried, "I *do* hope that man finds work!"[4] Yet, by the end of that year, Nixon had already reclaimed a place on Gallup's list of "most admired men." And throughout the rest of the decade, with the exception of 1964, Nixon remained there.[5] His supporters could be forgiven for hailing his reemergence in 1968 as nothing less than miraculous. Earl Mazo and Stephen Hess opened their 1968 campaign biography by predicting that "Nixon may still prove to be a political Lazarus."[6] Ralph de Toledano's third biography of Nixon, *One Man Alone* (1969), touted Nixon's victory as "the greatest political comeback in the history of the Republic."[7] But Henry D. Spalding's 1972 campaign biography, *The Nixon Nobody Knows*, surpasses them all in its celebration of the 1968 triumph, whipping up an indigestible mixed metaphor salmagundi of sports cliché (an "incredible comeback"), mythological allusion (reemerging from the ashes like the "legendary phoenix"), and Broadway show tunes (Nixon "dared to dream the impossible dream").[8]

Not surprisingly, Nixon's resurrection made him, for many, an even more potent symbol of the power of individual initiative. Warren King's post-election cartoon for the *New York News* depicted a solitary Nixon who has climbed the steps to success, scaling over obstacles like George Wallace's third party challenge, the greater number of registered Democrats, and his own loser image. A former assistant publisher of *American Heritage* magazine, Edwin P. Hoyt, in his 1972 biography, *The Nixons: An American Family*, conflates Nixon's genealogy with the story of the United States. By migrating from Delaware to Pennsylvania, Ohio, and, eventually, California, the Nixons acted out the national myth of settlers moving west, continually seeking a new start on new land. Richard Nixon's grandfather's philosophy of "root, hog, or die" displayed the resolute spirit of a people earning everything by their own hard labor. For the contemporary American, Richard Nixon's life "prov[ed] a reenactment of the American dream that any man (and someday any woman) can aspire to . . . the leadership of the nation."[9] If this rags-to-riches story only lacked the log cabin to evoke the memory of another Republican president, other representations of Nixon made the comparison explicit. In one button from the 1968 campaign, not even the obligatory ski-jump nose can obscure the Lincolnian jaw and forehead in Nixon's portrait. Like the rail-splitter from Illinois, Richard Nixon can be counted on to be "Of the People/For the People."

Other campaign items from the 1968 and 1972 elections also advertised Nixon as the epitome of national values. Urging America to give itself "another great president," one pin looked like an all-Republican Mount Rushmore, dominated by Nixon's photo in the center with smaller portraits of Lincoln, Theodore Roosevelt, and the safely Federalist George Washington circling his head. A second pin, though visually simpler, was

In this 1968 button distributed by local Republican Party organizations in Pennsylvania, Nixon's features take on a decided Lincolnian cast. Item from the author's personal collection. Photo by the author.

no less arresting. Here, the Uncle Sam of the iconic "I Want You" draft poster all but commanded our vote for Nixon, with the endorsement that "he's good enough for me in '68." Distributed by the A. G. Trimble Company, the producers of the "I Like Ike" slogan, both of these buttons insinuate that no true patriot could reject this spiritual son of Uncle Sam. In fact, Nixon's campaigns during both 1968 and 1972 boasted that almost literally no one opposed him. A poster from the 1968 election displayed an outline of the continental United States with the legend "Nixon Country" inscribed across it. A series of over thirty celluloid buttons from the 1972 campaign proclaimed a rainbow coalition of ethnic and multiracial support for President Nixon. The bandwagon grew so large that even his opponents endorsed him, or so maintained a whimsical lithograph pin that proclaimed the support of "Anti-Nixonites for Nixon."

Such extravagant claims made his downfall so hard to accept for Nixon and his supporters that, in their search to understand, they drew upon the jeremiad, which literary critics have classified as the first distinctive American literary form.[10] Originating with the Puritan ritual of the fast-day sermon, the American jeremiad detailed the colony's specific misfortunes, explaining them as God's punishment for the settlers' sinful failure to fulfill the divine mission that had brought them to the New World. Not meant to paralyze the Puritans with self-loathing, the jeremiad instead sought to renew their faith and rededicate them to their mission. According to Sacvan Bercovitch, the jeremiad functioned "to create a climate of

Borrowing the familiar iconography of the Selective Service poster, this button asserts that Americans in 1968 could best fulfill their patriotic duty to defend the United States by voting for Richard Nixon. Item from the author's personal collection. Photo by the author.

anxiety that helped release the restless 'progressivist' energies required for the success of the venture." This core purpose, in fact, far outlasted the Puritans themselves. By "transmitting a myth [of divine mission] that remained central to the culture long after the [Puritan] theocracy had faded and New England itself had lost its national influence," the Puritans "forged what was to become a framework for national identity."[11]

Although never one to bow to his critics, Nixon correctly anticipated that his pose as an American Jeremiah would not be accepted without doing some advance work to prepare his audience. After the interviews with David Frost aired, even his past ally and future eulogizer, Robert Dole, rejected the notion of any immediate role for Nixon in the Republican Party, suggesting that "it takes more than four interviews to properly rehabilitate Richard Nixon." The reviews of *RN* were, at best, mixed; quite often, they were openly hostile. John Osborne, writing in the *New Republic*, dubbed the memoirs "a really godawful book." The *Christian Century* dismissed it as "the chronicle of an unrepentant liar." *Newsweek*'s Peter Goldman tsked that Nixon was "still clinging to [excuses]—that he still consider[ed] himself guiltless of anything much worse than making mistakes." Former CBS news correspondent Daniel Schorr wondered at the total absence of the tragic in "Nixon's tenacious and lonely battle against an inevitable fate," ascribing the lack of nobility in the book's narrative of Nixon's demise to the man's lack of moral vision and to his being "so manifestly sorry for himself and so little sorry for the nation." Meanwhile, in the *New York*

Review of Books, John Kenneth Galbraith marveled at how a "rascal" like Nixon could seem to perceive "himself a deeply moral man—or, at minimum, [could believe] that he can so persuade any known audience."[12]

Ever the political pragmatist, Nixon conceded that no post-Watergate audience would accept his ascent to the moral high ground without a careful campaign to retrieve an image of integrity for himself. With that reality in mind, he methodically set about in the pre-scandal portion of *RN* to reclaim his reputation as a representative of America's most cherished myths. In a self-consciously apple-pie opening, Nixon begins with the simple declarative: "I was born in a house my father built" (3). This suggestion of a tightly knit, self-sufficient family leads directly into tributes to his parents that explicate the moral lessons they instilled in him. The Frank Nixon of the memoirs champions the "little man," living and preaching the central dogma of the gospel of success "that in America, with hard work and determination a man can achieve anything" (6, 7). From his mother's example and his family's regular attendance at Sunday morning, Sunday evening, and Wednesday evening Quaker meetings, Nixon learned that a healthy life must be based on a quiet spirituality. Speaking fondly of the home Frank and Hannah Nixon made for their children, he boasts: "It was not an easy life, but it was a good one" (*RN,* 5). At school, Nixon depicts himself as a determined overachiever, a well-rounded boy intensely involved in academic as well as extracurricular activities. But the college football practice field, in particular, offered him a forum for merging the hard-work philosophy of his father with that of his coach, who told his team "that if we worked hard enough and played hard enough, we could beat anybody" (*RN,* 19). In these early pages of the book, Nixon answers those critics who charged that he had no core beliefs by demonstrating that before his entry into public life his basic integrity had been formed by absorbing the values of family, church, and school.

Nixon also sets about polishing his tarnished Horatio Alger image. And so the narrative of his first campaign for public office—the U.S. House of Representatives race against the five-term incumbent Jerry Voorhis— models the classic American success story: Nixon wins because he works harder than his rival. Compensating for his political inexperience, he matriculates in a self-taught curriculum on Congress and campaigns: "Each night when I got home from work I pored over magazines, newspapers, and books" (*RN,* 35). Augmenting his industry, the narratives of all Nixon's early campaigns exhibit his political courage. In the elections of 1954 and 1958, likely disasters for the Republicans (as off-year races traditionally are for the ruling party), Eisenhower would not risk his reputation by campaigning for the GOP nationwide. But Nixon, despite warnings to stay out, insisted on working actively in these lost causes, sacrificing his prestige for the greater good of the party. In the final week of the 1960 presidential election, Nixon cancelled Ike's intensive campaign tour on his behalf to honor Mamie Eisenhower's fears that the stress might cause her husband to have another heart attack or stroke. In telling the story, Nixon publicizes his selflessness by explicitly noting the indisputable benefits he would have received from enthusiastic appearances by the president. Through moments such as these, Nixon justifies himself by claiming he typifies the hard work, fearlessness, and self-denial of the self-made man.

In a similar fashion, *RN* casts Nixon's pre-presidential career in the terms of the myth of American mission, consistently representing his idealistic awareness of America's special role as an exemplar nation. Far more than simple travelogues, Nixon's descriptions of his overseas trips from 1947 to 1967 call on his readers to fulfill America's duty to aid underdeveloped and captive nations. During Nixon's first visit to the Far East, South Korea's Syngman Rhee instructed him on the absolute necessity of American strength in Cold War politics: "The Communists think that America wants peace so badly that you will do anything to get it" (*RN*, 128). While visiting Pakistan in 1964, Nixon found his "old friend," President Ayub Khan, mourning America's support for the coup that killed South Vietnam's leader Ngo Dinh Diem, accusing the United States of complicity in the assassination, and taking the bitter lesson "that it is dangerous to be a friend of the United States; that it pays to be neutral; and sometimes it helps to be an enemy!" (*RN*, 256, 257). Yet, in relating these stories, Nixon has less interest in condemning his country than he has in correcting its wrong-headed policies—in urging it to learn from its mistakes so as to live up to its role as the hope of the world.

By resuscitating his "Ragged Dick" Nixon, American missionary persona, Nixon hopes to take his claims to virtuous character off life support and argue, as he did in *Six Crises*, that he deserved to be president. As the culmination of this effort, Nixon reports two testimonials. The first comes from Fina Sanchez, his Cuban immigrant housekeeper, who, on hearing of his decision to run for president in 1968, declared: "You are the man to lead the country! This was determined before you were born!" (*RN*, 294). The other comes from no less a luminary than Billy Graham, who told Nixon, "I think it is your destiny to be President" (*RN*, 293). These two endorsements complete the narration of preparation for the presidency, reasserting Nixon as a representative of America's dominant ideology and, hopefully, predisposing some readers to accept his use of the jeremiad.

Fully aware, however, that many post-Watergate observers would require further convincing, Nixon trumpets his first-term presidential accomplishments, portraying himself as the best president the United States has known. "I do not believe," he declares in the section of *RN* that deals with 1972, "that any administration in history has gone into a re-election campaign with a more impressive record. . . . There was no major area in American life in which we had not made progress or proposed dramatic new alternatives" (*RN*, 670). In fact, this strategy for reestablishing his credibility returns to a major theme of his 1972 reelection campaign. Shot in dramatic black and white, a poster from that year shows a contemplative Nixon, the indispensable leader, gazing out of the Oval Office into the Rose Garden. The caption running along the side of the photo valorizes Nixon as a man of substance, one who possesses "coolness," "intelligence," and "a sense of history." Rather than mere charisma, Nixon gives us both vision and accomplishments. Interestingly, the original version of the photo reveals not a heroic leader burdened by the unique responsibilities of his office but Nixon in conversation with Henry Kissinger—just one-half of a partnership. Yet the appearance of solitary leadership was so critical for Nixon that Kissinger had to be cropped out of the photo for use in the campaign. No less critical five years later, Nixon used the Frost interviews and his second autobiography to forcefully reclaim this powerful image, seeking not just to impress us with his handling of domestic affairs, Vietnam, and détente, but also to claim a place of honor in the pantheon of great American leaders.

In domestic affairs, Nixon characterizes himself as the principled defender of the ordinary American citizen: those "squares" he protectively referred to during the Frost interviews as "a lot of decent people too, even though they may not have gone to college."[13] Safeguarding their rights against an encroaching "Washington paternalism" (*RN*, 351), the Nixon of *RN*, like a mirror-image FDR, tries to restructure the federal bureaucracy and the Supreme Court, giving power back to states and local communities, to make government "more truly reflective of the rest of the country" (*RN*, 762). He draws on similar populist sentiments to explain his approach to calming the escalating racial tensions of the late 1960s and early 1970s. Improvement in the condition of blacks, Nixon asserted, must be combined with the realization that "the law cannot go beyond what the people are willing to support" (*RN*, 444). Real change in racism would

The nation needs
coolness more
than clarion calls;
intelligence more
than charisma;
a sense of history
more than a
sense of histrionics.

This poster from the 1972 reelection campaign, which sounds as if Nixon were still campaigning against JFK, presents a wise and lonely leader. Item from the author's personal collection. Photo by John Herr Photography.

The original photograph reveals what the campaign poster cropped out, namely that Nixon, far from being alone, was in the middle of a consultation with his national security advisor, Henry Kissinger. Oliver Atkins, Richard Nixon White House Photographs, Special Collections and Archives, George Mason University Libraries.

come not from federal legislation but from local solutions that would educate whites on "the wisdom and humanity that lay behind [the civil rights movement]" (*RN*, 440). In the end, Nixon claimed, his policy resulted in more, and faster, school desegregation than any other president had achieved.

The domestic threats posed by the antiwar movement required more active solutions. While in public Nixon vowed not to be swayed by the demonstrators, in private he plotted a secret campaign of surveillance and intimidation. His efforts peaked in 1970 with the proposal of the Huston Plan, a scheme that called for the various intelligence-gathering agencies to cooperate in surveillance, mail-opening, and covert-entry operations against suspected student revolutionaries. Aware of the extraordinary nature of such measures, Nixon defended the plan during his TV interviews with the claim that "when the President does it that means that it is not illegal." Challenged by Frost, Nixon compared himself to Lincoln bending the Constitution in order to preserve the nation during the Civil War. Because the nation was "torn apart in an ideological way by the war in Vietnam," Nixon dared take "actions which otherwise would be unconstitutional" to preserve the domestic peace.

As willful, judicious, and innovative as Nixon appears when discussing his domestic reforms, he exudes serene confidence that his foreign policy demonstrates his fundamental integrity. In Vietnam, Nixon asserts, he possessed the strength of character to conclude the war on favorable terms. As he told David Frost, when questioned about the enormous costs of continuing the war, "The most popular position to take on Vietnam . . . was to bug out and blame it on Johnson and Kennedy." Nixon had no intention, however, of surrendering to political expediency. When Hanoi launched an offensive in the winter of 1969, he responded with "Operation Breakfast," a series of secret bombing runs against communist guerrillas hiding in Cambodia. "I was prepared to continue," he says in his memoirs, indicating his willingness to take upon himself the entire burden of the war, "despite the serious strains that would be involved on the home front" (*RN*, 413). Bill Roberts, a cartoonist for the Scripps-Howard news syndicate, celebrated Nixon's handling of Vietnam, drawing him, on January 27, 1972, as a coolly collected poker player. While all the other figures at the table seem worn down by nerves, only Nixon sits straight and tall. Even though he has put all his cards on the table, he appears to be the one in control. Later that year, when the North Vietnamese, hoping to break America's resolve, twice stalled the peace process, Nixon answered swiftly with the mining of Haiphong harbor and the bombing of Hanoi in the spring and heavy B-52 attacks in the last weeks of the year. Though these actions were opposed by significant sections of the population, Nixon insists that his resoluteness is what made the 1973 peace settlement possible.

Moreover, Nixon asserts that these same qualities of will and vision achieved not only the end of the Vietnam War but also détente with the Soviet Union and the People's Republic of China. Through his easing of the tensions between the United States and its two most implacable enemies, Nixon claims to be on a mission for the entire world. To bolster this impression, he recalls the French writer André Malraux's parting words to him before the trip to the People's Republic: "All men who understand what you are embarking upon salute you!" (RN, 559). By balancing an awareness of the philosophical and strategic conflicts between the United States and its adversaries with a perception of their areas of mutual interest, Nixon imagined that the détente process could, as he told Brezhnev in 1973, allow "your children and grandchildren to grow up in a world of peace" (RN, 883). Nixon retains such confidence in his foreign policy achievements that, in response to Frost's request that he admit mistakes in the handling of the Watergate affair, he instead lists the summits with the Soviet Union, the China initiative, maintaining the fragile Vietnam peace accord, and progress toward peace in the Middle East, declaring, "I owe it to history to point out that from that time on, April 30th, until I resigned on August 9th I did some things that were good for this country."

Well before Watergate, by Nixon's exhaustive account, he had established a character that personified America's most cherished values. The old debater in Nixon, however, could never permit a goal as important as self-redemption to depend solely on one argument—no matter how well sustained. So he takes a different tack: seeking to diminish the judgment of Watergate, contending that it was not a serious matter when compared to America's interests on the world scene.

Nixon's dogmatism about Watergate's triviality derives from his certainty that everyone in government engaged in the activities for which his administration was condemned. During the Frost interview, as Nixon clung to his story that his concern during the early days of the Watergate scandal was entirely with containing its political damage, he remarked in passing that if such actions were corrupt then "President Truman would have been impeached." This throwaway comment foreshadowed more sustained efforts to come. In *RN*, such finger-pointing produces an itemized list of Democratic crimes matching, and exceeding, anything seen in Watergate. If his 1972 campaign engaged in illegal fund-raising practices, then so did Joseph Montoya of the Senate Watergate Committee. Charged with spending taxpayers' money for renovations of his homes in Florida and California, Nixon shows that Johnson and Kennedy had done the same for their residences.[14] Had Nixon deducted the gift of his personal papers to the National Archives? Well, so had Pat Brown, John Kenneth Galbraith, George Wallace, Hubert Humphrey, Arthur Schlesinger Jr., and Theodore Sorensen.[15] By protesting that such activities "were standard political practice by both sides" (*RN*, 643), Nixon hoped to blunt any moral outrage directed toward him.

Even before Nixon's resignation, a core constituency proved receptive to this argument. Southern rockers Lynyrd Skynyrd spoke to these people in their Top Ten hit song "Sweet Home Alabama," released in April 1974, which followed praise for Governor George Wallace with the challenge: "Now Watergate does not bother me / Does your conscience bother you?"[16] By the time *RN* appeared, recent events proved to be Nixon's strongest ally in expanding the audience for such sentiments. In 1975, a commission led by Vice President Nelson Rockefeller and a Senate committee chaired by Frank Church of Idaho had separately unveiled disturbing illegal acts and abuses of power that U.S. intelligence agencies had carried out at the behest of presidents from Truman through Johnson. CIA-sponsored coups and coup attempts, assassinations and assassination plots dotted the globe from Cuba and Guatemala to Iran, Congo, and South Vietnam. Nor had American citizens been safe from mischief. At home, the CIA had experimented with the effects of LSD and other mind-altering drugs, turning unwitting individuals into laboratory rats, while the FBI mounted a massive counterintelligence sabotage effort against antiwar and civil rights movement leaders, including the wiretapping of Martin Luther King Jr.[17] Meanwhile, political scandals, like a metastasizing cancer, seemed to race through the body politic. Federal grand jury indictments of politicians and other government officials grew more than fivefold in the first six years of the 1970s. Former governors, sitting judges, mayors, and aldermen found themselves facing charges. More than 60 percent of these cases ended in convictions.[18] In 1976, the *Washington Post* charged that nearly one-quarter of the House of Representatives had accepted bribes from South Korean lobbyists. Leon Jaworski, former Watergate special prosecutor, headed the investigation into what the media dubbed "Koreagate."[19] Less than a year later, Bert Lance, Jimmy Carter's director of the Office of Management and Budget and his personal friend, stood accused of financial improprieties while running the National Bank of Georgia. The ensuing congressional investigation and court case became known as "Lancegate."[20] In fact, the ubiquitous appearance of the suffix "gate" in any newsworthy scandal turned what had been accepted at the time as a unique constitutional crisis into a seemingly everyday event.

Moreover, Nixon and his supporters wanted the country to believe not just that "everybody does it" but that everybody else did it first. In 1977, Victor Lasky published *It Didn't Start with Watergate*, a Wagnerian-length recital of crimes committed by previous Democratic administrations. Apparently, such arguments resonated enough to be taken seriously by a good portion of the reading public because Lasky's book camped out on the best-seller list for twenty-four weeks, a total exceeded by only four other nonfiction books during 1977.[21] One of the few journalists Nixon trusted personally, Lasky also wrote the scathing exposé *JFK: The Man and the Myth* and (co-authored with Ralph de Toledano) *Seeds of Treason*, a book on the Hiss case, which depicted Nixon so heroically that his 1950 Senate campaign staff sought to circulate 500,000 copies of the *Readers' Digest* condensation.[22] From the first page of *It Didn't Start with Watergate*, Lasky proves that his friend's trust was not misplaced, articulating this classic defense: "Precisely what is Nixon accused of doing, if he actually did it, that his predecessors didn't do many times over?"[23] In this masterly formulation, Lasky doubles the doubtfulness of Nixon's guilt: first by casting it as a question and then as a hypothetical embedded inside the query. In *RN*, when Nixon admits the existence of Gordon Liddy's plan for intelligence gathering on the Democrats, he points out that this scheme did not use the FBI, a favorite tactic of Lyndon Johnson's. And, although conceding that he wanted to pressure the Internal Revenue Service into harassing his enemies, Nixon characterizes his attempts to do so as "tentative . . . feeble and amateurish in comparison to the Democrats" (*RN*, 676). At every turn, he dismisses the charges of corruption made against him by drawing attention to the superior skill and cynical effectiveness with which others played the political game.

At the same time, Nixon's defense rested on the belief that his foreign policy successes should outweigh any of his alleged wrongdoings. As Nixon himself phrased it, "Watergate mattered so much less than the things I did well" (*RN*, 973). *RN* forcefully drives home the comparative inconsequentiality of the scandal by narrating the events of October 1973 in short passages that alternate between descriptions of the Yom Kippur War and the procedural details of Watergate. For twenty-four pages, the suspenseful story line of Nixon's struggle to avoid nuclear confrontation with the Soviets over their threat to unilaterally enforce a cease-fire between the Israelis and the Arabs keeps being interrupted by the legal minutiae of a case of breaking and entering. Even those who believe Watergate to be important must admit that it is not as momentous as nuclear Armageddon. Such self-described "realistic" thinking can be found throughout *With Nixon*, a memoir by presidential speechwriter Ray Price, which, although it never reached best-seller status, was offered through the Book-of-the-Month Club and was selected by the *New York Times Book Review* as one of the "noteworthy titles" of 1977 for providing "the most eloquent defense of Nixon so far."[24] In venting his frustration with how Watergate hampered Nixon's handling of the Yom Kippur War crisis, Price displays a pragmatism that, for some, might be better described as an unsettling nonchalance about the rule of law in a democratic society. That Special Prosecutor Archibald Cox could demand compliance with subpoenas for tapes during this international emergency, Price insists, gave "a compelling illustration of the utter asininity of the doctrine that where the interests of the courts conflict with other national interests, the courts alone should set the priorities."[25] Regarding Watergate and its place in the history books, Nixon and his supporters take the firm line that "ten years from now . . . this will be a few paragraphs. In fifty years it will be a footnote" (*RN*, 839).

By establishing the representative quality of his character and the insignificance of Watergate, Nixon creates the expectation that the scandal should have had no power to harm him. Instead, the reader of *RN* witnesses an incarnation of the nation's ideals being hounded from office. In *Six Crises*, Nixon found a redeeming excuse with which to absolve his fellow countrymen for the results of the 1960 election. Here Nixon offers no pardon, detecting instead a growing weakness in the national character. Watergate succeeded in toppling him from the presidency because an irresponsible Congress, a reckless news media, and, most significantly, a lazy populace suffered from a "fashionable negativism which . . . reflected an underlying loss of will, an estrangement from traditional American outlooks and attitudes" (*RN*, 762–763). In short, to explain his fall from power, Nixon turns to his own version of the jeremiad, prophesying the decay and impending downfall of the United States.

In truth, Nixon and his supporters never needed an excuse to bash Congress. Even before his treatment of Watergate, Nixon had already accused

Capitol Hill of a variety of crimes, persuading him "that Congress had become cumbersome, undisciplined, isolationist, fiscally irresponsible, overly vulnerable to pressures from organized minorities, and too dominated by the media" (RN, 770). Nixon's opinion of the legislative branch dropped even lower during Watergate. As Nixon scripts the story, the Watergate investigation was a fraud nurtured by the publicity-mad members of Senator Sam Ervin's committee. Asked by Frost to admit wrongdoing in Watergate, to confess to abuse of presidential power, and to apologize for those offenses, Nixon filibustered, complaining about "that enormous political attack that I was under. It was a five-front war with a fifth column" led by "a partisan Senate committee staff." In RN, Nixon denounces the committee members and staff who frequently leaked materials prejudicial toward him and his aides, while withholding information regarding corruption in Democratic campaigns. When Nixon's men testified before Ervin's group, "their treatment was in direct response to their willingness to grovel and to implicate others" (RN, 895). Such charges provide the context for Lasky's claim that "Richard Nixon was less the sinner than he was sinned against."[26] In this view, the abuses of the Ervin committee in perpetuating the scandal constitute a greater crime than the break-in itself.

But the condemnation poured over the Senate committee merely previewed the indignation the pro-Nixon forces reserved for the conduct of the House Judiciary Committee the next summer. In what Nixon loyalists viewed as a shameful display of political opportunism trumping ethical behavior, the committee members approved three articles of impeachment, without ever agreeing on the definition of an impeachable offense. But, as Ray Price charges, legal niceties could not have been more beside the point; the Judiciary Committee aimed to concoct "a climate of hostility" in which impeachment would seem inevitable, because "the public either would be disposed to believe the worst or would grow so disgusted that evidence of specific impeachable offenses would become unnecessary."[27] Because viciously partisan liberals dominated the proceedings, the committee almost did not deign to permit Nixon's lawyer an appearance. One of the rabid Nixon-haters, John Conyers of Michigan, told the *New York Times Magazine* that it was his duty to make sure Judiciary Committee chairman Peter Rodino did not "get *too* damn fair" (RN, 990). Such men and women postured as impartial judges in front of the television cameras, even though, as Nixon scoffed, "the votes were in even before the witnesses had been heard or a defense had been made" (RN, 1041). In these scathing words against the institution where the voice of the people is supposed to speak in the affairs of government, one can almost hear Jeremiah's admonition to a wayward Israel: "The wise men shall be put to shame. . . . What wisdom is in them?"[28]

The jeremiad's choice of a second culprit, the national news media, also raises few eyebrows. A constant throughout his career—from the time of the Alger Hiss case through the Fund crisis to his defeat in the 1962 campaign—Nixon's certainty that the media took special delight in skewering him provided his political polestar, illuminating and guiding his career. By 1972, as Nixon charges in *RN*, the liberal-dominated press had united in conspiracy against him. He quotes *Washington Post* publisher Katharine Graham as proclaiming during the campaign, "I hate [Nixon] and I'm going to do everything I can to beat him" (*RN*, 684). So, as Jeremiah castigated "the false pen of the scribes," Nixon berates the American press for its biased reporting during Watergate.[29] After maintaining his composure for much of the Frost interviews, he bitterly condemned the media when he discussed his wife's recuperation from the stroke she suffered in 1976. Seeming to blame her condition on her having read portions of Woodward and Bernstein's *The Final Days*, Nixon, without naming his targets, lashed out: "As far as my attitude toward the press is concerned, I respect some, but for those who write history as fiction on third-hand knowledge, I have nothing but utter contempt. And I will never forgive them. Never." The motivation behind all Nixon's attacks on the press crystallized in the moment when Frost only half-facetiously asked Nixon if he felt that he would have had more power had he been president of a television network instead of president of the United States. "Oh yes," Nixon replied, almost blandly: "The greatest concentration of power in the United States today is not in the White House; it isn't in the Congress and it isn't in the Supreme Court. It's in the media. And it's too much."

Part staged, but also part very real, Nixon's outraged critiques of the press describe a monster gone amuck—living outside, and in contempt of, the Constitution. In *RN*, Nixon embroiders this well-developed theme, asserting that the media invented derogatory images in its lust to topple him. When the White House undertook a campaign to assuage the public's doubts about Watergate, certain cynical members of the media dubbed the effort "Operation Candor," a label the remainder of the press used as if the administration had named the program. As the scandal grew to a national obsession, Nixon accused reporters of circulating rumors that he was emotionally unbalanced and then studying his behavior for confirming signs of their concocted allegation. More interested in creating reality than reflecting it, the media, as depicted in *RN*, live in an insular, incestuous world.

Conservative contempt for the media's behavior during Watergate runs so deep that some tried expressing their outrage in literary forums. In *With Nixon*, Ray Price confessed the political right's unfamiliarity with literature, dubbing it "basically a 'liberal' enclave."[30] Nevertheless, the anonymous author of *Nixon and the Foxes of Watergate* took a stab at mock-epic poetry. Composed under the pseudonym Aldebaran for the Walter Bagehot Research Council, the poem insists in its first section that Watergate originated not with the planning, or even with the actual break-ins at Democratic National Headquarters, but with the moment that the *Washington Post* decided to make its accusations.[31] The second section, the Epilogue, first printed in December 1974, opens with an attack on the paper's publisher, Katharine Graham: "Because the *Post*, owned by an Eastern Hen / Disliked both Nixon and his Western men / And would not let a caper be a caper, / For such was Watergate, save to her paper." In this conspiracy theory, one newspaper exerted an unlimited sway over the entire country. In fact, Aldebaran paints venerated CBS news anchor Walter Cronkite as a pawn of Katharine Graham, Ben Bradlee, Bob Woodward, and Carl Bernstein: "Some say he is a king with a dark mandate / From hidden Foxes who built Watergate / And pay him well to dignify the news / That they may slant at will to fit their views."[32]

But the press needs to have an audience receptive to gossip and innuendo for its sleazy tactics to work. Distributed in 1974 by the Bible publisher Thomas Nelson, Sabrepen's *I Quit! A Fable from the Dead Issue Scroll*, an illustrated moral tale, lifts Watergate out of its historical era by drawing Nixon as an unnamed chivalric knight forced to resign by opponents who "made it impossible for him to otherwise do further service for the country." While he has harsh words for the media, Sabrepen points toward what would become the final target in Nixon's own jeremiad: the gullible American people. In their quickness to echo the words they hear from the media, ordinary people operate with a herd mentality. Telling of "one leader of thought" who announces that the knight should resign and "the responding chorus [that] quickly adjusted its refrain accordingly," Sabrepen draws one man thinking, while over his shoulder can be seen two men with their eyes glued on him, turning thumbs down. On the next pages, this one opinion multiplies, blindly echoing "from pulpits . . . and from pool halls. From houses of distinction . . . and from houses of ill-repute. In civic club luncheons and in professional gatherings." This society's utter stupidity can hardly be more apparent to the reader than when we look at the manner in which Nixon the knight is represented: no five-o'clock shadow, a face-lift tightens the jiggling jowls, and even the famous nose draws no undue attention. Instead, Sabrepen's Nixon exudes dignity in the mournful sadness with which he holds himself in carrying out his selfless gesture of resignation. Underneath that armor, his uniform of service to the community, the knight dresses in the simple clothes of the common citizen. Piling such images of Nixon's nobility one upon the other, Sabrepen lampoons the foolishness of the people who would turn against such a faithful public servant.[33]

Despite what his loyalists were saying, when it came time for the Frost interviews, Nixon refused to blame the people of the United States for his downfall. Characterizing his resignation as a "voluntary impeachment," Nixon shouldered as much responsibility for the Watergate scandal as he ever would. "I let down the country," a teary-eyed Nixon told Frost. "I let down our system of government and the dreams of all those young people that ought to get into government, but think it's all too corrupt and the rest. . . . I let the American people down, and I have to carry that burden with me for the rest of my life." Strategically, Nixon realized that, in his first public statements since his resignation, he would not be taken seriously unless he offered some kind of confession of culpability for Watergate. During a break in the taping of the Watergate portion of the programs, Nixon aide Jack Brennan insisted that his boss would "go further than mistakes and misjudgments [in admitting his responsibility]. He wants to make a full accounting."[34]

But mea culpas, even limited ones, never proved congenial to Nixon. So not surprisingly, once freed from the requirement of facing an interrogator, he began blaming the American public for his downfall. In fact, Nixon's mood turned gloomy almost as soon as the red light on the cameras turned off. During their last visit, in May 1977, as the interview programs were being aired, Frost found a melancholy Nixon, one who was "pessimistic, almost apocalyptic in his view of the United States and where it is heading. He talk[ed] freely about the 'end of the American era,' perhaps even of Western civilization."[35] *RN* cozies up to this despairing story line, insisting that Watergate destroyed Nixon's career because the decadence of Congress and the media had spread into the public at large. Until the Watergate portions of the book, Nixon idealizes the majority of Americans as a source of unyielding, albeit silent, moral strength. He glories in their limitless potential for achievement. When they "decided a particular goal was worth reaching, they could surmount every obstacle" (*RN*, 984). Ordinary citizens could be relied upon to understand Nixon's reasoning when he took actions unpopular with the "establishment." More than the Congress or the media, therefore, Nixon trusted the American public to see Watergate in proper perspective. That they did not indicated to him a failure of character.

And so he turns the focus of his jeremiad directly on those upon whom he had counted for support. Later sections of the book, such as the story of the "missing" Watergate tapes, chronicle the public's appalling lack of vigilance in seeking the truth. The special prosecutor subpoenaed certain conversations between Nixon and his aides because the White House, mistakenly, had told him they had been recorded. Disregarding the explanations of this error, the public took the White House's failure to produce these nonexistent tapes as evidence of a cover-up. The allegations of Nixon's misuse of public funds for remodeling his homes in Florida and California and of illegal deductions on his income taxes illustrated the people's quickness to judge without proof. By the time investigators determined that the money spent on Nixon's residences had all been government authorized and that the tax write-off had been an accountant's mistake, for which he was liable but not personally responsible, Nixon complained, "I had already lost the case as far as public opinion was concerned" (*RN*, 960–961). If, as Nixon once unguardedly suggested, the American public is like a child in a family, then, as depicted in *RN*, this child, impatient and excitable, gets too easily distracted to note the slow emergence of the truth. At times Nixon's assessment seems more pessimistic. Following the resignations of Haldeman and Ehrlichman, Nixon withheld an answer about his involvement in Watergate because the public was "waiting for a yes or no answer," and he knew that "a totally honest answer would have been neither a simple yes or no" (*RN*, 849). The difficulty here rests entirely with the American people's simplemindedness. Only an uncomplicated story holds their attention, and, by its nature, this kind of truth isn't true. In Nixon's critique of the public's faith in reductive answers, once again, we can hear the words of Jeremiah: "Behold you trust in deceptive words to no avail."[36]

In sum, Nixon finds support for his jeremiad in the public's lack of discipline, the media's lack of scruples, and Congress's lack of responsibility: three elements plotting to destroy all that is good about the country. Consequently, he sees the United States disintegrating where it had been most strong. Its educational system deteriorates because college professors and high school teachers seek to "blame somebody else for their own failures to inspire their students" (*RN*, 685). American credibility in foreign affairs, which had soared high after World War II, collapsed when "twelve years of sacrifice and fighting [in Vietnam] were lost within a matter of months" (*RN*, 889). Even economic good fortune weakened the country by encouraging national complacency. The danger, Nixon warns, is that "as people [get] more material goods they [become] less 'hungry,' [lose] their drive, and become almost totally obsessed with self" (*RN*, 1033). Through the lens of his fall from power, Nixon detects a pervasive corruption threatening to destroy the United States.

And such hand-wringing played before receptive audiences. Fears of national decline resonated throughout the 1970s. After the boom of the 1950s and 1960s, the economy suffered some of its uneasiest years since the Great Depression. Inflation soared, yet gross national product and the stock market both dropped drastically while unemployment levels grew; this supposedly impossible confluence of both inflation and recession—dubbed stagflation—seemed to portend the end of the known economic world.[37] In 1974, Federal Reserve chairman Arthur Burns worried aloud about "the future of our country [being] in jeopardy."[38] The OPEC oil embargo in 1973 and 1974 and accelerating price hikes in the months after oil began flowing to the United States drove the economy into even more precarious territory, with major American cities suspended over the chasm of financial collapse. In the period 1975–1976, New York City dodged bankruptcy only after its teachers' union provided an eleventh-hour loan, which, combined with municipal government budget cutbacks, convinced the federal government to help in the bail-out efforts. Honesty required President Ford to concede the obvious during his January 1975 message to Congress: "The state of the union is not good."[39] By the end of April, the country received a blow to its self-image as an international power when South Vietnam fell to the North Vietnamese army. Along with the nation's first military defeat, Americans had to endure photos of a chaotic evacuation of U.S. diplomatic and military personnel, surrounded by Vietnamese begging not to be left behind. In one picture, an American official was caught planting a right to the jaw of a South Vietnamese man attempting to jump on board a severely overloaded departing airplane.[40] At home, a civil war of sorts raged in some cities over the issue of busing, a court-ordered solution to providing racial balance in the public schools of the North. In Boston, the 1974–1975 school year saw riots and random acts of violence, as the white working-class residents of South Boston rose up against enforced integration.[41] Nothing summed up the nation's continuing racial strife as brutally as a photo taken in downtown Boston during the July 1976 celebrations of the nation's bicentennial in which a gang of young white men attack a middle-aged black man dressed in a three-piece suit. While one holds the victim, another youth, holding as a spear a metal flagpole with Old Glory still attached, prepares to gore the African American man.[42] Little wonder then that disaster movies proved to be box-office staples of Hollywood films during much of the 1970s: *The Poseidon Adventure*, *Earthquake*, *The Towering Inferno*, and *Airport 75* pictured a world that seemed to guarantee that whatever could go wrong would. Moreover, Nixon's memoirs appeared during the grimmest, most dour period during that anxious time. Describing the widely held idea that the nation was "teetering at the edge of an abyss," James T. Patterson declares that "the mood of the late 1970s was in important ways the gloomiest in late twentieth-century American history."[43]

Nobody told this story better, and few commanded larger audiences, than Richard Nixon. All the same, many of his supporters joined in, echoing his jeremiad. In writing about the resignation, Ray Price turns elegiac. After Nixon had left for San Clemente, Price visited the former president's hideaway office in the Executive Office Building and saw the desk, strewn with pipe tobacco, reading glasses, and pens and paper "just as he had left them Thursday afternoon. Just as if 'our long national nightmare' had been only a bad dream. Just as if, stepping out of the office that Thursday, only his day's work had been interrupted. Just as if all that Richard Nixon had begun in the world could still be completed."[44] Price's version of the loss of Eden explicitly identifies what had been taken from the United States—a hardworking man of virtue—while, implicitly, seeking out the Adam and Eve whose original sin cast us all out of paradise. The bittersweet subtlety of Price, in less capable hands, could quickly turn acrid. Vermont newspaperman Franklin B. Smith's Watergate-era editorials read as a catalog of sour recriminations. During the final days of the scandal, Smith reprimands a debased nation, which in casting off Nixon "rejected greatness through means which disgraced everything for which this nation used to stand." In Smith's eyes, the United States, in its treatment of Nixon, committed suicide. "The heart of America stopped beating this week," he claimed on the morning of the resignation. In the first week of the Ford administration, he reported the beliefs of "many who feel, beyond the horrible injustice done to one man, that the Constitution is now a dead document."[45]

And if the United States had lost touch with its founding principles, then it had lost God's blessing as well. In *Nixon and the Foxes of Watergate*, Aldebaran envisions the scandal as a struggle for the country's soul: "O Sirs! Which clan must be the Nation's Host? / The Christians? or the Pagans with their *Post*?" Sabrepen uses a lighter touch in *I Quit!* Nixon the knight resigns, expecting, in fairness, that anyone else "who has ever been even suspected of falling short of his duties or of violating his professed code . . . also will resign." As a result, society ceases to function—politicians, reporters, teachers, and ministers all step down because they too are not pure. Sabrepen sets up the piece's punch line by having a voice cry out of the chaos, "Oh, Lord, what shall we do?" In the fable's final section, God responds—using lightning to carve into a mountainside "the simple words: Don't Ask Me I Quit!" Because of this foolish scheming to get rid of Nixon, God abandons the United States to its own sinful devices.[46]

But jeremiads do not merely prophesy doom. Aldebaran, for example, means for *Nixon and the Foxes of Watergate* to rally the remaining faithful Americans: "But Christians! Look beyond this sad event / And gather in your fallen President."[47] Similarly, in *RN*, Richard Nixon diagnosed America's illness so that his country might heal itself. Jewish theologian Rabbi Abraham Heschel once described the Hebrew prophets with words Nixon might have applied to himself: "It was not his vested interests, honor, or prestige that the prophet was fighting for. He was fighting for the physical survival of his people."[48] Fearful that America will succumb to "the danger in advanced nations[, the] . . . weakening of character" (*RN*, 1033), Nixon tries to make his memoirs more than personally vindicating; he attempts to stimulate a national revival, a return to his vision of America. To this end, he argues that his presidency attempted to reinspire the United States, to make it a place where the "spiritual hunger which all of us have" (*RN*, 465) would be satisfied. Nixon's pursuit of world peace by improving relations with America's most dangerous enemies, the People's Republic of China and the Soviet Union, applied this abstract goal practically. His ritualistic solemnity on receiving the formal invitation to visit China speaks to the key role détente played in his plans to satisfy America's "spiritual hunger." On the night that Kissinger delivered the news, Nixon dedicated the triumph with a toast "not to ourselves personally . . . or to our administration's policies . . . [but] to generations to come who may have a better chance to live in peace because of what we have done" (*RN*, 552). Domestically, Nixon called for a healing reunification of a deeply divided country. His presidency offered the opportunity to bring about "a new rebirth of optimism and decisiveness and national pride" (*RN*, 764). Understood in proper context, the scathing criticisms of this jeremiad recall the American people to Nixon's moral and spiritual agenda. By doing so, this Jeremiah at San Clemente reconciles his love for his country's ideals with his condemnation of his countrymen's failure to live by them. He enables himself to believe that he had not betrayed America; it betrayed itself, and he is its reluctant doomsayer.

Richard Nixon dedicates nearly eleven hundred pages of rhetorical gymnastics to the effort to convince us that he earned his prophet's role. But the original jeremiad interpreted the misfortunes of the community, while *RN*, at heart, deals with the misfortunes of Richard Nixon. He cannot see, or will not admit, that he really only defends himself. Nixon's own descriptions of the Watergate scandal provide the evidence against him; here he struggles most transparently to redeem himself from history's judgments—and fails most nakedly. His prophetic posturing remains incredible because Watergate contradicts the image of righteousness he so laboriously crafted in the earlier sections of the memoirs. After having been conditioned to *always* accept Nixon's actions in idealistic terms, we find his character changing—suddenly and without explanation. Almost as if he had lost all drafts of the first two-thirds of the book, Nixon the author seems to have lost track of Nixon the character. The "completely pragmatic" and "cynical" reactions of the Watergate president do not harmonize with the young man whose Quaker family taught him the difference between right and wrong (*RN*, 628). Nor do justifying political espionage and lying to Congress and the public illustrate any of the personality traits enshrined in the orthodox success ethic. Horatio Alger's heroes never said, "Everybody does it."

But the quick recourse to this excuse points to a contradiction between American myth and American experience: the ability to wed a near-evangelical sense of personal and national purpose to an amoral pragmatism. For example, Ray Price can, on the one hand, describe his collaboration with Nixon on the first inaugural address as trying to express something "rooted in the human spirit." At the same time, he defiantly defends Nixon's mendacity: "If the country were ever to be restored to its senses, the public would have to recognize that a measure of scheming and duplicity are necessary in the real world of power politics."[49] Far more than mere surface hypocrisy, the problem here is the inability to perceive any problem at all. The all-too-familiar conviction that a pure end sanctifies any means—this cohabitation of high-minded righteousness with gutter morality—sanctioned the break-in at Daniel Ellsberg's psychiatrist office, because punishing the man responsible for the leaking of the Pentagon Papers seemed more important than protecting individual civil rights. And it fostered Watergate, with its mind-set that ensuring Richard Nixon's reelection justified any tactic.

In its extreme form, this unquestioned conviction of personal and national righteousness scapegoats opponents. Steeped in suspicion of the unchosen, Aldebaran's *Nixon and the Foxes of Watergate* attempts to craft, or so the Foreword to the 1974 edition tells us, "a truly national literature . . . [that mirrors] our anger at what has been a brazen, alien-minded violation of America's integrity." We do not have to wait long for the source of this desecration; from the poem's earliest lines, Aldebaran insists that Katharine Meyer Graham, publisher of the *Washington Post*, fabricated Watergate. The reason for using her maiden name has little to do with the requirements of poetic meter: "What's in a name? Much more than meets the eye, / *Post*-editor Simons challenged Chiefs on high, / And called in Rosenfeld and Sussman too, / And Lewis and a Bernstein, for his crew; / And added Woodward as a Trojan Horse, / As owner Meyer, backed it all, of course." Thus, a "Jewish cabal"—though not the one at the Bureau of Labor Statistics that Nixon once asked White House aide Fred Malek to investigate—extracts its "pound of flesh" and destroys God's servant.[50]

Used in this manner, the jeremiad permits the majority culture, the sources of real power in society, to see themselves as embattled underdogs. Witness the claim of the editor of *The Foxes of Watergate* that Christians in the United States are an endangered, embattled group: "The Christian view of life" he writes, "will not disappear either by wishful thinking or by campaigns to denounce it. . . . Just as the Jews who respect their own special laws and their great masters, and their holy Book are allowed to stand firmly on what they believe, so too the Christian must be allowed that same privilege." As the passage's second portion illustrates, the jeremiad often identifies villains who possess less cultural influence than those in the mainstream. In a similar vein, Gary Allen, author of *None Dare Call It Conspiracy*, an inspirational text for the militia movements of the 1990s, published *Richard Nixon: The Man Behind the Mask* (1971) to rebuke Nixon for his betrayal of true conservatives. Allen explains Nixon's apparent shift to the political left as part of a conspiracy by the super-secret Council on Foreign Relations and international banking interests to abolish the United States and establish a one-world government. Nixon, the man behind the mask, sold out those who supported him for the promise from what Allen calls the "Insiders" that he will be established as the first king of the universe. While these fat-cat Insiders remain mostly a faceless abstraction, Allen draws a much more detailed picture in targeting welfare deadbeats. In an astounding reversal of reality, he pictures the welfare mother as part of some burgeoning class of venture capitalists, "simply in the baby business for fun and profit," making a comfy living off of government largesse. Far from antiquated absurdities, such language finds expression today in the rhetoric of some in the Republican right wing about welfare mothers and the United States as a Christian nation. Yesterday's extremist poison threatens today to go mainstream.[51]

In addition to these general concerns about the jeremiad's uses, Nixon's specific manipulation of the form ultimately doesn't make sense. In the Watergate portions of the memoirs, Nixon appears incompetent and foolish, an administrator not in charge of his operation. As the first Watergate trial neared, Nixon received reports about the despondency of one of the defendants, Howard Hunt: "Implicit in [his] growing despair was a threat to start talking, although I was never sure exactly about what" (RN, 776). Oddly, although this scandal presents a growing threat to his administration, Nixon would have us believe that he had been unable to gather even the most elementary information about it. Displaying this same strange passivity, he confesses to doing nothing about suspicions that his aides were not telling him everything they knew. Nine months after the break-in, Nixon still had not asked his friend John Mitchell about his knowledge of and involvement in Watergate. Trying to hide behind a shield of uncertainty, Nixon claims that "where Watergate is concerned I have learned not to be categorical" (RN, 746). But, just as the decisive politician who caught Alger Hiss, tested wits with Khrushchev, and eased relations with China and Russia has never been anything but definitive, the muddling, befuddled Richard Nixon of Watergate destroys the internal consistency of the narrative in RN.

Most important, Nixon's efforts to diminish the importance of Watergate fail because it was one of the supremely significant events in recent American history. Richard Nixon—not Congress, the press, or the public—lied to the American people, obstructed justice, and abused presidential power with a display of a deep contempt for the legislative and judicial branches of the federal government. Gallup polling from 1974 through 1992 indicates the widespread belief that Nixon's own actions brought on—and warranted—his resignation; 65 percent of those polled in August

1974 said that Nixon deserved such a fate. By June 1982, the number had grown to 75 percent, dropping off to 71 percent in May 1986 and 70 percent in June 1992.[52] In a famous *Doonesbury* strip from the Watergate period, Garry Trudeau drew a crew of faceless hard-hatted workers erecting a brick wall between the White House and the outside world. In the background of the first three panels, we read Nixon's words from a tape transcript, directing his staff to "stonewall it . . . plead the Fifth Amendment," anything to impede the progress of the inquiries into the scandal. Moving through the strip, the barrier grows higher, obscuring Nixon's words, until, in the fourth panel, the last brick plops in place, and all we can see is the wall. For the first time, Trudeau suggests, our leader cut himself off from us—a situation that, far from being a footnote to history, is a crisis in the truest sense of the word.[53]

Idealistic rhetoric aside, Nixon's jeremiad actually relies on the corruption in America's citizens that it pretends to condemn. In spring 1977, David Frost imagined an angry Richard Nixon: "No, [he] would say, people have a short memory. A conveniently short memory."[54] But Frost fails to see that, ever resourceful, Nixon can use this short-sightedness. Uncritical readers will miss the internal contradictions in his Watergate alibis and accept his self-portrait as a wholly virtuous man. They will lack the patience to compare his story to journalistic and historical accounts, instead docilely accepting *RN* as the definitive source on his presidency.[55] Consequently, the success of Nixon's campaign to restore his reputation indicates the degree to which we, as a people, have repudiated the values we claim to espouse. So, although we cannot accept Nixon as a prophet, we can take the outcome of his comeback campaign as prophetic.[56] For if we embrace Richard Nixon, we embrace our own moral bankruptcy, "[our] lot," adopting the words of Jeremiah, "because [we] have . . . trusted in lies."[57]

Yet such moral outrage, while justified, should not obscure the existence of a responsive audience for Richard Nixon and his call for national revival. In 1976, the film *Network* imagined a city filled with disgruntled, angry citizens throwing open their windows and screaming out into the night: "I'm as mad as hell, and I'm not going to take this anymore." While screenwriter Paddy Chayefsky and director Sidney Lumet had a more liberal critique of American society in mind, the populist outrage of the mid- to late 1970s and its attendant call for an American renaissance belonged to the birth of the New Right. Hungering to "feel once again a sense of mission and greatness," conservatives rallied to Ronald Reagan's cause in

This August 12, 1974, Doonesbury *strip summed up, three days after the resignation, what many saw as Nixon's defining act as president—his decision to isolate himself from the nation he was elected to serve.* DOONESBURY © 1974 G. B. Trudeau. *Reprinted with permission of* UNIVERSAL PRESS SYNDICATE. *All rights reserved.*

the 1976 presidential primaries, with a support so passionate that, even in defeat, they dominated the Republican convention.[58] In the two years leading up to the publication of *RN*, evangelical Christians, led by the singer Anita Bryant, formed a "Save Our Children" campaign that successfully overturned a Miami, Florida, antidiscrimination law extending civil rights protections to homosexuals.[59] Picking up on her crusade in the spring of 1978, voters in several cities also struck down existing laws protecting gay people from discrimination.[60] During the fall of 1977 and the spring of 1978, foreign policy conservatives preached against the evils of President Carter's determination to relinquish control of the Panama Canal. Fearing that the return of the canal presaged a declining will to protect the nation's national security, antitreaty groups mobilized letter-writing campaigns to senators and launched advertising blitzes, such as the American Conservative Union spot that insisted: "There is *no* Panama Canal. There is an *American* Canal in Panama. Don't let President Carter give it away."[61] In 1978, the year *RN* hit bookstores, the big electoral news was California's Proposition 13, sponsored by a seventy-five-year-old anti–New Deal activist, Howard Jarvis, which passed by a two-to-one margin. Immediately cutting property taxes by 57 percent, Proposition 13 also upped the ante on any new public revenue, requiring a two-thirds vote of the state legislature to raise state taxes and the same majority of local voters to increase municipal levies.[62] More than just a rebellion against taxes, Proposition 13 ignited what Pat Cadell, Jimmy Carter's pollster, dubbed "a revolution against government." From his forced retirement, Richard Nixon, who got a $27,500 reduction on his taxes because of Proposition 13, joined in the antigovernment groundswell, declaring: "Let us hope that California's message will be heard loud and clear . . . across the nation."[63]

And the exile of San Clemente wasn't just hopping on someone else's bandwagon. When Barry Goldwater, the modern conservative movement's favorite son, flamed out in the 1964 presidential election, losing to Lyndon Johnson by what was at that time the greatest margin in history, Richard Nixon had been there to pick up the pieces. Campaigning loyally for Republicans across the country during the 1966 off-year elections, he won over the Goldwater partisans who had taken control of the party structure on the local level. As Rick Perlstein describes Nixon's path to victory in 1968: "[The other national Republican politicians] sat on their hands, [and Nixon] would be the one to court the conservative foot soldiers who now owned the precincts, grateful that at least someone in the Establishment hadn't sold them out." Goldwater may have coined the phrase "the Forgotten American" in 1961, but it took Richard Nixon to adopt it (it would later evolve into his "silent majority") and to harness it to a successful presidential campaign. Those who had known in their hearts that Goldwater was right were ready to embrace the miniature jeremiad of the Nixon campaign's apocalyptic 1968 slogan: "This time, vote like your whole world depended on it." And with Nixon's calls for "law and order," his questioning the wisdom of recent Warren Court decisions, and his attacks on the welfare programs of the Great Society, conservatives felt certain that "he's one of us . . . again."[64]

Although after Watergate Ronald Reagan served as the effective spokesperson and genial face of the conservative renaissance, much of the groundwork for this political realignment came from Nixon's efforts. The significant elements of Reagan's ruling coalition—"white blue-collar workers, southern white foes of civil rights, Republicans who opposed big government, and socially conservative Catholics and evangelical Protestants"—reads like a page out of Nixon's 1972 campaign playbook.[65] The convergence of these disparate groups, which would form the New Right, made up the key elements of Nixon's landslide reelection victory. In explaining his fund-raising success, direct mail specialist Richard Viguerie (known as the "godfather" of the conservative resurgence) gave an answer that alluded to and credited the man responsible without actually using his name: "There really is a silent majority in this country, and the New Right has learned how . . . [to] mobilize them."[66] Moreover, the intellectual core of the new conservative movement owed much to Richard Nixon.

November 5, 1980

WE'LL HAVE PLENTY OF ELDER STATESMEN

LANDSLIDE

One day after Ronald Reagan's victory, Pat Oliphant detected behind it all the most powerful
influence on modern Republicanism—Richard Nixon. OLIPHANT © 1980 UNIVERSAL PRESS
SYNDICATE. Reprinted with permission. All rights reserved.

The goals of the movement, described by cultural historian Peter Carroll as "restor[ing] a world of simpler virtues, an old America based on family, church, and the work ethic," echo much of the rhetoric of *Six Crises*, as well as mirror precisely the organizing themes of the early pages of *RN*.[67] Particularly auspicious for Nixon, the growth of the New Right in the late 1970s depended on the resuscitation of the self-made man mythology, the very narratives with which he had identified his life and career and on which he was depending for his revival.[68] Even Ronald Reagan's rejuvenation of the myth of national mission— quoting John Winthrop about the United States being a "city on a hill" and reminding Americans that they lived in "an exceptional, liberty-loving nation whose democratic institutions were destined to spread about the world"—even this characteristic Reaganism derived from Richard Nixon.[69] Reagan's words in rejecting a foreign policy of limitations—"Shouldn't we stop worrying whether someone likes us and decide once again we're going to be respected in the world?"—sounds like a paraphrase of Nixon on the same subject: "The United States appears so lost in uncertainty or paralyzed by propriety that it is either unable or unwilling to act."[70] In fact, Reagan's speechwriters often took notes from Nixon, frequently lifting passages from his 1980 book, *The Real War*, directly, and without credit, for the candidate's foreign policy speeches.[71]

Thus, the Jeremiah at San Clemente tapped into a deep pool of anxiety about national moral decay, making Nixon the beneficiary of a resurgent right wing readying itself for a rise to power. In an editorial cartoon called "Landslide," which appeared just following Reagan's 1980 victory over Carter, Pat Oliphant drew the president-elect sliding downhill, bringing in his wake Henry Kissinger and a rehabilitated Richard Nixon, gleefully celebrating by flashing his "V for Victory" salute. Offering confirmation of Oliphant's prophecy, Reagan appeared in a photo from the early days of his presidency, emerging from his helicopter on the south lawn of the White House, carrying a copy of *The Real War* under his arm. As impossible as it might have seemed to his critics, Nixon was back.

CHAPTER THREE

"ANYONE CAN BE THE PRESIDENT"

BEHIND THE MASK OF SUCCESS

In "Pink Houses," a 1983 tribute to blue-collar middle America, rock musician John Mellencamp remembered a childhood when young boys were told that they might one day grow up to become president and lamented: "But just like everything else those old crazy dreams just kinda came and went."[1] Although the singer may doubt its validity, the talismanic incantation "anyone can be the president" still carries clout as a mythic story, both for him and for his culture at large. Even steadfast Nixon opponents often concede that he was the prototypical self-made man. In 1960, William Costello, author of the first critique of the man and his career, celebrated Nixon as "an authentic product of the American pioneer tradition" who succeeded because "no effort was impossible, no goal unattainable."[2] All the same, Nixon and his self-made ways made some people a little queasy. In 1956, Herblock drew Nixon in front of a wardrobe containing the costumes of the All-American boy, the statesman, the political huckster, and the dirty-trickster, portraying a man without core convictions who merely switches from one role to another as political convenience dictates. As the 1968 Republican presidential primaries began, Herblock rendered the politician as an unscrupulous used car salesman, foisting "the Nixon," a broken-down ruin of a car, on a dubious public. A 1972 Andy Warhol silkscreen print visualized uneasiness transformed into outright nausea, with a photo of Nixon splashed with stomach-turning colors—a seasick green head, with orange lips and pink splotches in the eyes, sitting atop pink shoulders, set against a bright-orange background. Nor did a decade of distance ease the discomfort. In a fall 1982 episode of the situation comedy *Family Ties*, Stephen Keaton, former 1960s radical turned PBS station manager, admits that "my vocal cords can be very stubborn. It took them six months to say President Nuuh-Nixon." His reflexive stammer, however, betrays his inability to accept his nemesis's success, even fourteen years later.[3] A 1990 *Doonesbury* cartoon, published after the opening of the Nixon presidential library, shows that, even to a child, Nixon's mendacity was perfectly clear. Discovering his parents watching Richard Nixon on television, the boy sits down in front of the set, watching silently, until, finally, he declares: "He's lying right now, isn't he?" Underneath the humor lurks a suspicion that, if Richard Nixon could be president, something is terribly wrong.

For some playwrights, poets, filmmakers, political cartoonists, television writers, novelists, and social critics, reinventing Richard Nixon presents an opportunity to explore ugly truths hidden behind the adage "anyone can be the president." At the opening of Robert Altman's film *Secret Honor: A Political Myth* (1984), Nixon, speaking as if he were a defense attorney for himself in a courtroom trial, promises to reveal "the reasons behind the reasons" for the Watergate affair so that "you, ladies and gentlemen of the American jury, shall look at the face that is under the mask."[4] Lawrence Ferlinghetti's poem *Tyrannus Nix?* (1969) contemplates Nixon's inscrutable public face: "What've you got under it That's what I've / been trying to fathom."[5] And, in the first extended fictional treatment of Richard Nixon, Gore Vidal's play *The Best Man* (1960) uncovers a nominating convention's behind-the-scenes power struggles. For these and other critics, going "under the mask" of Nixon's self-made-man persona exposes the American success mythology's failure to produce a moral, meaningful life and raises troubling questions about the value of democracy, the nature of individualism, and the possibility of integrity in the public sphere. Looking at these fictionalized versions of Richard Nixon as they developed over time, we observe how the critics of the self-made-man mythology offer sharper and more astute critiques of the orthodox ideology's failings, all the while growing ever more despairing about finding any remedy. In 1960, Vidal, for instance, displays a confidence that, while the best person cannot rise to the top, not just anyone can be president: the best—the most intelligent and moral—individuals will block the worst man from taking the prize. By 1969, Ferlinghetti, conceding that a true self-made man can be president, proposes a communal vision of our shared humanity as an antidote to the poisonous fruits of our destructive individualism. Fifteen years later, the failure of this utopian dream is immediately apparent in the world of Altman's film, which endorses the idea that anyone can be president as long as one is willing to discard one's honor—either by choosing to betray one's values or by ceding one's autonomy to shill for the corporate entities that really control America. But while offering a sharp critique of the irredeemable corruption of American political, social, and

"What You Need Is Something New, Like This"

This Doonesbury strip, which appeared following the Nixon Library dedication ceremonies, makes two important assertions: first, that Nixon's basic falsehood is transparent, and, second, that "the torch has been passed to a new generation" of Nixon-haters. DOONESBURY © 1990 G. B. Trudeau. Reprinted with permission of UNIVERSAL PRESS SYNDICATE. All rights reserved.

business life, *Secret Honor* leaves no countermyth, no vision of an alternative way of living. To understand that anyone can be the president means that the only sane action is to withdraw from public life altogether.

Gore Vidal's *The Best Man* premiered on Broadway on March 31, 1960, at the Morosco Theatre, a venue with a "reputation as the classiest house for serious drama," which had seen such productions as Thornton Wilder's *Our Town*, Arthur Miller's *Death of a Salesman*, and Tennessee Williams's *Cat on a Hot Tin Roof*.[6] The grandson of the populist Oklahoma senator T. P. Gore, Vidal, though he had written eight works of fiction by 1960, was best known for being a movie scriptwriter (*Ben-Hur*) and a television dramatist (his *Visit to a Small Planet* drew favorable notices as a television play before running on Broadway for 338 performances in 1957).[7] He was also famous for being Gore Vidal. A frequent guest on Jack Paar's *Tonight Show*, he made a December 1959 appearance as himself, narrating a live-broadcast television play about his grandfather, on NBC's *Sunday Showcase*. Vidal had enough name recognition to believe that he could win the House seat in New York's heavily Republican 29th congressional district in the 1960 fall election.[8] In an impressive display of public-relations savvy, Vidal dropped hints about his intentions while *The Best Man* was in rehearsal and timed the announcement of his candidacy for the first week of the play's run, letting the stories in the *New York Times* aid both efforts.[9] Despite strong competition during its run, *The Best Man* held its own against *The Sound of Music*, *A Raisin in the Sun*, *Bye, Bye Birdie* (with Dick Van Dyke), and Julie Andrews and Richard Burton in *Camelot*,[10] receiving unanimously enthusiastic reviews and running for 520 performances before closing in July 1961.[11] Within two months of opening night, United Artists purchased the film rights for the play, giving the project at first to Frank Capra, until Vidal insisted on his removal. The film, released in April 1964 with a screenplay by Vidal, won universal critical praise, including a successful showing at the Cannes Film Festival that May.[12]

Set in 1960, *The Best Man* dramatized the contest between the two front-runners at a presidential nominating convention: one was a high-minded intellectual, portrayed by Melvyn Douglas, the husband of Helen Gahagan Douglas, the woman Nixon had branded "the pink lady" during their bitter 1950 California Senate campaign; the other was a ruthless, no-holds-barred young politician played by Frank Lovejoy, an actor who bore a strong physical resemblance to the front-runner for the 1960 Republican nomination. Having risen to celebrity by exploiting his role during congressional hearings on domestic espionage, Senator Joseph Cantwell also evokes the spirit of Richard Nixon, whom Vidal viewed even then as "a splendid twentieth-century archetype."[13] Like his counterpart, Cantwell grounds his political identity in his humble origins: "I was born to this," he declares to his opponent. "I understand the people of this country. Because I'm one of them."[14] In the 1964 film version, Cantwell (played by Cliff Robertson) unabashedly exploits his socioeconomic roots. His first speech, set during a televised news conference, finds him declaiming with studied sincerity: "I think it's a pretty swell thing that in a nation like this someone like me can be here to speak for the real people of this country. Where else but in America could a boy from a poor family run for the greatest job in the world?"

So, yes, anyone can be the president. And *The Best Man* recoils at the thought. If Joe Cantwell represents the poor boy's potential to win the White House, Vidal shows that this miraculous ascent comes only by jettisoning any political ethics. The play's hero, William Russell (an Adlai Stevenson–like intellectual of unquestioned public principles), conceals damaging secrets about marital infidelities and nervous breakdowns, which Cantwell plans to exploit to steal away the front-runner's seemingly assured nomination. Playing with words to insinuate that Russell is "apt to crack up under stress" (*Best*, 108), Cantwell reshapes the truth like Play-Doh, implying that his opponent tried to kill himself. When challenged, he points out that he only alleged that Russell had "suicidal *tendencies.*" However, Cantwell's disavowal leaves an impression of the smear's essential validity; Russell *could* commit suicide after all, if things got bad enough (*Best*, 107–108). This morally slippery rhetoric echoes Nixon's famous branding of Truman and Stevenson as "traitors to the high principles in which many of the nation's Democrats believe," a jibe that, without literally saying so, made people think of his opponents as treasonous.[15]

Under these terms, being the "best" man means being the most skilled at playing politics. Joe Cantwell may deal in clichéd and pious hypocrisies, but, as his name indicates, he is very good at doing so. Former president Art Hockstader, a character based closely on Harry Truman, grudgingly admits that the despicable smearing of Russell is "clever as all hell" (*Best*, 122). First, Cantwell threatens Russell with the release of damaging information. Unless Russell withdraws, Cantwell's team will deliver neatly bound copies of the psychiatric file to each convention delegate. Meanwhile, Cantwell, posing as a model of fairness, plans to propose that Russell should be examined "by a non-partisan group of psychiatrists to determine if he is sane" (*Best*, 109). Aware that his opponent will decline to cooperate, Cantwell stands ready to proclaim that Russell's refusal "means he has something to hide" (*Best*, 109). Here, too, Cantwell's language borrows directly from Nixon, this time from the Fund episode, when he fought off corruption charges by making a complete financial disclosure and pronouncing that if the Democratic candidates did not do likewise, "it will be an admission that they have something to hide."[16] This remorseless pursuit of any advantage illustrates Cantwell's boast: "I knew from the time I won my first election I was going to be President and nobody was going to stop me" (*Best*, 153). Not only *can* someone like Joe Cantwell become president; such a cutthroat political operator holds the inside track.

In betraying such concerns about the nation's condition, *The Best Man* displayed the era's anxious spirit. In 1957, the Soviet Union had launched Sputnik, the first satellite, stoking fears that fueled multiple jeremiads, particularly ones bemoaning the state of America's education system. But even the country's successes proved worrisome, as social critics saw dangers in the prosperity of 1950s postwar America. Sloan Wilson's 1957 novel, *The Man in the Gray Flannel Suit*, took on the materialistic, spiritually vacuous lives of middle-class suburbanites, trapped by the weight of their possessions in lives they despised.[17] John Kenneth Galbraith's 1958 best seller, *The Affluent Society*, attacked the imbalance between spectacular private wealth and paltry public services, and he scorned the intellectual complacency—"the bland lead the bland"—that permitted private interest to trump any vision of the common good.[18] Many feared the influence of the popular new medium of television. Elia Kazan and Bud Schulberg's film *A Face in the Crowd* (1957) traced the rise of a hard-drinking, womanizing ex-convict, re-created as populist television celebrity, "Lonesome" Rhodes, whose folksy on-air persona attracts sixty-five million viewers a week, giving him the power to sell everything from bogus energy pills to presidential candidates. (In advising the colorless conservative senator who would be president to craft a more lovable, engaging persona by trading in his Siamese cat for a dog, Lonesome reminds his client that "that mutt [meaning Checkers]" had helped Dick Nixon connect with the average American—a remark that appears to be the earliest Hollywood reference to the man.)[19] And if audiences could dismiss Schulberg's message by pointing to the clearly amoral nature of his low-life fictional character, the public couldn't dismiss the troubling truth of 1959's quiz show scandals, when investigators discovered that one of television's most popular game show champions, Charles Van Doren, the son of a highly regarded Columbia University professor, had taken $129,000 in bogus winnings from rigged contests.[20] So uneasy was the national mood as the country entered the presidential election of 1960 that three different commissions conducted investigations into and published reports on the nation's sense of purpose.[21]

Vidal's anxiety centered on the realization that, if anyone can be the president, the best person becomes less likely to triumph. The most intelligent, truthful, and moral politician *cannot* win without fatally compromising his character. Told he might have to "pull a Nixon" (*Best*, 116), the original script's sole direct reference to Cantwell's model, Russell refuses to demean himself by going on television to "cry on the nation's shoulder" (*Best*, 116). This fundamental dignity prohibits any retaliation against Cantwell, even when handed an ultimate weapon. Having unearthed rumors of his opponent's homosexuality, Russell refuses to spread scurrilous gossip. Remaining convinced that Cantwell must never be president, Russell imagines a politically unthinkable solution: withdrawing to support the convention's dark-horse candidate—an acceptable, if not the best, man. Even such a qualified happy ending, however, could be reached only after some revisionist thinking; *The Best Man*'s first draft had Cantwell taking the nomination. "After much thought," Vidal confessed, "I changed my mind. Cantwell could not prevail—at least nowadays—because in its idiot way our system, though it usually keeps us from having the very best man as President, does protect us from the very worst."[22]

Yet more than a whiff of patrician snobbery wafts from *The Best Man*'s sneering dismissal of Joe Cantwell. Never having wanted for anything in life, Russell can afford his conscience—especially his principled decision to withdraw. While Cantwell counted pennies to pay for his daughter's braces, Russell lived in a mansion called Watch Hill, dined at the country club, and sent his sons on European tours. Even though Russell concedes that self-made men have no choice but to "fight" their way to the top (*Best*, 153), Cantwell still stands condemned for lack of morals *and* class. Hockstader sneeringly threatens to return the upstart senator to "the insurance business" if he goes through with his threatened smear attempt (*Best*, 111). Such condescending treatment of a self-made figure forces the realization that, culturally, we may have associated Horatio Alger with the notion that any boy can grow up to be president, but, in his own fiction, the writer never told that story. Alger's poor boy heroes merely rise to middle-class respectability. To escape the insurance office and compete with the power and authority of the ruling class, perhaps the Joe Cantwells of the world must resort to every available weapon. And it is the job of the nation's elite, those from the best families, who went to the best schools, read the best books, those, in short, who are too good to succeed in a democratic system, to exert the moral leadership necessary to make sure that Cantwell fails.

So in 1960 *The Best Man* had enacted every liberal's cherished fantasy: the political death of Richard Nixon. But eight years later, Nixon was back, and many observers struggled to explain this amazing event. *Baltimore Sun* reporter Jules Witcover resorted to the language of religious miracle—his book on the 1968 election was entitled *The Resurrection of Richard Nixon*—to capture the improbability of the man's return. Impressionist David Frye made this Jesus parallel the premise of his comedy album *Richard Nixon Superstar*, with its title nodding to the Rice/Lloyd Webber rock opera and its cover art parodying the Protestant Sunday school staple, Warner Sallman's *Head of Christ*. In one of the record's opening sketches, Frye, speaking as the Reverend Billy Graham, acknowledges the mystery of Nixon's triumph: "Richard Nixon, Superstar, who would have thought you'd ever go this far!"[23]

Laugh or cry, critics could no longer deny that, indeed, anyone—even Nixon—could be the president. Now that the worst man could no longer be kept out of power, they had to ask what that failure meant. One of the first to do so was Lawrence Ferlinghetti, whose *Tyrannus Nix?*, published in November 1969, joined a series of "political-satirical tirade[s]" by the beat poet.[24] Accustomed to controversy, Ferlinghetti, co-owner of San Francisco's City Lights Bookstore (the first shop in the United States to sell only paperbacks), had braved a 1957 obscenity trial for publishing Allen Ginsberg's *Howl and Other Poems*.[25] Dedicated to making poetry a "vital and popular art," Ferlinghetti experimented with reciting his work backed by a jazz combo, releasing the results on a 1958 Fantasy Records album. The printed versions appeared that same year in his collection *A Coney Island of the Mind*, which became one of the most popular works of contemporary poetry. While some beats preferred to adopt an apolitical stance, Ferlinghetti often used his poetry to express "the heated activist protest of the rebel spokesman whose social consciousness still burned to transform the world."[26] The first of these works, May 1958's "Tentative Description of a Dinner to Promote the Impeachment of President Eisenhower," was followed by "One Thousand Fearful Words for Fidel

Having returned from the political dead to attain the presidency, Richard Nixon elicited serious metaphoric comparisons to Lazarus as well as comic ones to Jesus Christ. Artist: Sandy Huffaker. Reprinted with permission. All rights reserved.

Castro," a January 1961 poem that predicted the U.S. government's various attempts to overthrow and assassinate the Cuban leader, and, finally, "Where Is Vietnam?," a 1966 poem that satirized Lyndon Johnson as "Colonel Cornpone."[27] For its part, *Tyrannus Nix?* seemed to have struck a responsive chord. The New Directions book version of the poem sold approximately 45,000 copies, and Berkeley's Fantasy Records released a recitation of the poem on vinyl.[28]

Ferlinghetti wrote *Tyrannus Nix?* during May and June 1969, a time when the nation waited to see how the new president would bring the war in Vietnam to a close. The initial signs seemed hopeful: Nixon requested a reform in the Selective Service system, establishing a lottery that would reduce the period of time when young men were vulnerable to the draft to one year instead of seven, and announced his plans to Vietnamize the war, that is, begin a phased withdrawal of American troops while slowly turning the major responsibilities for fighting over to the South Vietnamese army.[29] However, by the time New Directions published *Tyrannus Nix?*, the antiwar movement had stopped waiting, staging a Moratorium against the war on October 15, with protests in all the nation's major cities, constituting the largest protest against war in U.S. history. To follow up, the organizers called for all protesters to assemble in Washington, D.C., at a unified rally on November 15. In an attempt to defuse the Moratorium, Nixon went on national television on November 3 to explain his strategy for ending the war and to call on "the great silent majority" to unite behind him, insisting that "North Vietnam cannot defeat or humiliate the United States. Only Americans can do that." But while Nixon's approval rating jumped to 68 percent, 250,000 protesters made their way to Washington for the November Moratorium, actions which seemed to support *New York Times* columnist James Reston's lament that Nixon's rhetoric would "merely divide and polarize debaters in the United States."[30] In this atmosphere of heightened tension, the readers of *Tyrannus Nix?* saw Ferlinghetti liken Nixon to a mediocre baseball player who miraculously connects with the bases loaded, driving the ball deep into the outfield. Uninterested in admiring Nixon's unlikely achievement, Ferlinghetti focuses instead on its results: "Where will / it come down Fair or Foul." The question elicits more than a sporting interest, because Ferlinghetti's Nixon exemplifies the sterility of middle-class America. On its surface, Nixon's lifeless mask, with its "nowhere eyes," betrays an emptiness that is "the true story of America," revealing "no face at all behind the / great seal of the United States." Without something waiting to be discovered under Nixon's "American Gothic Bold Face," the fruits of his success can only be poisonous.[31]

For Ferlinghetti and other social critics, the ideals of competitive individualism by which Nixon lived produced a prosperous, but spiritually barren, America. *Tyrannus Nix?* envisions Nixon's devastated hometown, "run / over by a freeway like the lost home- / town of every American transplanted heart."[32] The small-town farming community in which Nixon grew up has vanished, but he, and the America he represents, has no nostalgia for this lost world. To the contrary, in the documentary film *Millhouse: A White Comedy* (1971), director Emile deAntonio includes footage of Nixon at a 1962 campaign rally seeming to celebrate the destruction of his past. "The orange groves and the lemon groves and avocado groves, for the most part, are gone," Nixon tells the approving crowd; in their place stand "houses, homes, by the thousands, shopping centers—progress." In *Tyrannus Nix?*, Ferlinghetti rants against this unrestrained embrace of commercial development. Bisected by the highway that connects the factory to its labor supply and decorated with monstrosities of free enterprise—"six supermarkets four drive- / ins sixteen fillingstations," America's Whittiers and Yorba Lindas have willingly swapped community, the shared experiences of family and neighbors, for easy access to thirty-one flavors of ice cream.[33]

This spectacularly bad trade typifies America's inauthentic, dehumanizing culture. In a passage from "Howl, Part II," to which Ferlinghetti makes a passing allusion in *Tyrannus Nix?* and which expresses what became countercultural orthodoxy fourteen years later, Ginsberg inveighed against the soulless demonic power that defines mainstream American culture, chanting: "Moloch whose blood is / running money. . . . Moloch whose soul / is electricity and banks."[34] By 1967, the film *The Graduate* could get comic mileage out of a shorthand version of this appraisal of America's materialistic and artificial soul—the single word "plastics," uttered by the creepily sincere family friend who acts as if he's handing Benjamin Braddock the keys to the kingdom. *Tyrannus Nix?* understands that, in its tasteless commerciality, America commodifies everything. Even death. "They're using the same footage for the / War," Ferlinghetti complains, "as for the Soap Opera with the same sponsor." Vietnam, a regular feature of the nightly TV news, has become indistinguishable from *As the World Turns;* the producer of bathroom tile cleaner also creates chemicals to incinerate human beings.[35] Following the inhuman logic of the marketplace, America's business is business, and "war is good business."[36]

To strive for success under such terms, therefore, proves self-mutilating. All manner of cultural commentators saw something oddly mechanical about Richard Nixon in his drive to become president. Impressionist David Frye mocked such mindless determination in a comedy routine that imagined Nixon's campaign for third-grade blackboard monitor. While his opponent, in a quavering falsetto, lisps promises to wipe the board and clean the erasers, Frye's Nixon, in adult voice, objects to his teacher's calling him "Dickie"—"that's Richard, if you please"—and vows to root out faceless, unnamed "chalk thieves." Cut off by the teacher as his promises escalate, he whispers, "Cue the balloons." The joke works because we can easily imagine this Nixon in knee pants—preternaturally industrious, humorlessly methodical—pursuing his electoral grail.[37] Just as Frye's Nixon unhesitatingly misleads his classmates with false promises, the culture that champions individualism cares little for the individual. In a December 1971 episode of *All in the Family*, "The Man in the Street," a CBS reporter interviews Archie to get a working man's thoughts on Nixon's economic policy. Effusive in his praise, Archie anticipates the joy of watching himself defending his president on network television. Just as Archie is introduced, however, Nixon preempts the news for a special announcement. Frustrated, Archie moans: "That Nixon is going to open his mouth once too often, and he ain't going to have Archie Bunker to kick around no more." Despite such threats, Archie willingly suffers more abuse. In "Archie's Fraud," aired on September 23, 1972, he complains about Nixon's wage freeze but denies speaking against any part of his president other than "the dumb part. The part that runs over to Russia and China and sits on my wages." Having endured disappointment before, Archie remains loyal; Nixon's "forgotten Americans" don't abandon him, even when he forgets them.[38]

Archie Bunker never could make the leap from personal complaint to a critique of the system itself. By contrast, *Tyrannus Nix?* probes the inherent contradictions in mainstream American ideology. Referring to a protester's death during the May 1969 Berkeley People's Park confrontations, Ferlinghetti scorns Nixon's allegiance to an America that systematically represses individual Americans, demanding to know "if you actually believe you can serve / the people and the State at the same time." In reality, individual citizens are silenced so as not to contradict that faceless, abstract group that Nixon presumes to represent because, as Ferlinghetti explains, "people are / a danger to the public." Faced with the sterility of Nixon's America, Ferlinghetti must hope that Tyrannus Nix "might / yet learn to unmask [his] Self." But, although time remains—Nixon's fly ball is still in play—unless the wind changes, his success will be irredeemably foul.[39]

And the necessary changes involve nothing less than scrapping America's belief in individualism. In a line borrowed from a George Harrison contribution to *Sergeant Pepper's Lonely Heart's Club Band*, Ferlinghetti warns Nixon away from militaristic adventurism: "You may lose your life like Ahab / in strange China Seas if you don't ever ever / see 'We're all one and life flows on within you / and without you.'" Because humanity is indivisible, acts of violence against another are actually attacks on oneself. Ferlinghetti's Whitmanesque rhapsody of praise for the "unfamous

men" of America aspires to universality: "The People Yes / and No including Indian chiefs and tyrants queers / kings hausfraus athletes parents
policemen bosses / soldiers sex-offenders jewish newspapermen [and]
long- / haired students." As his accompanying "notes to allege various
thefts and plunderings" indicates, Ferlinghetti's vision brings together an
ecumenical congregation of literary allusions (Allen Ginsburg, e. e. cum-
mings, Vachel Lindsay, Bertolt Brecht, Herman Melville, William Blake,
and Shakespeare), pop music lyrics (Dylan and the Beatles), mainstream
political commentary, New Left underground press political broadsides,
and countercultural spirituality tracts.[40] His anarchic, visionary belief in
a brother- and sisterhood of humanity unified in an effort to reconstruct
"a lost message Peace Music / Love Revolution Joy" makes space even for
Richard Nixon. The final words of the poem reach out to and embrace
Tyrannus Nix: "And the air is alive with love / and we are charged with
loving You too."[41]

By proposing the green flag raised in May 1969 over People's Park in
Berkeley as a new national symbol ("I think I'll sing the Green Flag Rag
rather than the / Blood Spangled Banner"), Ferlinghetti selects an event
that, for him, symbolized the revolutionary possibilities of combining political action with cultural rebellion.[42] In the spring of 1969, local activists
had attempted to claim as a public park a vacant, litter-strewn lot south of
the University of California campus that the administration had decreed
would become a parking lot and soccer field. A combination of student
activists and local residents came together and appropriated the land from
the university, claiming it in the name of "the People," and began, during several weekend work sessions at which as many as 3,000 people
arrived daily, to plant grass, trees, and a garden, install swings, and dig a
barbeque pit. Describing the construction of People's Park as "a trace of
anarchist heaven on earth," Todd Gitlin, the third president of Students
for a Democratic Society and later professor of sociology at Berkeley, New
York University, and Columbia, noted that this project managed to bring
together, "in harmonious combination," what often proved to be the oil-
and-water mix of the New Left political organizers and the counterculture
hippies and other lifestyle and personal consciousness rebels.[43]

Unfortunately, Ferlinghetti celebrated not a beginning but an ending.
Even sympathetic chroniclers say the People's Park confrontation signaled
the death of the 1960s student movement. The university administration, spurred on by Governor Ronald Reagan and conservative members
of the university system's Board of Regents, responded by posting "No

Trespassing" signs and closing off the surrounding eight-block area. When thousands of protesters decided to march from the campus to reclaim the park, they found their way blocked by Alameda County sheriffs, who sprayed buckshot into the crowd. Over a period of several hours, the police fired on protesters, reporters, and bystanders, even at students who were merely walking across campus. By the end of the day, one man was fatally wounded, another was blinded, and at least fifty, perhaps as many as a hundred, more had been shot. Reagan, still itching for a fight, ordered 3,000 National Guardsmen into Berkeley. According to Gitlin, the realization, one year before Kent State, that the government was prepared to kill white middle-class young people "ended up driving a wedge" between the factions of the movement and the counterculture.[44] The New Left activists promptly splintered further. The SDS convention of 1969 proved to be the last, as Leftists battled Marxist-Leninists and Maoists, until the Weathermen, a cadre "committed to enlisting the working class in revolution through immediate terrorism," walked out with 700 of the 1,500 total delegates.[45] In October Chicago police arrested hundreds of Weathermen as they vandalized downtown stores throughout the Loop during their "Days of Rage," and early in March 1970 several members of the underground group blew themselves to pieces while manufacturing bombs in a New York City townhouse.[46] According to Gitlin, "The Weathermen heightened the general self-hatred, darkened the darkness that already spilled over the Left."[47]

The counterculture got far better press. August 1969's Woodstock Music and Art Fair (and its celebration in the 1970 Academy Award–winning documentary film) seemed to presage the birth of a new nation dedicated to "peace and music . . . and love." Impressed by reports that, despite horrible overcrowding, uncooperative weather conditions, inadequate toilet facilities, and a short supply of food, nearly half a million people lived together for three days with no recorded violent acts, the *New York Times* saw Woodstock as a "declaration of independence" for the youth culture. Thrilled by this brave new world, Charles Reich, a Yale Law School professor, in his 1970 best seller *The Greening of America*, heralded the dawn of a new level of cultural consciousness—one that jettisoned outdated belief systems like the work ethic or the corporate ethos that preached the joys of "power, success, [and] status" in favor of free self-expression and communal living. One counterculture enthusiast, interviewed for the movie *Woodstock*, when asked if he "could ever communicate with a guy like Nixon," replied, in Ferlinghetti fashion, that he "hope[d] so," yet he went on to dismiss the president as "neurotic or psychotic." Insisting that "[*he did not*] need all that power," the young man rejected the orthodox mythology's traditional definition of ultimate success. "I don't have to become President of the United States. . . . I don't have to make the climb because there's nothing to climb for because it's all sitting right here."[48]

Yet this vision abandoned the political sphere. When Abbie Hoffman tried to speak at Woodstock, asking for donations to the legal fund for the defendants charged with conspiracy to incite riots during the 1968 Democratic convention, Pete Townshend of The Who crowned the Yippie with his guitar. Reich dismissed the New Left's political agitation as "a hopeless head-on fight against a machine," and Theodore Roszak, in his notable 1969 study *The Making of a Counter-Culture*, insisted that "the New Jerusalem of the young would begin not with class or party or race but 'at the non-intellective level of personality . . . [because] building the good society is not primarily a social, but a psychic task.'"[49] The counterculture seemed to believe that it could change the world by changing individual consciousness and living arrangements. But what happened was a diversion of "the energies of the rebellion of the young." The counterculture, without the threat of political action, "posed no present danger to the state and small potential threat to the academy."[50]

So, though he could not know it at the time, Ferlinghetti's dream of "Peace Music / Love Revolution Joy" was in its death throes even as he sang its praises.[51] Indeed, by 1973 Ferlinghetti had already recanted his guarded optimism. During that year, *Tyrannus Nix?* began appearing with an outer mini-sleeve called the "Watergate Rap," a twelve-line poetic denunciation that railed against Nixon as "A too-true caricature / of yourself, too truly fantasized in this 'populist / hymn' sent to you unheeded years ago." For these many reasons, the early 1970s reader of *Tyrannus Nix?*, greeted by Ferlinghetti's utopian vision, was confronted with the reality that, to borrow the words of John Lennon, "the dream [was] over."[52]

Viewed through the prism of Watergate, Ferlinghetti's tentative hopefulness about a Nixon presidency seems naive because the unmasking he desired revealed an even more disheartening reality. *Secret Honor*, Robert Altman's 1984 film, imagines no kinder, gentler Nixon. Instead, we find a suicidal drunk spewing a ninety-minute rambling monologue purporting to offer the secret explanation of Watergate. Donald Freed and Arnold M. Stone's play *Secret Honor: The Last Testament of Richard M. Nixon* debuted in June 1983 in a Los Angeles Actors' Theatre production. A founding member of a Los Angeles support group for the Black Panthers, Freed was best known as the author of politically based novels and plays, such as *Inquest*, a drama about the accused atom bomb spies Julius and Ethel Rosenberg, which played for twenty-eight performances on Broadway in 1970.[53] Stone, Freed's co-author, had been a former National Security Agency analyst and Justice Department lawyer in charge of mafia investigations. During its Los Angeles run, Robert Altman, captivated by the show, determined to bring it to New York City and to direct a film version.[54] The play opened Off-Broadway on November 8, 1983, at the Provincetown Playhouse, where both Eugene O'Neill and Edward Albee had launched their careers.[55] After only forty-seven performances—but with a strongly positive notice from Mel Gussow in the *New York Times*—*Secret Honor* moved to the University of Michigan (where Altman held a visiting position) for filming in late January 1984.[56] Bankrolled by $350,000 of Altman's own money, *Secret Honor* previewed on May 28 of the same year, during the Seattle Film Festival, before a mid-July premiere at the Cannery Theater, a 300-seat cinema in a Fisherman's Wharf shopping complex, just before the Democratic National Convention opened in San Francisco.[57] From November 1984 through September 1985, the film collected excellent reviews—making the Top Ten lists of the nationally syndicated television movie critics Gene Siskel and Roger Ebert—and played in art-film houses across the country.[58] By comparison to the top box office draws of 1985—movies like *Back to the Future* or *Rambo, First Blood Part Two*, *Secret Honor* couldn't compete.[59] But on its own terms, the film succeeded. By September 1985, Altman had recouped half of his investment. And, in Nixonian fashion, *Secret Honor* survived, stubbornly and slowly widening its circle over the years—from its cable television premiere on the Bravo network in September 1986 to its release on VHS video in 1987 to its release on laserdisc in 1993. Twenty years after the film's original release, it earned the distinction of being included in the prestigious Criterion Collection, a DVD series dedicated to preserving the finest of world cinema.[60]

By the time of *Secret Honor*'s original theatrical production, years of hard economic realities for middle-class and poor Americans had severely challenged the myth of success. Reagan replaced Carter, but the change in administrations did little, at least initially, to improve the economy. Unemployment grew from 6 percent during the second half of the Carter presidency to nearly 10 percent in 1982–1983. Poverty rose by 25 percent during the same period. Millions of minimum and low-wage workers scrambled just to survive. Meanwhile, the administration, having slashed federal money to school lunch programs, proclaimed ketchup a vegetable so as to pretend that meals served in the nation's public schools would still meet basic nutritional standards. Cut off from the day-to-day realities of struggling Americans, Reagan adviser Ed Meese wondered out loud whether "genuine pockets of hunger" existed in the United States or whether reports of deprivation were merely "anecdotal things from which some members of the press and political opponents are generalizing."[61] Organized labor suffered devastating setbacks in the 1980s; after the president fired 11,000 striking air traffic controllers in 1981, the Reagan era saw the fewest number of strikes per year of any administration. At the same time, Reagan's tax cuts during the early 1980s benefited the wealthy and exacerbated the nation's growing economic inequality. In these harsh facts, those on the left perceived "an apparent war on the poor" and the working middle class.[62]

Written in this depressing atmosphere (only in retrospect would it be clear that an economic recovery began during 1983), *Secret Honor* re-creates the American myth of success as a phantasmagoric nightmare. The movie's theatrical release poster, a lurid cartoonish drawing, displays a distant White House under a full moon. Trudging relentlessly forward— head grotesquely oversize, his hair and body covered with dirt clods—a Dennis-the-Menace gone bad skulks toward the presidential mansion, pulling a wagon packed with dynamite sticks. Next to the boy, the mythic words "Anyone can be the President" pasted together like a ransom note, announce that the American dream has been taken hostage. For the first clue to the identity of the kidnappers, we need look no further than the word "winner," one of the most repeated terms in the screenplay. Nixon reveres successful people, especially a group he refers to as the Committee of 100, the Republican businessmen operating out of a California retreat called Bohemian Grove.[63] These men had supported Nixon from the beginning of his political career, inspiring him with "a vision of the riches and power of this world." The traditional success mythology had promised its disciples a "true success," one that elevated the soul through the practice of virtue and, as a by-product, delivered the goods of this world—money, power, and fame.[64] But this orthodox vision of success fails to describe twentieth-century American politics. When Nixon outlines the first two points of his 1950 Senate campaign platform, "I believe in America, and I believe in real estate," he seems to equate the two. And if America is real estate, then people win or lose by virtue of how much they sell, like the real-estate agents of David Mamet's 1984 Pulitzer Prize–winning play *Glengarry Glen Ross*, who compete in a contest in which first prize is a Cadillac, second prize is a set of steak knives, and third prize is a pink slip.[65]

Secret Honor's Nixon subscribes entirely to this unmerciful logic. Tormented by his perceived inadequacies, he narrates his autobiography as a recital of failures. A taste of defeat taints even his triumphs: "When I won that scholarship to Duke, I had the last laugh. But I still wasn't a winner. A winner doesn't have to break into the Dean's office like I did to find out what my grades were." To live with this conception of success and to be an ordinary American means that, effectively, one does not exist: "We are all small fry, nothings," Nixon laments, "compared to the boys at Bohemian Grove." In his brutal self-denigration, *Secret Honor*'s Richard Nixon exemplifies one of the dynamics of what sociologist Michael Lewis called "the culture of inequality." Internalizing an ideology of unlimited individual opportunity, which tells us we should be personally censured for our failures, the majority of Americans in the last quarter of the twentieth century were left with massive guilt when faced with the realities of their very limited personal and professional successes. "The obvious consequence of this state of affairs," Lewis concluded, "is a large number of people in a varied array of personal circumstances who are . . . haunted by a sense that they are inadequate no matter what they have actually achieved."[66] Dismissed by the elite, the majority of Americans work dead-end jobs and live drearily ordinary lives—like Archie Bunker, whose sole comforts at day's end are to sit in his favorite armchair, drink a can of beer, and watch television. Or like the 15,000 lonely, insomniac failures who listen to callers share their troubles on the all-night radio talk show featured in Stanley Elkin's 1970 novel, *The Dick Gibson Show*, which ends with Richard Nixon calling in for foreign policy advice: "Bebe Rebozo and I are terribly concerned about what's been going on in Vietnam." Or like Lazlo Toth, the pen name of Don Novello (also known as *Saturday Night Live*'s Father Guido Sarducci), who, during the Watergate years, wrote letters soliciting support for Nixon that mindlessly spliced together sports and self-help book clichés. In his first of the published *Lazlo Letters*, Toth exhorts a beleaguered Nixon to "Fight! Fight! Fight! I'm with ya!"—a message he echoed to Gerald Ford after Nixon's resignation. If there is any equality of opportunity in this America, it is the opportunity to be mediocre.[67]

Paradoxically, *Secret Honor*'s Nixon believes that his strong identification with the sad lives of his countrymen is the very thing that will bring him success. Despised for his crassness by the Bohemian Grove clique,

"Anyone Can Be the President." This staple of faith from the American mythology of success takes on an ambiguous and decidedly sinister cast in the Robert Altman film Secret Honor. Reprinted with permission of Robert Altman and Sandcastle 5 Productions. All rights reserved.

he employs his used-car-salesman persona to his own advantage: "I would be a winner because I was a loser!" But not only does success on these terms accede to the elite's contemptuous dismissal of him; it also creates a political myth that undercuts his storybook success.[68] Nixon became a winner not because of his own determination but because the Committee of 100 employed him as their front man, as Bohemian Grove's Willy Loman. Substantially passive in his ascent to the White House, Nixon acts as a receiver for the messages he refers to as the "blueprint for my life." Well before the event, the Committee of 100 informed Nixon of his destiny, telling him that "it's only a matter of time" until he becomes president. By accepting the committee's support in the congressional election of 1946, he strips himself of any free agency forever after: "Then I answered that *goddamn* ad in that *goddamn* paper for Congressman, from that point on . . . I couldn't do anything."

Nixon's claim of powerlessness prefaces his main revelation: that he committed Watergate's minor crimes to cover up the treasonous acts he perpetrated for Bohemian Grove. Specifically, Nixon alleges that his supporters hungered for the untapped markets of the Far East. (The heroin trade of southeast Asia appealed especially to the committee's mafia contacts.) Having underwritten his political career, understandably they had no desire to see Nixon leave the White House. Accordingly, in exchange for the promise that America would stay in Vietnam through the mid-1970s, South Vietnamese president Thieu redirected millions of dollars of U.S. aid to Nixon's 1972 campaign fund, the excess to be used in 1976—after Congress passed a constitutional amendment permitting a third term.[69] Yet, even in disgrace, Nixon's compulsion to be a winner drives him to claim some measure of success: that his resignation stymied the Committee of 100's master plan. For without Watergate, Congress and the media would eventually have discovered Thieu's "blood bribery," a revelation that would have resulted in unprecedented social upheaval: "We're talking shooting it out in the streets; I mean civil war in this country by 1977." To hear Nixon tell it, Watergate is a sacrificial act: to save the nation, he makes himself a criminal outcast. Rather than continue as an accomplice to the Committee of 100's chicanery, Richard Nixon chooses "secret honor."

Even so, Nixon does not count himself a success. Immediately after lauding his own selfless integrity, he betrays his real feelings: "Sure, secret honor, and public shame." This Nixon, utterly unlike the one of the autobiographies, derives no solace from his private virtue: "And what do I get for following orders for thirty goddamn years. Is this it? A fucking pardon in disgrace?" The entire action of *Secret Honor* argues against the value of anything other than a publicly acknowledged success. In this way, Nixon acts out an ironic version of Christopher Lasch's observation that "success in our society has to be ratified by publicity," that the modern American politician or business leader "confuses successful completion of the task at hand with the impression he makes or hopes to make on others."[70] But Nixon's achievement here is an impression that American democracy still exists, and the moment he publicizes his story he destroys the illusion by revealing the system's corrupted reality. Equally important, his video security system of four television monitors and a mini-cam on a tripod testify to Nixon's pathetic clinging to symbols of authority to ward away his fear that nobody is watching. Confronted with his failure and his inability to live without the fame that substituted for real achievement, a solitary Nixon turns on his tape recorder, clutches the microphone, and plays to the television camera in a desperate search for the identity he otherwise lacks.

If there is no other jury, we, as the film's audience, must render a verdict on Richard Nixon. Yet *Secret Honor* makes judgment difficult, blurring the lines of fact and fiction by blending radical, sometimes conspiratorial, conjecture with real events and the politician's actual words. And, although the movie opens with the disclaimer that the screenplay is "a work of fiction, using as a fictional character a real person, President Richard M. Nixon—in an effort to understand," some reviewers condemned liberties taken with the historical record. For example, Iain Johnstone of the *Sunday Times* (London), who called the movie "unfair," suggested that "only the fact that the former president has been villified [*sic*] so frequently in public can have inhibited him from challenging them in court."[71] Treating Freed and Stone's claim of fictionality as mere legalistic cover, many reviewers failed to accept that *Secret Honor*'s subtitle, "A Political Myth," alerted us to the film's attempt to tell a story that expressed a kind of truth that went beyond the bare facts. Even more telling, few reviewers considered a second reading of the subtitle: that Nixon had fabricated his confession. And, ironically, if we doubt his story, then we grant him his success. As a man who rose from lower-middle-class beginnings, his life offers proof of the mythic assertion that in America any young boy who works hard enough can grow up to be president of the United States.

But this orthodox success mythology recognized no contradiction between success and salvation. However, *Secret Honor*'s Nixon, like a modern-day Faust, long ago sacrificed his spiritual values to his all-consuming ambition. Living with the hangover of his success, thinking back to the inspiration for his public career ("I really did want to grow up to be Abraham Lincoln"), Nixon articulates the disillusioning cost of his success: "I found out that the world is nothing more than a bunch of second-generation mobsters, and their lawyers, and the P.R. guys, and the new money crooks who made theirs in the war, and the old money crooks who made theirs selling slaves and phony merchandise to both sides in the Civil War." A November 1983 episode of *Family Ties* used Nixon to deal with the same theme. In "Speed Trap," Alex Keaton struggles to decide whether to take amphetamines to help him prepare for a week filled with papers, tests, and a crucial college entrance exam. Turning to his hero for advice, Alex asks his framed photo of Richard Nixon: "What would you do? Pressure mounting from all sides. Your entire future, your career, hangs in the balance. Would you do something you knew was wrong?" Immediately betraying embarrassed awareness of his question's irony, Alex, convinced he cannot perform without the drugs, turns the photo face down on his bedside table. Days later, with the help of his father, Alex breaks out of the drug's addictive cycle, realizing that worthy ends never justify unethical means.[72] By contrast, *Secret Honor*'s Nixon sold out his idealism and virtue, forcing him to deal with the guilt of not having lived as he was taught he should.

In an adult life defined by betrayals, Nixon's abandonment of his mother's values haunts him most. Early in the film, Altman captures the tormenting contradictions of Nixon's life in a close-up shot of the former president's desk on which sits a whiskey glass next to a framed photograph of Hannah Nixon with her family. Having repudiated the religious principles of his pacifist mother, who never drank or swore, he cannot live at peace with the life he created. Instead, he suffers a poignant nostalgia for his youth: "When I was a child, the sweetest sound I ever heard was the sound of the Santa Fe railway." Revealingly, however, this dream engine carried him away from home, separating him forever from his mother's purer world. He can testify to her influence ("Only you I owe, Mother"), yet resent her for the saint-like example he repudiated in his own life. Near the film's end, Nixon turns down the lights, hopelessly attempting to hide from her eyes—which he feels to be "searchlights of truth burning into each crisis in my miserable life." The idea of his dead mother judging him evokes both rage and shame, revealing the conflicting tensions of loyalty and rebellion inherent in their relationship. In Nixon's predicament, we observe aspects of the cultural dilemma created by America's radical devotion to individualism. The authors of the 1985 best seller *Habits of the Heart* dissected America's belief in an autonomous selfhood that, to develop, required one to leave both the parents' home and the church, a declaration of independence that ultimately "places the burden of one's own deepest self-definitions on one's own individual choice." The result is "a classic case of ambivalence" in which Americans, on the one hand, hold to the importance of self-reliance for the individual, while, at the same time, "we deeply feel the emptiness of a life without sustaining social commitments."[73] Caught between conflicting emotions, in the end, Nixon's anger erupts. At first believing that his mother wants him to kill himself, Nixon refuses, because "I did not elect myself. They elected me. Not once. Not twice. But all my goddamned life. And they would do it again." Defiantly, Nixon repeatedly chants his final malediction: "Fuck 'em!," cursing ambiguous enemies, trying vainly to exonerate himself and assuage his guilt.

At its most basic level, *Secret Honor* protests that America has forgotten what success means. One of the 1980s' most successful films, *The Big Chill*, which opened in the weeks before *Secret Honor* made its Off-Broadway debut, spoke to this same fear, portraying the reunion of a group of 1960s student activists who had all become successful in material terms, but who felt unsettling intimations that, spiritually and politically, their lives had taken a wrong turn. Most Americans of the time, however, did not seem to suffer such pangs of conscience. Popular television programs like *Dallas* and *Dynasty*, with their unabashed veneration of wealth and power, seemed to reflect as well as promote a new Gilded Age. The 1983 holiday shopping season, with its Cabbage Patch doll mania, marked an opening salvo in what one historian of the decade called "a grand national shopping binge," a celebration of the improving economy that for the next several years was marked by "a compulsive acquisitiveness, a moral and spiritual vertigo."[74] The dominant economic orthodoxy of the day, supply-side economics, preached that giving wealth back to the rich and to the largest businesses would accomplish the common good when that money "trickled down" to those on the bottom rungs of the economic ladder, a theory that, critics complained, really offered "nothing more than the old selfishness dressed up in new garb for the 1980s."[75] And while the priests of this "new Gospel of Wealth" spouted homilies shamelessly plagiarized from Horatio Alger, they made the CEO and the entrepreneur, like Lee Iacocca of the Chrysler Corporation or the real-estate mogul Donald Trump, into the new national heroes, the patron saints in

America's glorification of success.[76] But all these Americans, like *Secret Honor's* Richard Nixon, confused the sacred with its symbols. Riches and power were to be merely the outward signs by which to recognize those of virtuous character. In their longing for an authentic public honor, Freed and Stone seem to call for a return to the original purity of the American dream—with one crucial difference. For in its initial formulation, true success merged public with private rewards. *Secret Honor*, however, excludes the possibility of public integrity. In America, honor, if it exists at all, exists in secret.

Such a conclusion, however, effectively abandons the field to Nixon's successor. Freed and Stone seem to acknowledge as much when, late in the film, Nixon, pointing to Bohemian Grove's seemingly inexhaustible resources, seems to speak of the Reagan presidency: "They've got a million guys down there. They can send down to Central Casting and get some dummy that looks good on the tube." And in late 1983 through 1984, the American viewing audience, by and large, responded enthusiastically to the Great Communicator and his overarching theme of America's "great renewal." In January, Reagan announced his intention to run for reelection, reminding people of the nation's recovery from the brink of economic collapse and America's return from military weakness—in October 1983, Reagan had sent 5,000 U.S. troops to the Caribbean island of Grenada, where in two days of fighting they defeated the pro-communist forces there, an act trumpeted as an exorcism of "the Vietnam curse." "America is back," Reagan insisted, "and standing tall."[77] While Altman screened his film in San Francisco in the days leading up to the Democrats' convention, the Reagan reelection campaign readied its proclamation that it was "morning again in America," preparing to air a series of "soft focus, God Bless America campaign ads" so moving that reportedly even some staff members of the Democratic nominee, Walter Mondale, cried when they viewed them. With its scathing critique of the American myth of success, *Secret Honor*, like the Democrats, who in 1984 offered only "narrow economic appeals" to special interest groups, failed "to sing a song that could inspire and unite America." Yet so ready were many Americans for that song of inspiration that they waved their flags at Reagan campaign rallies and bellowed out the refrain of Bruce Springsteen's "Born in the USA," ignoring the verses' depressing story about an unemployed Vietnam veteran. "Angst was out, affability was in." Tired of stories suggesting the bankruptcy of treasured national myths, "most Americans were happy to enjoy the good times."[78]

What's more, by 1983–1984, far from being holed up in his study and drinking himself into oblivion, Richard Nixon was carefully treading the comeback trail. In July 1983, just weeks after *Secret Honor* premiered in Los Angeles, Nixon wrote *Real Peace*, a warning to Reagan that "unremitting hostility toward the Soviet Union was a misguided policy." As Altman was preparing to film the play, Nixon sat down to film a video biography— thirty-eight hours of conversation with a former aide, for which CBS producers paid half a million dollars to air ninety minutes, split between *60 Minutes* and *American Parade* and spread over three nights in April 1984. During the summer, while Altman tested his film in San Francisco, Nixon was already at work on his next book, *No More Vietnams*. Published at the end of April 1985, on the tenth anniversary of the fall of South Vietnam, the book vigorously defended Nixon's handling of the war. Panned by the major newspapers, Nixon's fifth book "found a receptive audience" and garnered "substantial sales."[79] At the end of *Secret Honor*, a defiant Nixon promised that he would not go quietly into that good night, raging, "If they want me dead, they'll have to do it." Less than two years after the play's debut at the Los Angeles Actors' Theatre, it was perfectly clear that the American public was too squeamish to pull the trigger.

As we have seen, Richard Nixon often gets reinvented to explore key ideological pressure points in the American myth of self-reliant individualism. Once accepted almost unquestioningly within the dominant culture, the promise of material and spiritual rewards for those with the character to labor diligently enough to earn them has faced challenges from inside, as well as outside, of the American mainstream—questions that continued throughout the 1980s and the 1990s to the present. Anthropologist Katherine S. Newman has argued that during the 1980s and early 1990s even those baby boomers who made careful financial plans and deferred extravagant purchases found their dreams strangled by "skyrocketing prices, stagnating wages, dissipating promotion prospects, and the relentless pressure of an economy that just does not seem to work any more."[80] Nor did the prosperity of the Clinton boom years resolve these tensions. Barbara Ehrenreich's *Nickel and Dimed: On (Not) Getting By in America* chronicles her unsuccessful 1998 experiment in living on a working woman's wages: as a waitress and hotel maid, as a cleaning woman and nursing home aide, and as a Wal-Mart associate. "Something is wrong, very wrong," she concludes, "when a single person in good health, a person who in addition possesses a working car, can barely support herself by the sweat of her brow."[81] Under such circumstances, the old verities about the American dream no longer make sense.

And reinventing Richard Nixon remained an activity that permitted social critics to explore these tensions. In fact, by the mid-1990s, Nixon had become a shorthand emblem for the mainstream culture's unbounded obsession with success. In February 1994, during the Winter Olympics and the height of the Nancy Kerrigan/Tonya Harding affair (Harding's boyfriend had, one month earlier, hired a goon to injure Kerrigan, the favorite to win the gold medal in women's figure skating), *Newsday* political cartoonist Doug Marlette called on a familiar iconic image. In the drawing, one coach confides to another: "I think the stress is starting to get to Tonya." Meanwhile, skating past our eyes, diminutive frame turned dumpy and pear-shaped, Harding has morphed into Richard Nixon. With this cartoon, Marlette explains Harding's working-class-background resentment of and paranoid obsession with the Massachusetts-bred media-darling Kerrigan and confirms Nixon's status as the cultural symbol of the American dream's devolution into an ends-justifies-the-means thuggery. Two years later, "Awards Show," an episode of the TV sitcom *NewsRadio*, took the Richard Nixon self-made-man myth to dada-esque heights. Because news director Dave Nelson is frustrated by gloomy predictions about the station's chances at the annual regional broadcasting awards ceremony, station owner Jimmy James attempts an inspirational story about a fellow classmate who yearned to play football: "Coach wouldn't let him because he wasn't big enough. But, did he give up? . . . No, just made him try harder and harder. I mean, the kid ate like a wild animal every day. I mean, he pumped iron all night long. And, after two months, he got a hernia. [Pause.] Makes you think, huh?" When Nelson admits to utter confusion with this self-help anecdote gone awry, James realizes he has left out the key piece of information: "That kid's name . . . was Richard Nixon." When Nelson remains baffled, James stumbles, trying to explain an elusive moral: "The point of the story *is*. . . ah let's see, hernia, wild animal, Nixon . . . ah hell, it's in there somewhere." Spoofing the wave of tributes to Nixon as the diligent man who never quit that flooded popular culture in the years following his death, the "Awards Show" episode gave us a cultural mythic narrative so frequently invoked that it has lost all meaning—for its storytellers as well as for its audience.[82]

The Best Man, Tyrannus Nix?, Secret Honor, and the other representations of Richard Nixon we have seen in this chapter belong to a rich tradition in American literature and popular culture focusing on the failure of

According to cartoonist Doug Marlette, skater Tonya Harding and former president Richard Nixon shared an ends-justifies-the-means kinship in their ruthlessly practical responses to having to fight against media darlings from Massachusetts. © Tribune Media Services, Inc. All rights reserved. Reprinted with permission.

success. In Vidal's play, we are granted a temporary reprieve from our cultural mythology; anyone *cannot* be president—or, at least, not just yet. The truly best person can still find a way to win by keeping evil out of power. By 1969, Nixon had triumphed, and cultural observers had to decide what to make of this proof that anyone, indeed, could now be the president. According to Lawrence Ferlinghetti in *Tyrannus Nix?*, the struggle for the American dream was dehumanizing and was creating an amoral world. Somewhere along the way, in the pursuit of success, authentic nurturing community and a sense of personal integrity are lost. In the post-Watergate era, "anyone can be the president" took on another, more cynical, meaning. Robert Altman's film *Secret Honor* suggests the possibility that it doesn't matter who is president because this person is an interchangeable figurehead serving at the will of hidden financial interests. Success, of the traditional self-made variety, no longer realistically describes political, economic, and social realities. Put bluntly, the presidency has been taken hostage and democracy is dead. Or perhaps *Secret Honor* offers the same critique as *Tyrannus Nix?*—that the ideal of competitive individualism brings success at a cost that is too dear. The myth of the self-made man hides the reality of the self-unmade man who gains power at the expense of his soul. At the close of *The American Idea of Success*, Richard Huber wonders if "perhaps America has always been a dream incapable of realization, a promise too demanding to keep."[83] In the tentativeness that ends what had been, to that point, a detailed critique of the American obsession with success, Huber shares a problem with Vidal, Ferlinghetti, and Freed and Stone: exposé is easier than reform. None of our authors portrays a viable philosophy to supplant the traditional conception of success. If *The Best Man, Tyrannus Nix?*, and *Secret Honor* are unable to offer us a completely integrated alternative to American orthodoxy, it is because they are better at penetrating the mask of success than they are at fashioning a new face that can be worn at public as well as private occasions.

CHAPTER FOUR

THE SELF-MADE MONSTER

AMERICA AND THE MYTH OF

NATIONAL MISSION

Each year the myth's power intensified. Initially talking only in terms of winning or losing, eventually Nixon spoke of potential Armageddon. The episode of the groundbreaking documentary *Vietnam: A Television History* (1983) that deals with Richard Nixon's handling of the war in Indochina opens with three film segments taken from three consecutive years from the mid-1960s. Beginning in a relatively dispassionate and analytical tone, Nixon, in April 1964, uncertain about the goal the United States is setting in Vietnam, asserts that the objective must "be nothing less than victory." Ten months later he turned up the heat, casting the struggle as an episode in the continuing Cold War, by describing the nation's efforts in Southeast Asia as a message to the "Red Chinese" that America will not permit any country to lose its freedom to communist aggression. By May 1966, his detachment gone, a dogmatic Nixon crisply intones a doomsday prophecy that a U.S. retreat "from Vietnam would be a communist victory of massive proportions and would lead to World War Three."[1]

By the time American troops came home, the myth had him talking nonsense. After the January 1973 Paris Peace Accords, having finally settled for terms that some historians believe would have been available several years earlier, terms that provided little more than a "decent interval" between U.S. withdrawal and North Vietnamese victory, Nixon defiantly maintained that he had not been the first president to lose a war. Rather, he had achieved "peace with honor." Jules Feiffer, in a March 1973 cartoon, saw more than a hint of desperation in Nixon's monotonously insistent assertions of victory. Arms mechanically pumping up and down and across his chest, the typical Nixonian public-speaking gestures rendered as a kind of semaphore, Feiffer's Nixon's resolute repetitions of the phrase "peace with honor" slowly mutate into gibberish. "Honor" becomes "almonds," "almonds" becomes "onus," "onus" becomes "armor," until Nixon, who has been shrinking smaller and smaller, is left absurdly pronouncing, "We

are proud of peace with momma." In the final panel, a tiny, no longer ges-
turing Nixon is pathetically reduced to calling out for "momma, momma,
momma."[2]

This imprisoning power of the myth of national mission, with its
proclivity to restrict our vision of reality in irrational ways, emerges in
a cluster of Nixon characters—from Coover's landmark novel *The Public
Burning* (1977) to Ron Kovic's 1976 memoir *Born on the Fourth of July*,
Oliver Stone's 1989 film of the same name, the 1995 made-for-television
movie *Kissinger and Nixon*, and Jonathan Lowy's novel *Elvis and Nixon*
(2001). In each case, these artists do not complain about America's mythic
imagination; indeed, they believe that no other type of vision is possible.
Rather, their critique is that the nation's hegemonic culture has objectified
its belief systems. As each of these works argues, throughout much of the
twentieth century—for *The Public Burning*, the early Cold War years, and
for *Born on the Fourth of July* and *Elvis and Nixon*, the Vietnam era—the
mainstream culture accepted the myth of mission as unalterable dogma.
In these instances, reinventing Richard Nixon becomes a way to explore
the dangers of a country believing too literally in its own national mythology. In 1952, the year that Richard Nixon was first elected to national
office, the theologian Reinhold Niebuhr described the United States as a
nation so convinced of its own pure motives that Americans believed "only
malice could prompt criticism of any of our actions." Yet such pridefully
blind insistence on our national purity makes us dangerous. "Nations, as
individuals, who are completely innocent in their own esteem, are insuf-
ferable in their human contacts," Niebuhr insisted, and the refusal to shed
our cultural mythology of mission "will . . . plunge . . . us into avoidable
guilt by too great confidence in our virtue."[3] This paradox sits at the heart
of the myth of American mission, making it, as a result, the primary irony
of the United States and its relations with the world during the Nixon
era. Such blind conviction blocked out the emergence of possible counter-
myths and created a rigid American orthodoxy that took its temporal ideas
as timeless truths and, in the process, did violence to its believers and
those it named heretics alike. Yet because the critics have not been able to
move beyond the elements of the mission-myth story line, they have not
offered any new vision to replace the old narrative, sentencing us to fighting and refighting the same cultural battles over and over again.

Throughout his forty-year career, Robert Coover has been fascinated by
the mythic narratives humans create to order and give meaning to their

lives. During the late 1960s and through most of the 1970s, he used the figure of Richard Nixon as a vehicle to explore the creative, but ultimately destructive, power of America's national myths. In his novella *Whatever Happened to Gloomy Gus of the Chicago Bears?* (which appeared in a 1975 issue of *American Review*), Coover focused on the power of the success myth, imagining what would have happened had Nixon decided, while at Whittier College, to concentrate exclusively on the areas at which he was a failure: football and sex.[4] With single-minded dedication to the American mania for self-improvement, Coover's hero, Gloomy Gus, Nixon's nickname during law school, lives out the "rags to riches drama of the industrious American boy." In a grim parody of the "Art of Virtue," found in Part Two of Benjamin Franklin's *Autobiography*, Gus makes himself into the very things that, by nature, he is not, a process that first strangles his soul and finally kills his body.[5] Coover's masterwork, *The Public Burning*, transfers this lesson from the personal to the national level. Begun in the late 1960s as a short play on the Rosenberg atomic bomb spy case, the novel was planned as a group of set pieces, like a series of circus acts, held together by its clown/narrator Richard Nixon. But during his research into Nixon's public statements and his memoir *Six Crises*, Coover became interested in treating Nixon's voice sympathetically and involved him in the story line. Planned for publication during the 1972 presidential campaign, then delayed until the nation's bicentennial, Coover's novel was not released until August 1977, due, in large part, to the publisher's fear that Nixon might sue.[6]

Despite all the adversity, *The Public Burning* managed to register on the *New York Times*'s best-seller list on October 2, 1977, behind Tolkien's *The Silmarillion*, *The Thorn Birds*, and *Oliver's Story*, the sequel to *Love Story*.[7] Reimagining the final days of Julius and Ethel Rosenberg, the husband and wife who were executed in 1953 for giving the secret of the atomic bomb to the Soviet Union, and told alternately by an omniscient third-person voice and the first-person perspective of Vice President Richard Nixon, *The Public Burning* exposes the subjectivity that American orthodox ideology passes off as divinely ordained history. The novel's prologue, "Groun'-Hog Hunt," identifies a dominant narrative that encodes American experience as a cosmic design fulfilled in its special mission to bring "the Doctrine of Self-Determination and Free-Will and . . . the Light of Reason to the . . . superstitious nations of the earth."[8] Such a worldview, however, bifurcates the world into good and evil. Coover personifies one-half of this simplifying dualism through the legendary figure of Uncle

Years later, some historians would assert that Nixon had achieved neither peace nor honor. Even at the time, cartoonist Jules Feiffer felt that Nixon's insistent repetition of the phrase "peace with honor" had rendered the words nonsensical. © *Jules Feiffer. Reprinted with permission. All rights reserved.*

Sam, "[the] star-spangled Superhero and knuckle-rapping Yankee peddler," who, as leader of "the Sons of Light," convinces his "elected sons and daughters" to embrace the nation's "manifest dust-in-yer-eye." To oppose the chosen people, American mythology gives us the "Sons of Darkness" led by the evil Phantom.[9]

But objectifying subjective myths has deadly consequences. *The Public Burning* depicts Julius and Ethel Rosenberg's executions as a blood sacrifice to sustain the myth of national mission—regardless of the couple's actual guilt or innocence.[10] As Uncle Sam tells Nixon, "We ain't talkin' about trials now, boy, stay awake, *we're talkin' about the sacraments!*" The myth's narrative structure requires that America's seeming failure to control the world's destiny during the early days of the Cold War—the fall of China to communism, the stalemate of the Korean War, the Soviets' development of an atomic bomb—be explained as the acts of some satanic conspiracy. Having internalized this mind-set, Nixon blandly accepts fabricated evidence against the accused couple as "a routine part of police work." In the absence of any objective history—"The past is a bucket of cold ashes," Uncle Sam pronounces; "rake through it and all you'll get is dirty!"—myths compete with one another, and a courtroom trial simply places "one set of bolloxeratin' sophistries agin another." The guilty verdict against the Rosenbergs casts them as the spies who must exist to permit continued suspension of disbelief in the narrative of American omnipotence. America had to wash its feet in the blood of the Rosenbergs, Uncle Sam confesses, because "order ain't what comes natural . . . and a lotta people gotta get killt tryin' to pretend it is."[11]

Interestingly, given Coover's antipathy toward the real-life model, Nixon, alone among all the historical characters in *The Public Burning*, develops a critical awareness of myth-making as a defining human activity. In the days before the executions, the vice president, reading over the trial transcripts, notes an underlying dramatic structure to the case—its theme of good and evil and the Rosenbergs' tendency to act as if they were following "some larger script"—and envisions the case as his generation's morality play.[12] While the politician in him accepts fabrications in the FBI's case, the literary critic is disturbed that, even with the invention of testimony and evidence, the government, like a staff of hack writers piecing together a pulp novel on a deadline, cannot construct a plausible story line that, with any certainty, casts the Rosenbergs as the leaders of the espionage ring.[13] Spurred by the belief that Uncle Sam has chosen him for a special part in the execution ceremonies, which Coover moves from Sing Sing Prison to a stage erected in the middle of Times Square, Nixon identifies narrative writing as his role. His days spent wading through the minutiae of facts, physical evidence, and testimony suggest to him that what America needs is an author who can integrate the seemingly unconnected and contradictory elements of the Rosenberg case into a moral fiction: "I had to . . . *Write a speech!* . . . That was what language was for: to transcend the confusions, restore the spirit, recreate the society!"[14] All of his earlier literary experiments have been preparatory for this job of explicating the Rosenberg executions and creating a new vision of America.

But Coover's Richard Nixon also suffers orthodoxy's repression when he commits a sin almost as cardinal as unbelief—attempting to rewrite the national mythology. Led by his authorial instincts, Nixon accepts as fiction the story of the Sons of Light, a myth he had believed with a fundamentalist's faith. Analyzing the public record en route to the Rosenbergs' executions, Nixon reassesses the case, realizing the arbitrary linkages in any historical account: "There were no scripts, no necessary patterns, no final scenes, there was just *action*, and then *more action!*" Comforting in its neatness, the narrative that promises America's ultimate victory (despite territory lost to the communists since 1945 and the Soviet Union's acquisition of the bomb) is false. The myths of clear-cut good and evil and good's guaranteed victory are only, to borrow the vice president's words, "stuff we make up to hold the goddamn world together." With this message, Nixon believes he can redeem the American people by going to Sing Sing Prison to stop Uncle Sam's executions from happening. His duty is to "step in and change the script."[15]

However, he soon discovers a more personal reason for his rescue attempt: at the Sing Sing Death House, he finds himself confessing his desire for Ethel and trying to make love to her. However, his failure to recognize the human need for myth dooms his crusade. His vow to "change the script" betrays his irrepressible desire to weld discrete actions into a unified narrative; the script has been altered, not abandoned. Even while he kisses Ethel Rosenberg and tells her that they have been duped by the same lie of causation, he thinks to himself that his erotic desires were really what led him to Sing Sing. The trip to destroy the lie of purpose had its own objective: to invent a scene in which he, the leading man, gets the girl. More important, Nixon cannot recast America's orthodox mythology because he does not really control the events making up its plot. His seemingly spontaneous attempt at disrupting Uncle Sam's story turns out to have been written into the Yankee peddler's script; the "Ethel Rosenberg" that the vice president tries to free and attempts to seduce may really be a cross-dressing J. Edgar Hoover, who has been trailing Nixon in various disguises. And, as a final sign of supremacy, Uncle Sam tracks Nixon down after the executions and sodomizes him, making him submit to the national mythology's author.

Though details of the Korean War dominate the narrative—the time of the Rosenbergs' arrest, trial, and executions matches the span of the conflict almost exactly—the first readers of The Public Burning could not help but project beyond the novel's June 1953 time frame and see the Vietnam War as the most powerful example of the national mission myth's destructive power. In fact, in a sentence from the novel's Prologue, Coover links the two conflicts: "In Korea Uncle Sam has broken the intransigence of the Reds, bringing them to the conference table if not to their knees, while further down the coast pro-French candidates have won all localities except Hanoi in the first real democratic election those little yellow people of Indochina have ever known." Subsequent references to the French "losing their nerve in Indochina" and to hard-line Republicans objecting to Eisenhower's plan to establish a truce in Korea as "peace without honor" help us to understand Coover's novel as a reflection on the trauma through which the nation had just passed—to see that not just the Rosenbergs but the American public itself had been burned by Uncle Sam.[16]

Yet by no means was *The Public Burning* the first warning. In 1952, Niebuhr had already called for a more realistic, less messianic, approach to the Cold War, arguing that America's plan to quickly democratize underdeveloped Asian countries ran afoul of economic, social, cultural, and religious factors that made "many of the values of democratic society which are most highly prized in the West . . . neither understood nor desired."[17] Three years later, British novelist Graham Greene offered a strong cautionary tale in *The Quiet American*. The book's main character, Alden Pyle, a member of the U.S. Economic Aid Mission with covert ties to American intelligence, grounds his life in a missionary purpose: "He was determined," the book's narrator declares, "to do good, not to any individual person but to a country, a continent, a world." Convinced that the answer to Vietnam's problems is to create a "Third Force," an alternative to communism and colonialism, Pyle, "impregnably armoured by his good intentions and his ignorance," refuses to accept that his ally could be so vicious and corrupt that the United States might be harming, rather than helping, the Vietnamese.[18] Greene himself had visited colonial Vietnam four times, touring the countryside, flying reconnaissance with the French air force, so that—even as Vice President Richard Nixon was urging wider American involvement in Indochina, beginning with an effort to save the French garrison at Dien Bien Phu from the humiliating defeat that would drive the Europeans home—the novelist was in a position to witness what Robert Stone describes as "the beginning of a terrible mistake."[19]

Some American observers seemed to heed Greene's admonition, but, on closer inspection, they really did not comprehend it. William J. Lederer and Eugene Burdick's 1958 blockbuster best seller *The Ugly American*, which mixed episodes set in real Southeast Asian countries with its main plot centered on the struggle against communism in the fictional nation of Sarkhan, lambasted an incompetent U.S. foreign service, populated with ignorant, xenophobic, political appointees. But Lederer and Burdick's chief complaint is not with the mission myth; the novel's few admirable characters only want their country to better live up to its purpose. Gilbert MacWhite, on being appointed ambassador to Sarkhan, learned the language in less than four months, educated himself in the culture and history of the region, and, in general, "prepared for his new assignment with a thoroughness in the best traditions of missionary faith."[20] In fact, Lederer and Burdick's ultimately positive message provided fodder for Nixon's presidential aspirations in 1960, when he tried to co-opt *The Ugly American*'s notoriety for his own purposes, insisting that the United States "need[ed] to know the tactics and strategy of world communism" while, at the same time, affirming "why we love our country, and what it stands for."[21] In 1966, the same year that Nixon linked Vietnam to a third world war, J. William Fulbright's monograph *The Arrogance of Power*, asserting that buried "in all of our souls there is a bit of the missionary," criticized the United States for confusing its power for "a sign of God's favor, conferring upon it a special responsibility for other nations . . . to remake them . . . in its own shining image." Here too, however, criticism was meant to redirect the nation toward its true mission: "the service of her own example."[22]

Yet even these limited cautions did little good. Indeed, the mission myth created a set of ideological blinders that prevented many Americans from entertaining certain ideas about the war. First, as Loren Baritz has argued, because our national myth convinced us "that our intentions [were] pure, our motives good, and our behavior virtuous," Americans initially supported the war, certain that "we had a superior moral claim to be in Vietnam, and because, despite their queer ways of doing things, the Vietnamese shared our values." Such bland assumptions did not allow for the idea that the Vietnamese communists could also be nationalists. In the teleology of the Cold War, Third World communists could only be puppets of a monolithic block led by the Soviet Union and the People's Republic of China. As Neil Sheehan has described them, the narrative structures by which most Americans understood the world in the early to mid-1960s "halved [the globe] between darkness and light," preventing the United States from really understanding the country in which it operated. John Hellmann argues that Vietnam remained a mystery to Americans because, "when they thought about Indochina, [they] generally saw themselves . . . once again [as] 'western pilgrims' on a mission of protection and progress." By and large, for Americans, Vietnam was not about a civil war in Indochina; it was about defining the American character and national purpose.[23]

Furthermore, because we told ourselves that we were engaged in an altruistic mission, we were slow to understand the self-interested motives driving our international commitments. During the later years of the war, critics found the image of Richard Nixon to be a convenient emblem of this self-deceiving hypocrisy. In a savagely ironic scene from deAntonio's film *Millhouse*, Nixon, making a speech about Vietnam, declaims that, by the war's end, "we will have gained nothing for ourselves, except the possibility that the people of South Vietnam will be able to live in peace and choose their own way without any foreign domination." Although the United States possesses the power to "embark on conquest around the world," Nixon asserts that "we want for ourselves, and for the world, peace [and] freedom." But as he pontificates, a two-columned chart labeled "The US in SE Asia" scrolls up the screen, itemizing the dozens of American businesses—Alcoa, Pepsi-Cola, Shell, and Uniroyal—that had set up shop in South Vietnam.[24] In a July 15, 1970, editorial cartoon, Herblock ridiculed Nixon's defense of the domino theory, the Cold War staple that insisted that if one country in Southeast Asia were to succumb to the communists then they all would fall like a row of dominoes. Nixon, singing and soft-shoeing as Doctor Dolittle from the 1967 Rex Harrison movie, reveals the foundation of the U.S. relationship with Southeast Asia. With no interest in anything but reaping monetary rewards, the dominoes smile greedily, dance in step, and count the bills—one even picks Nixon's pocket. Meanwhile, another holds up a sign, "Dollars Spoken," indicating the true common language between the United States and these countries.

When he was interviewed for the 1975 Academy Award–winning documentary *Hearts and Minds*, former bomber-pilot Randy Floyd asserted that "America has tried, we've all tried, very hard to escape what we've learned in Vietnam." Yet Coover's novel appeared at a time when American culture was beginning to confront its recent past and actively seek to understand what had gone wrong.[25] Published in May 1977, just a few months before *The Public Burning*, Philip Caputo's memoir, *A Rumor of War*, portrayed the soldier's experience as a process of gradual, but fundamental, disillusionment: "When we marched into the rice paddies on the damp March afternoon, we carried, along with our packs and rifles, the implicit convictions that the Viet Cong would be quickly beaten and that we were doing something altogether noble and good. We kept the packs and rifles; the convictions, we lost."[26] Within the next two years, Hollywood released major films dealing with the war's legacy. The first of these, Hal Ashby's *Coming Home*, won the 1979 Best Actor and Best Actress Oscars. Taking as its subject the traumatic physical and emotional scars of the war's returning soldiers, the film concluded with one veteran, who, after receiving a Purple Heart for a self-inflicted accidental wound, drowned himself in the Pacific, unable to forgive himself for failing to live up to his dreams of being a noble warrior.[27] Michael Cimino's *The Deer Hunter*, the 1979 Best Picture Academy Award winner, told the story of three steelworkers

"If You Could Walk With The Dominoes, Talk With The Dominoes . . ."

from Clairton, Pennsylvania, sent off by their community from a wedding reception hall draped in red, white, and blue bunting and with a banner reading "Serving God and Country Proudly" to a war that was as brutal and meaningless as a game of Russian roulette.[28] Released in August 1979, Francis Ford Coppola's *Apocalypse Now* grafted the plot of Conrad's *Heart of Darkness* onto America's experience in Vietnam.[29] Eager for "a mission," Captain Willard (portrayed by Martin Sheen), a soldier from heartland America on his second tour in Vietnam, is sent into Cambodia to assassinate the renegade general Walter Kurtz (Marlon Brando), one of the army's brightest stars, who falls victim to "unsound" practices— among other things, he scrawls "DROP THE BOMB EXTERMINATE THEM ALL!" across the typed manuscript of a study he was preparing on Vietnam for a California think tank.[30]

Born on the Fourth of July, a memoir by Vietnam veteran Ron Kovic, led the vanguard of this revisionist wave. Published by McGraw-Hill in August 1976, the book appeared at a time when critical reevaluations of the United States were fixtures on the best-seller lists—from Gore Vidal's novel *1876* to Woodward and Bernstein's *The Final Days* and Lillian Hellman's *Scoundrel Time* (taken together, a bookend study of Nixon's career from its beginning during the days of the House Un-American Activities Committee to the last months of the Watergate scandal).[31] The recipient of "overwhelmingly positive" reviews, *Born on the Fourth of July* contends that the myth of national mission destroyed the United States as much as it did Vietnam.[32] Raised a true believer, Kovic begins his book with the familiar "Ask not" passage from Kennedy's inaugural address and describes a generation conditioned to assume the morality of American power. Gunslinging patriotism and religion blended seamlessly for Kovic, who, fed a steady diet of John Wayne movies, had "a cowboy hat on my head and two six-shooters in my hands" during his first Communion. This mythic vision, however, ravages all the lives Kovic touches. For his first kill, he accidentally shoots one of his comrades, creating a confusing and traumatic guilt: "He'd never figured it would ever happen this way. It never did in the movies. . . . The good guys weren't supposed to kill the good guys." Even so, Kovic refuses to jettison his mythic narratives. In fact, he begins to take greater risks, guided by his desire "to prove to myself that I was a brave man, a good marine." Only after receiving the wound that paralyzes him from the chest down, unable to feel his legs, choking on blood from a wounded lung, does Kovic begin to question the beliefs that brought him to volunteer for two tours of duty in Vietnam.[33] If his war experiences did not play out according to script, neither did his homecoming. Shipped to horrific VA hospitals, including one where rats would nibble on the paralyzed limbs of the wounded, Kovic endured callous and degrading treatment. At his hometown's Memorial Day parade, no one waves as he is driven down the street, and at the ceremony no one invites him to speak. In fact, his post-Vietnam life makes so little sense that he can only process it as "one big dirty trick."[34]

And who better to serve as a symbol of this trickery than Tricky Dick himself? In Washington, D.C., to demonstrate against the Cambodian invasion and the killing of students during protests at Kent State University, Kovic instinctively moves toward the White House, in which he suspects an indifferent Nixon sits "holed up, probably watching television," but, finding the mansion surrounded by a protective wall of buses, the veteran marvels at how purposefully this president has isolated himself. At spring 1972 protests outside of Nixon's Los Angeles campaign headquarters, undercover police, posing as fellow Vietnam vets, rip Kovic's medals from his chest, dump him out of his wheelchair, and beat him so badly he ends up in the emergency room. Later that same year, he and his fellow Vietnam Veterans against the War conduct their "last patrol," a cross-country convoy headed for the Miami Beach Republican National Convention "to tell Nixon a thing or two." Using his friendship with a West Coast television producer to get into the convention hall, Kovic plans to disrupt the president's acceptance speech, the act that he imagines as payback for "what had been done to me and a generation of Americans by all the men who had lied to us and tricked us, by the man who stood before us in the convention hall that night."[35]

Ironically, despite what the myth has done to him, Kovic still needs a missionary vision of himself to function. In the months before the trip to Miami Beach, the hero myth revitalizes him, ending a period of lethargy and depression: "He would come back very soon and he would make it like all the stories of baseball players he had read when he was a kid. '. . . *Kovic is making a terrific comeback, folks! A terrific comeback.'*" Unable to escape the need for a grand vision of himself and his life, Kovic describes the "strange caravan" of Vietnam veterans he leads to the Republican Convention as "a historic event like the Bonus March," fulfilling a transcendent purpose "to reclaim America and a bit of ourselves." Used to combat in the jungles of Vietnam, these soldiers, in taking on Richard Nixon and his supporters, "know [they] are fighting the real enemies this time—the ones who have made profit off our very lives." Despite his deep sense of betrayal, Kovic still draws inspiration from the stories he claims to have rejected.[36]

Perhaps because the critics of national mission failed to imagine a truly new story, the years following *The Public Burning*'s publication only confirmed the myth's staying power. Decidedly rejecting Jimmy Carter's warnings about facing an age of limits, the nation turned to a man who promised that it was "morning again in America" (even if he could achieve this pledge only by mentally exiling everyone but upper- and middle-class white Americans to a different time zone), clinging to what Garry Wills called a belief in its "original sinlessness," a denial "not only [of] the Fall of Man but [also of] the ruin of Eden."[37] So, rather than reject the national mission myth, many Americans in the 1980s took the Vietnam experience as demonstrating the need to return to and uphold the narrative. When Ronald Reagan sent American troops to the small island nation of Grenada to protect American medical students during a leftist governmental takeover, conservatives thrilled to the idea that the Vietnam syndrome was over. And not just the conservatives celebrated; the *Washington Post* blared a banner headline: "Tidy U.S. War Ends: 'We Blew Them Away.'"[38] Similarly, when the United States bombed Libya in April 1986 to avenge an attack on a German disco used by American soldiers, over 70 percent of the American public, according to a Harris poll, supported the action, which many proclaimed as illustrative of America's new willingness to fight for freedom on the world stage.[39]

During these years, the entertainment industry produced highly popular vehicles that supported a revitalized sense of mission. Among the biggest box office draws of the decade were the Rambo movies—*First Blood* (1982), *Rambo: First Blood II* (1985), and *Rambo III* (1988). In the first film, Vietnam Special Forces veteran John Rambo, harassed and humiliated by local police and treated like a criminal derelict, declares war on an apathetic, and even hostile, American public ungrateful for the sacrifices he and his fellow soldiers made in the national interest. By *Rambo: First Blood II*, Rambo gets to refight the Vietnam War. Freed from the hellish hard-labor prison to which he was sent after his surrender at the end of *First Blood*, Rambo, who asks "Do we get to win this time?," triumphs over Vietnamese and Russian soldiers, single-handedly freeing still-captive POWs. By the final installment in the trilogy, Rambo, Vietnam's failures put behind him, returns to the global struggle against the tyranny of godless communism—this time on the side of the Afghan mujahideen against the invading Soviet forces.[40] Martial arts movie star Chuck Norris had his own Vietnam film trilogy, with the initial offering, 1984's *Missing in Action*, earning $22 million in the United States.[41] During 1986 alone, Hollywood saw two movies that boasted of an American triumph over the crippling legacy of Vietnam: Clint Eastwood's *Heartbreak Ridge* and the box-office smash *Top Gun*, which grossed more than $170 million in the United States alone.[42] A comic treatment of this same theme, NBC's hit TV show *The A-Team* ran from 1983 to 1986.[43]

Though Reagan provided the star-power glamour, Nixon, with a string of best-selling foreign policy books, supplied much of the intellectual muscle for the mythographers. So, for instance, *The Real War* (1980) stated its purpose in the plainest terms possible: "This book is a *cri de coeur* . . . to take hold before it is too late, and to marshal America's strengths so as to ensure its survival." Eight years before *Rambo III*, Nixon pled Afghanistan's case by making it America's, arguing that this seemingly remote country was "a testing ground for an ominous, brazen new phase in the Soviet expansionist drive." A decade after the fall of Saigon, Nixon took on the ghost of Vietnam directly. Opening his 1985 work *No More Vietnams* with a debunking of misconceptions about the Vietnam War, Nixon urged the nation not to abandon its role as a defender of freedom across the globe, arguing that, through his policies, the United States had achieved its goal of peace with honor. But Congress squandered the victory by refusing to permit any resupply of the South Vietnamese troops or bomber support from the U.S. Air Force. Properly understood, America's experience in Vietnam should not lead to weak isolationism; rather, Nixon insists, "'No More Vietnams' can mean that we will not *try* again. It *should* mean that we will not *fail* again."[44] And public opinion polling indicated that, by the end of the 1980s, Nixon received credit as the president who extricated the nation from the war's quagmire and that, of people associated with the era, only Henry Kissinger and the soldiers themselves were considered more favorably.[45]

Despite its reemergence, the myth of national mission never lost, and has continued to have, its skeptics. One of the founding groups of the punk rock movement, The Clash, railed against America's drive toward cultural, economic, and military hegemony, in "I'm So Bored with the U.S.A.," a song from their spring 1977 debut album. With American economic investments in an unhealthy symbiotic relationship with right-wing repressive regimes in the Third World, songwriters Joe Strummer and Mick Jones suggest replacing the American flag with a more truly representative symbol: "Let's print the Watergate tapes."[46] Scoffing at U.S. claims to represent freedom and equality, The Clash identifies the real voice of the United States to be the profanity-spewing, cynical, power-obsessed one of Richard Nixon from the transcripts. The next year, cartoonist Lou Myers captured this brand of venomous contempt in his 1978 drawing "Nixon's Memoirs." Through this rendering of a bestial-looking Nixon, who functions as a human B-52, dressed (from the waist up) as Uncle Sam, dropping two bombs and a dove out of his naked ass, Myers savages the hypocrisy of a man who mouths patriotic platitudes about peace while wreaking devastation on all in his path. Four years later, *Missing*, the first U.S. film by the Greek-born French director Costa-Gavras, told the story of the disappearance (and eventual execution) of Charles Horman, a young American documentary filmmaker, author, and freelance journalist, during the Chilean coup of 1973. As Horman's father (played by Jack Lemmon) and his wife, Beth (Sissy Spacek), try to locate Charles, they confront an American ambassador and other embassy officials whose eagerness to hide U.S. involvement in the coup obstructs the Hormans' efforts to find the truth—perhaps because the American embassy itself acquiesced in the young man's murder. In one scene, the U.S. ambassador chastises Ed Horman for suggesting that the American government might be working with the local police; as he does so, repeating emphatically that "no such operation exists," he stands in the shadow of a large framed photo of Richard Nixon.[47] For the film's 1982 audience, the presence of Nixon's face over the shoulder of this bureaucrat tells everything needed to judge his veracity and sincerity. That the film's characters never speak the word "Chile," keeping the setting a generic Latin American country, could not help but make its audiences think about Ronald Reagan's support for the anticommunist, but brutally repressive, Central American government of El Salvador and his attempts to wage war against communist Nicaragua by funding the counterrevolutionary soldiers known as the contras, forces that Reagan, in 1985, memorably described as the "moral equivalent of the Founding Fathers."[48]

Public distrust of Reagan's mythic invocations on behalf of his policies in Central America had everything to do with the history of U.S. involvement in Vietnam. The Boland Amendments of 1982 and 1984, which first barred CIA and Department of Defense financing for the contras and then, later, forbade even nonmilitary aid, spoke to Congress's deep concern that history was about to repeat itself.[49] By and large, the public shared these anxieties. A March 1981 poll, reported in the *Los Angeles Times*, indicated

NIXON'S MEMOIRS

The Mad Bomber. Penned in outraged response to the publication of RN: The Memoirs of Richard Nixon, *Lou Myers's drawing "Nixon's Memoirs" vented spleen at a man who still insisted that bombing his way to peace was patriotic and honorable. Reprinted with permission of Bernice Myers. All rights reserved.*

that 47 percent of Americans worried that Central America would turn into another Vietnam. In 1982, public opinion sampling pointed to strong opposition to the use of American troops in El Salvador, even if military intervention was the only way to prevent the government from falling to the leftists.[50] By 1986, the year the Iran-contra scandal brought to light just how far the Reagan administration was willing to go to provide support to the Nicaraguan resistance despite the two Boland Amendments, the number of people who feared Vietnam repeating itself in our hemisphere had grown to 62 percent.[51]

The American experience in Southeast Asia itself continued to evoke powerfully negative responses. A large majority of Americans—63 percent in 1985 and 74 percent in 1990—judged the war to have been a mistake.[52] In 1990, 63 percent averred that involvement in Vietnam had damaged America's prestige and power in the world, and 65 percent of the respondents in a 1991 poll pronounced Vietnam to have been an unjust war.[53] Oliver Stone's 1986 movie *Platoon* mocked as a foolish "crusader" its main character Chris Taylor, an upper-middle-class youth who dropped out of college to enlist in Vietnam because he did not believe that only the sons of the poor and lower middle class should have to defend America.[54] Nixon's efforts at self-justification in *No More Vietnams* attracted hostile reviews from the nation's leading newspapers. In 1991, Nixon biographer Stephen E. Ambrose labeled the book "contentious and shrill," as well as unreflective and self-promoting.[55] Attacking the former president's shamelessness, Paul Szep, the *Boston Globe*'s editorial cartoonist, pictured a brazenly eager Nixon flashing his trademark victory salute over the top of the Vietnam Veterans Memorial in Washington, D.C., a height he can achieve only by standing on an empty wheelchair, and even then only by standing on his tiptoes.

In his 1989 film version of *Born on the Fourth of July*, Oliver Stone uses Richard Nixon as a symbol of the missionary myth that destroyed Ron Kovic's body and turned the nation against itself. Originally under contract in 1978 as a vehicle for Al Pacino, *Born on the Fourth of July* lost its funding only days before shooting was scheduled to start, its backers fearing that the other Vietnam movies of that time had already saturated the market. Stone, who had co-written the screenplay, vowed to return to the project when he could, and, using the critical and popular success of *Platoon*, he made good on his promise.[56] During the opening credits of the film, which establish young Ronnie Kovic as a "Yankee Doodle Boy" ready to prove his manhood by being ready to fight for his country, Mrs. Kovic calls her son to join the family in watching JFK's inaugural address. When Kennedy promises that the nation will be ready to "bear any burden" in its defense of freedom, the television cameras cut to outgoing vice president Richard Nixon nodding his agreement. But if Stone recognizes that Kennedy provided the inspiration for America's initial involvement in Vietnam, Nixon becomes the emblem of a culture that refuses to let go of a harmful myth even after the soldiers' experience in Southeast Asia contradicts the promise of our missionary ideals. During the Syracuse University students' protest of the Cambodian invasion, Nixon's profile appears on a protest sign made to resemble a dollar bill, a burning effigy dangles from a pole, and a protester (played by former Yippie leader

Nixon still defends Vietnam on 10th anniversary of prisoner-of-war release.

"In Vietnam, we tried and failed in a just cause." When Richard Nixon uttered such sentiments (which he would eventually publish in his 1985 book No More Vietnams*), Boston Globe cartoonist Paul Szep saw only a man who was willing to deny reality, hoisting himself up into the public spotlight to promote his discredited ideas by standing on top of the bodies of the soldiers killed and maimed by his misguided direction of the Vietnam War.* © Paul Szep, Szep.com. *Reprinted with permission. All rights reserved.*

Abbie Hoffman) excoriates "Tricky Dicky Nixon" as the leader of those who "pulled the trigger that killed the kids at Kent State." Soon after, Kovic grows disillusioned with the war, and, returning home drunk one night, he enters his parents' house to be greeted by two symbols of the faith he no longer believes: the crucifix that has always hung just inside the front door and, next to it, a china plate decorated with Nixon's portrait.[57]

In the final scenes of the film, Stone moves beyond failed religions to emphasize a heroic war to reclaim the nation's soul. Unlike Vietnam, the soldiers in this battle can clearly identify the enemy. The Miami Beach scenes open with the Vietnam Veterans against the War marching outside the auditorium, carrying placards that scream out Nixon's personal responsibility for the war. One just reads "Nixon," but the words, written in white, appear on a solid black background, and a human skull replaces the letter "o." Another replaces the "x" in "Nixon" with a swastika. As the chanting veterans march by the entrance to the convention hall, the camera pulls up to a banner draped from the roof, proclaiming "Miami Beach Welcomes the 1972 Republican National Convention," and then reveals the special welcome that Nixon has in mind: armed police on top of the building. In the seconds before Stone cuts away to archival footage of the president addressing the convention, we see police in riot gear moving out to do battle with the veterans. And, if the repressiveness of the Nixon regime couldn't be more apparent, neither could its hypocrisy. As a smiling Richard Nixon piously advises the country to "reject any philosophy that would make us a divided people," his no-longer-silent Silent Majority, the convention delegates in their red, white, and blue polyester, shouts at Kovic and spits in his face, while security forcibly removes the paraplegic veteran from the hall. High above the mayhem, Nixon pontificates: "Let's give those who *have* served in Vietnam the honor and the respect that they deserve and that they have earned." All this clear villainy gives Kovic a chance to fulfill his heroic dreams. Outside the convention hall, an undercover policeman dumps him out of his wheelchair and attempts to arrest him. A black veteran swoops down and, in a moment that parallels the scene in which Kovic received his wounds, scoops him off the ground carrying him to safety. As the sound of helicopters overhead recalls the war, Kovic plans his group's advance on the convention hall and orders them forward, in best John Wayne fashion, with a terse "Let's move!" While the veterans move out, the camera pulls back to show their approach to the waiting policemen, just before the scene goes to black. Concluding the scene before the battle begins suggests that the bravery of these unarmed men in taking on the teargas and nightsticks of Nixon's security forces matters more than the results of the struggle.[58]

Even more than the memoir on which it is based, the film *Born on the Fourth of July* seems imbued with a missionary purpose. The screenplay Stone co-wrote with Kovic adds a final scene, not in the memoir, suggesting the possibility of a new, higher purpose for Kovic's life. Following the 1972 convention street battle scene, Stone re-creates Kovic's televised address to the 1976 Democratic National Convention. As a speaker declares that the Nixon-Ford era of rule by and for the few has ended, Ron Kovic makes his way backstage toward the podium, cheered by the crowds lining the hallway, hearing the encouragement of his fellow veterans. To suggest the healing of Kovic's fractured life, Stone weaves into this scene several flashback images from earlier in the film: Ron's mother telling him, while watching JFK's inaugural address, of her dream that he made a speech in which he said "great things"; his childhood war games and the Fourth of July parades in Massapequa; and his Little League home run. Finally, Kovic fulfills the promise of his idyllic all-American childhood. Signing a copy of his book, as the convention's band plays "The Grand Old Flag" in the background, he expresses the hope that "just lately I've felt like . . . I'm home. You know. Like maybe we're home." In an interview with *Today* show host Bryant Gumbel, Stone, who likened his first two Vietnam films to the *Iliad* and the *Odyssey*, characterizes the narrative arc of *Born on the Fourth of July* in epic terms, describing Kovic as one who had gone "to war to be a certain kind of hero. . . . And he goes through hell. And he comes back from hell, and he's grown into a better man than what he intended to be. And he's become a different kind of hero." In short, *Born on the Fourth of July* fulfills what Stone, paraphrasing Elie Wiesel, calls the "sacred mission [of survivors]: to serve as witnesses and teachers of what they suffered, thereby preventing such catastrophes from occurring again."[59]

These grand dreams, however, fell short of total realization as the national mission myth proved its continuing resilience. In fact, according to international relations scholar Andrew J. Bacevich, "the image of the United States leading the world to peace . . . [has] command[ed] broad assent in virtually all segments of American society [since at least the end of World War I]." Some elements among political activists, radicals, and the intelligentsia "might take umbrage at the prospect of a world remade in America's image and policed by American power, but out on the hustings the notion plays well."[60] On December 20, 1989, the day *Born on the Fourth of July* premiered, the United States launched Operation Just

Cause to overthrow Panamanian dictator General Manuel Noriega, an action that appeared to show the United States, in the words of a historian of the period, "shucking off its post-Vietnam blues."[61] In the first months of 1991, when the United States led a UN coalition of forces to free Kuwait from an invading Iraqi army, George H. W. Bush, flushed with 89 percent approval ratings in a *New York Times*/CBS News poll, boasted, "By God, we've kicked the Vietnam Syndrome once and for all."[62] The dismantling of the Berlin Wall and the collapse of communism in Eastern Europe and the former Soviet Union provided seeming confirmation that the United States, this "new Jerusalem, sent down from heaven," in the words of the revolutionary-era poet Philip Freneau, had a divinely ordained destiny to assume world political, cultural, economic, and military leadership. As Bacevich has noted, "In effect the New Jerusalem had become the New Rome, an identity that did not supplant America's founding purpose but pointed toward its fulfillment—and the fulfillment of history itself." For many, particularly those in the neoconservative movement, the events of the early 1990s proved that the United States stood "on 'the right side of history.'"[63] And, during this period, Richard Nixon continued to publish best-selling foreign policy monographs urging the United States to fulfill its special mission in the world. As he concluded his 1988 book, *1999: Victory without War*, Nixon looked forward to the turn of the century, asking whether "a new America [will] lead the way to a new dawn for all those who cherish freedom in the world." Marketing his 1992 tome, *Seize the Moment: America's Challenge in a One-Superpower World*, as a timely exhortation to rise to the challenges posed and opportunities offered by the demise of communism and the crumbling of the Iron Curtain, Nixon pronounced, "We must seize the moment to win victory for peace and freedom in the world." And in the final paragraph of his last book, *Beyond Peace*, published only weeks after his death in April 1994, Nixon insisted that American foreign policy be "driven by a higher purpose" and called upon his fellow Americans to "reach into the soul of this nation and recover the spirit and mission that first set us apart . . . so that our example shines more brightly abroad." Nearly twenty years after the Vietnam War ended, Nixon could still speak of the American exemplar and its mission in the world.[64]

Portions of the public, however, continued not to buy either Nixon's elder statesman image or the mythic narrative that it promoted. In fact, in the years following his death and the stream of eulogies celebrating a master representative of America on the world stage, the critical representations of Nixon tended, if anything, to harden. For instance, the Turner Network Television movie *Kissinger and Nixon*, first aired on December 10, 1995, portrays Nixon as a clueless captive of mainstream America's cultural mythology.[65] Written by Lionel Chetwynd, a Reagan-inspired convert to conservatism, the film received wildly varied responses—bitter denunciations from Henry Kissinger and Alexander Haig and a handful of mixed reviews, on the one hand, to generally positive notices from most television critics and nominations for Emmy, Gemini, and Writers and Directors Guilds of America awards. During the film's opening, which shows documentary footage of U.S. soldiers in Vietnam evacuating their wounded comrades, the narrator's voice grimly notes that by 1972 "it seemed that a war-weary United States would never find a way to finally end the conflict and bring the last American soldiers home." The blame for this desperate situation rests with the stale platitudes of American invincibility as mouthed by Richard Nixon (played by Beau Bridges, sporting a prosthetic proboscis worthy of a *Cyrano de Bergerac* revival). Wary of a negotiated settlement, Nixon insists that America's image in the world must be maintained. "No sir," Nixon swears to Haldeman and Colson, "we're going to finally prevail. I will not be the first American president to lose a war." Ensnared by this imperative, Nixon can only conceive of military responses. Though the situation on the battlefield is clearly at a stalemate, his thoughts keep looping back to unrestrained, massive force. Barring any "soft deals," Nixon sends word to Kissinger (played by Ron Silver) to threaten Le Duc Tho, the North Vietnamese negotiator, with the knowledge that "we're ready to bomb him to kingdom come. . . . Just because I brought our troop level down from over half a million to less than 30,000 doesn't mean I'm weak!" The Nixon idea of negotiating is, in essence, conducting war by other means.[66]

As conceived by Chetwynd's teleplay, Nixon's failure to imagine alternatives to the myth of national mission stands as a symptom of an inherent small-mindedness.[67] Uttering anti-Semitic comments—during his first speech, summoning Kissinger, he explodes, "Where the hell is my Jewboy!"—and holding a glass of scotch as a nearly constant extension of his right hand, he comes across not as a global strategic thinker but as a second-rate football coach. In his first scene with Kissinger, Nixon admonishes his national security advisor for being too independent, asserting that "we can't have the receivers calling plays the quarterback doesn't know." Much of his resistance to a peace settlement comes from his equating war with sports. So, when Kissinger proposes a negotiated conclusion, Nixon denies that the American people are tired of the war, insisting, "This is sudden death overtime; they want us to score the winner!" Such unquestioning commitment to an unrealistic conclusion renders Nixon useless to the peace process. Because he viewed the United States as an invincible defender of freedom across the globe and, therefore, could only envision the unattainable conclusion of victory on the battlefield, the escape rope from this quagmire must come from the North Vietnamese. After the opening narration, the film's first scene—a June 1972 Politburo meeting in Hanoi—shows Le Duc Tho arguing that the North should show flexibility, drop its demand for the removal of South Vietnamese president Thieu, and "force [Nixon's] hand" by offering him his "peace with honor." On the U.S. side, the hero's role, as the film's title suggests, belongs to Kissinger, who, through his own unsupported effort, ends the war. In fact, Nixon, whom Kissinger refers to as "this madman in the Oval Office," only acquiesces to the peace agreement after stories appear in the press implicating Haldeman and Colson in the Watergate scandal.

Six years later, first-time novelist Jonathan Lowy presented an even harsher view of Nixon. Though not widely reviewed, Lowy's *Elvis and Nixon*, released by Crown Publishers in February 2001, generated mostly positive notice, including praise in the *New York Times* and a place in *People*'s "Worth a Look" column.[68] In this fictional rendering of the days leading up to the December 1970 Oval Office meeting, during which a jump-suited King of Rock and Roll—addicted to prescription pills—volunteers as an undercover agent in the drug war, Lowy portrays Nixon as a casualty of the American dream. Even before entering politics, he succumbed to bitterness, taking a spiteful object lesson—"Fuck the bastards. . . . Fuck 'em all"—from his failure to win the Wall Street law firm jobs that his honors graduation from Duke Law School should have earned. While his rise to the presidency permits him to look back vengefully on those who ridiculed him over the years, the personal cost has been immeasurable. Something as natural as a smile requires his conscious, laborious effort. Gone too is any vestige of moral conscience. When Colonel Alex Sitorski, assigned by the Pentagon to brief the president on progress in Vietnam, reports the details of the My Lai massacre, Nixon shows more interest in creating plausible denials of the incident than in investigating how such an atrocity could have occurred. This cynical pragmatism distinguishes a White House governed by the catchphrase "Truth is what you get away with."[69]

Similar to *The Public Burning*, in which Coover portrayed a U.S. government convinced that its domestic political opponents must be agents of the Phantom, *Nixon and Elvis* depicts a paranoid White House mind-set in which to be perceived as opposing Nixon equals treason. Not even a military career man like Colonel Sitorski is immune from the not-so-tender mercies of Nixon's security apparatus. A true believer in the mission myth, the colonel not only encourages his son to enlist when Al Junior reaches draft age but refuses to use his influence to keep the boy from combat duty. Days before being shipped out to Vietnam, the son asks why the United States is fighting, and Sitorski offers a letter-perfect recitation of the domino theory. Confronted by his son's doubts—"Is that it?"—he fleetingly realizes that the national mission myth provides inadequate comfort, even though it remains "the only story he knew."[70] Despite these credentials, Sitorski draws Nixon's paranoid suspicions when, at the end of a briefing about Calley's upcoming court-martial trial, the president asks, "How will it play in Peoria?" The colonel, nonplussed, demurs because he lacks the expertise to assess My Lai's domestic political implications.[71] Unaware that Nixon has approved a covert public relations campaign supporting Lieutenant Calley, code-named Peoria, Sitorski, by his reticence, convinces the White House of his unreliability, thereby subjecting himself to FBI wiretaps and physical surveillance. Oddly, such malign attention does not mean that Lowy's Nixon hates his enemies. To the contrary, he loves them—not from any vestigial charity clinging to his dormant Quaker soul, but because he needs them for his own political success. After a White House ceremony to recognize disabled Vietnam veterans, during which the token African American honoree spits on his medal and, with his remaining arm, throws it out of the Rose Garden, Nixon does not fire the mid-level staff member responsible for planning the event. Instead, when Max Sharpe, John Ehrlichman's deputy, apologizes for the disaster, the president enthuses: "Wonderful scene. Exposes the fucking ugliness we're dealing with. We offer them honor, and they turn it into disgrace. Perfect." For Nixon, history's abiding lesson is that all great nations succeeded because they had something to hate. Without such fears, Nixon has nothing to rally his Silent Majority and cement his hold on power. As Ehrlichman explains the strategy, "Defeat the enemy, and we defeat ourselves."[72] Taken to this perverse conclusion, the myth of mission turns the nation upon itself.

Just a matter of months following the publication of *Elvis and Nixon*, after the devastating attacks in New York City, Washington, D.C., and rural Pennsylvania, Lowy's recycled critiques of the myth of national mission offered little insight or consolation. If Americans have tended to see themselves, as Reinhold Niebuhr described it, as tutors for humankind's "pilgrimage to perfection," then, as Bacevich claims, the horrors of 9/11 rallied most people in "their determination to complete the journey."[73] Consequently, George W. Bush's rhetoric following the terrorist strikes on the United States repeated the strains of a familiar national anthem. At the memorial service held at the National Cathedral on Friday, September 14, Bush proclaimed the United States' involvement in something more momentous than responding to the monstrous acts of one day. Rather, the nation's "responsibility to history" encompassed nothing less than to "rid the world of evil."[74] As Bob Woodward notes in *Bush at War*, the president saw himself and the nation as agents "in the grand vision of God's master plan."[75] Speaking with Woodward, the president used familiar Nixonisms in attempting to relate his grand moral vision for America's foreign policy, at one point declaring, "There is nothing bigger than to achieve world peace," a less-grandiose rendition of the words from Nixon's first inaugural address: "The greatest honor history can bestow is the title of peacemaker." By his September 20 address to the nation, Bush had settled on a word that reverberated more deeply in the nation's cultural mythology: in our response to the attacks, "we have found our mission and our moment."[76] In these mythic invocations, Bush summoned images of encounters with unquestionable evil, permitting us an unexamined certainty of our own innocence.

This kind of stubborn resistance to critiques of the myth on the part of the dominant culture, with its refusal to recognize the ironies inherent in its behavior, generates a violent dogmatic response from the critics. Though Robert Coover inveighs against the mythic imagination's absolutism through much of *The Public Burning*, in the end, even he succumbs. In the novel's brutal Epilogue, Uncle Sam tracks down an already publicly humiliated Richard Nixon, cowering in the spare room of his Washington, D.C., home, and sodomizes him. The literary critic Tom LeClair has argued that *The Public Burning* represents a brilliant, purposely excessive, demonstration of Coover's mastery over his readers and his narrative and, ultimately, of America's myth of divine mission.[77] But, as this condensed, and consequently milder, version of the rape indicates, the book's final scene proves more troubling than this triumphant reading suggests: "'*No!*' I cried. '*Stop!*' But too late, he was already lodged deep in my rectum and ramming it in deeper. . . . '*For God's sake!*' I screamed. '*You're tearing me apart!*' . . . . I was screaming and howling horribly but nobody came to my rescue. . . . I lay there on the spare-room floor, gurgling, sweating, half-senseless, bruised and swollen and stuffed like a sausage. . . . Nothing could match this. . . . Not without being fatal."[78] To this point, *The Public Burning* derived its strength from Coover's remarkable ability to balance sympathy with satire. The novel's conclusion loses this admirable flexibility, however, in its determination to put Nixon in his rightful place. Disturbingly, Coover renders the painfully graphic rape scene from the victim's point of view—seemingly as a way of mocking him: "And in he came, filling me with a ripping all-rupturing force so fierce I thought I'd die! This . . . this is not happening to me alone, I thought desperately, or tried to think, as he pounded deeper and deeper, destroying everything, even my senses, my consciousness—but to the nation as well."[79] Struggling to survive his ordeal, Coover's character falls back on a specious rationalization the real Richard Nixon often used: a purposeful confusion of his purely personal desires, fears, and troubles with the country's fortunes. Worse yet, this violated Nixon ultimately confesses love for his rapist. The scene's brittle satire works only by denying any remnant of empathy. We both blame—and laugh at—the victim; Nixon, finally, gets what he deserves. At the last minute, the novel tames its most subversive notion: that Richard Nixon could be something more than just Tricky Dick. The character who could raise questions about the Rosenbergs' guilt and see through the government's machinations in the case now acquiesces to both Uncle Sam's pose of righteousness and the superhero's confession that "I'se wicked, I is."[80] In this final characterization of a Nixon who eagerly embraces the evil of a wholly corrupt America, Coover replaces the questioning of all cultural truths with a creed of his own.

In many ways, the Richard Nixon of Lowy's *Elvis and Nixon* seems to take the one left at the end of *The Public Burning* and project him seventeen years into the future. In Ehrlichman's explanation of what his boss has taught him about history—"history is what is written about the past; nothing else. It isn't what happened"—we hear echoes of Uncle Sam's instruction to then vice president Nixon. And in his cynical transformation of truth into public relations, Lowy's Nixon appears as irredeemably evil. Even a doped-up King of Rock and Roll senses the depravity, seeing Nixon as a kind of satanic figure who with a wand-like index finger can melt the oil on the portraits of the presidents in the West Wing, stripping away "the distinguished mythic profiles" to uncover their true faces: "murky, cobwebbed, all with the crooked, ski-jump nose, arching brows, the sinister smiling face . . . by turns dark and brooding . . . of Richard Nixon." None of these other beloved presidents were pure; nevertheless, Nixon outranks them all, seemingly representing the Ur-face of America's corruption. In fact, Lowy's Nixon represents a vision of evil domesticated and homogenized. Nixon's ability to make the reprehensible bland stands out in his odd request to Max Sharpe: "If I'm assassinated, I want you to have them play 'Dante's Inferno.' And have Lawrence Welk produce it."[81]

So, while works like *Elvis and Nixon*, *The Public Burning*, and *Born on the Fourth of July* expose the destructive potential of cultural myths, they do little to tell us how to live with what Coover calls "these . . . necessary things."[82] Lowy's tale, a story with no survivors, takes on the tone of a funeral dirge. In despair, Al Sitorski Jr. self-immolates, like the Vietnamese Buddhist monks; the FBI murders the one-armed African American veteran who refused Nixon's medal at the White House ceremony; Colonel Sitorski, branded a security risk, bolts from an Oval Office interrogation just in time to witness his son's suicide; and Elvis would die without recapturing his youthful promise. Only the face of evil prevails: "Richard Nixon would outlive them all."[83] Both the book and the film versions of *Born on the Fourth of July* conclude just as Ron Kovic must start the real work of rebuilding his life. And in *The Public Burning*, Coover seems so consumed with debunking America's orthodox cultural mythology that, as the critic John Ramage notes, "no one is quite sure what, if anything, he is offering to replace the [narratives] he has just laughed out of existence."[84] The best advice Coover can provide is that, as a nation, we need to be more self-conscious about, and take more responsibility for, our communal fictions. We must realize that myths are only tools for explaining "what seem to be the truths of the world at any given moment," and, eventually, they will outlive their usefulness. So we must never forget to battle "against the falsehoods, dogmas, confusions, all the old debris of the dead fictions."[85] Failure to do so allows our myths to become monsters of our own creation, all the more tyrannical because they are our own.

CHAPTER FIVE

RICHARD MEPHISTO NIXON

FURTHER ADVENTURES IN

AMERICAN POLITICAL DEMONOLOGY

For Nixon critics, the most tyrannically controlling mythic narrative is the one that casts the man as evil incarnate. In more sanitized forms, these reinventions of Nixon find it too seductively easy to limit their portraits to simplistic, cardboard cutouts. Even an abbreviated tour of these characterizations suggests the addictive power of this reductive image. In 1973's *Gravity's Rainbow*, Thomas Pynchon transforms Nixon into the oily Richard M. Zhlubb, a Los Angeles movie theater night manager with a "chronic adenoidal condition."[1] Frank Zappa said it all with the title of his 1974 Mothers of Invention song "Dickie's Such an Asshole."[2] To Kurt Vonnegut, in his 1979 novel *Jailbird*, Nixon seemed a mechanical, joyless man, whose "unhappy little smile that invariably signaled that he was about to engage in levity . . . [resembled] a rosebud that had just been smashed by a hammer."[3] In his group Aquabox's 2001 song "Dick Nixon and the Rover," keyboardist Lee Curreri, best known as "Bruno" in the film and television versions of *Fame*, got comic mileage out of the image of Nixon as an artificial, strange man. As doctored audiotapes of moon-walking astronauts talking to Mission Control play over a synthesizer and drum machine background, one of the lunar explorers declines an invitation to meet with the president at Camp David, declaring emphatically, "I don't want to go . . . . He's *weird!*"[4]

For many of the 1970s-era reinventions of Nixon, the only dimension of the man worth presenting was his iconic dishonesty. The hero of Woody Allen's futuristic comedy *Sleeper* (1973), shown a snippet of the Fund speech, confirms the theory that Richard Nixon once served as president but did something "horrendous so that all records—everything—was wiped out about him," adding that whenever he left the White House, "the Secret Service used to count the silverware."[5] Muriel Spark's 1974 novel, *The Abbess of Crewe*, and its 1977 film version, *Nasty Habits*, portray Nixon as a spiritually corrupt nun who ensures victory in the election to replace the recently deceased abbess by having her underlings break into her opponent's campaign headquarters and by installing hidden microphones throughout the abbey.[6] Steve Martin kept telling Nixon jokes well after the resignation, perhaps because the material never failed: "All I had to do was mention Nixon's name," he remembered later, "and there were laughs from my collegiate audiences." In a routine from *Let's Get Small*, his debut album, Martin imagined a scheming ex-president, wandering the beach of San Clemente with "big old shorts on," searching for lost treasure with a metal detector.[7] The 1978 Peter Falk/Alan Arkin movie *The In-Laws* skewered Nixon for his lethal sanctimony. After awarding medals to his guests of honor, a hilariously unstable Central American dictator (played by the brilliant comedic actor Richard Libertini) turns them over to a firing squad, kissing their cheeks and lamely apologizing: "I am a pacifist by nature with a deep Quaker belief in the sanctity of human life. I wish I had the choice but to kill you."[8] In a first-season episode of the situation comedy *WKRP in Cincinnati*, which ran on CBS from 1978 to 1982, Nixon served as the poster boy for petty larceny. When an out-of-work announcer pulls a gun on one of the station's deejays, commandeering the microphone during a remote broadcast, Dr. Johnny Fever sympathizes with the unemployed man, helps him evade arrest, and promises to give a bad description to police sketch artists. In the concluding scene, a spoof of the *Dragnet* finale, Fever appears in a lineup and, with a slight smirk, displays a picture of a jowly, stubbly, glowering Richard Nixon.[9]

Into the 1980s and the 1990s, the image of Tricky Dick lived on. In Winston Groom's 1986 novel, *Forrest Gump*, a paranoid huckster President Nixon tries to sell Forrest one of the "twenty or thirty wristwatches" he keeps hidden under the sleeves of his suit.[10] Barry Levinson's 1987 film *Good Morning Vietnam* suggested a Nixon so fundamentally devious that even those who knew him best didn't trust him. "Why I wouldn't buy an apple from the son-of-a-bitch," declares the commanding officer of U.S. Armed Forces Radio, "and I consider him a good, close, personal friend."[11] Taking Nixon as an archetype of disingenuousness, the Chicago rock band The Bad Examples, in what became one of their trademark songs, morphed the used-car salesman into an insincere female ex-lover: "She smiles like Richard Nixon / Walks like Bridget Bardot / And I love her, but I can't trust her."[12] The British electronic band Depeche Mode sampled the phrase "I want to tell you my side of the case" from the Fund speech in the Capitol Mix version of their 1990 hit "Policy of Truth," a song that offers an arch tribute to the utility of lying.[13] Even after his death, Nixon still got mileage as a symbol of duplicity. In a 1995 episode of the prime-time cartoon series *The Critic*, a 1955 newsreel covering the opening of Disneyland showed what appeared to be Pinocchio's silhouette. As the narrator says, "And *here's* a mischievous character known for not always telling the truth," the camera pans ahead, and the shadow on the wall turns out to belong to then vice president Richard Nixon.[14]

Finally, our tour ends with those for whom Nixon functioned not just as a cartoonish symbol of individual evil but as a representation of something gone deeply wrong with the United States. The bridge of "Give Me Some Truth," a song from the 1971 album *Imagine*, proposes Richard Nixon as the progenitor of all contemporary society's ills, with John Lennon defiantly insisting that he will not be duped by any "short-haired, yellow-bellied son of Tricky Dicky."[15] Looking back on this period, Vietnam veteran and author Tim O'Brien sees Nixon as the shadow cast over post–World War II America. In *The Nuclear Age*, the novelist's 1985 follow-up to his National Book Award winner, *Going after Cacciato*, Richard Nixon appears as a politician deceitful enough to go before the United Nations and preach "eloquently of peace, of raising a 'great cathedral' to the human spirit," even as bombs fell on Cambodia as part of a military operation hidden from Congress and the American people. For the narrator, Nixon signifies America's decision to turn away from its true meaning; in choosing him, "America had misstated itself." But in his ability to embody this national self-betrayal, Nixon becomes precisely the "classy new villain" the New Left required.[16] By the 1990s Richard Nixon's villainy had become the standard by which a new generation of political bad guys was judged. Tim Robbins's 1992 film *Bob Roberts* assesses the vileness of its main character, a neoconservative folk-singing bard whose U.S. Senate campaign taps into white middle-class resentment and racism, by noting that "Bob Roberts is Nixon, only he's shrewder."[17]

As some of the examples from our quick tour have hinted, vilifying Richard Nixon can turn downright nasty. After the May 1970 killing of four Kent State University students by National Guard troops during protests of Nixon's decision to send U.S. troops into Cambodia, the rock group Crosby, Stills, Nash, and Young released the single "Ohio," which opens with an image of a homicidal president leading a small army against those who oppose him.[18] C. K. Williams's poem "In the Heart of the Beast," also written in response to Kent State, imagined the president as a cannibal or a butcher: "this is fresh meat right mr. nixon?"[19] In a sketch that first appeared in *Rolling Stone* magazine's coverage of the 1972 election,

Ralph Steadman drew Nixon as Godzilla, who left a leveled city behind him while crushing a soldier in one bloody paw and brandishing a document with the words "Peace in our time with Honour" in the other.[20] Even gentle George McGovern ran his presidential campaign, in large part, on the image of his opponent's depravity. One of his campaign posters featured a rumpled, pasty-faced, goose-stepping Nixon, carrying a tattered American flag that substitutes a dollar sign for stars. Accentuating the famous widow's peak as a narrow, elongated peninsula, the artist depicts Nixon as inhumanly ugly. His eyebrows bristle outward like feather dusters, thick tufts of hair jut out of ear and nose, and an exposed portion of his ankle reveals wiry strands—all these luxuriant growths outdoing even his trademark five-o'clock shadow. Unsatisfied just with labeling Nixon as personally malevolent, many proclaimed him the avatar of human depravity. During May Day demonstrations in 1971, the Nixon administration detained thousands at RFK Stadium in Washington, D.C., without charges. Soon after, the War Resisters League issued a button for the survivors of "Camp Nixon." Changing the middle consonant into a swastika celebrated the protesters' bravery by creating an emblem of their enemy's total immorality.

In 1987, Michael Rogin, a political scientist at the University of California at Berkeley, described a process of "inflation, stigmatization, and dehumanization of political foes" that he took to be the central feature of mainstream American politics. Calling this practice "political demonology," Rogin suggested that "the demonologist splits the world in two, attributing magical, pervasive power to a conspiratorial center of evil."[21] But the Left's treatment of Richard Nixon clearly indicates that the Right has no monopoly on political demonologies. Indeed, many works of fiction, film, television, and the graphic arts, such as Philip Roth's *Our Gang* (1971), Gore Vidal's *An Evening with Richard Nixon* (1972), Ishmael Reed's "D Hexorcism of Noxon D Awful," and Kathy Acker's *Don Quixote* (1986), confirm Richard Nixon as the Left's favorite fiend. Each of these works reduces Nixon to one dimension, making him the quintessence of political nefariousness—if not the devil himself, then, at least, a particularly malignant spirit. For Philip Roth and other liberals, Nixon appears as a singular source of evil whose removal will restore an otherwise sound political system to working order. Yet, during the revelations of the Watergate scandal, even some adherents of this benign take on American society worried that Richard Nixon was too strong and too crafty to be easily eliminated. As Gore Vidal and other more radical voices saw it,

Vote McGovern. As this 1972 campaign poster suggests, Richard Nixon, in all his materialistic, authoritarian ugliness, gave voters almost as much reason to vote for George McGovern as did McGovern himself. Item from the author's personal collection. Photo by John Herr Photography.

American Führer. For many of Nixon's opponents, it was not enough to think that he was simply wrong or that he was merely immoral. Rather, in their imaginations, Nixon had to be the epitome of all human evil. As broadly insinuated by this button distributed for those May Day 1971 demonstrators detained at RFK stadium in Washington, D.C., without any legal charges being filed, Nixon was the new Hitler. Item from author's personal collection. Photo by the author.

removing Nixon, while desirable, would not solve anything because the man symbolized America's systemic failures to live up to the promises of its democratic vision. Frequently high-handed and preachy, these voices too often express contempt for their fellow citizens. Taken to extremes, these radicals fall into despair over changing American society, descending, in the worst cases, to a perverse symbiotic relationship in which they require Nixon's existence as the man they love to hate. Those marginalized by mainstream culture, such as African American and feminist artists, tend to avoid this love/hate relationship with Richard Nixon; instead, for them, he symbolizes all that stands in the way of their liberation. For these voices, reimagining Richard Nixon offers a pointed reminder of the necessity of forging a racial or gender identity separate from a corrupt and oppressive mainstream. Yet that effort too often leads the victimized to adopt the victimizer's behavior. Rather than take Nixon, his followers, and their values seriously, many on the Left have tried to trivialize the politician and the ideals he represents—thereby denying legitimacy to those with opposing beliefs and values.

Written between April and mid-July 1971, *Our Gang* grew out of Philip Roth's disgust with Nixon's "gross opportunism and moral stupidity." The triggering incidents occurred during the first week of April. Nixon issued a statement opposing abortion as a procedure that "I cannot square with my personal belief in the sanctity of human life—including the life of the unborn" and then ordered the release from prison and review of the sentence of Lieutenant William Calley, convicted only days before for leading his army platoon in the killing of over 500 Vietnamese civilians, including women and children, in the village of My Lai. Roth wasn't the only one who was unhappy; in fact, he wrote *Our Gang* during the nadir of Nixon's first term. Both high inflation and high unemployment persisted. On August 15, as Roth's book was being typeset, Nixon was forced to announce wage and price controls and to take the dollar off the gold standard. Earlier that summer had marked the publication of the Pentagon Papers, a collection of CIA, State Department, and Defense Department documents, many of them classified, revealing how Johnson and Kennedy had lied about American involvement in Vietnam. And throughout this period, Democratic front-runner Edmund Muskie frequently bested Nixon in Harris poll trial heats for the 1972 election.[22]

Our Gang satirizes Nixon, renamed Trick E. Dixon, whom Roth views as "this Tartuffe of ours," a man for whom "scheming, plotting, [and] smearing" are "ordinary human activities."[23] Notwithstanding a tepid critical response, the book, which was published on November 8, 1971, spent eighteen weeks on the *Times*' best-seller list, sharing top-ten honors with John Updike's *Rabbit Redux*, Herman Wouk's *The Winds of War*, and William Peter Blatty's *The Exorcist*.[24] By June 1974, over one million copies of the book were in print.[25] Prefacing his satire with a passage from Orwell's "Politics and the English Language," condemning politicians' manipulation of language to make the despicable sound honorable, Roth starts with a quotation from the real Nixon opposing "abortion on demand" and stating his conviction that the "yet unborn" have rights "recognized in law, recognized even in principles expounded by the United Nations."[26] Putting these words into his "Tartuffe's" mouth, Roth then takes us through six episodes, all rendered in dramatic formats: a conversation between Tricky and a citizen, who wonders how to square Dixon's professed belief in the sanctity of human life with the My Lai massacre; a press conference during which the president reaffirms the rights of the unborn; a White House strategy session on how to address widespread Boy Scout protests that Tricky's support for the unborn means that he favors sexual intercourse; a presidential address announcing military action against the "pro-pornography" Danish government for harboring the scapegoat Dixon's advisers concocted for the Boy Scout protest (Curt Flood, the former

St. Louis Cardinal outfielder who challenged Major League Baseball's reserve clause); press coverage of Tricky's assassination; and, finally, Dixon's campaign speech as he seeks to unseat Satan as ruler of Hell.[27]

Tricky personifies Orwell's worst fears, a politician for whom language exists merely as a tool for creating politically advantageous images. When his pro-life stance elicits Boy Scout demonstrations against him as a supporter of fornication, Dixon, in conference with his political "coaches," drops the mask: "Let's look at the record. I said *nothing*! *Absolutely nothing*! I came out for 'the rights of the unborn.' I mean if ever there was a line of hokum, that was it." Tricky has learned that a little wordplay—calling an amphibious landing by American troops near Hamlet's Castle in Denmark a liberation—can make evil actions appear good. An invasion by another name does sound sweeter.[28] Equally insistent in the view that Nixon "degrades both the office he holds and the nation," Roth concludes *Our Gang* by assassinating Tricky and dispatching him to hell, where he immediately campaigns for lower office. A greater devil than the Devil himself, Tricky smears Satan for his weakness in the "deadly competition [between Hell and] the Kingdom of Righteousness" and his appeasement of God in "the famous Job case." *Our Gang* ends with the one who made human existence for so many a "Hell on earth" blighting the underworld with his unique talents.[29]

But this condescending treatment diminishes Roth's political message. By naming his Nixon character "Tricky," Roth transparently signals his attempt to totally discredit the man and his political positions. Thus, the complexities of America's involvement in Vietnam reduce to the genocide of My Lai. Roth invalidates Billy Graham's conservative social and political agenda by satirizing him as "the Reverend Billy Cupcake," who delivers Tricky's eulogy as an insipid catalog of *Webster's Dictionary* definitions. And, most provocatively, Roth ridicules the antiabortion movement through Dixon's proposed constitutional amendment to give voting rights to fetuses, a proposal in which the movement's political champion does not truly believe: "These rights . . . don't even exist! And . . . I wouldn't care about [them], even if they did!"[30] What seemed unthinkably absurd to Roth in 1971—that a fetus could be considered to have rights—has become an extraordinarily successful political rallying point for an army of evangelical Christian political soldiers in the decades since.

Painting himself into an ideological corner, Roth cannot construct a plausible explanation for the politician's success. In fact, Roth would have us believe that Dixon was elected president without *any* popular support.

When Tricky is assassinated, drowned in a water-filled baggie while at Walter Reed Hospital to remove his lip's sweat glands, Roth at first dwells on the lack of reaction; indifferent citizens in Chicago, Los Angeles, and New York proceed with "their ordinary, everyday affairs as though nothing had happened."[31] However, this explanation contradicts Roth's ostensible satirical point. The closing epigraph of *Our Gang*, a quotation from Revelation, speaks of the Devil being sealed in a pit so that "he should deceive the nations no more."[32] But if apathetic voters elected Dixon, how can he be blamed for the corruption of American politics?[33] And, ultimately, Roth's portrayal of the hours following Dixon's assassination refutes public apathy toward the president. To the contrary, people flood the streets of the nation's capital, carrying signed confessions and accosting policemen, all attempting to claim credit for the assassination. Strangely, *Our Gang* omits any sense of the people's responsibility for Dixon. In doing so, Roth accuses one man of degrading the presidency and the nation and, unlike Orwell, denies, or at least minimizes, any systemic problems. Like the band Chicago's "Song for Richard and His Friends," an encore number they performed during 1971, which calls on Nixon to "Please be gone / Go away and leave us alone," Roth suggests that getting rid of the devil solves everything. Ultimately, he proposes nothing more than politics by exorcism.[34]

Following *Our Gang* by less than two years, the shocking revelations of the Watergate affair also inspired a variety of re-creations of Richard Nixon that imagined him as a demon whose removal from public life would redeem the nation. Written in direct response to the events of the unfolding scandal were a series of Shakespearean and Greek drama parodies: from Robert J. Myers's *The Tragedy of Richard II* (1973), Dana G. Bramwell's *The Tragedy of King Richard* (1974), both unproduced scripts published by small presses, to the Yale Repertory Theatre series of sketches titled *Watergate Classics*, which ran from November 1973 through January 1974.[35] Yet, at the time, a much older work, a nearly decade-old folk song, had more of an impact on public consciousness. "It's Alright, Ma (I'm Only Bleeding)" received a contemporary updating from audiences during Bob Dylan's 1974 comeback tour as they roared approval and applauded every night when he reached the line "but even the President of the United States sometimes must have to stand naked."[36] Mapping out exactly how Richard Nixon had come to be so completely exposed, Alan J. Pakula's film version of the Carl Bernstein and Bob Woodward book *All the President's Men* premiered on April 4, 1976, grossing $70 million at the box office and collecting four Academy Awards, including one for best screen-play.[37] Refusing to use an actor, Pakula effectively conveys Nixon's insidi-ously malign power by making him an absent player. The audience views Nixon's image only through news footage of his triumphant return from the first Moscow summit and the pomp of the second inauguration. Yet underneath these political and diplomatic successes lurks a hidden story. The opening scene transitions from the smiling face of Richard Nixon before a joint session of Congress to the break-in at the Watergate com-plex, implicitly commenting on the illegal measures taken to maintain Nixon's rule. But *All the President's Men* uses Richard Nixon's corruption to reaffirm that the system works. A classic David and Goliath story, Wil-liam Goldman's screenplay shows two junior reporters for the lowly Metro desk of the *Washington Post* bringing down the most powerful man in the United States. In the film's final scene, Nixon appears on a television set in the *Post*'s newsroom, taking the oath of office for his second term. To the right of the set and in the background, the reporters sit at their desks, oblivious to the television coverage, fingers dancing across their typewrit-ers. From the reporters, the shot cuts to a teletype machine, printing out Watergate headlines that end with the one announcing Nixon's resigna-tion. Diligence and determination defeat entrenched power—and save the nation.

Yet, almost from the start, some feared that Nixon would not be easy to drive off. Louis Rossetto Jr.'s 1974 novel *Take-Over* imagined a power-hun-gry, but deeply unstable, Richard Nixon, who has already undergone one round of electroshock treatments, conspiring to use his emergency pow-ers to grab control of the government, thereby preventing his impeach-ment.[38] *Dick Deterred*, a musical parody of *Richard III*, which opened at London's Bush Theatre in February 1974, offered further Orwellian over-tones. Written by British playwright David Edgar (best known for his 1980 adaptation of *Nicholas Nickelby*), *Dick Deterred* begins by secretly videore-cording the audience's arrival inside the theater. Immediately following the Act One blackout, the tape is played, and "this, with reactions, is re-taped."[39] Within the action of the play itself, Edgar's Richard, an amoral schemer ready to sacrifice his most loyal aides to maintain power, scours the stage at play's end, while under attack by Richmond's forces, pleading for "A goat! My kingdom for another Scapegoat!" Just as in Shakespeare, Richmond triumphs and, in the final song, assures the audience that "It's definitely / All over now." But, Richard, left for dead in his coffin, resur-rects himself, reclaiming the crown with a sly "Wanna bet?" Richmond's soldiers stop at the sight of Richard, and "in one beat, like lightning, [they] whip around to point their carbines at the audience." To underscore that Richard Nixon will not go quietly, Edgar directs that the exiting crowds be shown their recorded reactions to the surveillance tape that played during intermission.[40]

Even after the resignation, many were apprehensive that the man would return from the dead. On March 25, 1978, as *RN* was published and critics proposed a boycott, *Saturday Night Live* cast Nixon as a vampire who would terrorize the country unless his memoir was destroyed. To prevent "the stench of San Clemente" from infecting a nation of readers, horror-film veteran Christopher Lee drove a stake through the center of the manuscript, while Dan Ackroyd hissed and collapsed in typical B-movie fashion. The skit's punch line, however, fretted that Nixon's evil transcended even supernatural remedies; once Lee departs, Ackroyd pops up from behind his desk, shifty eyes searching the room, and sits down to write the book all over again.[41] In the 1980s, the decade that witnessed Nixon's miraculous restoration to public life as best-selling author and elder statesman, getting rid of Richard Nixon moved to the wish-fulfillment of alternative-reality science fiction. Published in late 1987, as one year of Iran-contra scandal headlines drew to a close, Michael Bishop's novel, *The Secret Ascension: Philip K. Dick Is Dead, Alas*, imagines a substitute history for the United States, one made nightmarish by Nixon's demonic possession. "At some point during his presidency, perhaps the year after the U.S. win in Indochina," Bishop's narrator informs us, "Richard Nixon's own evil cunning began to give way to the evil cunning of a greater malefactor." In the novel's climactic scene, the heroes, advised by the spirit of the recently deceased science fiction writer Philip K. Dick, perform an exorcism on Nixon, hoping to reset time in favor of "a saner reality."[42] But even in science fiction, the effort to rid the nation of Nixon can fail. Philip K. Dick's own novel, *Radio Free Albemuth*, published posthumously in 1985, remakes Richard Nixon as President Ferris Fremont, the leader of a totalitarian United States. Like his real-life counterpart, Fremont comes to Congress from southern California and grabs the spotlight through investigations of un-American activities, which he intensifies by claiming that the U.S. Communist Party is really just a front for a secret organization, named Aramchek, responsible for all evil done to the nation. Once in office, he proposes his "New American Way," a name reminiscent of Nixon's promised "New American Revolution," which seems to be a plan to so badly scare people about shadowy enemies that they will spy on and identify their neighbors as potential traitors. Dick's two main characters, Nicholas Brady and a writer of science fiction named Philip K. Dick, struggle to topple the Fremont government using instructions they receive from Valis, a "Vast Active Living Intelligent System," speaking to them from a faraway star. And, although the two friends discover the truth—that Fremont, the rabid anticommunist, is, in actuality, a communist operative—they fail to bring down his regime.[43]

At the end of Robert Altman's *Secret Honor*, Richard Nixon, in refusing to commit suicide, threw down a gauntlet to the American public: "If they want me dead, they'll have to do it."[44] By the late 1990s clearly the deed still remained undone. L. A. Heberlein, in his 1996 debut novel, *Sixteen Reasons Why I Killed Richard M. Nixon*, chronicles a series of fantasy claims to have murdered this "dark figure in the American psyche." Beginning in 1974, when he started receiving phoned confessions while working at a crisis hotline, the narrator painstakingly archived the accounts, such as a poem from the doctor who insists that he snapped the neck of Frank and Hannah Nixon's newborn baby or the confession of Pat Nixon who wishes that she had strangled her abusive husband with a hair dryer cord. Because Nixon's public rehabilitation has profound implications for America's moral health, the narrator envisions himself on a crusade: "My nation still has not learned to fear and despise its Nixon. When he died this last year they eulogized him . . . called him a statesman." Meant to combat such perverse twisting of America's ideals, these Nixon death stories offer hope: "As long as my country still follows its Nixon, feeling souls across this land still rise up spontaneously to kill him off."[45] By 1997, Philip Roth, too, came to recognize that Nixon's evil portended some deeper, darker truth about American society. In *American Pastoral*, the grandfather of a baby-boom-child-turned-political-terrorist unleashes scathing tirades that indulged his "uncensored hatred of Nixon." For him, the idea of destroying this adversary possesses miraculous power: "If we can just tar and feather Nixon, America will be America again, without everything loathsome and lawless that's crept in, without all this violence and malice and madness and hate. Put him in a cage, cage the crook, and we'll have our great country back the way it was!"[46] But as the events of Roth's novel, indeed the readers' experiences of 1990s America, make clear, staking national redemption on the removal of one man is a false hope.

What Roth points to in *American Pastoral*, however, is a perspective that was obvious years earlier to many others. For these cultural critics, a cartoonish, demonized Nixon makes sense not because he is so uniquely wicked but because his evil nature best sums up a sick national culture. In their 1984 song "Lost," The Meat Puppets, a pre-grunge rock band cited as a major influence on Kurt Cobain, used Nixon as a metaphor for total cultural alienation, lamenting that they are "tired of living Nixon's mess." Novelist Thomas Pynchon resurfaced in 1990 with *Vineland*, his first novel since *Gravity's Rainbow*. A book that deals with the uncertain legacy of the 1960s and early 1970s, *Vineland* uses Nixon, whose name appears fourteen times, to personify a nightmarish America, in which selling out friends and loved ones to federal agents becomes so routine that the government has bureaucratized the procedures and funding for betrayal. When the New Left movement at College of the Surf collapses—sold out by one of its leaders, the sordid scene plays beneath "the black rearing silhouette" of a Richard Nixon statue, which dominates the campus of this institution that had been designed to train people to serve "Southern California money, oil, construction, [and] pictures."[47]

Interestingly, tracing this mode of reinventing Richard Nixon back to its source leads, yet again, to Gore Vidal. His second literary representation of the man, *An Evening with Richard Nixon*, had its Broadway opening on April 30, 1972, just as the president's popularity was rebounding from the doldrums of 1971. To some degree, an election-year economic upturn helped solidify Nixon's favorable ratings, but in large part the president's peacemaker image explained his new momentum.[48] On July 15, 1971, just as Vidal was beginning to write the play, Nixon took the first step in establishing his foreign policy reputation, with the announcement that he had been invited to visit the People's Republic of China in February of the next year. Securing a promise for a May 1972 summit meeting in Moscow followed almost exactly three months later. By the time the play opened, Nixon was riding so high that not even renewed bloodshed in Vietnam could dull his luster. Forced by a seeming collapse of the South Vietnamese army in the spring of 1972, Nixon had first stepped up the bombing, then announced that he was mining Haiphong harbor to cut off Hanoi's war supplies. Despite this escalation, Nixon arrived in Moscow on May 22 and days later signed the Strategic Arms Limitations Treaty.[49] *An Evening with Richard Nixon* would not be as successful. Staged on Broadway in the Shubert Theater, a venue usually reserved for musicals, Vidal's play lasted only two weeks, closing after lukewarm reviews and only thirteen performances.[50]

Part of the reason for the play's failure could be that Vidal's second monochrome portrait of Nixon as an opportunistic, amoral, and self-aggrandizing schemer displays more cynicism and less hope for the future than does *The Best Man*. The play, hosted by George Washington, begins with the curtain already up, suggesting that Nixon is never offstage. At the announcement of his birth, Richard appears "dressed as he is always dressed: in a blue suit, all set to run for President." For this perpetual campaign, Nixon sacrifices his integrity to gain political advantage. He can hurl names at Adlai Stevenson ("Adlai the Appeaser who got a Ph.D. from Dean Acheson's College of Cowardly Communist containment") and Harry Truman (a traitor "to the high principles in which many of the nation's Democrats believe"), while piously claiming that he has "never engaged in personalities in campaigns." Willing to accept money to protect the interests of oil companies, to play on the racial resentments of white southerners in return for votes, and to continue the war in Indochina indefinitely, Vidal's 1972 Nixon, like his 1960 version, Joe Cantwell, lacks any moral scruples.[51]

Yet Vidal makes clear that Nixon embodies only a "more naked" example of America's corruption by pitting the iconic moral authority of George Washington against both the current president and his predecessors, Dwight Eisenhower and John F. Kennedy, who appear as commentators on, and participants in, the play's action. When Kennedy defends U.S. policy in Vietnam by claiming that Washington cannot understand the complexities of "great empires," the Father of Our Country accuses his successors of having betrayed "the people and the Constitution, for no democracy, no republic, can survive once it aspires to dominion over other people in other lands." Under the guise of carrying the light of democracy abroad, Nixon and friends have compromised America's true mission, making it "the sort of country from which your ancestors fled."[52]

Using an assortment of quotations from the public record, *An Evening with Richard Nixon* condemns its targets with their own words and takes on the collective lack of memory that allows the public figure to "reinvent himself every morning." Thus, Vidal assumes a historian's role, even appending a bibliography and nineteen pages of endnotes to the published script.[53] However, he is not entirely honest about his endeavor. Although composing nearly every speech of his Nixon using the real-life model's words, Vidal crafts entirely new contexts for them: in one notable case, splicing together one speech out of comments from three separate incidents—each reported in a different source. Worse yet, he misuses sources, as when he quotes Hannah Nixon asking her son to give up the Hiss case because "no one else thinks Hiss is guilty," without revealing that she spoke out of concern for her son's health and that he convinced her that the investigation must continue.[54] Cloaking his well-honed axe in the priestly robes of objectivity, Vidal dresses up polemic as history.[55]

Curiously, he assumes an equally high-handed tone toward his audience, insulting those he wishes to persuade.[56] In his first speech, George Washington presupposes a group of spectators so ignorant that he must introduce himself. Once the drama begins, Vidal's Kennedy chastises the audience because they "fell for" Nixon's nonexistent plan to end the war or because "they've even forgotten the first act."[57] An exercise in smugness, *An Evening with Richard Nixon* exists to showcase the political enlightenment of its author and his followers. Stanley Kauffmann captured the self-satisfied nature of the drama, calling it "an anti-Nixon polemic whose effect—at best—is to make anti-Nixonites feel better about themselves."[58] But anti-Nixonites were a fairly small audience in 1972. Nixon took 60.7 percent of the votes in the presidential election that year, winning every state in the Union except Massachusetts. Like the minister making an altar call on Friday night of a weeklong revival meeting, Vidal preaches only to the already converted.

Despite the pessimism, however, Vidal does preach. The United States may be a corrupt empire, but, as his detailed endnotes suggest, he still harbors some faith in the reforming power of facts. But once cynicism soured people's faith in public life, many opted instead for tales of private redemption. By the time the "Carlson for President" episode of *WKRP in Cincinnati* aired, on November 5, 1979, viewers had endured the shocks of the mid-1970s—the troubling revelations by the Rockefeller Commission and Church Committee and the culture of scandal that seemed to proliferate after Watergate. Moreover, they were reeling from the news of the day before, that Iranian students had taken approximately seventy hostages at the U.S. embassy. Americans were hardly likely to have much confidence in the political system. To underscore these kind of doubts regarding public life, writer Jim Paddock uses Richard Nixon's career to gauge station manager Arthur Carlson's campaign for the Cincinnati City Council. Borrowing language from the Watergate tapes, Carlson wrestles with his temptation to make political capital out of his opponent's drinking problem: "We can't use it. [Long pause.] Course, uh, we *could* use it.

[Shorter pause.] But that would be wrong." Despite his principled intentions, Carlson completes his transformation into Tricky Arthur during the televised debate after being goaded into revealing his opponent's secret. But *WKRP* suggests an alternative to the history its audience just lived through. After his moment of weakness, Carlson requests that Herb Tarlek, his polyester-suited, white-shoed huckster of a sales manager, "get down on [his] knees with me and pray for guidance," a scene re-created from Woodward and Bernstein's *The Final Days*. But instead of a seemingly inebriated president offering self-justifying prayers, *WKRP* gives us a man seeking redemption. Losing the election on purpose after pulling a series of dirty tricks on himself, Carlson regains his self-respect, which suggests that integrity can only be maintained by retiring to private life. Public service makes Nixonian crooks out of even the best-intentioned.[59]

Opening on August 4, 1999, one day shy of the twenty-fifth anniversary of the release of the "smoking gun" Watergate tape, the Columbus Pictures film *Dick* further undercuts the Watergate conventional wisdom that "the system worked."[60] In writer/director Andrew Fleming's spoof, Nixon's fall results not from the journalistic heroics of Woodward and Bernstein but from the purely accidental luck of two fifteen-year-old girls. Betsy Jobs (Kirsten Dunst) and her best friend, Arlene Lorenzo (Michelle Williams), stumble across G. Gordon Liddy (played by Harry Shearer) in the middle of the Democratic National Committee break-in as they sneak back into Arlene's Watergate apartment after mailing an entry in to a "Win a Date with Bobby Sherman" contest. To silence the girls, Nixon (portrayed hilariously by Dan Hedaya) appoints them "Official White House Dog Walkers," an act that unwittingly dooms his presidency. Having stumbled upon a tape recorder when the dog's leash gets caught in Rose Mary Woods's desk drawer, the girls play the tape and are shocked to hear Nixon's profanity, bigotry, and, most horrifying to them, his abusive treatment of his dog. Angry, they call Bob Woodward, using the name "Deep Throat," a nod to Betsy's doper brother, who got caught sneaking into the infamous movie. Pilfering one of the tapes and turning it over to the *Post*, the girls force Nixon's resignation. But their victory is limited. Out shopping when Nixon resigns, Betsy and Arlene watch the speech on a department store television, unable to resist self-satisfied smiles. "It's going to be different now," Arlene insists, a proclamation that Betsy affirms with a heart-breakingly innocent prediction: "They'll never lie to us again." But, having lived through Reagan's "mistakes were made" Iran-contra obfuscations,

George H. W. Bush's "read my lips, no new taxes" broken promise, and Bill Clinton's "I did not have sexual relations with that woman" mendacities, the film's original audience knew better. Thus, in the long term, the girls' success is purely personal. According to the film's epilogue, Betsy's brother made a fortune inventing Quaaludes. And, with a loan from this drug money, the girls open a roller disco re-creation of the Oval Office—complete with spinning mirrored ball and ABBA blasting on the sound system. From their seed money to the investment itself, the girls' success symbolizes the national hedonistic retreat into the self that followed Watergate.[61]

Moreover, once Americans turned suspicious of public life, it didn't take long for cynicism to turn to despair. Former Nixon adviser John Ehrlichman's first two novels, written in the immediate aftermath of Watergate, share this hopeless vision of the United States. Published in 1976 by Simon & Schuster, *The Company* pits a Nixon figure, President Richard Monckton, who thrives in Washington's backstabbing universe, against a wily director of the CIA, in a battle to control the files regarding a Bay of Pigs–style invasion in the Dominican Republic.[62] Ehrlichman's sophomore effort, *The Whole Truth* (1979), gives us a victimized hero, a whistleblower who finds that honesty about a CIA coup in Uruguay (modeled on the 1973 overthrow of Salvador Allende in Chile) cannot outdo the duplicity of this novel's Richard Nixon stand-in.[63] Nor were such harsh depictions limited to disgruntled (and self-interested) Nixon staffers. In 1978's *Death of a Politician*, Richard Condon, author of the classic 1960s political thriller *The Manchurian Candidate* and 1972's *The Vertical Smile*, which recast Nixon as "Funky Dunc," a transvestite Wall Street lawyer turned presidential candidate, also found America's malignity so overwhelming that it was not worth preaching anymore.[64] On August 9, 1964 (exactly ten years before the real Richard Nixon would resign the presidency), former vice president Walter Bodmore Slurrie is found shot to death following a meeting during which high-level party operatives had decided that this controversial Texas politician, credited with creating the anticommunist frenzy and riding it from Congress to the vice presidency, would be the party's nominee in 1968. But his death offers no hope of a national moral restoration, because Slurrie owed his political career and hidden wealth to Horace Riddle Hind, a reclusive Howard Hughes–like businessman, and Abner "Nudey" Danzig, a Florida mob figure. For these secret benefactors, Slurrie performed such odious services as prolonging the war in

Southeast Asia for the lucrative heroin trade. Even worse, he and his law school roommate, Charles Coffey, a counselor for the governor of New York, joined the conspiracy surrounding JFK's assassination by arranging the killing of the Oswald-like fall guy. Disgusted with himself, his friend, and the entire political process, Coffey murdered Slurrie solely as retribution, not as an act that would save the country.

Condon's and Ehrlichman's gloom about Richard Nixon's America seems positively tame, however, compared to the venomous fury of Hunter S. Thompson. In his freelance work in 1968 and his coverage of the 1972 campaign for *Rolling Stone* magazine, Thompson granted Nixon most-favored-villain status, depicting him as "the dark side of the American spirit" and "a monument to all the rancid genes and broken chromosomes that corrupt the possibilities of the American dream." His 1972 electoral landslide, Thompson mourned, broke the hearts of those who had believed in America's goodness and high-mindedness.[65] Scoundrel though he is, Nixon remains essential to Thompson; his world did not cohere without its evil genius. As if in confirmation of this twisted symbiotic relationship, the film *Where the Buffalo Roam*, starring Bill Murray as Thompson, and the first of Nixon's best-selling foreign policy books, *The Real War*, were released within a week of each other in the spring of 1980. What's more, without Nixon, *Where the Buffalo Roam* would remain an impossibly disjointed story.[66] Desperate to meet an impending magazine deadline, Thompson relates several vignettes involving his one-time-attorney-turned-gun-running-revolutionary, Carl Laslo, a man who refused to succumb to "the age of Nixon"—a "fast, strange time" when it was best "to keep your head down."[67] Nixon, portrayed by the noted impersonator Richard Dixon, appears twice in the film, most memorably in an airport bathroom during a 1972 campaign tour. Having trapped Nixon at a urinal, Thompson extemporizes about the screwheads ("savage tribal thugs who live off illegal incomes") and their victims, the doomed ("the young, and the silly, the honest, and the weak"). Unfazed by this over-the-top tirade, Nixon displays his contempt for the have-nots, ending the harangue with a contemptuous "Fuck the doomed!" As if in response to such heartlessness, the film indulges in juvenile fantasies of vengeance: in one manic scene, Laslo and Thompson spray everyone aboard the Nixon campaign plane, the president included, with the on-board fire extinguishers. Yet such a moment offers no productive political alternatives to Nixon. Instead of imagining a way to reclaim a place for the rebel in American political and social life, *Where the Buffalo Roam* celebrates a withdrawal from the world, glorifying Thompson's hermetic life with his guns, his booze, and his drugs. In the final scene, he sits on the floor holding a Nixon mannequin and denies that either the president or Laslo have disappeared for good: "I don't think I'm going to believe that until I can gnaw on both of their skulls with my very own teeth. . . . Because it still hasn't gotten weird enough for me." Far from wanting to expunge Nixon, Thompson embraces the demon.

No such self-indulgent nihilism lurks in fictional re-imaginings of Richard Nixon by African Americans during the late 1960s and 1970s. Instead of a perverse love/hate relationship with a satanic Nixon, black essayists, fiction writers, musicians, editorial cartoonists, and television writers all display a grim determination to tell the truth and shame the devil. For them, reinventing Richard Nixon has nothing to do with Thompson's adolescent brinkmanship games with magazine deadlines—it's a matter of their race's survival. With such absolute stakes, emotions run high. In March 1974, during a ceremony at which the Cathedral of St. John the Divine in New York City presented him with a medal recognizing "the artist as prophet," James Baldwin preached a brimstone jeremiad, calling Richard Nixon a "motherfucker."[68] However, this sort of scalding antipathy had not always been the reaction Nixon received from the African American community. In the earlier years of his career, he fancied himself a progressive on race, taking a leadership role in ensuring passage of the Civil Rights Act of 1957. Martin Luther King Jr., dazzled by the vice president's "apparent sincerity" during a two-hour Capitol Hill strategy session, wrote to a journalist that "if Richard Nixon is not sincere, he is the most dangerous man in America."[69] For the 1960 Republican Party platform, the candidate endorsed a strong civil rights plank, and Nixon always had a handful of African American celebrities endorsing his presidential runs: from Jackie Robinson in 1960 and Wilt Chamberlain in 1968 to Sammy Davis Jr. in 1972.[70] Nevertheless, Nixon's failure to show any public sympathy for, or take any action on behalf of, King during the civil rights leader's October 1960 arrest and imprisonment started a process of radical estrangement from the African American community. From 1960, when Nixon garnered approximately 33 percent of the black vote, to 1968 and 1972, when he received only about 12 percent and 13 percent, respectively, of what the Gallup Poll called the nonwhite vote, Nixon's standing dropped almost out of sight.[71] Even the president's men recognized the deep-seated hostility. In his autobiography, Born Again, Charles Colson confesses that, when he learned of a plan to kill him in prison, he assumed the plotter was a black man bent on revenge for the administration's civil rights policies.[72]

In truth, such antagonism was not reserved for Richard Nixon alone. Black nationalism had emerged from the interracial civil rights movement before 1968. The Student Non-Violent Coordinating Committee (SNCC) and the Congress of Racial Equality (CORE) had welcomed participation by sympathetic whites during the Freedom Rides of 1961 and the voter registration projects in Mississippi in 1964.[73] But two years later, Stokely Carmichael, recently elected leader of SNCC, tried to exclude whites from a march in Mississippi, then led the crowd in calling for "black power," which he defined as "a call for black people in this country to unite, to recognize their heritage, [and] to build a sense of black community."[74] Although both SNCC and CORE banned all white participation in their organizations, they were soon supplanted by the Black Panther Party of Oakland, California, as the vanguard of black nationalism. Calling for economic, political, and cultural independence for black people and sponsoring free breakfast programs for inner-city children, Panther Party founders Huey P. Newton and Bobby Seale taught self-defense as a means of protecting blacks from police brutality, educated party members in their legal rights, and advised them to carry unconcealed guns (lawful in California at the time). From fifteen members in late 1967, the Panthers grew into a potent force of two thousand members in twenty-five cities nationwide by the time Nixon prepared to take the oath of office as president.[75]

For their part, the Panthers initially saw Richard Nixon as no different from any other white politician. In his cartoons on the 1968 presidential race in *The Black Panther*, the party's weekly newspaper, Emory Douglas (who signed his work as "Emory") drew all candidates as filthy pigs, identifiable only by their names being written underneath. Indeed, even after the presidential race settled down to a three-man contest between Humphrey, Nixon, and American Independent Party candidate George Wallace, he never pictured one politician without the other two. On October 19, 1968, Emory drew the swinish troika worshipping before a star-spangled swastika labeled "Law and Order." One week later, his cartoon depicted Nixon waving a placard emblazoned with the slogan "*Vote for Me / Law and Order / White Supremacy*," while a tearful Humphrey pig tries to grab the sign, protesting "I Said It First."

Notwithstanding claims that all white politicians were essentially the same, some African Americans saw Nixon as an enemy worth singling

HUBERT   NIXON   WALLACE

For Emory Douglas (Emory), cartoonist for The Black Panther, *the weekly newspaper of the Black Panther Party, all white politicians in 1968 were essentially the same. Reprinted by permission of David Hilliard and the Dr. Huey P. Newton Foundation. All rights reserved.*

out. Early in a long and diversified career as teacher, publisher, activist, and critically acclaimed writer, Ishmael Reed published the short story "D Hexorcism of Noxon D Awful."[76] Released in February 1970, "Noxon" stands as one of the earliest appearances of Richard Nixon as a literary character and provided Reed with "the seed" for his 1972 masterwork *Mumbo Jumbo*.[77] Described by its author as a "primitive piece" using the gris-gris dolls of HooDoo religious ceremonies, "Noxon" experiments with purposefully cartoonish writing—the title page describes what follows as "one of those mean incoherent frequently nonsensical hallucinogenic diatribes." Having read how "an enemy could be destroyed or fixed merely by the idea one put out," Reed conjures up a spell on Richard Nixon, appearing in this story as a grotesque otherworldly demon, "Noxon the Noxious of [the planet] Ob."[78] Everyone recognizes Noxon's inherent evil: New York governor Rin Tin Rover (a Nelson Rockefeller caricature) dials 666 to call him on the phone, while the narrator pegs him as one "who eats his own and carries dirt in his heart."[79] But, if Noxon is a devil, he's America's devil. Exemplifying the American dream, Noxon, who peppers his speech with "Boy o boys" and "Gee whizzes," starts at the bottom to become master of ceremonies of the United States and, most importantly, a "Property Owner." This American story, however, has another layer to it. Despite his apparent success, Noxon is nothing more than the flunky who provides comic relief to the economic interests in control of the United States, a secret society known as the Left Hand Path. As the Left Hand Path watches its televisions, Noxon approaches the camera, "smeared with Blackface and . . . waving goodbye with his white gloves. The writing on the screen That's All Folks means that America is signing off after another day of vigorous cartooning."[80] Far from giving in to Noxon's looney-tunes, however, Reed levels a HooDoo curse on the enemy of the people. The story's main figure, Papa LaBas, a conjurer who escaped from a slave ship and killed his captors, takes on Noxon D Awful, calling a meeting of his coven and setting their password: "Nix on Noxon."[81]

This kind of critique of the underlying madness of the Nixon administration and white society's refusal to make good on America's promises of freedom contrasts with Nixon's own self-promotion as a civil rights leader. In his 1972 reelection campaign and in his 1978 memoirs, Nixon touted the number of schools desegregated during his first term and the number of contracts offered to minority firms through the Philadelphia Plan, his affirmative action policy. Since the early 1990s, certain revisionist historians have endorsed this line of thought, quoting the same statistics to promote Nixon as the last, and most successful, liberal president. By themselves, the numbers do seem to tell a tremendous success story. For instance, during Nixon's administration, the number of children attending all-black schools dropped from 40 percent to about 12 percent nationwide.[82]

But such interpretations work only if one ignores certain facts about the legal challenges to continuing segregation, the images that the Nixon White House was careful to convey to the white South, and the felt experiences of most black Americans of the time. First of all, the desegregation of American public schools came about not because Nixon championed integration but because, in *Alexander v. Holmes County*, the Supreme Court declared unanimously that segregation in school districts across the United States had to end without further delay.[83] Put simply, Nixon had no choice but to act as he did. As historian Kenneth O'Reilly has noted, "Some degree of civil rights enforcement was inevitable because the law was crystal clear."[84] In nearly every other way possible, however, Nixon did his best to signal his displeasure with the Court's rulings and his sympathies for the feelings of southern whites. Repeatedly ordering the Department of Justice and the Department of Health, Education, and Welfare to "do only what the law requires, not one thing more,"[85] Nixon tried to appoint justices to the Supreme Court who appeared likely to be hostile to civil rights cases: in August 1969, Clement Haynsworth, a South Carolina Appeals Court judge with "a segregationist background" and, when the Senate rejected him, G. Harold Carswell, an eminently unqualified man who had declared, during a run for the Georgia state legislature, that "segregation of the races is proper and the only practical and correct way of life."[86] Nixon was also not shy about voicing his displeasure with the Supreme Court's April 1971 decision supporting mandatory busing as a means for achieving school desegregation, going so far as to undercut his own administration's plans in Austin, Texas, and trying to legislate an explicit national busing prohibition.[87] A Jeff MacNelly editorial cartoon in the *Richmond (VA) Times-Leader* from the period captures Nixon's public persona on the issue, depicting the president as a burly, southern law enforcement officer, complete with sunglasses, single-handedly stopping a school bus driven by a crazed Supreme Court justice. Such actions made Nixon into what O'Reilly has called the "white man's champion against the special pleadings and privileges of the blacks." By mixing together anxieties about race and socioeconomic class status, Nixon, through his "southern strategy," saw a way to win the previously Democratic votes of the South and of the northern white working class, thereby splitting the old Roosevelt New Deal coalition and transforming the Republicans into the majority national party.[88]

Entirely less ambiguous was the racial cast to Nixon's call for law and order. In one of the early moves of his first term, Nixon introduced the District of Columbia Court Reorganization Act, referred to as the D.C. Crime Bill, which was meant to serve as a model for the rest of the nation. At its most controversial, the D.C. Crime Bill proposed "preventative detention," which permitted judges to hold suspects in jail for sixty days

'YOU IN A HEAP O' TROUBLE, SON.'

Hoping to draw support from what had been the solidly Democratic South, Nixon played up his opposition to busing as a means of achieving racial desegregation of public schools. Cartoonist Jeff MacNelly captured the spirit of Nixon's appeal. © *Tribune Media Services, Inc. All rights reserved. Reprinted with permission.*

before a trial, as well as a "no-knock" provision (sanctioning police entering homes without displaying a search warrant). According to O'Reilly, "Because [Nixon's law and order efforts] began with the nation's capital, heavily black and crime ridden, no one had any illusions about the message or intent."[89] Songwriter Gil Scott-Heron got the message right away. His song "No-Knock (*to be slipped into John Mitchell's Suggestion Box*)," which appeared on his 1971 album *Free Will*, dismisses Nixon's attorney general's claim that the D.C. Crime Bill was enacted for the benefit of the largely African American population of the nation's capital. Instead, Scott-Heron displays a keen awareness of the bill's real targets: "For my protection? / Who's gonna protect me from you?"[90]

In fact, for many blacks, Nixon's name served as a sad one-word epitaph on the tombstone of the 1960s civil rights movement. James Baldwin, a heralded novelist, was perhaps even better known for his collections of essays, *Notes of a Native Son* (1955), *Nobody Knows My Name* (1961), and *The Fire Next Time* (1963), books that, in the words of one critic, "did much to free the impasse in racial discourse" in the late 1950s and early 1960s, making him, at that time, "the most widely read black author in American history."[91] In *No Name in the Street* (1972), after having prophesied nine years earlier "no more water, the fire next time" if "the relatively conscious" blacks and whites failed "to end the racial nightmare, and achieve our country, and change the history of the world,"[92] Baldwin laments that Nixon's first term as president effectively destroyed black America's naive trust in the mainstream culture's ability to remake itself in the name "of honor and knowledge and freedom." For Baldwin, Nixon encapsulates white backlash, offering, "very accurately and abjectly," a précis of the self-centered, cowardly refusal of white America to "atone" for its sins. In other words, Nixon's presidency represents the time when white America told African Americans that it wasn't really interested in social, political, and economic justice. As such, Nixon and his administration laid bare, "in all their unattractive nakedness," the rancid operating values of mainstream America.[93] Through the apprehensions evoked by his law-and-order rhetoric and the authoritarian repression it condones, Nixon and his administration "can rule only by fear," justifying the bigotry of the white ghetto policeman, encouraging him in his efforts to "cow the natives." Nixon finally reached the White House because, in striving to repress African Americans, "the bulk of the people desperately seek out representatives who are prepared to make up in cruelty what both they and the people lack in conviction."[94] As such, Nixon embodies the terminal condition of mainstream white society.

As if to underscore Baldwin's thesis that white America was unprepared to deal honestly with the race issue, *No Name in the Street* made considerably less impact than Baldwin's previous nonfiction. Dial Press released the book in mid-May 1972 (in the week after Vidal's play closed on Broadway), promoting it as a momentous work, one expected to create the same sort of stir as had *The Fire Next Time*. An ad in the *New York Times* on May 17, 1972, boasted of the book's selection by the Book Find Club and the Saturday Review Book Club and indicated that *No Name in the Street* had gone into a "second printing before publication."[95] Yet the reviewers' respectful notices lacked the enthusiasm his previous works had garnered, and the book never managed to claim a spot on the *Times'* best-seller list. Instead of confronting Baldwin's blunt analysis of race relations in the United States, readers of nonfiction in the spring of 1972 preferred the consoling assurances of *I'm OK—You're OK*, the elegiac celebration of baseball's glory days in *The Boys of Summer*, or the titillating redefinition of sexual fidelity in *Open Marriage*.[96] Adding to Baldwin's frustration, while confirming the worst fears of *No Name*'s jeremiad about mainstream America's unwillingness to face the truth, "white Americans were complaining of his 'ingratitude.'"[97]

Yet these grumblings were coming at a time when many blacks felt that members of their race faced economic conditions that made even basic survival difficult, if not impossible. Even as Nixon's most liberal domestic adviser, Daniel Patrick Moynihan, was opining in a January 1970 memo that "the time may have come when the issue of race could benefit from a period of 'benign neglect' [because] the subject has been too much talked about," African Americans began to lose some of the economic gains they had made during Johnson's Great Society.[98] The unemployment rate for blacks, which in 1969 had reached the lowest level—6.4 percent—in the thirty years from 1960 to 1990 jumped by nearly 2 percent in 1970, going as high as 10 percent in 1972. By 1975, the rate ballooned to 14.8 percent and remained in double digits for the next fifteen years.[99] Not surprisingly, blacks made up a disproportionate share of Americans living below the official poverty level. In 1974, the year Nixon left office, according to U.S. Census Bureau figures, 22.6 percent of all African Americans between eighteen and sixty-four years of age were poor. The number for blacks under eighteen was 39.8 percent; and 34.3 percent of those over age sixty-five lived in poverty. By contrast, the numbers for white people in the same age categories were 6.6 percent, 11.2 percent, and 12.8 percent, respectively.[100] Even those men fortunate enough to have work did not find their relative earnings making much progress toward equality with white males. Between 1959 and 1969, African American men had progressed from $612 for every $1,000 earned by white men to $694. But in the ten years beginning in 1969, black males gained only $21. And the next ten years proved even worse, netting a gain of only a single dollar more.[101]

Given these hard economic realities, it is not surprising that for some of these people Nixon's iconic name measured the daunting obstacles blacks faced in simply trying to live in white America. In "Please, Mr. Nixon," a song recorded in the early 1970s, the acclaimed blues, jazz, and country musician Clarence "Gatemouth" Brown begged the president not to end welfare. Mixing images of a well-heeled majority driving luxury cars while the poor minority live in hovels, Brown lashes out at Nixon's ability to tolerate such inequities, "sitting there in the White House / As happy as you are."[102] Around the same time, Texas blues singer Thomas Shaw's "Richard Nixon's Welfare Blues," which contained the repeated refrain "I don't want to go to the welfare store," expressed the indignity, shame, and, ultimately, pride, of welfare recipients who are treated "mean" by callous bureaucrats and who, rather than accept such degrading behavior, refuse the money offered there.[103] Premiering during the spring of 1974, the situation comedy *Good Times* suggested Richard Nixon's responsibility for the plight of black people in the ghetto who, no matter how hard they worked, could never get ahead. In fact, he merited mention in three of the show's first five episodes.[104] Set in the housing projects on the south side of Chicago, *Good Times* was created by *All in the Family* (and later *The Jeffersons*) co-star Mike Evans and Eric Monte (the screenwriter for the 1975 film *Cooley High*). Although it was only a mid-season replacement, this spin-off of the Norman Lear hit *Maude* did well enough to come in at number seventeen in the Nielsen ratings for the 1973–1974 television season.[105] In the show's third episode, "Getting Up the Rent," aired on February 22, 1974, Nixon's name cropped up barely five minutes into the program. As the Evans family faced eviction from their apartment because their matriarch Florida Evans (played by Esther Rolle) had required expensive emergency surgery, which used up the rent money, James Evans (John Amos) still held out hope that the housing project wouldn't evict them. Michael, the youngest and the militant one in the family, tells her that his father was assured by a man named Monty that everything would work out. To that set-up, Florida deadpans, "That's the *same* Monty that said Nixon was gonna be poor folks' best friend."[106]

As African Americans struggled during Nixon's first term in office, black nationalists began to accept Nixon as a particular symbol of this degradation. On November 15, 1969, at an anti–Vietnam War protest in San Francisco's Golden Gate Park, David Hilliard, a founding member of the Black Panther Party, cursed Nixon as "an evil man"—the leader of a counterinsurgency against the Panthers that spied on them, disrupted their inner-city breakfast programs, and, finally, imprisoned and murdered their leadership—ending his impassioned speech with the threat: "We will kill Richard Nixon. . . . We will kill any motherfucker that stands in the way of our freedom."[107] Such extreme rhetoric was not unprovoked. From the moment he took over the Justice Department, John Mitchell gave J. Edgar Hoover the green light to step up the Counterintelligence Program (COINTELPRO) started in 1967 and designed to destroy black nationalist movements. While not originally a target of the FBI's efforts, the Panthers, in September 1968, had made the top of Hoover's list of internal security threats, and Mitchell ordered wiretaps to be placed on party members and supported raids on Panther headquarters across the country. After Hilliard was jailed for his comments about the president, the FBI and Chicago police moved against Fred Hampton, a rising star in the party, killing him in an early morning attack at his apartment. Of the nearly 300 COINTELPRO operations directed at black nationalist groups, 233 were directed against the Panthers. As the police arrested more and more party members, the Panthers found their attention distracted and their treasury nearly exhausted by their legal defense efforts. Imprisonments decimated their ranks; during Nixon's first term, the number of Black Panthers in prison nearly reached one thousand.[108]

Reflecting an awareness of the struggle in which the party found itself, gradually the artwork in *The Black Panther* began to move beyond the early representations in which Nixon was indistinguishable from any other white pig politician. By 1973, Nixon most frequently appears drawn in wholly human form, making the attacks more personal. In a full-page cartoon in the March 10, 1973, issue, a scowling Nixon stands in the door of a building marked "Community Day Care," heartlessly turning away a black woman and her child. Just a month earlier, even Emory had drawn Nixon as Nixon—this time laughing with Henry Kissinger about "Good Old American Peace," as a bomb pierces a globe labeled "Third World." With Nixon clearly the dominant figure in the drawing, the stance that one white man is just as evil as another had been modified. The Panthers now saw Nixon as an enemy worth recognizing.

And, as such, he represented an obstacle to African American freedom that had to be removed. In "Watergate Blues," from his final album *The Back Door Wolf* (recorded in August 1973 and released on Chicago's renowned Chess Records), blues legend Howlin' Wolf mischievously imagined that at least one black working man, the Watergate complex's security guard, had already taken action against Nixon and cautioned white America of a larger racial reckoning if it continued to wrong the black minority: "We'll blow the whistle on you / just like we did the Watergate."[109] Amiri Baraka's warnings and his calls to action were considerably less playful. By the time of Howlin' Wolf's final album, Baraka had established himself as an influential figure in African American literature: first, under the name LeRoi Jones, as a beat-inspired poet, a playwright of the Obie Award–winning *The Dutchman* (1964), and an avant-garde novelist; then,

By February 1973, Emory had joined other cartoonists in The Black Panther *by drawing Nixon as a source of an individual, and a particularly noxious, evil. Reprinted by permission of David Hilliard and the Dr. Huey P. Newton Foundation. All rights reserved.*

after his name change, as a founder of the Black Arts movement, which advocated separation from white society and promotion of black people's pride in their history and culture. In a 1973 poem, "Afrikan Revolution," Baraka presents Nixon as a piece of refuse to be swept away in the wake of an inevitable pan-African nationalism: "Nixon is a sick thief why does he / remain alive? Who is in charge of killing him?" In an interesting adaptation of Franklin's "Art of Virtue," Baraka declares war on poverty, sickness, ignorance, and racism, exhorting Africans from around the world to discipline themselves through a rigorous program of self-education: "Meet once a week. Once a week. / All over the world." Once Nixon and the evils of his world have been removed, Baraka exudes confidence in the coming utopia: "Love is our passport to the perfectibility of humanity / Work & Study / Struggle & Victory."[110] Two years later, Baraka had rejected black nationalism, sensing the need of a Marxist-Leninist revolution to change the structures of economic power. In "When We'll Worship Jesus," a poem from the 1975 collection *Hard Facts*, Baraka uses Nixon as a symbol of established black churches' failure to really help their people. Employing Nixon as a test of whether Christ deserves to be worshipped, Baraka proclaims that blacks will turn to Christianity only when Jesus stops "helpin / nixon trick niggers." The time has come, Baraka insists, for Jesus to take *some* action against those who oppress and exploit black people, proposing that Christ "blow up the white house / or blast nixon down."[111]

Such militant language, however, appeared at precisely the time of backlash against the gains of the civil rights movement. In 1974, the Supreme Court refused to take on de facto segregation, ruling in *Milliken v. Bradley* that suburban schools could not be required to merge with those in the inner city, creating unified districts that would accomplish racial balance by busing white and black students throughout entire metropolitan areas. Busing, where it existed, often faced bitter, violent opposition. On Boston's first day of public school in the fall of 1974, white mobs lobbed racial insults, bottles, and rocks at the few black students from the Roxbury section of the city brave enough to attempt to attend school in predominantly Irish American South Boston. Later in the same year someone stabbed a black student, and South Boston High had to shut its doors for a month. Although later in the decade the vocal opposition to busing abated somewhat, it did so in large part because many white parents either sent their children to private schools or they abandoned the city for the suburbs. Simultaneously, opponents of affirmative action began to speak of "reverse racism" suffered by whites, due to purportedly preferential treatment given to African Americans. In June 1978, in the first in a series of challenges over the past thirty years that have threatened to roll back affirmative action, the Supreme Court ruled in the *Bakke* case that racial quota systems violated the Constitution.[112] So although African Americans did make some progress in the 1970s, these symptoms of a growing white resistance to true racial equality left large numbers of blacks, especially middle-class African Americans, dispirited and, in what historian James T. Patterson calls "one of the sadder legacies" of the period, "increasingly pessimistic about a number of things, including the intentions of white people. Some seemed to be doubting the American Dream."[113]

Time only sharpened the American Left's hatred of Richard Nixon and, continuing the vicious circle, saw the fury of the conservative backlash grow stronger. Fourteen years after Vidal's play and eleven after Baraka's poem "When We'll Worship Jesus," Kathy Acker's blistering treatment of Nixon in her novel *Don Quixote* denounces a male-created culture of aggression and greed. Novelist, performance artist, and poet, Acker, once described by the *New Republic* as "combining the high rebelliousness of postmodernism with the low rebelliousness of punk," produced a screenplay, ten novels, and numerous essays and short works of fiction between 1975 and her death from breast cancer in 1997. *Don Quixote*, her seventh novel (third with the prestigious Grove Press, publishers of Samuel Beckett, Henry Miller, and William Burroughs), appeared in the United States in late fall 1986. In this dream-novel, said to be "her most explicitly feminist" work, Acker's protagonist, suffering from the trauma of an abortion, names herself after Cervantes' knight and has a vision in which she opposes the forces that make human love an impossibility. At its midpoint, the novel turns to political analysis, because, "to defeat the evil enchanters of America, Don Quixote first had to find out how the American government works"—a lesson that leads her to Richard Nixon.[114] Notable even within Nixon demonology, this subgenre of extremely shallow characterizations, *Don Quixote* strips the man of his humanity, referring to him by the genderless pronoun "it" and casting him as a beast that "barks" and "woofs." Having called upon the Angel of Death "to level the spirits of Americans," *Don Quixote*'s Nixon serves as a perfect emblem of America's moral devastation.[115] Yet Don Quixote's quest brings her to discover that, when nature itself is an abomination, "Nixon, a minor fact in nature, no longer mattered." Because he only serves the country's "evil enchanters," those who control the social, intellectual, political, and economic realms of everyday life, "defeating Nixon isn't defeating America." The myths and ideologies of American orthodoxy themselves reek of corruption. The dream of success plays out as a nightmare of isolation and unhappiness. "The self-made American dog has only itself," Acker's character Thomas Hobbes, the Angel of Death, states. "It isn't able to love." Like Vidal, Acker dismisses America's rhetoric of national mission as a smoke screen for economic hegemony. In the unique position after World War II of being able to "impose its hatred of nonmaterialism—its main ideal—on the remainder of the world," America built an empire based on "large export markets and unrestricted access to key materials." The ideology of the Cold War doesn't protect freedom; it safeguards America's financial empire.[116]

Sermonizing against the dominant culture's corruption, however, is not just futile; it's an impossibility. Those on the fringes of society cannot protest because they have no real voice. As the prologue to the second section of Don Quixote explains: "BEING BORN INTO AND PART / OF A MALE WORLD . . . [Don Quixote] / HAD / NO SPEECH OF HER OWN." Stripped of language and, consequently, of identity, women are left with only the male world of "the enchanters," one in which "the only English (or language) is despair." Only through building a community outside the mainstream can Acker's heroine "find a meaning or myth or language." As God tells Don Quixote at the end of her dream: "Now that you know I'm imperfect, night, that you can't turn to Me: turn to yourself." To grasp the world that lies before them, the outsiders must, in a subversive use of the traditional value of self-reliance, band together among themselves. For this reason, some literary critics view Acker's novels as "terroristic cultural assaults"— a call for women to "overthrow their education" by destroying the practices of patriarchal society to build a new kind of selfhood.[117]

Ironically, however, Acker strives to give a voice to the voiceless by adopting the hegemonic culture's methods, stripping away the names of the powerful, calling them simply the "owners" and "enchanters." What's more, Acker denies the free and reasoned judgments of all those people— male and female—who support the dominant culture's orthodox values, insinuating that they have been duped into compliance. Honest opposition is unimaginable. Acker's protagonist instead posits "an increasing separation between the universal military government and the national civilian populace." While Acker bemoans the silencing of the dispossessed and accuses the mainstream of not hearing the cries from the fringes, she mutes her ideological and political opponents. The novel concludes as Don Quixote "awoke to the world which lay before me," but, if Acker's outsiders build their community by the same scarring methods of exclu-sion, how will this new day improve upon the old nightmare?[118]

To be fair, *Don Quixote* may be making precisely this point. As Ellen G. Friedman suggests, the search for "a new healing myth" may be a fool's quest, leading "to silence, death, nothingness, or reentry into the sado-masochism of patriarchal culture."[119] According to this ironic reading, *Don Quixote* purposefully demonizes its opponents. Nixon is referred to as an "it" because the culture teaches only these dehumanizing terms. Douglas Dix insists that Acker reveals "the tendency of any revolutionary group to fall into the hegemonic practices it is combating."[120] If so, the novel seems nothing more than a howl of outrage against the impossibility of building a more humane world. And, at the time of *Don Quixote*'s publication at least, it seemed that Acker had given up on American culture. Explaining why she chose to live in London, Acker described herself as someone who "like[s] the middle ground. [But] I didn't see it possible to maintain that middle ground [in the United States]."[121]

Far from being a centrist, however, Acker, in *Don Quixote*, reflects a radical vision of feminist individuality, more than a decade after such an extreme version of identity politics had split the women's movement. In 1966, three years after *The Feminine Mystique*, Betty Friedan began NOW (the National Organization for Women), dedicated to equality in the work-place and at home and the insistence that "American women [be brought] into full participation in the mainstream of American society now."[122] Al-most immediately the organization faced criticism from those who felt equality was too conservative a goal, that liberation from a patriarchal sys-tem was the proper focus of feminism. Robin Morgan, author of the 1970 best seller *Sisterhood Is Powerful*, lambasted NOW's complacent willing-ness to accept mere reforms of male-dominated structures of power that guarantee the "second-class citizenship of women."[123] Instead, groups like the Redstockings declared women to be "an oppressed class," who must band together to understand their "personal suffering as a political condition."[124] Other organizations, like the Women's International Terror-ist Conspiracy from Hell (WITCH), staged outlandish events of public theater—such as hexing the New York Stock Exchange or crashing a bridal show at Madison Square Garden while singing, "Here comes the slave, off to her grave"—intended to publicize what they saw as the systemic oppression of women.[125]

Despite such internal divisions, the women's movement managed some remarkable successes in the early 1970s, particularly congressional approval of the Equal Rights Amendment (ERA) in 1972 and its quick ratification by twenty-eight states in just over one year and the early 1973 Supreme Court decision in *Roe v. Wade*, which, based on the right to privacy precedent, argued that access to abortion was a constitutional right.[126] But the movement's factionalism left it vulnerable to a powerful counterattack from the right. Phyllis Schlafly, a conservative activist who had balanced a career with raising six children, organized an effective counterrevolution against the ERA, which expressed elemental "fears about changing gender roles, the fate of the family, and the state of masculinity."[127] Under this potent assault, support for the amendment stalled, and, despite receiving an extension of time for ratification, it died.[128] As historians of the period have noted, Schlafly's successful movement pulled together antifeminist women, political conservatives, white southerners, blue-collar workers, and evangelical Christians—a broad coalition that would bring success to Ronald Reagan and which, with few exceptions, "foreshadow[ed] the electoral geography of modern-day Republicanism."[129] Throughout the late 1980s and early 1990s, using the forum of his highly rated radio talk show and his best-selling books, Rush Limbaugh inveighed against "femi-Nazis" and argued as one of his "Thirty-Five Undeniable Truths of Life" that "feminism was established so that unattractive women could have easier access to the mainstream of society."[130] Nor, as journalist Susan Faludi has noted, was the backlash against the women's movement limited to the right wing. Mainstream magazines and newspapers subjected feminism to harsh, critical analysis. Meanwhile, Hollywood produced a string of films like *Fatal Attraction* (1987), which turns the character of an unmarried career woman into a psychotic would-be man-killer, and *Baby Boom* (1987), which, by having its main character abandon her Manhattan career to raise a child in rural New England, suggests that high-powered women business executives could not have it all.[131]

Yet in its adherence to a radical vision of feminism, *Don Quixote* seems not to comprehend the possibility that the accomplishments of the women's movement could suffer a rollback. For in the midst of this backlash, the women's movement could not take solace in having safely won the legal struggle for equality. Ironically, Acker's use of abortion as a symbol of the conditions of a male-dominated society that drive women insane seems to take legal access to the procedure for granted, even as the Supreme Court was turning more hostile to abortion rights. The summer of 1986, just a few months before *Don Quixote*'s publication, saw William Rehnquist, former John Mitchell Justice Department lawyer and Nixon appointee to the Supreme Court, become chief justice, along with the appointment to the Court of archconservative Antonin Scalia. Furthermore, Acker's stance on abortion seems to overlook that access to safe, legal abortion, far from being a symbol of male control, served for most early feminists as a sign of the movement's greatest victory.

Acker's brand of separatism led ultimately to a self-defeating isolation of radical feminists from the majority of American women. During the late 1980s, historians observed the strange trend of large numbers of women endorsing the movement's goals but, at the same time, shying away from being identified with the movement itself. By the early 1990s, only 33 percent of all women in national polls identified themselves as feminists. And, for college-age women, the numbers were even more sobering. Only 20 percent of eighteen to twenty-two year olds embraced feminism. Elizabeth Fox-Genovese saw most of feminism's problems stemming from a radical elite insisting on views that were alienating most women from the movement. Naomi Wolf blames this estrangement on "old habits left over from radical feminism's rebirth from the revolutionary left of the 1960s," describing these "habits" in words that would serve as an apt summary of much of Don Quixote's ideology: "reflexive anti-capitalism, an insider-outsider mentality, and an aversion to the 'system.'" Although such an ideology was "once necessary and even effective," Wolf asserted, it is "now getting in our way."[132]

Finally, even for radicals, Acker's opting out of the mainstream doesn't make sense. For Marxists like Antonio Gramsci, the process of disrupting the hegemonic culture requires one to work within society, gradually expanding the influence of oppositional voices until a new cultural consensus can be formed. In other words, overthrowing the existing power structures is not achieved through "a sharp rupture at a single moment" and cannot be effected from outside the civil society.[133] Acker wrote herself out of the process of cultural change, accepting her marginalization, by embracing the role of an outlaw bent on the destruction of an entire culture. So, despite its forceful critique of mainstream society, Don Quixote's unyieldingly confrontational stance toward orthodoxy subverts the political effectiveness of its message because Acker opted out of the work of building what British cultural studies critic Raymond Williams called "our common life together."[134]

For liberals, Richard Nixon serves as more than an easy target—he functions as a touchstone for the validity of their values. In "Angst for the

Memories," a September 1993 episode of *Murphy Brown*, a situation comedy about a *60 Minutes*–like television newsmagazine, Murphy (played by Candace Bergen) lands an interview with the reclusive author of a landmark 1960s novel, *Technicolor Highway*. The excitement over this scoop fades when Murphy discovers that her literary hero has become a virulent neoconservative. Commiserating afterward at their favorite tavern, Murphy and her co-workers admit that they too have changed. One by one, these denizens of the liberal media offer confessions—one now believes that many welfare recipients are lazy, another has considered purchasing a gun—until one of them cuts to a final test: "Does anybody here think Nixon might have gotten a raw deal?" Instant denials reassure them, and, with great relief, Murphy and her colleagues clink glasses, toasting, "At least we've still got that," affirming Nixon's villainy as their one bedrock belief.[135]

Such certainty surfaced frequently in Matt Groening's long-running TV cartoon *The Simpsons* and his cult-favorite *Futurama*. In an October 1993 *Simpsons* episode, when Homer sells his soul for a doughnut, the devil, coming to collect on the contract, assembles a "jury of the damned" to judge the case, which includes a reluctant Richard Nixon, who relents only when reminded that he owes the devil a favor. But, although Nixon keeps his promise to Satan, he cannot be trusted otherwise. In "Duffless," when Homer tours the Duff brewery, he views old television commercials, including a spot recorded during the 1960 presidential debates. Stepping away from the podium, JFK smiles and, to the cheers of the studio audience, tells the viewers how much he enjoys Duff. But when Nixon offers his self-conscious, halting endorsement—"I'd, uh, also like to express *my* fondness for that particular beer"—even Homer sniffs out the basic insincerity, sneering, "The man never drank a Duff in his life."[136] Groening's *Futurama*, a science-fiction cartoon set in New New York City in the year 3000, features numerous gleefully malevolent cameo appearances by Richard Nixon's head (all historical twentieth-century figures appear in the fourth millennium as severed heads stored in fluid-filled jars). In "A Head in the Polls," Nixon's head runs for President of Earth, threatening to "get Cambodian on your asses." When the show's regular characters attempt to interfere with his plans, he explains: "I've become bitter, and, let's face it, *craaazy* over the years, and once I'm swept into office, I'll sell our children's organs to *zoos* for meat. And I'll go into people's houses at night and wreck up the place. Muhuhahahaha." Series creator Matt

Groening embraces responsibility for all the Nixon-bashing, describing it as retribution for past psychic traumas: "I was so mad at Nixon, you know, as a kid growing up. He was just such a jerk. . . . If I could have known back then that, in 1999, I'd still get to make fun of him, ahhh, it would have cheered me up."[137]

Often these demonized reinventions of Richard Nixon exist to ridicule the idiocy of his supporters. The Funky Nixons, self-proclaimed house band of Berkeley's People's Park, included a song on their 1996 CD "Still Not Crooks" that expressed such contemptuous feelings. Wondering how American voters could possibly have supported Nixon (and his Republican successors Reagan and Bush), the singers provide a simple explanation, which gives the song both its refrain and title: "(You must be) stupid!"[138] The Dick Nixons, a 1990s punk band from Donaldsonville, Louisiana, dramatized this stupidity. Over half of the songs on their only CD, 1992's *Paint the White House Black*, are paeans to Richard Nixon, like "The Patriot Song," which proposes a way to restore the nation—"vote Richard M. Nixon in 1992." But the song lyrics, scrawled on the back of the CD's front insert (and including multiple cross-outs, missing apostrophes, and gross misspellings), put into context the claim that Nixon is the "Virgin Mary second sun." Anyone who idolizes Nixon must be mentally defective.[139]

When Richard Nixon sought to justify his political dirty tricks, he cast himself as a victim of similar tactics. During the 1972 campaign, he insisted that his staff understand that "we were finally in a position to have someone doing to the opposition what they had done to us."[140] At the same time, he fantasized about dire consequences should his political agenda fail: "The country simply can't afford to have the likes of Kennedy and McGovern as even possible Presidents."[141] Too often, Nixon's detractors embraced his perversion of the Golden Rule: doing to others as you imagine others have done to you. While answering real provocations, the artists looked at in this chapter deliberately provoked in return. Instead of seeking balanced rhetoric and perspectives, they indulge in imagining a nearly unlimited evil residing in their nemesis. Consequently, the political visions contained within these works fail. *Our Gang* and *An Evening with Richard Nixon* flirt with irrelevancy: Roth by blaming Nixon for all America's ills and Vidal by sanctimoniously promoting his own ideological agenda as objective history. *Don Quixote* and the African American artists present a more complicated case. On the one hand, they advocate the empowerment of those who have been excluded and exploited by the mainstream culture. But they end up undercutting this position by descending to the same hateful tactics of the oppressors and, in Acker's case, seemingly denying the effectiveness of any rebellion against the dominant culture. The common lesson is this: casting Nixon as the devil, however emotionally satisfying it might be, adds little of use to the debate of cultural values.

CHAPTER SIX

"NEVER GIVE UP"

AMERICAN ORTHODOXY,

REVISED STANDARD VERSION

Most of the man's critics just didn't get it. They thought they had finally gotten rid of Richard Nixon. In his mid-1990s song "1974," British rock musician Robyn Hitchcock mocked the complacent self-congratulatory certainty with which liberals celebrated their supposedly final triumph over their nemesis, crowing after Nixon's hurried exit from the White House: "They'll never rehabilitate that mother / No way."[1] Yet many people kept repeating the mistake. The play *Frost/Nixon*, written by Peter Morgan, known for his screenplays *The Last King of Scotland* and *The Queen*, owed much of its success to its highly dramatic retelling of the 1977 David Frost interviews with the ex-president as a comeback battle between two former giants that only one can win. After he obtains from Nixon the "confession" and apology that American journalists had failed to elicit, Frost reclaims the spotlight, while the play's final words on Nixon assure the audience of his ultimate defeat: "Despite being buried with full honours in 1994, Richard Nixon never again held public office of any kind, nor achieved the rehabilitation he so desperately craved."[2]

What Nixon's critics failed to understand was that they could expose the man's crimes and dissect the cultural myths he held dear, but, without an alternative story to supplant them, the traditional cultural narratives wouldn't go away. Indeed, much of the American Left simply does not understand the intrinsic need for shared stories to make sense of our national experiences. As Garrison Keillor observed, too many liberals "trusted scholarship and experience," neglecting to express their ideas in mythic narratives, "and a man who has no story is a man with no truth to offer."[3] Consequently, the belief systems Nixon represented for his supporters, and which he defended in *Six Crises* and *RN*, rebounded to fill the mythic vacuum of the post-Watergate era.

During the mid- to late 1970s, popular culture clung to the story of underdogs who eventually triumph because they refuse to give up. Within two years of Nixon's resignation, Sylvester Stallone made millions at the box office and won an Oscar for *Rocky*, the story of the perennial loser from a neighborhood gym in South Philadelphia who, despite dropping the decision of his heavyweight title fight, gets the chance to prove he has the heart of a champion. In the 1979 sequel, Rocky's virtue wins him the material reward of the champion's belt. The same year saw the surprise hit *Breaking Away*, which concluded at Indiana University's Little 500 bike race with the triumph of a team of lower-middle-class, small-town boys against a field filled with rich fraternity snobs.

This revitalized cultural mythology played just as well in American politics. Campaigning in 1980 against Jimmy Carter, Ronald Reagan appealed to his fellow citizens with the slogan "Let's make America great again," an optimistic message promising nearly unlimited possibilities for the nation that did not give up on itself. Four years later, when Reagan declared that "America is too great for small dreams," he increased his share of the popular vote from the 1980 figure of 50.9 percent to 59 percent.[4] Nixon's comeback chances benefited from Reagan's popularity and successes, but Nixon, like a blocking lineman, had done much to open the field for the Gipper. In a real sense, the much-hyped "Reagan Revolution" should also be recognized as a second chance to fulfill Nixon's promised "New American Revolution." Even at the time, some observers pointed out this complicated relationship. The editorial cartoonist Pat Oliphant has always been insistent on this point. We've already noted his morning-after-the-election cartoon from 1980. During the transition period, Oliphant suggested Nixon as a guiding influence on Reagan, drawing the former president as a bird on the shoulder of the president-elect, whispering the suggestion of Al Haig (the Watergate-era White House chief of staff) for secretary of state. Even as far into Reagan's administration as 1986, Oliphant still saw Nixon as the visionary force. When Antonin Scalia was added to the Supreme Court, Oliphant drew the new justice together with newly installed chief justice William Rehnquist as a parody of Grant Wood's "American Gothic," that iconic symbol of heartland America and its staid conservatism. In the bottom left corner of the cartoon, we find not the president who made the appointments but a skulking Richard Nixon, celebrating his triumph over an activist judiciary with his "V for Victory" salute. The Nixon Library also guides its visitors to see Reagan as Nixon's political godson. In fact, the first person seen in the museum's orientation film, "Never Give Up: Richard Nixon in the Arena," is Reagan, appearing as a defeated presidential candidate at the 1968

Although some credited Reagan for the old-fashioned American Gothic values represented by a newly conservative Supreme Court, according to Pat Oliphant those who looked closely could see the handiwork of an earlier master. OLIPHANT © 1986 UNIVERSAL PRESS SYNDICATE. Reprinted with permission. All rights reserved.

Republican convention, asking for the delegates to make Nixon's nomination unanimous.

Demoralized and disarmed by conservatism's ascendancy in the 1980s, the American Left offered little effective opposition to Nixon, the values he embodied, and his campaign for rehabilitation. In these last years of his life, the symbolic presentations of the man reiterated the earlier mythic images but also began to take on a new cast. Nixon now also represented unceasing determination and the refusal to give up. In short, he was a triumphant survivor. As such, he appeared for many as an American sage, at peace with himself, still ready to struggle for the causes in which he believed. Not simply did Nixon critics lack a compelling, persuasive countermyth, but some of them, seduced by the power of this story, actually participated in reinventing Richard Nixon as a mythic hero. In so doing, they accepted compartmentalized moral judgments of the former president's life and career, precisely the gambit Nixon himself had been using since the David Frost interviews and the publication of *RN*. Such a surrender on his terms by some of those he saw as his natural enemies made Nixon's task that much easier as he moved into the final phase of his struggle for redemption—the publication of his final book of memoirs, *In the Arena*, and the opening of his presidential library in 1990. In the absence of any truly effective opposition, this revised standard version of America's orthodox myths enjoyed a revitalized power in U.S. politics and culture, one that proved as resilient in the face of critique as Nixon himself.[5]

Even before the Nixon Library opened, Nixon's drive for rehabilitation had succeeded to the point that he could, on occasion, extract from his critics the concessions that he hoped for. Suckers for the comeback story, *Newsweek*, in its May 19, 1986, issue, heralded Nixon's ultimate victory over his critics. The cover shouted "He's Back," promising the exclusive story of "The Rehabilitation of Richard Nixon." What was more shocking? That a magazine controlled by the *Washington Post* declared his restoration? Or the cover photo of a relaxed Nixon, flashing a genuine smile? Katharine Graham, owner of the *Washington Post*, ordered the story after witnessing Nixon's virtuoso performance during an April 1986 foreign policy presentation to the American Newspaper Publishers Association.[5] And the *Newsweek* staff complied by relating Nixon's twelve-year-long march out of the valley of the shadow of Watergate as a comeback tale that owed solely to his own calculation, patience, and skill. One of Nixon's friends marveled: "He has planned all this for years in a very cautious and painstaking fashion." After the success of *RN*, Nixon produced a series of foreign policy books that passionately argued for America's return to the world stage. Complementing this public role, Nixon established himself as a private counselor to President Reagan. According to a *Newsweek*/Gallup Poll taken in the weeks just before the story, he had convinced 39 percent of the American public that he should return to public life as an ambassador or adviser.[6]

Yet even as it heralded the comeback, the media's inclination toward skepticism regarding Richard Nixon tried to reassert itself. Having offered a favorable portrait, *Newsweek* couldn't help gagging on its own compliments. In equal measure, the story acknowledged Nixon's renaissance while raising doubt about, if not actually denying, his success. Quoting Henry Kissinger on Nixon's "legacy of solid achievement," the reporters turned to two historians who "see that record as a house built on sand." Uncomfortable about the heroic image of Nixon the story promises, the magazine hints that this current rehabilitation may not be the final scene: "He has triumphed, failed and survived; always he came back, and always he found new ways to defeat himself."[7]

All the same, *Newsweek*'s critical words, buried inside the story, could not erase the message of its cover. If the seven letters printed in the "My Turn" pages of the June 9, 1986, issue reflected the general reaction, readers understood the magazine to be promoting Nixon's comeback. For all but one of the writers, this perception led to harsh criticism: "To treat such a man as an honored statesman is the lowest form of hypocrisy." But whether they were critical or approving, such as the woman who welcomed Nixon back because he "still has much to contribute," most people read the headline "The Sage of Saddle River" and skipped over the fine-print qualifiers.[8]

Soon, however, some of the traditional Nixon opponents stopped gagging when they celebrated the man as a foreign policy guru. The moment always most likely to establish Nixon's diplomatic legacy had come on February 21, 1972, when he strode across a Beijing tarmac with his hand outstretched to the premier of the People's Republic of China, Chou En-lai, and ended decades of angry silence between the two nations. For his own part, Nixon had cultivated the seeds of this event's mythic possibilities, seeing in them his best chance to remove Watergate's stain on his legacy. In *RN*, he fancies himself a latter-day Christopher Columbus, "embarking upon a voyage of philosophical discovery as uncertain, and in some respects as perilous, as the voyages of geographical discovery of a much earlier time," and equating his handshake with Chou with the opening of a new historical "era" so momentous that it "changed the world."[9] Through careful husbanding of his image, Nixon infused much of his grand version of the China initiative into the collective memory of the trip. In the minds of many, he became U.S. diplomacy's great visionary, pursuing a policy for peace that he alone had the skill, the farsightedness, and the tenacity to fulfill. *New York Times* publisher C. L. Sulzberger, in a 1987 book on U.S. foreign policy, nearly out-Nixons Nixon, lauding the China initiative as "the greatest diplomatic coup" of the leader who understood foreign affairs better "than any American president this century."[10] Indeed, by the end of the 1980s, the phrase "only Nixon could go to China" worked its way into the political lexicon—and, improbably, into the repertoire of modern American opera.[11] The creation of three alumni of Harvard University (an institution Nixon disdained as much as he did the *New York Times* or the *Washington Post*), *Nixon in China* premiered at the Houston Grand Opera on October 22, 1987.[12] Avoiding the hyperbole of both *RN* and Sulzberger's monograph, librettist Alice Goodman, composer John Adams, and director Peter Sellars present their Richard

Nixon as an Everyman figure who prevails despite his middle-American provinciality.[13] In a 1987 interview, John Adams described the Nixon of Goodman's libretto as a man who feels keenly his own limitations: "You see the beads of sweat on Nixon's forehead as he tries to show the Chairman that he's not the rube Mao might think he is."[14] Rather than diminish Nixon, however, this refusal to take a larger-than-life view of the man, in actuality, leads the opera to salvage and recycle the orthodox values of mainstream U.S. culture.

First of all, by rendering Nixon on a human scale, Goodman and company reaffirm the American myth of success. Though not a Superman, he remains a hero, struggling for world peace against severe obstacles, the first of which are the inherent limits of human achievement. By choosing to begin the opera with its highest moment of drama, the arrival of an American president in Beijing, its creators suggest the imperfection of even the greatest accomplishments. For in the afterglow of triumph, Nixon fears failure. In his opening aria, contented thoughts give way to anxiety: "There's murmuring below. / Now there's ingratitude!"[15] Without immediate diplomatic results, Nixon expects harsh criticism, both from Democrats, who would say that he had lost a great opportunity, and from the Far Right, who would use any setback to question the wisdom of dealing with the communist Chinese at all. At the same time, China's internal politics impedes any possible dramatic breakthroughs. Act Two, Scene Two, which features a staging of Madame Mao's ballet, *The Red Detachment of Women*, dramatizes the revolutionary fervor obstructing Nixon's plans for détente. Blatantly political, the ballet dramatizes the peasants' oppression by a ruling class specifically identified with the United States through the inclusion of Kissinger in the role of the landlord's evil factotum. When Nixon leaves the audience to join Pat in saving a peasant girl from Kissinger, Madame Mao herself crosses over into the opera to prevent the president from escaping the message that if his national security advisor is the landlord's factotum then he must be the landlord. Supplying her dancers with rifles, Madame Mao sets them upon the capitalists, crying, "What are you gaping at? / Forward Red Troupe! Annihilate / This tyrant and his running dogs!" This ballet within the opera dramatizes the anti-American zeal of Mao's fundamentalist followers, who "speak according to the book." In pitting him against these limiting forces, both personal and political, the creators of *Nixon in China* perpetuate the "only Nixon could go to China" myth by lionizing a president who, facing great odds, dares to dream of world peace.[16]

To be sure, Nixon's heroism also resides in his embrace of this idealistic sense of national mission. In one of the few times that Adams sets Nixon's words to melodic strains, the president explains his motivations: "We send / Children on our crusades, we bring / Children our countries, right or wrong. / Then we retire. Fathers and sons, / Let us join hands, make peace for once." Because the "children" sent on their father's "crusades" probably refers to American soldiers, particularly those in Vietnam, we see here a redefinition of America's redemptive mission, transferring its goal from the propagation of democracy through violence to the achievement of peace. Typical of the rhetoric of national mission, Nixon sets up America as a model for the rest of the world. On his arrival in Beijing, Nixon imagines his countrymen back home viewing him on television: "The three main networks' colors glow / Livid through drapes onto the lawn. / Dishes are washed and homework done, / The dog and grandma fall asleep." In this small town idyll, America appears as a harmonious society, a safe haven of shelter for home and family. As the first scene of the opera concludes, Nixon hopes his efforts in China will bring this peaceful life to the rest of the world: "The nation's heartland skips a beat / As our hands shield the spinning globe / From the flame-throwers of the mob. / We must press on." With this recasting of the redeemer nation myth, the creators of *Nixon in China* offer a picture of a country dedicated to harmony among the world's nations.[17]

But the opera elicits our admiration for a purposefully imbalanced image of Richard Nixon, one that, oddly enough, accedes to the limited moral judgments of his career that he worked so hard to elicit, willingly cutting him precisely the slack that he needed to fuel his comeback. Seemingly without recognizing the implications of his admission, Adams told a reporter for the *Marin (CA) Independent Journal*: "At times, I would see the real Nixon on TV and I'd become angry. You see, I became so attached to *my* Nixon that I forgot what a jerk the real Nixon is."[18] Wishful thinking aside, however, Adams cannot escape so easily—a fictional Richard Nixon still, in some sense, stands for the historical Nixon—particularly when this fictional character was created almost entirely out of the accounts in Nixon's and Kissinger's memoirs. Alice Goodman defended their choice by asserting: "Having started out blissfully ignorant, I was not going to become wise after the fact."[19] Yet additional wisdom might have alleviated their dependence on one of the crucial assertions of Nixon's version: that his laudable foreign policy record stands untouched by his problematic domestic legacy and his controversial handling of the Vietnam War. By opening the opera with the arrival in China and concluding before the return flight home, Goodman and company suggest that Nixon's days in the People's Republic stand outside time. As crucial an issue as Vietnam receives little direct discussion, nor are there any specific references to the domestic and social upheavals of the late 1960s and early 1970s.[20] In *Nixon in China*, the antiwar movement and the demonstrations on college campuses—not to mention Nixon's plans to engage in illegal surveillance to combat them—disappear. Even more notably, the opera neglects to foreshadow the Watergate scandal. By February 1972, the White House had authorized and carried out a break-in at the California office of Daniel Ellsberg's psychiatrist; Dwight Chapin, the president's appointments secretary, had recruited a college friend, Donald Segretti, to enact a campaign of sabotage against the Democratic presidential candidates; and the Committee to Re-Elect the President had started discussions that would result in a plan to spy on the Democrats. By omitting any suggestion of these activities, Goodman, Adams, and Sellars miss the opportunity to explore the paradox of this man who brought peace between nations but also did much to destroy his own country from within.[21]

Furthermore, *Nixon in China* ignores the dangerous legacy of the kind of secret diplomacy used to achieve the China opening. Arguing that total confidentiality was necessary to permit the delicate negotiations with the People's Republic to take root and develop, Nixon used Henry Kissinger as his clandestine envoy to China, keeping William Rogers, his longtime friend and secretary of state, wholly uninformed. Not only does the opera not question the advisability of running a covert government, but it erases Rogers from history. For, though he made the trip to China, the secretary of state neither appears nor merits a mention in the opera. Yet Goodman, Adams, and Sellars's opera premiered after nearly a full year of Iran-contra scandal headlines, revelations that should, at the very least, have raised reservations about the fruits of secret diplomacy. The October 1986 crash of a plane carrying military supplies being sent to the contra rebels at war with the communist government in Nicaragua led eventually to the exposure of members of the Reagan administration carrying on covert operations contrary to its own stated policy and in violation of the law. Despite loud protests that the U.S. government never negotiated with terrorists, Reagan had sought to free some American hostages in the Middle East by selling weapons to Iran. The money generated by those sales was then used to provide military support for the contras, contrary to the letter and spirit of two different acts of Congress. In February 1987, the

Tower Commission, a presidentially-appointed investigative body, issued a report highly critical of both the arms for hostages plan and the diversion of funds, as well as Reagan's lax oversight of his underlings. Throughout the spring and summer, Congress continued the investigation, with televised hearings, into what amounted to "a covert policy inspired by a secret decision to support a group that the American people had decided overwhelmingly *not* to support." Thus, *Nixon in China*'s veneration of what an individual can achieve and its glorification of the country's missionary aspirations is a reaffirmation bought on the cheap. For the revised standard version of America's orthodox myths that *Nixon in China* gives us—much like the Reagan era out of which this work came—revives the traditional national mythology only by ignoring events that shook the foundations of American culture.[22]

With the ground softened for him by some of his supposedly implacable enemies, Richard Nixon was ready to enter a new phase of his rehabilitation efforts—the opening of his presidential library and museum. Timed to precede the midsummer dedication of his library, Nixon's third autobiography, *In the Arena: A Memoir of Victory, Defeat, and Renewal*, published in April 1990, appeared in stores, along with George F. Will's baseball book *Men at Work* and Robert F. Caro's *Means of Ascent*, a scathing biography of Lyndon Johnson, and just five months before John Updike's Harry "Rabbit" Angstrom returned—another figure surrounded by decades of controversy—in 1990's Pulitzer Prize winner for fiction, *Rabbit at Rest*.[23] At first glance, Nixon's book seems a disjointed collection of mini-ruminations on single-word topics, such as "Family," "Risks," and "Twilight." (In the audio abridgement of the book, Nixon reveals that he dictated the first draft, thinking of each chapter as if it were a speech.)[24] Yet this final autobiography proves just as purposeful as the first two memoirs. While it trots out all the predictable old anecdotes, using much the same language as before, *In the Arena* makes its real story the presumption of Nixon's total rehabilitation: that he can offer advice on living, not just with the belief that those chestnuts will be accepted, but that, through his persistence, he has *earned* the right to assume the wise man's role.

If *Six Crises* and *RN* each try to explain a setback in Nixon's life, *In the Arena* celebrates his survival. The three chapters of the first section set out what Nixon sees as the cycle of life: "Peaks and Valleys," "Wilderness," and "Renewal." Beginning on the day of his 1972 arrival in Beijing, Nixon opens with his greatest presidential achievement. But, for Nixon, defeat and victory intertwine inextricably. The chapter's remaining segments relate Nixon's resignation in disgrace and its aftermath. At the bottom of the deepest chasm he ever experienced, Nixon despaired: "I was a physical wreck; I was emotionally drained; I was mentally burned-out. . . . I could see no reason to live."[25] Yet, as he explains in the book's second chapter, "Wilderness," the truly great figures of history often suffer a setback as a prelude to their triumphant return to the public stage. And, despite having "no precedent for what faced [him] in the 1970s," Nixon methodically achieved the unprecedented.[26] Rebuilding his physical strength through daily golf games, recovering his spiritual health by relying on his family and a sustaining network of caring friends and loyal supporters, Nixon reestablished his financial and mental health by writing his second autobiography. At the end of these years of personal recovery, Nixon could dedicate himself to the third principle that he claims sustained him during his wilderness period: "Devote your time to a goal larger than yourself." The final chapter, "Renewal," gives a quick world tour, proffering Nixon's wisdom, because "I had some unique experience and had developed some strong views about the mistakes that had been made in the past and the need for new policies in the future." By regaining this selfless perspective, Richard Nixon moves forward. Remembering a friend's counsel that "life is ninety-nine rounds," Nixon, in the section's final paragraph, picks himself up off the canvas, dusts off his gloves, and continues the fight: "The battle I started to wage forty-three years ago when I first ran for Congress is not over. I still have a few rounds to go."[27]

As one who has met defeat, sojourned in the wilderness, and returned, spiritually and intellectually renewed, to the arena of public life, Nixon uses the rest of *In the Arena* to muse about life, politics, and the United States. In Section Two, he suggests that the kind of character he exhibited in surviving Watergate and its aftermath originates from basic values such as family, religion, teachers, and struggle—each serving as a chapter title. In a return to the rhetoric of jeremiad that served as the organizing principle of *RN*, Nixon celebrates each serving as a American culture's failure to value it. Our current fascination with the culturally trendy, Nixon asserts, has led many mainline Protestant denominations to jettison "timeless moral and spiritual issues" for "pathetic attempt[s] to be 'relevant' on current political issues" and educators to seek to "mold students into culturally and politically correct citizens of some ideal world." In the end, this obsession with the new blinds us to what is truly worthwhile, rendering America into a "society whose rock stars were more admired than great teachers; beautiful people more than interesting people; scandal more than good deeds."[28]

In Sections Three and Four, the core of the book, Nixon turns to pragmatic advice for daily living. He may write about reading, conversation, memory, thinking, and recreation, but each topic's interest stems from an opportunity to practice and master self-control. In the tradition of Franklin, Nixon shares with his readers his methodical program for encouraging thinking—a plan that includes sitting in an austere office with one's back to the window to avoid distraction and scheduling daily time for thought in isolation from other people. Cutting through the surface of these maxims, like an iceberg in the North Atlantic, floats the assumption that the world is a harsh, stark place, making struggle a moral imperative.[29] Section Four, the longest of *In the Arena*, turns to the practice of politics. Worried about the debilitating effect of television, rising campaign costs, the dominance of special interest groups, and an overriding obsession with placating rather than leading public opinion, Nixon pleads for a courageous brand of rule-breaking politician. With shocking frankness, he concludes: "The Constitution, extraordinary document that it is, cannot by itself produce a moment of peace or an instant of prosperity. Only the will and the vision of leaders, exercised through the democratic system, sometimes restrained by it, *occasionally even exceeding it*, can bring about these goals" (emphasis mine). Lacking any sense of the big picture, our political culture reveres the process, the "how" rather than the "what," the goal itself. A true leader, when necessary to evade the obstructionists, may use undemocratic means to bring about the greater good. And, Nixon assures us, there will be deliberate obstructionists—for the chapter "Friends" leads, naturally, into the chapter "Enemies." If politics is understood as a "battle," enemies inspire and rally the loyal troops to action. The number of his foes measures a true leader's effectiveness.[30]

From the pragmatism of Sections Three and Four, Nixon moves to larger questions, such as geopolitics, war, and peace. But even the eternal "search for higher meaning" cannot be separated from practical concerns. Nixon's description of the nation's founders as "neither woolly-headed utopians nor empty-headed pragmatists" sounds an awful lot like his own self-image. The distinguishing "hardheaded realism" of the Nixonian worldview recognizes the need for secrecy as a tool of diplomacy: "Covert operations per se are neither bad nor good. . . . Secrecy in these cases is bad only when the end is bad." All the same, Nixon tempers his insistence that the United States cannot rule out the use of force with the recognition that violence must be redeemed by some higher purpose. Balancing the ideal with the attainable, Nixon dreams of "striving to create a better world, to advance mankind's material, cultural, philosophical, and spiritual progress." Speaking with "reasoned optimism," Nixon declares that "we hold the future in our hands."[31]

That Nixon survived to offer his vision of America's future provided cause for celebration in "Twilight," the book's final section. Quoting Sophocles—"One must wait until the evening to see how splendid the day has been"—Nixon affirms that, although not over yet, his "day has indeed been splendid." Through all the crises, Nixon remained focused on his goal: "A world in which peace and freedom can live together." Such assurance permits Richard Nixon, the focal point of so much divisiveness, to assert that he has ultimately found "what my Quaker grandmother would have called 'peace at the center.'"[32]

This serenity seems to have been won, however, by a refusal to deal honestly with the past. Whereas he needed hundreds of pages to deal with Watergate in *RN*, unsatisfactorily even then, a decade later, he dispatches the scandal in a mere ten. Although he admits that Watergate was wrong and that he failed to take a "moral tone," Nixon trivializes its overall importance, calling the episode "worse than a crime—it was a blunder," at the same time insisting that he was the victim of "a concerted political vendetta by [his] opponents."[33] But these three components of the Watergate affair are hardly equal: the wrongdoing Nixon relates in one short paragraph; the blunder receives two paragraphs that total about one-half of a page; while the political machinations against Nixon run on for more than two pages. In fact, his admitted moral failures, upon closer inspection, turn out to be further digs at his critics: "Not taking a higher road than my predecessors and my adversaries was my central mistake." In the same breath, he asserts that he "long ago accepted responsibility for the Watergate affair," insisting that "I have paid, and am still paying, the price for it." But with the $21.95 hardcover version of the book spending more than ten weeks on the *New York Times Book Review* best-seller list and with his continued lack of understanding of his true culpability, the American people seemed to be the ones still footing the bill.[34]

On July 19, 1990, nearly three months after the publication of *In the Arena*, 40,000 people attended the opening of the Richard Nixon Library and Birthplace in Yorba Linda, California, an event that celebrated, and a place that honors, perseverance on a grand scale. Because Congress had stipulated in 1974 that Nixon's presidential papers and tapes could not leave the Washington, D.C., area, the Nixon library could not become a part of the National Archives and Records Administration (NARA) presidential library system and, therefore, would receive no federal funding for its operation. Instead, private contributors had to ante up the needed $21 million to build the facility as well as create an endowment for the year-to-year operation of the library. By dedication day, over 5,000 donors had pledged in excess of $27 million; Nixon personally contributed two million.[35] To stimulate the fund-raising, the Nixon Library and Birthplace Foundation provided numerous gift opportunities, including membership in the Richard Nixon Foreign Policy Round Table, which entitled any donor of $250,000 plus a yearly fee of $10,000 to a pair of personal briefings each year from Nixon himself, followed by dinner and a discussion session.[36] Though, unsurprisingly, its primary contributors were less likely to be cloth-coated Republicans than nattily dressed millionaires like Robert Abplanalp, inventor of the aerosol spray can, Bebe Rebozo, Miami banker and presidential best friend, or Walter Annenberg, founder of *TV Guide*, the Nixon Library still had had to beat uniquely tall odds, because no NARA presidential library had to raise money for anything other than initial building costs.[37] Little wonder then that at the opening of the *NBC Nightly News* on July 19, anchored from the library grounds, Tom Brokaw recognized the improbability of the day, declaring, with a mix of admiration and wonder, "He got his library."[38]

And the importance of getting the library can hardly be overestimated. Building one allowed Nixon to participate in what has become an almost required national ritual of memorializing a president and defining his legacy. Benjamin Hufbauer has noted how de rigueur presidential libraries (every president beginning with FDR has built one) have replaced memorials dedicated only to those presidents worthy of special veneration. An "assertion of ego and power," a sign of the imperial presidency developed during the twentieth century, the presidential library and particularly its museum participates in the commemoration of national saints, sacred places and objects, and ritual practices—elements that compose what Robert Bellah referred to as America's civil religion. So the presidential library presents a particular representation of its subject, but it also evokes a particular national image and ideology. As Hufbauer puts it, "For tourists, a presidential library presents an ideologically charged narrative that valorizes a presidential life, helping to incorporate it into the nation's civil religion."[39] At the Richard Nixon Library and Birthplace, in its original design, a message about the eventual triumph of dogged determination defines its interpretation of Nixon and of the United States: "Don't quit," the museum fairly shouts, "and the old cultural myths of self-reliance and national mission will prevail."[40]

All the same, the Nixon Library doesn't leave much to chance. It clearly expects all visitors to enter the museum via the orientation film, "Never Give Up: Richard Nixon in the Arena."[41] Once the visitor pays for admission at the gift shop cash register, the docent on duty in the lobby points out the entrance to the 299-seat theater, above which a digital clock announces, in glowing red numbers, "Time Remaining to Next Show."[42] In the museum's earliest days, visitors, once inside, were even instructed how to respond; one docent in charge of introducing the film encouraged the audience "to feel free to clap, cry, and cheer."[43] Announcing its theme in the first moments, "Never Give Up" begins with film clips from two of Nixon's most notable comebacks: his unanimous nomination at the 1968 Republican convention and his 1990 return visit to Capitol Hill. The narrator provides the moral of these two events—and the interpretive frame for the entire Library experience: Nixon, a man who "never failed to turn a setback into an opportunity," made "coming back from defeat the hallmark of his entire career." No defeat could permanently derail Nixon—not even Watergate. Over film of White House staffers weeping on the day Nixon resigned, the narrator intones: "He was in the deepest valley. He would not stay there long." After relating Nixon's resignation, "Never Give Up" dedicates over four of its twenty-eight minutes to document the triumphs of a rehabilitated elder statesman, and, at the film's conclusion, Nixon offers a sage benediction—among other things, urging young people to "never give up; take risks."

Outside the theater, the museum's floor plan reinforces the overall message by steering visitors quickly through the Nixon setbacks. His defeat in 1960 appears as one of a wall-long series of reader boards dedicated to the election. The ill-fated run for governor of California makes up only a part of the section treating "The Wilderness Years." And the reader boards for this period serve as the entrance to the space dedicated to Nixon's triumphant return in the 1968 presidential election. The most spacious rooms in the museum trumpet Nixon's achievements as president. While the library has publicized the Watergate display as one of the museum's largest, the scandal doesn't merit a room; instead that story gets told in a long but narrow and exceptionally dark passageway.[44] Although it does contain an encyclopedic amount of information, with a wall containing three rows of reader boards and photo panels, a bench for sitting, and several stations for listening to selections from the smoking gun tape, the Watergate gallery doesn't invite lingering.[45] Directly in front of the visitor at the end of the darkened hallway looms a wall-sized, brightly lit blow-up of the famous August 9, 1974, photo of Nixon standing on the steps of the presidential helicopter, waving goodbye to the White House staff. Virtually glowing, the photo exerts a magnetic pull on visitors, who naturally prefer the light at the end of the tunnel. As originally designed, evenly spaced ceiling lights were to leave a trail of small pie-shaped wedges of illumination on the carpet leading up to the Nixon photo, like runway landing lights directing us to a safe touchdown beyond the hallway. Don't wallow in Watergate's darkness, the museum urges, the real story resides in moving on.

The docent-led tours reinforce this message. Over a four-day period in May 2002, I witnessed eight different tours in the Watergate hallway: seven for classes of upper elementary or middle-school children, the other for a small group of French tourists. Five of the eight tours gave a short explanation at the head of the hallway and then marched the group through. Of these five, the most detailed narrative merely explained the lack of light ("because this was the darkest time" for Nixon) and told the group that Watergate was a commercial building where there was a break-in at the Democratic National Headquarters on June 17, 1972. Though Nixon did not order the break-in, "he made a mistake and tried to cover it up," an act that led to his resignation on August 9, 1974. The more bare-boned narratives suggested Watergate was too complex for the students to understand until they reached high school age. "As you get older," one docent explained, "you'll be bombarded with information. You'll have to decide for yourself what happened." The other three tour guides, solemn as pallbearers, mutely ushered their visitors through the hallway. For all the investment of text, photos, audio stations, and display cases put into the Watergate exhibit, the library hopes to elicit the response of the couple who looked around briefly and departed without another glance, one saying to the other: "We know enough about Watergate."

And when one does move on, the final stops of the tour epitomize the victory of Nixon's values. For, after exiting the museum portion of the library, the Visitor's Guide directs the guest out onto the grounds, past the reflecting pool, the Rose Garden, the Pat Nixon Amphitheater, the Nixon gravesites, and on to Nixon's birth house, a small, one-and-a-half-story white frame house that Frank Nixon built around one hundred years ago. This modest dwelling of a struggling middle-class family underwent an extensive $400,000 renovation so it could serve as the centerpiece of the entire multimillion-dollar facility. But this high price tag has paid tidy dividends in positive media attention for the library.[46] When Huell Howser, a popular California public television personality, brought his show to Yorba Linda, he dedicated the entire program to the birth house, which his guide, Julie Nixon Eisenhower, identified as the library's most popular attraction.[47] In 2001, CNN's *Larry King Live* took viewers into the museum, but the program began in, and gave special attention to, the house.[48] For both programs, the tiny structure's significance resides in its value as a symbol of the American dream. Howser's show opens with a black-and-white picture of the Nixon home, standing alone in the middle of Yorba Linda's citrus groves. While turn of the twentieth century–style folk music plays in the background, Howser offers a self-consciously mythic narration about how this "small, unassuming little house" provided shelter for "a hard-working, God-fearing family" and served as a physical representation of "the beginnings of their California dream."[49] If anything, *Larry King Live* makes the myth even more visible. In one of his trademark going-into-and-coming-out-of-commercial film clips, King lets Nixon serve as his own mythographer, asserting that the lesson of his birthplace is that "someone could come from a very modest house in a tiny little town of less than 200 and go to the very top in the United States."[50]

Indeed, the birthplace concludes a contemplation of the classic American success story begun upon entering the museum. While waiting for the orientation film, the visitor passes time by viewing reader boards that proclaim how the "hard but happy" life of Nixon's family in Yorba Linda found its roots in "hard working people of humble origins[,] . . . farmers and school teachers, pioneers who lived off the land," who had no inkling "that someday one of their offspring would become President of the United States." But, in rising to those heights, Nixon remained true to his origins. The gallery titled "Senate" sports a life-sized cutout photo of Nixon standing on the fold-down gate of a Woodie station wagon, recreating a 1950 Nixon campaign rally. The road signs—which place Los Angeles sixty-three miles away—and the small crowd intimate that Nixon ventured away from the big cities to meet the forgotten Californian. By contrast, a photo in the display case shows Nixon's opponent, Helen Gahagan Douglas, flying by private helicopter to a campaign rally in San

Francisco, casting the race as a contest between urban wealth and sophistication and rural, middle-class simplicity.

The Nixon presidency, as depicted by the museum, represents a culmination of this work ethic. To this point organized chronologically, the displays now are grouped by Nixon's achievements: one room, the hall of "World Leaders," shows his contact with international politicians; another gallery, "Structure of Peace," is given to his foreign policy accomplishments; and a third is titled "Domestic Affairs." Originally the only White House room re-created for the museum was the Lincoln Sitting Room— in Nixon's words "the smallest room in the White House and my favorite," largely because it made an excellent work space. On the wall opposite the replica, reader boards tell the story of the evolution of the Silent Majority speech, which is a narrative of Nixon's hands-on involvement in his presidency, down to the details that today's presidents farm out to others. Nixon took over this speech quite early in the process, we are told, because a draft written by a National Security Council member "did not get across the right message." In this display case, the visitor finds the deficient draft, Nixon's own handwritten notes, and a copy of the speech with Nixon's notes on its delivery.

Although forcing one to walk the gauntlet of the Watergate hallway, the museum affirms Nixon's values as ultimately victorious. The library grounds possess a reflecting pool and rose garden, reminders of the neoclassical grandeur of Washington, D.C., the graves of the former president and first lady, and the birthplace itself, inviting visitors to see Nixon's life in totality, the beginning revealing the end—and the end, the beginning. A plaque on a marker outside the house memorializes Nixon's exemplary life's journey: "We are proud of our native son, a man who has spared nothing of himself to help build a great nation." Despite the setbacks and defeats he suffered, Nixon vindicated America's belief in the unlimited possibilities of individual initiative. Noting that the library drew almost exclusively a white middle-class audience during the first weeks after its dedication, the British magazine the *Economist* wasn't surprised, observing, "It is a museum to middle-class aspirations."[51]

Upon exiting the museum, just before reentering the lobby, visitors encounter a remarkable painting, titled *Nixon at Andau*, the work of Ferenc Daday, a Hungarian émigré artist. Completed in 1971, the work commemorates Nixon's 1956 visit to rebels fighting against the communist-controlled Hungarian government.[52] The painting's foreground overlooks a river valley. The sky above roils, filled with either churning dark clouds or the swirling smoke from distant battle fires. In the far right foreground, a man waves a tattered Hungarian flag, its red stripe melting into the sky itself, suggesting the bloodshed below. A young man in the left foreground leans on a crutch. Just right of center, a child carries a bandaged arm in a sling. Into this world of gray and black strides a white-trench-coated Richard Nixon, who pulsates with a light seemingly emanating from within. At the painting's center, a group of supplicants pleads for his help. Down the hill, another cluster of refugees rejoices at the vice president's arrival. Meanwhile, the figures behind Nixon seemingly soak up the warmth of his glow. A husband and wife, surrounded by their worldly belongings, regard him with a mixture of hope and calm, the mother holding a nursing baby at her breast. Another father carries his son on his shoulders so that the child can glimpse their savior. The politician himself exudes determined compassion. Extending his left arm to steady the young freedom fighter, at the same time he rests his right hand on the head of a child, who stands on tiptoes to offer a sprig of flowers. In an interesting twist, Daday depicts the face not of the 1956 Nixon but of the older man, much as he appeared in 1971 at the time when the painting was completed.[53] Through this visual anachronism, Daday implies that Nixon rose to presidential stature in this impulsive visit to bedraggled refugees, twelve years before he actually won the office. Now on permanent loan to the library and hanging in the museum's "Legacy of Peace" gallery, Daday's *Nixon at Andau* venerates Nixon as a messianic hero who brings the light of freedom to a world imprisoned by tyranny.

Once again, the Nixon Library works from the moment we enter to prepare us for its message. A frosted-glass panel placed just inside the lobby doors, one of the first things the visitor sees, offers a quotation from Nixon's 1969 inaugural speech: "The greatest honor that history can bestow is the title of peacemaker." The early exhibits in the museum show us the evolution of a statesman: from Nixon's detailed country-by-country evaluation notes from his 1947 trip to war-wrecked Western Europe, to an entire display case titled "Reshaping the Vice Presidency," which defines Nixon as the "first Vice President to assume a major role in the making of foreign policy." The hall of "World Leaders," the room one enters after the museum's coverage of the 1968 campaign, proclaims the end of Nixon's apprenticeship. Facing the front of the room, looking above the statues of such figures as Churchill, Mao, Sadat, and Meir, one reads Nixon's words inscribed on the wall: "They are leaders who made a difference. Not because they wished it, but because they willed it." Though he does not appear as one of these leaders, the next room, the "Structure of Peace" gallery, dispels any doubts that Nixon belongs among this select company. At the gallery's entrance, a world map etched on glass suggests a statesman who, at a glance, saw the world whole. Inside, the room celebrates his foresight in opening dialogue with communist China, his fortitude in taking the right, rather than the popular, course in ending the Vietnam War, and his commitment to hard-headed détente as a means of thawing relations with the Soviet Union. Just in case anyone missed the message, the museum added statues of Nixon and Chou en-Lai shaking hands to the gallery, which are identical in size and style with those in the hall of "World Leaders," broadly hinting that Nixon belongs in the Great Hall's pantheon.

After the Watergate hallway, the museum immediately reestablishes Nixon as a peacemaker. A re-creation of his Park Ridge, New Jersey, study commemorates the philosopher statesman: his desk is displayed just as it was on April 18, 1994, the day he suffered a stroke after finishing corrections to his last book, *Beyond Peace*. The reader boards remind us that during this last phase of his life Nixon served as a counselor to five presidents, traveled eleven times to China and the Soviet Union, met with the most important world leaders of the day, and authored eight books. Triumphantly summarizing his career, the museum eulogizes: "Thus had the Cold War statesman who had transformed the world, making it safer and saner for hundreds of millions of people, brought his vision as an elder statesman to bear just as fruitfully upon the unique new problems of the post–Cold War world."

This well-prepared interpretive frame shapes our vision of Daday's *Nixon at Andau*. What might seem simply over-the-top at some earlier point in the museum makes sense at the end, where it gives a mythic significance to Richard Nixon's career as a statesman. The painting reminds us that Nixon's dedicated efforts on behalf of peace, freedom, and democracy in the years following his resignation, more than just a ploy to achieve rehabilitation, fulfilled a lifelong mission. And so when visitors enter the library grounds and walk back to the gravesites, they find in Nixon's epitaph—"the greatest honor history can bestow is the title of peacemaker"—the same words that greeted them upon entering the library. Despite the trials of Watergate, Nixon refused to give up and, as a result, ensured his triumph.

The library does not encourage paying much attention to Watergate, but, nevertheless, it accedes to the imperative that the story must be told. And, in this recognition, it does more than many presidential libraries in acknowledging, if not actually facing, awkward truths. For instance, the Kennedy Library nearly ignores the Bay of Pigs fiasco; the Reagan Library almost completely skips over the entire Iran-contra scandal; and the Clinton Library only mentions Monica Lewinsky twice.[54] That said, the Nixon Museum's concession to reality comes with visible ambivalence. The entrance to the Watergate passageway differs from the entrances to the galleries, which have wide openings and, often, the name of the exhibit printed above. As visitors finish perusing the "Domestic Affairs" gallery, they face an unassuming set of double doors, propped open, with the familiar backlit "Exit" sign above. Because the hallway is so dark and its ceiling drops a couple feet lower than the gallery, one could almost believe the janitors accidentally left the fire exit open. Only after entering the hallway and turning to the left does one see the title "Watergate: The Final Campaign."

More than just a means of urging visitors to leave, the Watergate hallway's darkness underscores the museum's content. Unlike all the other moments of Nixon's life, Watergate, a murky aberration, can't be seen clearly. Even the term has an uncertain definition. As the hall's first text panel claims: "Watergate is a word that has come to mean many things to many people. . . . The story of Watergate is enormously complex. Even today, basic questions remain unknown and perhaps unknowable." Furthermore, the hallway's narrative deviates from those in the rest of the museum because, this time, Richard Nixon, the master politician and statesman, didn't control events. One of the reader boards sports a reproduced page from the White House transcripts, with John Dean stating, "You don't know everything I know," and Nixon replying, "That's right."

At the same time, references to events seemingly unrelated to the scandal confirm the image of Nixon as an otherwise competent, accomplished man. The Watergate time line, which runs across the top of the reader boards, follows the entry indicating the Watergate burglars' guilty pleas with two dates: one touting Nixon's 1973 inaugural vow to "Make [the] Next Four Years America's Best," and the other proclaiming the end of the Vietnam War. The time line records the second summit between Nixon and Soviet leader Leonid Brezhnev as the sole event of June, despite this month being when John Dean began his testimony before the Ervin Committee. And, borrowing a technique Nixon already used in *RN*, the October 1973 entries alternate between the Watergate investigation and the Yom Kippur War, pitting access to the White House tapes against Nixon's skillful managing of oil embargoes and threats of Soviet military intervention in the Middle East.

Yet what should have been a minor scandal ended the Nixon presidency, and it did so because, this once, Nixon's enemies outmaneuvered him. During one school tour, a docent told the children that what they most needed to know about Watergate was that it "was a minor incident that should have been left alone and wasn't." The first reader board in the hallway announces the museum's thesis: "At the time, commentators sought to portray Watergate strictly as a morality play, as a struggle between right and wrong, truth and falsehood, good and evil." However, this conventional wisdom fails to capture Nixon's opponents' purely cynical side. "Given the benefit of time, it is now clear," the museum insists, "that Watergate was an epic and bloody political battle fought for the highest stakes, with no hold barred." Supporting the position that the scandal was nothing but politics, the hallway's reader boards downplay Watergate's import. The attempts to pin the crime on Nixon can be measured in quantifiable detail ("millions of dollars, thousands of leads, hundreds of interviews, and countless hours were spent"), but, after this gargantuan investigative effort, nothing was found to implicate him in the break-in. And the things that the library admits that Nixon *did* do (such as tape record phone calls and office conversations), it claims, were not unprecedented. An aggrieved sense of habitually unfair treatment pervades the text on the reader boards in the Watergate hall. This sense is at its most explicit in the histrionics of Indiana representative Earl Landgrebe, one of only two congressmen to still publicly support Nixon after the smoking gun tape was released, who melodramatically imagined his own martyrdom: "I'm sticking by my President, even if he and I have to be taken out of this building and shot."[55]

At its most extreme, this sense of persecution created a view of Nixon's political opponents as treasonous. Under a section titled "The Drum Beat Swells," which relates the growing call for Nixon's resignation, the museum reproduces a letter of encouragement from the wife of a former Vietnam War POW, urging, "Don't let the bastards get you down Mr. President." This phrase—the exact words used by the residents of the

Hanoi Hilton to survive their brutal treatment by the North Vietnamese—demonstrates a startling incapacity to understand Nixon's critics as anything other than un-American—as being, in fact, at war with America itself. Whatever "inexcusable misjudgments" Nixon may have made during Watergate, they shrink in comparison to the venomous bad faith of the president's enemies, those who, as the museum insists, "ruthlessly exploited those misjudgments as a way to further their own, purely political goals."

Yet, even in this dark time, Nixon found a way to offer redemption—by sacrificing his personal interests for the good of the country. Attempting to rewrite the conventional wisdom that Nixon was *forced* to resign because the June 23, 1972, tape revealed his guilt in the Watergate cover-up, the museum insists that here Nixon regained control of events. The title of this section of reader boards, "The Decision to Resign," emphasizes Nixon's deliberate plan of action, which had everything to do with his love of country. By August 5, 1974, Nixon "had decided that he could not ask the nation to endure the agony of an impeachment debate." Moreover, Bill Clinton's impeachment and Senate trial have proven a useful tool in making this point. During one tour for middle-school students, an excellent docent, skilled at keeping the attention of early adolescents while offering them a fair amount of information, explained Nixon's resignation in these terms: "He got caught. He did wrong. But he didn't have to resign. It was his choice. President Clinton made a choice to see what would happen. President Nixon could have done that too. But President Nixon didn't want to cause problems. He wanted to 'Bring Us Together.'" In this compact little morality play, Bill Clinton's egotism contrasts with a Nixon who so loved his country that he gave up his own presidency rather than prolong a constitutional crisis. With this spin, the museum transforms Watergate shame into glory—Nixon's darkest moment becomes his most presidential.

Like the man himself in his single-minded pursuit of rehabilitation, the Nixon Museum separates means from ends, never permitting facts to obstruct the overall mission. For instance, the reader boards covering the Vietnam War blame the North Vietnamese for torpedoing the fall 1972 peace negotiations without acknowledging that the October agreement failed because South Vietnam refused to sign. Some of the distortions seem shockingly small. Explaining why Nixon returned to a job in Whittier after graduating from Duke Law School rather than go practice law in New York City, the museum neglects to relate that he had no other of-fers, pretending instead that he "decided against starting out in such an expensive city." Other moments border on disinformation. The museum's sloppy version of the Kent State killings—seen in both its bad research and its atrociously edited narrative—implies that the Ohio National Guard responded to immediate threats of violence against them: "The guards-men . . . were pelted wht [sic] rocks and chunks of concrete. Tragically, in the ensuing panic, shots rang out. Four studnets [sic] lay dead." Yet the witness testimony and photographic record of the minutes leading up to the shooting clearly show the National Guard in the process of leaving the scene unmolested; the students closest to the soldiers carried books, not rocks or bricks; and the four students killed were between 265 and 390 feet away. Most unconscionably, the museum's misleading account—with its lapse into the passive voice—professes doubt about the Guard's responsibility for having fired the first shot.[56]

When it comes to Watergate, the museum trades individual distortions for full-blown revisionist history. In particular, the June 23, 1972, White House tape receives a painstaking reinterpretation. At a Watergate hallway listening station, visitors don headphones expecting to hear the famous smoking gun conversation but instead must endure two minutes and twenty-eight seconds of introductory comments. The announcer declares that the tape, long thought to show Nixon's participation in obstruction of justice, is "not what it once appeared to be." Basing its claim on the dubi-ous premise that an attempted obstruction of justice must be successful to be illegal, the museum proposes that Nixon's order to pressure the CIA to impede the FBI investigation of the break-in no longer matters. Rather, as the reader board on the June 23 tape declares, "it is equally important to ask whether the FBI did, in fact, curtail its investigation in response to a request from the CIA." However, this ingenious interpretation seeks to unload the smoking gun after it has already been fired, because the FBI had already slowed its investigation—a point the museum's taped intro-duction implicitly concedes. After confessing that Pat Gray, acting FBI director, complained to Nixon about interference with his agency's efforts, the museum narration offers a new defense: "But if the President set in motion a cover-up, he abruptly ended it two weeks later." Strategically, the museum seeks to rewrite the most famous Watergate question, "What did the president know, and when did he know it?," posing as an alternative, "What did the president do, and when did he do it?" But even this suppos-edly exculpatory formulation doesn't provide absolution. By his decision not to report all that he knew about the break-in, Nixon perpetuated the cover-up, making the real question, perhaps, "What didn't the President do, and when didn't he do it?"[57]

So the museum shamelessly shades, shaves, and, on occasion, shatters the truth to promote Nixon as a symbol of America's traditional values. But, while the worst offender among the various presidential museums, the Nixon Museum's fault is in the degree, not the originality, of the sin. What *has* made it unique is its willingness to commercialize itself and its namesake in order to survive. In its own quirky way, the Nixon Library Gift Shop may well be the ultimate symbol of Richard Nixon's tenacious endurance. Despite its relatively small size, the gift shop overflows with more trinkets than a roadside Stuckey's. In 1997, library officials were boasting that the gift shop had "a higher sales volume per square foot than Bloomingdale's."[58] Its catalog displays a remarkably inventive number of things Nixonian: presidential china patterns, flag lapel pins, books and videos, sportswear, coloring books, and autographed golf balls. In 1993, one could purchase a birdhouse replica of Nixon's birthplace; 2002 saw an appeal to fans of the TV show *Friends*, with "certifiably hip" Nixon "custom surf logo" cappuccino cups. And a virtual cottage industry grew out of items commemorating Elvis Presley's 1970 visit to the Oval Office. They have sold as many as twelve Elvis-meets-Nixon selections: from the expected T-shirts and refrigerator magnets, to whimsical items like the "Nixon and Elvis Throw," a fifty-three- by sixty-five-inch cotton comforter version of the famous Oval Office handshake. But, for sheer chutzpah, what could compete with the library gift shop of a president undone by an illegal break-in and secretly tape-recorded conversations offering, as a child's toy, the "Ultimate Spy Kit"—a package that, among "a range of super-sleuth gadgets," contained "a ready made listening device." The perfect present for any Plumber-wannabes on your holiday gift list. In the Nixon Library Museum Store, the visitor can see most clearly what has been said of the library as a whole, that it is "a shrine to the unstoppable procession of free-market capitalism."[59]

In fact, the gift shop offers only one clue to the library's aggressive commercialism. Other presidential libraries encourage memberships. The Nixon Library practically commands them. On a display stand set several yards in front of the entrance doors, a sign proclaims in bold red type, "Free Admission for Library Members Today and Everyday." Then, in blue ink, starts the sales pitch: "Become a member of the Nixon Library." The next words, the masterstroke, switch back to red: "The only

The Nixon Library Gift Shop produced a multitude of trinkets featuring Nixon and Elvis. But for the truly hard-core fan, no other purchase could match that of the fifty-three- by sixty-five-inch cotton throw that replicated the famous Ollie Atkins photo. Item from author's personal collection. Photo by John Herr Photography.

Presidential Library that does not accept taxpayers' funds," making its financial insecurity part of the hard sell. This vigorous entrepreneurialism defines Nixon's Library. The Sales and Event Department publicizes itself on the website and with a display of "BOOK THE LIBRARY" brochures in the lobby. No event seems beyond the imagination: "Board Meetings, Sales Seminars, . . . Movie Premieres, . . . Silent Auctions, . . . Proms, . . . Holiday Parties, . . . and more." And let's not forget the weddings. As ridiculous as the idea might appear to others, to the true believer, the Nixon Library Rose Garden makes the ideal location for tying the knot. Asked by a clearly incredulous British reporter why they would want to be married at the Nixon Library, one groom-to-be responded, "We always loved Nixon, and I want to feel that he's blessing our union, too." In the first five and one-half years of the library's operation, over one hundred couples had held their weddings at the Nixon Library. By mid-1996, the price of a Rose Garden wedding and reception was a flat fee of $2,500, plus an additional $2.95 for each guest. Nine years later, the number of weddings had quadrupled to more than 450.[60]

Sporting a convenient location, close to major cities, airports, and Disneyland, as the brochure manages to mention twice, the library dubs itself the perfect location for "Truly Presidential Events." In its quest for financial stability, however, the library also developed a penchant for hosting decidedly unpresidential events. On Sunday, May 5, 2002, I visited the Nixon Library, to discover that the parking lot, which runs the length of the better part of a city block, had nearly every space full, even though it was barely past noon. As I prepared to enter, two docents stationed outside the library's entrance asked me if I was there for "the wedding show." Admitting that I was only interested in the museum, I was told to use the exit doors. Those attending the show entered via a rose-topped trellis, marked by signs declaring the program's sponsorship by an Internet wedding planner service. Inside, visitors received a gift bag and then wandered the lobby and the library grounds, perusing the stalls of dance bands, caterers, photographers, limousine services, and travel agents. Over 1,300 persons visited the library that day, but not to learn about Richard Nixon. Yet in such moments we see the Nixon Library enacting advice Nixon's paternal grandfather, Samuel, once gave his family: "Here we are . . . and it's root, hog, or die."[61] Faced with an acute need of money, the library displays a willingness to sell itself to the highest bidder, a disposition that ensures its continued survival, at the cost of degrading itself. The wedding show's trellis and welcoming banners obscured the glass panels displaying inspirational quotations from Nixon's farewell to the White House staff and his first inaugural address, passages that introduce two of the museum's main themes and which are normally the first objects the visitor sees upon entering. Like the lobby, the grounds had mutated into a market of competing vendors hawking their wares—one dance band blared its demo tape while caterers circulated with trays of food. The backyard of Nixon's birthplace became a kind of outdoor café, where people could sample the tuna and caviar canapés and plan their dream weddings.

But in a root, hog, or die world, it is easy to lose sight of one's purpose. By inviting the wedding show onto its grounds, the Nixon Library reveals itself as a true child of the American dream while exposing how pursuing that dream cheapens Nixon's legacy. After passing by the trellis, and unaccountably feeling under surveillance, I spot the eyes of a naked man and woman gazing back at me. Set up on an easel, an elaborately framed black-and-white study of a nude woman and man promotes the work of a specialist in erotic wedding photography. The woman lies on her stomach, awkwardly cradling the man, who rests on his back, his head propped up on the woman's left forearm. How can one even begin cataloging how wildly tacky this thing is? Well, for a start, there's a photo of buck-naked people on display in the lobby of a presidential library. Although some wags might claim that such a thing wouldn't be out of place at the Kennedy or the Clinton libraries, we're talking about Richard Nixon here, a man who wore wingtips to walk on the beach. The president's flag-draped casket had lain in state just a few yards from where this easel now stands. And there's another odd thing: the bride and groom exude as much eroticism as two people waiting at the dentist's to get their teeth cleaned. Strangest of all, nobody seems to notice. The photographer's stall is just one of scores in this one-stop-shopping wedding mall.

This mentality ensures the library's continuance but keeps it from being able to ask questions of appropriateness. One doesn't judge customers; one simply accepts their money. Escaping to the Rose Garden and the Pat Nixon Amphitheater for a snack, I listened to the salsa music play on the sound system while sitting at tables set up in the backyard of the Nixon home, wondering what Hannah would have made of these uninvited guests, if by some quirk of the space-time continuum she should emerge from the kitchen door, mixing bowl in hand, beating fresh California air into her angel food cake batter. Rising to leave, I spotted a large plastic trash can, stenciled in white capital letters with the word NIXON. Just downhill, a mere hors d'oeuvres–toss away, library visitors were paying their graveside respects to Richard and Pat Nixon, ground which has been officially sanctified and deeded to the Society of Friends church.[62] What would this most notoriously private of public couples think about their place of eternal peace being surrounded by milling crowds comparing notes on dance music and assorted finger foods? For, in its insistent commercialism, the Nixon Library and Birthplace becomes just another enterprise on a commercial strip. Across and up Yorba Linda Boulevard stands a mini shopping center named for the Sunkist plant where Hannah Nixon and her sons sometimes worked. Visible from the Nixon Library parking lot, Packing House Square hosts a grab bag of commercial establishments—Gold N Baked Hams, Sylvan Learning Center, California Patio and Spa, and, closest to the library, a real estate office—united by no internal logic other than the ability to pay the rent. Across the street, another strip mall, Yorba Linda Station, decorated in a train motif, competes for customers. Seemingly bent on creating a "Field of Dreams" school of commercial land use, contemporary American developers don't ask about the demand for more retail space, espousing instead the mantra, "If you build it, they will buy." We consume to the limits of our capacities—and beyond. And surviving in our culture generates a lot of trash. Consequently, as the Nixon Library has learned, better buy a big garbage can.

Say what you will, however, the Nixon Library's tenacious survival instinct seems to have made it, like its subject, an illustration of how redemption comes to those who never give up. Though it has struggled financially, losing $1.5 million in its first two years alone, the Nixon facility has always been one of the biggest draws among the presidential libraries, holding steady at between 150,000 to 200,000 visitors a year.[63] And years of determined struggle have eventually brought a more solid financial future. Understanding that his library's continued existence depended upon the growth of its endowment, Nixon instituted a lawsuit to be compensated for his confiscated presidential papers, resulting, six years after his death, in an $18 million settlement that netted the Library Foundation $6 million.[64] When the Nixon sisters mediated their much-publicized battle over whether the Nixon Foundation would be headed by a large professionalized board of directors or a small family-controlled one, the Nixon Library, flush with the $20 million bequest from Bebe Rebozo's estate released by the daughters' settlement, was ready for its final campaign—transfer of Nixon's tapes and papers to Yorba Linda and entrance into the NARA system.[65] While it constructed a $15 million extension, nearly doubling the building's size and including an East Room replica, more gallery space, and a basement archival and research area, the library hired a Washington firm to lobby Congress to change the Watergate-era prohibition against Nixon's presidential materials leaving the nation's capital. By February 2005, the library had gained an understanding that it would become part of the federal system, which saw fulfillment in October 2006 with the arrival of Dr. Timothy Naftali, a Cold War historian and expert in presidential recordings, as the first federal director of the Nixon Library. Less than a year later, on July 11, 2007, the National Archives made the transfer to the federal government official: the Richard Nixon Library and the Birthplace was now the Richard Nixon Presidential Library and Museum.[66]

Despite harsh critiques, the revised standard version of mainstream America's orthodox myths and ideology—absent any real challenges to

*As visitors pay respects on the sanctified ground of the grave sites, a trash can stenciled "NIXON"
stands under one of the pepper trees planted by Frank Nixon ready to receive the garbage of the
wedding show customers. Photo by Joel W. Martin.*

it—didn't just survive; it thrived. When Saddam Hussein invaded Kuwait
two weeks to the day after the library's dedication ceremony, President
Bush put together a combination of diplomatic and military responses
that was positively Nixonian in outlook—a UN Security Council Resolution supporting a worldwide coalition of American-led troops in Operation Desert Storm. Firmly defending U.S. economic interests in the world
(the Persian Gulf region supplied the United States with 25 percent of
its oil), Bush also put the upcoming war in the context of the myth of national mission, labeling Hussein as "worse than Hitler" and defining the
struggle as one to liberate a captive nation.[67] The next year, then defense
secretary Dick Cheney and his deputy undersecretary Paul Wolfowitz endorsed the Defense Planning Guidance, a strategy for the United States to
"maintain unrivaled superpower status as a colossus against all comers,"
a stance that seemed taken from the pages of Nixon's many foreign policy
tomes.[68]

Meanwhile, social conservatives took up Nixon's language of the jeremiad, so dominant in his memoirs and in *In the Arena*, to warn about America's moral decline. Forming a growing chorus of conservative naysayers, books like Dinesh D'Souza's *Illiberal Education* (1990), Robert Bork's *The Tempting of America* (1990), and William Bennett's *The De-valuing of America* (1992) fulminated against a decadent culture that fostered "sexual immorality, violent crime, vulgarity and sensationalism in the media, schools without standards, trash that passed as 'art,' and just plain bad taste."[69] Far from cries of despair, these pronouncements, like all jeremiads, were meant to rally the troops for battle. Former Nixon speechwriter Pat Buchanan, expanding his former boss's southern (and northern white working-class) strategy, ran a guerrilla campaign against the first Bush in the 1992 Republican primaries, raising the specter of unregulated abortion and a society dominated by feminist and homosexual threats to "family values." Sounding the alarm, Buchanan prophesied that the United States faced "a cultural war as critical to the kind of nation we shall be as the Cold War itself. This war is for the soul of America."[70]

The energy released by such alarms generated political success, when, in 1994, Newt Gingrich and the Republicans took control of the House of Representatives away from the Democrats, promising a "Contract with America" that glorified individual initiative and small government. Doing much to lead the groundswell of the so-called Republican Revolution of the 1990s, radio and TV commentator Rush Limbaugh preached his version of the American dream—"people being free, to do the best they could for themselves using the original American culture of rugged individualism, self-reliance, virtue, [and] honesty." On his television program, he sent a camera crew out into Manhattan to take a sampling of public opinion on the question, "Is the American dream dead?" Limbaugh presented clips of eight individuals as his proof that, even in cynical New York City, the dream lives on. "The key today is people have to work," one man declared. "We have too many people in our society today that do not want to work. They expect the government and the welfare system to support them." Another man held fast to the belief that anyone can make it in America, regardless of race, color, or creed: "Greater opportunities are available to everyone," he lectured. "You just have to find them." As the video clip of this man played, Limbaugh's own voice chorused his agreement: "*That's* the key!"[71]

Similar to his role in the Reagan renaissance, Richard Nixon was seen by some as the ideological founding ancestor for Limbaugh, Gingrich, and the "Contract with America." On November 11, 1994, opening the first *Saturday Night Live* to air after the Republicans' stunning election victory, "It's a Wonderful Newt," a parody of the Frank Capra classic "It's a Wonderful Life" suggested the genealogical lines between Nixon and Gingrich, the new Speaker of the House. With a slouching walk, hands clasped in front of his body, and a leering smile, guest host John Turturro threw himself into an oddly manic impersonation, a weird hybrid of Nixon, Ed Sullivan, and Groucho Marx. Set at Christmastime in 1998, the sketch shows Gingrich, ready to commit suicide because $8,000 is missing from the House Bank, wishing that he had never become Speaker. His guardian angel, Richard Nixon, telling Newt that he had had a wonderful life, takes him on a trek through a Gingrich-less Washington, D.C., a place where affirmative action was never rescinded, Martini's Gun Shop became Martini's Minority Teen Empowerment Center and Abortion Clinic, and, worst of all, Hillary Clinton sits in the Oval Office. Waking from his nightmare, Gingrich happily embraces his life as Speaker. Without doubt, the politics of this satire are readily apparent. Responding at the sketch's opening to Gingrich's certainty that Nixon had made it into heaven, the ex-president stammers, "Ah, not quite, but I'm working on it." And, at the conclusion of the skit, Gingrich's wife discovers an autographed copy of *RN*, and reads the inscription: "Every time a bell rings, I get poked in the ass with a pitchfork." The writers may hate what these two men stand for, but they clearly believe that these Republicans share the same political DNA.

So pervasive was Nixon's presence that even Gingrich and company's hated political opponents showed his influence. Bill Clinton, the only effective Democratic president in the last quarter of the twentieth century, took many of his successes from the Nixon playbook. The crime bill Clinton steered through Congress in 1994, with 100,000 new police nationwide, construction of new prisons, and a "three strikes and you're out" provision, denying parole to individuals convicted of three federal law violations, smacked of the law and order measures, like the D.C. Crime Bill, proposed by the Nixon administration. Clinton's vocal support of the Defense of Marriage Act of 1996, affirming marriage as an exclusively heterosexual union, played well with some children of the Silent Majority generation.[72] And, in keeping a campaign promise to "end welfare as we know it," Clinton's passage of the Personal Responsibility and Work Opportunity Act" delivered what Nixon's failed Family Assistance Plan could only dream of achieving.[73] Part of the visceral hatred of Clinton by conservative Republicans may have come from the political threat posed by his embrace and successful co-optation of some mythic narratives that they felt belonged to them.

More recently, after Arnold Schwarzenegger became governor of California, the Nixon Library made sure that Americans knew that even the Terminator also belonged to Nixon's political family. Running for governor in 2003, and again at the Republican National Convention in 2004, Schwarzenegger spun a mythic tale about his 1968 immigration from Austria to a United States where everything seemed "so big, . . . so open, so possible." Watching that year's presidential campaign unfold, Schwarzenegger decided he was a Republican, because Richard Nixon, who spoke "about free enterprise, getting the government off your back, lowering the taxes and strengthening the military," was Republican.[74] Although not quite equaling its Nixon and Elvis series, nevertheless the Museum Store quickly turned out coffee mugs, key chains, and T-shirts with a photo of Schwarzenegger and Nixon in front of the Nixon Library seal and the words "I am a Republican because of Richard Nixon" printed at the bottom.

Clearly, then, never giving up had its advantages. Because the political Left has not offered a mythic alternative, and because some of its members subscribed to the traditional stories, Nixon and his ideological children have successfully reasserted themselves in the debate over national identity. Because of its tunnel-visioned view of history, *Nixon in China* allows us to celebrate the foreign policy genius without having to deal with the lawbreaking politician. By refusing to face up to the full meaning and legacy of Watergate, Richard Nixon begins, in *In the Arena*, to reinvent himself as the sage of Saddle River, an elder statesman sharing his wisdom with the nation. And with its tailoring of the truth to fit its overriding message, as well as its succumbing to crassly commercial instincts, the Nixon Library venerates the memory of a man who refused to acknowledge the meaning of the word "quit." These and other messages about the power of individual achievement and persistence survive—if in a revised standard version—ready to fight on in the cultural wars to define the meaning and direction of the United States.

CHAPTER SEVEN

NIXON, NOW MORE
THAN EVER

Who could possibly embroil Thomas the Tank Engine in controversy? Yes, Nixon's the one! On April 27, 1994, the morning of Nixon's funeral, the New York City and Washington, D.C., public television stations aired a *Shining Time Station* episode in which the town's mayor battles for reelection against a "mysterious" newcomer known as "Mr. Richhouse." *Shining Time Station*, a program geared for preschoolers, combined live-action segments set in the Shining Time village train depot with model-train stagings of the famous Thomas the Tank Engine series of children's stories.[1] Parents watching the episode would have had little difficulty in identifying the historical source for the Richhouse character, who was portrayed by Nixon impersonator Richard Dixon. In addition to the choice of guest actor and the blending of Nixon's first and middle names, the episode trotted out familiar Nixon mannerisms and rhetorical formulations. When the press photographer instructs the mayor's opponent to just "look natural," he switches on a big grin and flashes the two-armed "V for victory" salute. Addressing the crowd as "my fellow Shining Timers," Richhouse declares that "some of my enemies" have questioned his reasons for entering the mayor's race.[2] Seeing those parallels and angered at this episode being shown on the national day of mourning for Richard Nixon, twenty-two people called to complain. Their outrage elicited immediate public apologies.[3]

Viewed dispassionately, though, the episode hardly ridicules Nixon. Instead, Shining Time's incumbent mayor, Osgood Flopdinger, takes the comic pratfalls. Hoping to avoid having to listen to the townspeople's complaints, Flopdinger hires Shining Time Station's resident bad boy, a character named Schemer, to be his campaign manager. In exchange for the position of "Secretary of Money," Schemer shares his "system of success" with Flopdinger—a plan that people vote based only on the candidate's appearance. When the mayor's attempts to follow this system backfire, Flopdinger fires Schemer and apologizes to the voters. With this atonement, the mayor wins reelection by one vote. In defeat, Richhouse proves a gracious loser, confessing to the children of Shining Time that he will move on from town to town, looking for a chance to serve, because "I've made some mistakes in the past, but, if I ever win another election, I *promise* you my only job will be to help *all* the people." Assuming a teacher's role with the children, he explains the democratic process: "Any politician who gets elected who doesn't try to help *all* the people doesn't deserve to win."

Yet, on this day, even an avuncular reinvention of Nixon raised hackles. Hours before the eulogizers and the talking heads prattled on about national reconciliation, we had convincing evidence that such talk was a polite charade. Certainly no one called in because a toddler was distraught that *Shining Time Station* had been mean to Richard Nixon. One can only imagine the festering resentments, the sense of a lifetime of media injustice toward, and lack of public appreciation for, their hero that could drive adults to find fault with this gentle program. Taken as a microcosm, the *Shining Time Station* episode encapsulates the entire period of Nixon's illness and death. For if we look at the media coverage and people's reactions during this time, we find that almost no one was satisfied. Belying all the rhetoric of national healing, the old hostilities surfaced again. Liberals (and some right-wing critics) complained that Nixon received embarrassingly glowing treatment, while other conservatives protested even the smallest of perceived slights, taking them as evidence that the media was kicking their hero around yet one last time. And, in the years since the funeral, the fight over Nixon and his meaning in U.S. culture has continued, particularly during the Clinton impeachment. At the same time, creative artists in theater, film, and literature have given hints of a possible new Nixon story: one that doesn't abandon a critical perspective but that treats the man with sympathy and forgiveness. But this new healing possibility seems lost on both Nixon loyalists and critics, who insistently, and undeviatingly, stick to their mythic story lines and their views of the United States. Over a decade after his death, he's still not bringing us together. Nixon, now more than ever, symbolizes cultural division.

During the period of national remembrance, some voices on the left complained that the media failed miserably in speaking the truth about Richard Nixon: at best, giving him a bye, and, at worst, whitewashing his crimes. Russell Baker led the chorus, complaining of "a group conspiracy to grant him absolution." Garry Trudeau offered a visual representation of the rush to suspend judgment on the former president with reprints of some of his *Doonesbury* strips, altered to suit "contemporary standards." Thus, the famous May 29, 1973, panel of disc jockey Mark Slackmeyer, drunk on Nixon-hatred, chanting "He's guilty, guilty, guilty, guilty," gets a new look. Now Nixon is "flawed, flawed, flawed, flawed."[4] In truth, there were plenty of media voices that did praise the man. ABC opened its evening news broadcast on Saturday, April 23, by declaring that Nixon was "finally being remembered the way he wanted to be: as a loyal friend, a respected states-man, and a world visionary."[5] For its part, the *Dallas Morning News* urged a reevaluation of his legacy: "History ultimately should show that despite his flaws, he was one of our most farsighted chief executives."[6] The obitu-aries most often praised his doggedness. In the *Baltimore Sun*, Jules Wit-cover, noting Nixon's lifelong ride on "a political rollercoaster that might have broken a less determined man," paid tribute to a person who liked to describe himself as one who would "keep fighting . . . when it seem[ed] that the odds are the greatest."[7] Of course, the media also praised his vision and achievements in foreign policy. Syndicated cartoonist Ranan Lurie's April 26, 1994, drawing depicts a faceless figure labeled "History," standing in the clouds, measuring the importance of Watergate versus China, with Nixon's foreign policy achievement decidedly outweighing the scandal. Dressed in a white robe and with angel's wings protruding from his back, Nixon appreciatively accepts heaven's judgment that "Richard, you've earned your halo."[8] But the press also noted a growing reappraisal of Nixon's handling of national affairs. The obituary stories almost uni-versally noted that the Environmental Protection Agency (EPA) and the Occupational Safety and Health Administration (OSHA) were founded during the Nixon administration; that he proposed the Family Assistance Plan, which amounted to a guaranteed income for the poor; and that his Justice Department moved ahead with school desegregation in the South. Even George McGovern suggested that his 1972 opponent ended up being "pretty good on domestic policy."[9]

Moreover, some of these songs of praise *did* proclaim Nixon's com-plete rehabilitation. The *Montgomery (AL) Advertiser* perceived redeeming life lessons in the post-resignation period: "He dealt with his downfall with class—no whining, no excuses." Meanwhile, William Safire anointed Nixon "America's greatest *ex*-president." The *Cleveland Plain Dealer's* editorial cartoonist visualized this improbable reinstatement, showing a marble Nixon taking a long stride to reach the top of the pedestal for his

Garry Trudeau protested what he saw as revisionist history after Nixon's death by altering some of his earlier Doonesbury *comic strips to match the nonjudgmental mood of the day.* DOONESBURY © 1994 G. B. Trudeau. Reprinted with permission of UNIVERSAL PRESS SYNDICATE. All rights reserved.

statue in a gallery of the "Most Important Figures of This Century." The inscription shows Nixon's triumph over his past; the judgment "Redeemed Statesman" erases his status as a "Disgraced President."[10] But even more than the perspectives of pundits and politicians, the voices of ordinary citizens figured in much of the media coverage during Nixon's illness, death, and funeral. From Monday, April 25, through Wednesday, April 27, the national outpouring of affection and respect dominated the news. When the library opened for mourners, an estimated 42,000 people filed past Nixon's coffin, waiting in a line that, at its height, extended for three miles, weaving in and out of cul-de-sacs. One woman reported an almost transcendent moment, claiming the "most emotional experience I've been through, including my marriage and the birth of my children."[11]

Despite these celebrations, however, nowhere in the coverage of Nixon's death did Watergate go unmentioned. The first paragraphs of newspaper stories, if not the leads, almost invariably featured the scandal. Often we were reminded of Nixon's disgrace even before being informed of his death.[12] The *Dallas Morning News* opened its obituary with a syntactically tortuous sentence that veered from disgrace toward praise and back to disgrace again—all without mentioning the subject's demise: "Richard Nixon, forced by the Watergate scandal to resign as president after a tumultuous career that ranged from crusades against Communists at home to accommodation with them abroad, was the most controversial president in modern American history." With few exceptions, editorial pages reminded us of Nixon's failings—and his corruption. The *Baltimore Sun* dubbed Nixon "the angriest president," a leader who possessed neither "greatness" nor "virtue." And, twenty years later, Watergate still didn't play in Peoria, Illinois. The *Journal-Star* summed up Nixon's presidency as a "sad triumph of cynicism over potential." Jack Ohman, editorial cartoonist for the *Portland Oregonian*, captured the inevitable duality of Nixon's legacy by rendering a Nixon Memorial made up of two opposing statues. The Foreign Policy Nixon strides over the Great Wall of China, an olive branch in his extended hand. But this progress toward world peace is about to be suffocated by a noose leading back to the second Nixon statue, this one on a pedestal labeled "Watergate." The rope turns out to be audiotape, and an oblivious Watergate Nixon, headphones over his ears, intent on trampling on the Constitution, cannot see that he is about to hang his more virtuous alter ego.[13]

Throughout the period of Nixon's death and funeral, Russell Baker's complaints to the contrary, numerous columnists and commentators reminded us of Nixon's dark side. Frank Rich, in the *New York Times*, equated Nixon-hating with patriotic duty, asserting that he had "learned to despise Richard Nixon around the same time I learned to recite the Pledge of Allegiance." Tom Teepen, of the *Atlanta Journal-Constitution*, blamed Nixon for making "the party of Lincoln into the party of white backlash," a cynical elevation of political pragmatism over idealism from which we have yet to recover. Even his much-vaunted resilience came under fire. Dick Feagler, in his *Cleveland Plain Dealer* column, found nothing praiseworthy in Nixon's refusal to quit: "He kept getting up from the canvas because he lacked the ability to know when he was disgraced. Only drunks, buffoons, and politicians count that as a virtue."[14] Letters to the editor and "on the street" polls also elicited more than just celebratory eulogies. Of the twelve people the *Manchester (NH) Union Leader* asked about Nixon's legacy, only three had entirely positive assessments. A man named Nixon, from the Portland, Oregon, area, brutally dismissed the person he claimed as a cousin: "He was a selfish [expletive deleted] whose most precious legacy to this nation is the resonant reminder that people should not trust their elected representatives." Meanwhile, one reader of the *Atlanta Journal-Constitution* refused to participate in the national day of remembrance, declaring flatly, "I will not mourn him."[15]

Yet this balance in media coverage pleased almost no one. Certain liberals seemed content only if Nixon received no credit for having done anything worthwhile. Syndicated columnist Donald Kaul, still stewing over Kent State, the Christmas bombing of Hanoi, the secret war in Cambodia,

To capture the complexity of the Nixon legacy, Jack Ohman, editorial cartoonist for the Portland Oregonian, drew dual monuments, showing the promising achievements of Nixon's foreign policy being sacrificed by the paranoid, criminal excesses of Watergate. © Tribune Media Services, Inc. All rights reserved. Reprinted with permission.

and the masked racism of the southern strategy, wondered aloud as to why this "anti-Christ" deserved a national day of mourning, nearly spitting: "So what if he's had a bad week and is dead? He's still Richard Nixon."[16] By contrast, a few voices from the Republican right wing couldn't forgive what they saw as Nixon's apostasy. Robert D. Novak spoke best for them when he cataloged Nixon's sins: betraying Taiwan, selling out the South Vietnamese in order to get a peace agreement with Hanoi, tilting the balance of power toward the Soviets by pursuing détente, and extending the Great Society. "All that was really 'conservative' about the Nixon administration," he observed, "was its futile effort to slow racial integration in the South."[17]

For their part, the Nixon loyalists bristled at *any* criticism. A caller to C-SPAN's *Sunday Journal* program on April 24, 1994, declared that "now [was] the time to put away all those foolish things that we don't like about a man, . . . give up criticizing him and show a little more compassion, a little more kindness, and a little more grace." Many local-reaction stories and letters to the editor in newspapers across the country defended Nixon and attacked the idea that there was anything that needed defending in the first place. At a gathering of his Whittier College classmates, Hubert Perry, the son of the man who solicited Nixon to run for Congress in 1946, insisted that Watergate had "been blown completely out of proportion," that the scandal contained absolutely "no moral implications," and lectured the press to "quit calling it a crime. It was a sad misunderstanding."[18]

A late April and early May 1994 cycle of editorial cartoons, juxtaposed with responding letters to the editor, play out on a small scale these conflicting responses to Nixon's death. Creating a whole new subgenre in the history of caricatures of the former president, these cartoons could be called the "Richard Nixon at the pearly gates" series. Some of them were celebratory, like the Ranan Lurie cartoon or the sketch by Rob Rogers of the *Pittsburgh Post-Gazette* showing Nixon striding in triumph through the gates of heaven, arms waggling his familiar "V" salute.[19] In an interesting reversal, Dick Locher, the *Chicago Tribune* cartoonist, had St. Peter offer the victory sign while he inscribes Nixon's name in the heavenly rolls. A few seemed relatively neutral. Dana Summers, of the *Orlando (FL) Sentinel*, pictures St. Peter leaning over his podium outside Heaven, calling out "Next," as Nixon's arms, outstretched in his trademark gesture, emerge through the clouds.[20] John Trevor, the cartoonist for the *Albuquerque (NM) Journal*, depicts a sheepish St. Peter reporting to another angel that, when Nixon sat on the heavenly scale of justice, the enormous weight of his contradictions broke the scale.[21] In Jim Borgman's drawing in the *Cincinnati (OH) Enquirer*, St. Peter orders his administrative assistant to "cancel my appointments," as Nixon waves his ubiquitous four-fingered greeting and makes his claim for entrance into heaven. Before St. Peter sit two equally overstuffed files, one labeled "Good Dick" and the other "Bad Dick."[22] Then there are those cartoons that cannot forgive Nixon's sins. In a Bill Schorr sketch, which originally appeared in the *Kansas City (MO) Star*, St. Peter admonishes a hump-shouldered Nixon: "You're in luck. *He* doesn't keep an 'enemies list.'"[23] Other critics could not imagine that Richard Nixon would throw himself on the mercy of even the most forgiving jury. Joe Heller, of the *Green Bay (Wisconsin) Gazette*, pictures Nixon at heaven's admissions desk, his cat-who-ate-the-canary expression telling all, as a befuddled St. Peter thumbs through his papers, wondering aloud who could possibly have stolen the Nixon file from his office. Suggesting that Nixon would never even have risked such an interview, the *Philadelphia Inquirer*'s Tony Auth draws St. Peter discovering the Pearly Gates with the lock picked and a "Welcome President Nixon" banner hanging above.[24]

Within days of these last three cartoons' publications, incensed letters to the editor illustrate the passions that Richard Nixon continued to inspire. One woman, from Peoria, Illinois, declared the Schorr cartoon "disgusting" and seemed ready to enlist in a reconstituted Plumbers unit: "I would like to look into the background of each and everyone of you who works at the *Journal Star* and see if your life has been without sin."[25] In Boise, Idaho, seven people complained about the Joe Heller drawing.[26] Within days of the Tony Auth piece appearing in the *Philadelphia Inquirer*, the paper published two letters upbraiding the artist. One writer, pronouncing the piece as a failed effort "to settle some type of score against Mr. Nixon," suggested that if Auth found cartoons about the dead funny, the *Inquirer* "should consider a continuing series. Vince Foster [Bill Clinton's Deputy White House counsel who committed suicide in 1993] could be the next subject."[27]

And so the battle continued—with the outcome far from certain. Jeff Koterba's cartoon in the *Omaha World-Herald* displayed an awareness that Nixon's legacy was not likely to be resolved in the near future. In this drawing, America looks eagerly over the shoulder of an artist labeled "History," who sits before a huge framed canvas, which already has a nameplate reading "Nixon." Trying to get some working room, History urges his audience to sit down, implying that the process will take some time, because "this portrait is a little more complicated than most."[28]

Since 1994, the contest to define Nixon and the United States has continued to simmer. During the Clinton impeachment and trial, it boiled over—with Nixon serving as a touchstone for all sides. Right-wing pundits wallowed in Watergate analogies as they made their case. For them, Richard Nixon served as a weapon to confirm the corruption of Bill Clinton and the hypocrisy of his liberal defenders. Former Reagan secretary of education William J. Bennett, in his 1998 book *The Death of Outrage: Bill Clinton and the Assault on American Ideals*, compared Clinton's handling of his scandals to Richard Nixon's defenses during Watergate. Bennett makes his argument almost solely by juxtaposing the words of Clinton and his defenders against those of Nixon, suggesting from the rhetorical similarities of the language used in both cases that anyone who found

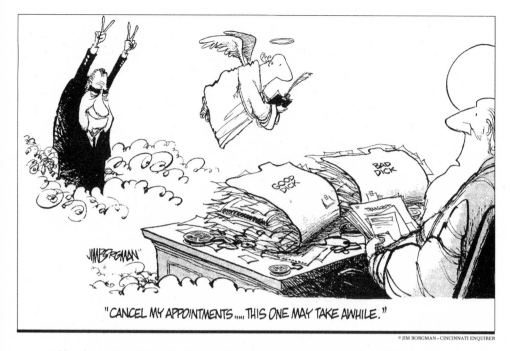

"CANCEL MY APPOINTMENTS ..... THIS ONE MAY TAKE AWHILE."

Unlike Ohman, Jim Borgman, Cincinnati Enquirer *editorial cartoonist, found it harder to predict history's verdict on Nixon. JIM BORGMAN* © *1994* Cincinnati Enquirer. *Reprinted with permission of UNIVERSAL PRESS SYNDICATE. All rights reserved.*

Watergate significant would, in all honesty, have the same response to Clinton. In fact, for some, the Watergate parallels offered a way to argue that Clinton's offenses were *worse* than Nixon's. In *High Crimes and Misdemeanors: The Case against Bill Clinton* (1998), Ann H. Coulter appropriated John Dean's Watergate metaphor of a "cancer growing on the presidency" to minimize Nixon's faults while maximizing Clinton's transgressions. Now, as one of Coulter's chapter titles indicated, the "Cancer [Was] on the Country." Depicted as the work "of some bad apples who had worked their way into positions of influence," Coulter's version makes Watergate seem entirely removed from Nixon. Unlike Clinton, who is personally culpable, Nixon merely suffered a "staffing problem."[29]

In the political battle that was the real-life impeachment struggle, the meaning of Richard Nixon and Watergate shifted, depending upon which side of the aisle the member of Congress sat. *Washington Post* reporter Peter Baker claimed that Republicans and Democrats alike looked to use the impeachment crisis of twenty years before, "each side interpreting

Watergate to its own favor, embracing its lessons when they were useful and dismissing them when they were not." Republican representative Steve Buyer of Indiana, in presenting the case to the Senate, also echoed John Dean's words, arguing that "the impeachment process is intended to cleanse the executive . . . office when it is plagued with such a cancer as perjury or obstruction of justice." Senator Phil Gramm of Texas, in casting his guilty votes, compared Clinton to Nixon, to the younger man's disadvantage: "Nixon had some shame" and had resigned rather than put the country through the ordeal of impeachment and trial in the Senate. By contrast, Representative John Conyers of Michigan, who sat on the House Judiciary Committee that approved the articles of impeachment against both men, scoffed at the Republican efforts against Bill Clinton, harrumphing at all the hysteria over nothing more than a matter of marital infidelity. In making their case before the Senate, the president's lawyers used a similar "it ain't Watergate" line of defense. In the analogy between the two presidents, both sides could avoid coming to terms with the real culpability of their heroes. The Nixon partisans could diminish the import of Watergate, and the Clinton supporters escaped facing the seriousness of the legally questionable means employed to frustrate Ken Starr's investigation of the president's relationship with Monica Lewinsky.[30]

Editorial cartoonists enjoyed skewering liberals with the uncomfortable parallels between this Democratic president and their despised archenemy. In a March 25, 1998, cartoon, Ben Sargent drew Nixon teaching Clinton the joys of impeding investigations through claims of executive privilege. Throughout the late spring and summer of 1998, several cartoons appeared that referred to the White House tape in which Nixon instructed his staff to "stonewall it." Most notable was the July 28, 1998, Oliphant sketch in which Nixon, observing Clinton's work building a wall around the White House, offers the compliment, "You do nice stonewall." During the 1998 Christmas season, Stuart Carlson couldn't resist the Dickens "Christmas Carol" opportunities, drawing Nixon as Marlow's Ghost, telling Scrooge/Clinton that "I Wear the Chains Forged in Life"—to which the ever-empathetic Commiserater-in-Chief responds, "I Feel Your Chains." Yet, in the end, some cartoonists backed off the Nixon/Clinton analogies, wanting to draw some distinctions between the two. Tony Auth, who started 1998 with his own "Christmas Carol" cartoon, using Nixon's ghost to warn about Clinton's future, concluded the year by asserting that whatever Clinton's guilt, it was of a far lesser level than Nixon's. His December 9, 1998, drawing shows a towering Nixon—labeled as "Genuine

WITNESS FOR THE DEFENSE

GENUINE HIGH CRIMES

AUTH

12-9-98 THE PHILADELPHIA INQUIRER. UNIVERSAL PRESS SYNDICATE.

Throughout the impeachment deliberations and the Senate trial, Bill Clinton's defenders and his prosecutors relied on comparisons to Richard Nixon and the Watergate scandal. The Philadelphia Inquirer's *Tony Auth initially was part of the group of editorial cartoonists who saw similarities between Clinton and Nixon. But, by the time the House of Representatives was preparing to vote on the articles of impeachment, Auth had changed his mind. AUTH ©1998 The Philadelphia* Inquirer. *Reprinted with permission of UNIVERSAL PRESS SYNDICATE. All rights reserved.*

High Crimes"—being called as a witness for the defense in the upcoming Clinton impeachment trial.

Interestingly, *Saturday Night Live* provided one of the few balanced assessments of the two scandals. In a September 1998 "Fun with Real Audio" cartoon, creator Robert Smigel took the audio track of Clinton's speech to the nation following his grand jury testimony, animating it as a series of outtakes. As Clinton tries to plead his innocence, Special Prosecutor Kenneth Starr continually pops in behind the president displaying evidence of his guilt—a blue dress, a pair of women's dress shoes, even a goat, all dripping with semen. Suddenly, Richard Nixon's ghost materializes, rips the text from Clinton's hands, and begins dictating the words from his own resignation speech. The audio track then skips quickly from the resignation to the "I am not a crook" press conference, to the Checkers speech. What seems to start as an elder statesman recommending the high road ends up as a reminder of Nixon's scandal-filled career. Rather than take the advice, Clinton calls on the Secret Service to arrest the ethereal Nixon. Instead, the ghost president takes possession of Clinton's body, forcing him to speak the words from Nixon's farewell to the White House staff: "Always remember, those who hate you don't win, unless you hate them. And then you destroy yourself." As Nixon's spirit departs, Clinton and Starr embrace, a national reconciliation that lasts for a few seconds— until, doglike, Clinton tries to hump Starr's leg.[31] This satire doesn't give either side exactly what it's looking for. On the one hand, the cartoon seems to propose resignation as the selfless choice, while alternatively it renders Clinton's sins farcical and less serious than Watergate. Far from showing any signs of dissipating, the battle to define Richard Nixon and his meaning for American culture raged on.

But, in the years following his death, some re-creations of the man began to imagine new ways to represent him. Developing a line of thought that had surfaced as early as the mid-1970s, Neil Young's song "The Campaigner" had made what for many was the astonishing claim that "even Richard Nixon has got soul." And a number of dramatists, screenwriters, novelists, and short story writers found ways to envision Richard Nixon that included not just understanding but even some measure of acceptance and forgiveness.[32] Opening in a March 1996 Off-Broadway production by the Shubert Organization after a September 1995 premiere by the Manhattan Class Company Theater, Russell Lees's *Nixon's Nixon* takes the famous last meeting between Nixon and Kissinger before the resignation as a starting point for a new story. After a highly successful New York run, the play received a major staging every year for the next eight years throughout the United States, as well as in Edinburgh, London, Toronto, Hong Kong, and Sydney. In each city it collected critical raves, like Vincent Canby's gushing *New York Times* review of the Off-Broadway production, which proclaimed *Nixon's Nixon* as "both a serious work of the imagination and a fully realized political satire of the sort that American theater seldom sees." In the fall of 2006, the Manhattan Class Company Theater staged a well-received tenth-anniversary revival of the play with the original cast members.[33]

Central to the play's success is its refusal to turn Richard Nixon into a cartoon. Lawrence Van Gelder, reviewing the play's 1995 opening, remarked on Lees's admirable restraint in dealing with an easy target: "The Nixon of 'Nixon's Nixon' is a rounded portrait: a powerful President, a formidable statesman, a wily politician, a foul-mouthed adversary, a wounded animal loathing himself as the instrument of his destruction."[34] Taking the few agreed-upon elements of the event—the president and Henry Kissinger meeting in the Lincoln Sitting Room and eventually kneeling together in prayer—Lees speculates that what went on between these two powerful men was the play-acting of one scene after another: Brezhnev meeting Nixon and Nixon meeting Mao—even invented dialogues between Golda Meir and Henry Kissinger and between Julie Nixon Eisenhower and her father. Initially at least, this role-playing, far from a frivolous distraction, offers Nixon a Watergate survival strategy: to outlast the scandal by acting like himself. "Americans like fighters. Underdogs. The scrappier the better. That's me, now. . . . Now I'm the guy to root for." In fact, he believes that this role explains his success: "I appeal to the Richard Nixon in everybody."[35] But Nixon's Nixon is just a front. Having hidden too long behind his public persona, Nixon now finds that the mask no longer comes off, leaving him without any core values. Sensing this vacuum, Kissinger goads his boss, mocking the president's obsessive private replaying of the White House tapes as a futile attempt "to discover an inner, more honorable Nixon." In his more honest moments, Nixon confesses the terrible moral consequences of his kind of success: "But then I fell. I fell like Satan tossed from Heaven." Like Milton's Satan, preferring to rule in hell rather than serve in heaven, Nixon readily sacrificed everything to get his hands on power.[36]

Deciding that he must, under no circumstances, give up the presidency, Nixon conscripts Kissinger into service by blackmailing him with the release of incriminating White House tapes. The secretary of state's task is to covertly provoke an international incident with the potential to escalate into a nuclear superpower showdown that only the president would have the foreign policy credentials to avert. Improvising through this scenario, Nixon stumbles upon a brilliant confidence game: begging for the public's forbearance on impeachment until he can avert Armageddon, he will promise to resign once the job is done. After such a gesture, Nixon reasons that the people will deem him indispensable and demand his return to public life. Although the plan calls for Nixon to step in and save the world, both men—at this stage drunk with alcohol as well as with their own sense of omnipotence—seem seduced by their power to destroy. Dialing the CIA, Nixon orders the telephone operator to "blow the fuckers up. . . . Start with small fuckers, then blow up bigger and bigger fuckers."[37]

Yet, having forged the weapon by which he can hold on to the presidency, Lees's Nixon discovers a conscience that refuses to let him pull the trigger. Overwhelmed by his capacity for evil, he turns reflective, forcing Kissinger to recite their shared death toll, numbering 800,005, from Vietnam, Cambodia, Laos, the Chilean coup (including Salvador Allende), and the four students at Kent State. As if only just comprehending the magnitude of his guilt, Nixon wonders how he can continue: "Now I spend the rest of my days wading in a swimming pool of blood?" At this point, Lees re-creates the famous moment of Nixon in prayer not as satiric send-up but as a soul-searching moment of wrestling with sin and its atonement: "Here I am, on my *knees*. Just to get You to help me realize that sometimes the courageous thing isn't to struggle on. Sometimes, it takes more courage, more honor to, to throw in the towel."[38] Before he can go through the public performance of resignation, however, Nixon needs one more round of role-playing—this time, to beg forgiveness of his daughter: "Julie. I did do things. I did. And if I let you go saying over and over that I hadn't—it's just that nobody ever showed me that much love before. I didn't know how to tell you that your dad was a bum." Moved by Nixon's remorse, Kissinger, speaking as Julie, offers a daughter's pardon. Reassured, Nixon faces the humiliating pageant of his exile, launching into the words from his farewell to the White House staff. As sounds of a helicopter fade in, he acts out the famous goodbye wave, having finally lost himself in a truly heroic role. Suddenly, the resignation, which Nixon had conspired to make *appear* statesmanlike, actually becomes a noble act. Faced with the death and destruction his will to power has caused, Nixon finally says "no more." To everyone's surprise, Lees's play discovers the impossible—"an inner, more honorable," Richard Nixon.[39]

Oliver Stone's film *Nixon*, released on December 20, 1995, also gives us an unusually sympathetic portrait of a man driven to destruction by his desire for success.[40] Yet the idea that *Nixon* might be participating in a fresh evaluation of the man and the country he led often got overshadowed by the controversy generated by most Oliver Stone efforts of this period. Almost from the start, the film struggled against adversity: the lead role took time to fill (Stone reportedly considered Tom Hanks, Robin Williams, and Dustin Hoffman, among others, before deciding on Anthony Hopkins); the first producer backed out just two months before filming was set to begin; and the film failed to make up its $43 million production costs, grossing a mere $13 million in the two months after its release.[41] Still, the movie, and particularly the media's discussion of it, reached possibly the largest audience of any reinvention of Richard Nixon. At its height, *Nixon* appeared on nearly 1,000 screens across the country and received widespread—and heated—press coverage.[42]

Outside the movie review pages, most observers missed the compassion in Stone's film. Conservative editorial writers pontificated about the director's disregard for history, even as some showed little regard for fact-checking in their own work. Robert Novak groused about Stone's creating the impression that Nixon lost the 1960 election because Kennedy used his knowledge of secret CIA plans to overthrow Castro to out–red-bait his rival during the televised debates, sniffing, "Cuba was not even a peripheral issue in Kennedy's win." Yet Nixon himself spends over five pages in *Six Crises* describing precisely this incident.[43] What's more, Stone took a beating on supposedly liberal op-ed pages. Particularly hostile, the *New York Times* launched a barrage of scornful barbs—from Maureen Dowd's characterization of Stone as a director who "poison-coats" the past, to Howell Raines's cutting assessment that Stone "has harnessed his great storytelling ability to an infantile political intelligence."[44]

To some extent, Stone did invite these misreadings. Many stereotypical anti-Nixon chestnuts appear in this movie. Our first glimpse of him shows a pathetic man: holed up, vampire-like, in a darkened Lincoln Sitting Room, popping sleeping pills and guzzling scotch. After this beginning, Stone rehashes the standard critiques of Nixon's early red-baiting days and shows a president who bombs Vietnam and Cambodia merely to prove his masculinity. What's more, Stone again indulges his conspiratorial imagination, suggesting that the Watergate cover-up tracks back to JFK's murder. From Nixon's enigmatic reference to the FBI's investigation of the Watergate break-in as "open[ing] up the whole Bay of Pigs thing again," Stone speculates that Nixon feared an investigation of E. Howard Hunt and his Cuban agents might reveal the American government's attempts to assassinate Castro, efforts which Nixon helped initiate and which led to Cuban retaliation against Kennedy. His dread of public exposure accounts for the eighteen-and-a-half-minute erasure in the "smoking gun" tape, as well as his resignation.[45] Distracted by these controversial moments, many people characterized Stone's overall portrait of Richard Nixon as a hatchet job.

Yet the hidden-in-plain-sight secret of the film is that, despite his reputation as card-carrying liberal, Oliver Stone had created an empathetic portrait of Richard Nixon. Interestingly, most movie critics got the message, even if their editorial boards, columnists, and feature writers did not. Pulitzer Prize–winning critic Roger Ebert confessed that he had "expect[ed] to see Attila the Hun in a suit and tie" but found, instead, a portrayal that "may amaze Nixon's enemies more than his friends."[46] From the film's opening epigraph, the fair-minded viewer understands that *Nixon* seeks a sympathetic approach. With the words of Matthew 16:26 ("For what is a man profited, if he shall gain the whole world, and lose his own soul?"), the film insists that Nixon had a soul to lose, hardly a small point, given the viciousness of some representations of the man. Furthermore, Stone's young Richard Nixon—earnest, bright, and eager to please—is scarred by a hopeless desire to please his judgmental mother. Confronting her second son about a corn silk cigarette his older brother had given him, Hannah admonishes Richard with words that echo the Parson Weems story of George Washington and the cherry tree: "Do not tell a lie, Richard."[47]

As an adult, Stone's Nixon continues to maintain this cruelly bred conscience. In running for president in 1960, he runs a principled campaign. In his rendering of the famous debates, Stone shows Kennedy exploiting information about the Eisenhower administration's covert support for anti-Castro Cuban exiles. Gambling that Nixon will not jeopardize these secret military operations, Kennedy accuses Eisenhower of having "lost" and ceded Cuba to the communists. Flabbergasted, upper lip dripping sweat, an honor-bound Nixon stammers, unable to answer, as we hear JFK's voice taking the presidential oath of office. To make matters worse, on election night Nixon learns that the margin of Kennedy's victory comes from suspect vote totals from the Democratic strongholds of Chicago and Texas. Nixon, nevertheless, refuses to endanger the national interest by insisting on a time-consuming recount. With a portrayal of a man with a strong sense of honor and a battle-tested knowledge that ends do not justify the means, Stone gives us a Nixon who knows that some things are simply out-of-bounds.

Even after he adopts the corrupt rules of the secret game he discovered in 1960, Stone's Richard Nixon still manages to maintain some basic integrity. To ensure that he will never again be outspent by his opponents, he travels to Texas in November 1963 to meet with an oil company owner named Jack Jones, who promises that he and his friends will raise money in record amounts, enough to deliver Texas and the entire South to a Republican presidential candidate, an enticement he accepts in 1968. Despite these shady dealings, however, Nixon proceeds with his own agenda, stubbornly refusing to stay bought. During their 1972 meeting, Jones angrily confronts the president about the phased withdrawals from Vietnam, the opening to China, détente with the Soviets, federally mandated school desegregation, and oversight of his oil company by the Environmental Protection Agency. Boldly, Nixon declares that he is beholden only to the American people, slyly observing that IRS audits are considerably worse than EPA inspections. When a stunned Jones tries to clarify whether Nixon has been "threatening" him, Nixon responds coolly, "Presidents don't threaten. They don't have to."[48] Rising to a heroic level, Stone's Nixon stands by principle in defiance of his financial backers.

Although Nixon commits crimes that result in his downfall, in many ways he also seems a victim. The news that Howard Hunt participated in the Watergate burglary obviously stuns him. A pensive Nixon realizes that, for the truest of national security reasons, cover-up is the only possible answer: "Howard Hunt? . . . Jesus Christ, you open up that scab . . . and you uncover a lot of pus." What most Watergate scholars have seen as a transparently self-serving cover story—that the FBI's probe into Watergate would "open up the whole Bay of Pigs thing again"—Stone and his co-writers take on faith. This Nixon falls on his sword in a vain attempt to preserve the American public's innocence about the actions of its secret government.[49]

And, in the end, Stone envisions this story as a vehicle of forgiveness between the generations. Eleven years earlier, the poet Sharon Olds, in "The Victims," had used Nixon as a universal measure of contempt to help others understand the depth of the speaker's hatred for her father by comparing her delight when her mother filed for divorce to the glee the American public felt when Nixon was forced to resign the presidency.[50] By contrast, Stone dedicates his film to his father, a move that takes reinventing Richard Nixon into mostly unexplored territory. During the closing credits, Stone inserts film clips of the former president's funeral. With the National Anthem concluding in the background, footage of the honor guard carrying Nixon's casket leads to Stone's final image: a black-and-white still of the actor who played the young Richard Nixon, face expectant and fresh and, as the screenplay says, "eyes all aglow with the hopes of the new century." As the screen fades to black, Stone superimposes the words: "FOR LOUIS STONE / 1910–1985." In this poignant final gesture, Stone transforms his film into a son's reconciling tribute to his conservative Republican Wall Street father, making dealing with Richard Nixon a way to heal generational rifts.[51]

This same healing message dominates both Karen Kovacik's *Nixon and I* (1998), a collection that alternates between poems about the speaker's father and those that explore Richard Nixon's character, and Michael Cahill's 1998 novel *A Nixon Man*, set during the Watergate years, which tells the story of a son's growing up to appreciate the quiet virtues of his father, a steadfast Nixon believer, who unlike his hero is truly not a quitter, despite a life of failed dreams, hardships, and a troubled marriage.[52] But it is another novel, published the same year, Mark Maxwell's *nixoncarver*, that entertains the more radical notion that America needs a reconciliation with Richard Nixon. Confronting the harm perpetrated by fathers, mothers, and other family members—as well as the unfriendly fire we inflict on ourselves—*nixoncarver* opens during the immediate post-resignation exile with a humiliated former president, cowering in his San Clemente office, flailing himself with insults.[53] Mourning his loss of power and worrying over Pat's hospitalization following a stroke, Maxwell's Nixon sets off north along the Pacific, where he meets the writer Ray Carver, whose battle with lung cancer has sent him restlessly traipsing the coastline southward from Washington. Under the watchful eye of the book's unnamed narrator, the two men meet and form an instant intimacy, a bond that both men need—most obviously Nixon, who is clearly damaged goods. Even as a little boy, he loathed himself as unclean, as bestial: "Make me human, Momma," he begs. "Straighten my hair. Plug up my sweat glands. Shrink my big dumb forehead. I'm an ape, Momma."[54] Yet this insecurity, instead of creating a compassionate person, results in a sneaky, aggressive dishonesty—in short, the birth of Tricky Dick. In high school, for example, Nixon wins a debate by fabricating sources on the spot to cynically manipulate the judges. This teen-aged cheater foreshadows the adult to come: the one who was, as he confesses to George McGovern, late in life, "spared by the hand of God so I could fuck the Constitution up the ass."[55]

Yet *nixoncarver* accepts, without dwelling on, Nixon's crimes. In fact, Maxwell often seems ready to excuse them, picturing a man doomed by a twisted family life to turn out exactly as he did. As a Yorba Linda neighbor reminisces: "I'm not afraid to say that I wasn't surprised in the least about what became of him when he went to Washington. None of us were—none of us that really knew the family anyway."[56] But Maxwell moves beyond just sympathy, imagining a Richard Nixon who experiences the consolation and healing power of friendship. In their meeting on the beach, halfway between San Clemente and Port Angeles, Washington, Carver and Nixon experience an instant camaraderie. Their handshake, "a greeting of condolences," suggests a spiritual connection that "erases the space between them."[57] And through the ordinary interactions of friendship, Maxwell's Nixon seems to gain as much forgiveness as any person can. Eating pizza while cleaning out the garage at San Clemente or sitting down for endless games of poker—and, whatever they are doing, telling their life stories, Carver, Nixon, and the narrator establish a human connection that can help the ex-president toward if not catharsis, then, at least, some kind of self-understanding. As they boast about their "dreams of greatness," they also relate their "missed opportunities" and their "ridiculous failures," all so they can "laugh at [their] pathetic lives." Nixon can admit to this group, as he could never say in life, "I'm a total fuckup." Because of these shared experiences, he has someone to turn to during traumatic times. Returning from the hospital following Pat's stroke, Nixon, for solace, calls Carver, who gently instructs him that Pat's illness "is not part of your punishment" and urges him to "call me again . . . if you need to be reminded."[58]

As his response to Pat's illness indicates, not even Richard Nixon is beyond the redeeming power of love. On the first morning in San Clemente after the couple left Washington for good, he finds his bedroom filled with his most prized possessions: a first edition of *The Grapes of Wrath*, his law school diploma, an autographed baseball, and his mother's family Bible. Nixon realizes that Pat had secretly filled her own luggage with these items and in the middle of the night had decorated her husband's room with these familiar objects, "thinking he would need to wake surrounded by the things that would remind him of who he was." In the years immediately following the resignation, Pat sustains her husband. As he sits, day after day, brooding in his office chair for hours at a time, she joins him—sitting silently, pouring him a drink, reading aloud from the newspaper, or, on one memorable occasion, seducing him on the den floor. Knowing that without her daily presence "he'd be in a straitjacket some place," Nixon can only marvel at the strength of her devotion: "She loves him. The stupid stupid woman." Aware of how Pat had saved her husband and of how much Nixon loves her in return, Carver prognosticates the grief the real Nixon displayed at his wife's 1993 funeral: "Ray imagines when Nixon buries his wife, there will be a picture of him in the paper, his whole face flooded with tears." Thinking about his last visit with his friend, the narrator muses: "Somebody once said, 'Dick Nixon was the saddest man I ever knew.' Sometimes I think that's the only true thing anybody's *ever* said about him." Even more effectively than Bill Clinton's plea during his eulogy at Nixon's funeral, Mark Maxwell's novel tells us to stop judging Richard Nixon. The time has come for mercy.[59]

If *nixoncarver* offers forgiveness to Nixon, "Nixon Under the Bodhi Tree," a short story by Gerald Reilly, imagines an even-more-difficult task: getting Nixon to forgive himself. Reilly's story, which first appeared in the *Gettysburg Review* and was selected for the 1999 O. Henry Prize anthology, focuses on Dallas Boyd, a forty-three-year-old gay actor, who, after twenty years of struggling through the "freak shows and supporting roles," has finally landed "his crowning achievement," the part of Richard Nixon in a one-man show titled *Nixon at Colonus*.[60] Though he draws stellar reviews and inquiries from Hollywood casting directors, Boyd, who suffers from the advanced stages of AIDS, cannot reap the rewards of his breakthrough because he barely has the energy now to sustain his two-hour performance. The story's action takes place fourteen months into the play's run on a late April 1994 evening, in the hours prior to the curtain, as Boyd learns, almost twenty-four hours late, that Richard Nixon is dead.

At first, Reilly's Nixon elicits more censure than pity. After months of practice, Dallas Boyd has finally captured the essence of Nixon's character—his audacious hubris, grotesquely oversized ego, and grandiose aspirations. Boyd's performances capture this terminally imperfect man— one who in his "bristling awkwardness" always fails to rise to the occasion, offering words that forever "seemed to be uttering just the wrong sentiment"—who, nevertheless, pursues greatness. Unlike *nixoncarver*'s hero, the Nixon of "Nixon under the Bodhi Tree" feels neither guilt nor remorse for his actions. Dallas Boyd sees his subject as a profane, petty man, obsessively raging "about all the Jews and liberals out to get him just because he wasn't as charming or Ivy-League connected as Jack Kennedy." He's a man who can secretly drop a holocaust from the skies on Cambodia and, without a shudder of embarrassment or regret, watch as his underlings and friends one after the other go to prison for things they did for him, claiming that his sole failing is being "too softhearted."[61]

Nevertheless, Dallas Boyd, who has developed a fascination with Buddhism, theosophy, astrology, and channeling, has come to believe in an authentic Richard Nixon who exists outside the man's physical shell. Through his intense identification with the role he plays on stage, Boyd has been inviting this genuine Nixon into the actor's body. Enticing this spirit to experience the play might permit the man's tortured soul to slough off the "prejudices and stubborn self-images" that imprisoned the historical Nixon throughout his life.[62] The point of all Boyd's efforts of these past

fourteen months, he comes to realize, is to provide some form of expia-
tion for the disgraced former president: "I've already forgiven myself. It's
all for Tricky Dick from here on out." As he prepares for his performance
each night, Boyd meditates, channeling all of Nixon's "anger and hatred,"
transforming it into "the most peaceful, wonderful feelings." Exploring
Nixon's guilt permits the actor to realize that Nixon's chance to exorcise
the demons of his past might redeem us all. As Boyd, transformed into
Richard Nixon, makes his entrance on stage, the walls and ceiling of the
theater evaporate. The stars of the Milky Way shine overhead while, below,
the dead from Cambodia and Kent State join the audience, along with Pat
Nixon and the actor's dead lover. Together, all these imperfect people, "as
flawed as Dallas, as flawed as Richard Nixon," desire simply "a glimpse of
the truth." And that release, through Boyd's spiritual performance, seems
only moments away.[63]

The Four Tops got it wrong—at least when it comes to the Nixon-haters
and his true believers. It *is* the same old song, but with the *same* meaning
since he's been gone. While some of Nixon's critics have, in the years since
his death, been able to reevaluate, sympathize with, and even offer forgiveness to their old nemesis, his implacable foes have kept whistling the
same tune. The 1989 AT&T-sponsored television movie *The Final Days*
offered a pitch-perfect rendition of Woodward and Bernstein's 1976 portrayal of a physically graceless, socially awkward president who, though
he knows his guilt, lies to even his family and staff, desperately hoping to
keep the truth from being revealed.[64] Phil Bosakowski's *Nixon Apologizes to
the Nation*, which received its first full staging in 1995, used the disgraced
former president as a symbol of "a country grown too comfortable with
duplicity."[65] Twenty-three years after Nixon left the White House, James
Taylor offered no new insight into Nixon's character. The opening verse of
his 1997 song "Line 'Em Up" casts Nixon's farewell to the White House
staff just as liberals saw it at the time—a calculated acting job crafted for
the cameras by a selfish, cynical old manipulator who works the crowd
with a "tiny tear in his shifty little eye."[66] Offered the chance to collaborate
with British DJ Paul Oakenfold on a track from the million-selling 2002
album *Bunkka*, Hunter Thompson merely rehashed his old grievances
against Richard Nixon. From the sound of the tape, his contribution to the
cut "Nixon's Spirit" was literally phoned in and could have appeared in a
1974 issue of *Rolling Stone*.[67] Tom Carson's 2003 novel *Gilligan's Wake*, a
hilarious postmodern pastiche of twentieth-century U.S. history through

the lens of the characters from the 1960s sitcom *Gilligan's Island*, imagines Thurston Howell as an associate of Alger Hiss, forced to testify against his old friend, who equates the young representative from Orange County, California, with incurable disease, calling him "young Congressman Cancer," and refers to a bleak medical prognosis as having "been diagnosed with terminal nixon."[68] Although well written and magnificently acted, the 2004 Sean Penn film *The Assassination of Richard Nixon*, based on the real-life story of Samuel Bicke, who, in 1974, attempted to hijack a plane in order to have it crashed into the White House, merely replays earlier critiques of the American dream. "What happens," he asks, "to the land of plenty when there's plenty for the few, and nothing for the plenty?"[69] And, in a magnificent restatement of liberal grievances against Richard Nixon, the television drama *24* gave us the crafty, conniving Charles Logan (played by Greg Itzin), a California president who, at one point during the show's fifth season, asks his closest adviser to kneel in prayer with him. Forced to resign for plotting to corner the world oil market for U.S.-based business interests, a conspiracy that resulted in the assassination of one of his predecessors, Logan gets his comeuppance in Season Six when his estranged wife, Martha (Jean Smart), plunges a paring knife into his chest. Whether he dies or whether we'll still have Logan to kick around some more was left unresolved—at least until Season Seven.[70]

At least as monotonously insistent as the liberals, Nixon's supporters, like American conservatives in general, continue to sing the same aria, note for note, without variation. On August 5, 2004, five days ahead of the anniversary of the resignation, the Richard Nixon Library and Birthplace sponsored "The Legacy of Richard Nixon: A 30th Anniversary Conference." Promising a "landmark discussion" led by "a diverse panel of experts," the flyer announcing the event, decked out in red, white, and blue ink—and substituting a star for an apostrophe, invited the public to "COME JOIN THE GREAT DEBATE ON PRESIDENT NIXON*S LEGACY." Indeed, the panel was distinguished enough: Dr. Herbert Parmet (author of *Richard Nixon and His America*), Dr. Walter A. McDougall (a Pulitzer Prize–winning historian from the University of Pennsylvania), Dr. Lewis Sorley (who served in both the army and the CIA and who wrote a history of Nixon's handling of the Vietnam War), Ray Price (Nixon's head White House speechwriter), and, finally, Len Colodny (who co-authored *Silent Coup*, an admittedly "unorthodox," but best-selling, explanation of Watergate's origins). Yet, despite the scholarly credentials of most of the participants, no real debate took place—nor was it meant to. The library had invited only panelists known to have positive things to say about Richard Nixon. The conference's honored guest, given a seat in the center of the first row of the library's auditorium, was the president's brother, Ed Nixon. Clearly, the deck was stacked from the start.

Yet, for some, not even this sanitized environment felt safe. As one couple, both volunteer docents for the library, settled into their seats in the half-filled theater, the husband, perusing his program, grumbled: "Which one of these guys am I not going to like?" In introducing the panel, the library's executive director, the Reverend John H. Taylor, groused that both Parmet's and Colodny's books were no longer commercially available and, although each one had been published fourteen years before, suggested conspiracy as the reason: these pro-Nixon books were out of print *"because of their considerable virtues."* This aggrieved perception of perpetual be-leaguerment extended to some on the panel itself. When, at the beginning of his presentation, Colodny had trouble getting the video equipment to work, he joked: "They've been trying to silence me for years!" With fierce insistence, Walter McDougall held that historians will come around to the proper perspective on Watergate, but only "some day, after all those who have a psychological stake in hating Nixon are dead." On this day, histori-cal disagreements seemed explainable only as bad faith or some form of psychosis.

Once the panel presentations began, the well-rehearsed Nixon stories reappeared. Almost as if it had gathered to listen to a greatest hits album, the audience waited for the familiar refrains. Watergate wasn't Nixon's fault, Colodny consoled them; John Dean lied to the president, initiated a cover-up, and withheld vital information about Haldeman aide Gordon Strachan's prior knowledge of the Watergate break-ins. Ray Price dismissed the smoking gun tape, echoing the library's line that the June 23, 1972 con-versation with Haldeman mattered less for what Nixon said than for what he actually did. In domestic affairs, the panel heralded Nixon as a cham-pion of the working class. Relating how his neighborhood pizza parlor still displayed a photograph of the former president, Herbert Parmet laughed about how he "became a local hero for doing a book on Nixon." McDougall ran through a checklist of Nixon's domestic accomplishments—ending the draft, extending the vote to eighteen-year-olds, creating OSHA and the EPA, and imposing wage and price controls, a list that most Demo-crats would be proud to claim. Yet "liberals give Nixon *no* credit." As for foreign policy, Lewis Sorley commended Nixon for abandoning a failed policy in Vietnam and, through his Vietnamization of the war, bringing

American involvement to an end with a South Vietnam that had a chance to determine its own future, thereby upholding America's credibility as an ally in the rest of the world. McDougall, posing the rhetorical question of whether Nixon should be seen as "a relic of the Cold War" with little relevance to today's world, rebutted this unattributed opinion by affirming Nixon's "mighty legacy," although (again unnamed) "scholars and journalists might take decades to own up to that." Claiming that Nixon ascended to the presidency under more difficult circumstances than anyone else (presumably even Abraham Lincoln), McDougall praised Nixon's appeal to renewed discipline and patriotism, a firmness embodied in policies and diplomatic efforts that "laid the foundation for winning the Cold War."

The question-and-answer period that followed the presentations managed to replay key themes of the Nixon Library's preferred story. Not coincidentally, library executive director John Taylor carefully controlled the Q&A, taking for himself at least the first thirty of the allotted seventy-five minutes. In the remaining time, audience members by-passed probing questions for a slew of parlor-game "what ifs?" Each scenario allowed the panel and audience to ponder how much better the world would be today if only Richard Nixon had received a fair shake. Fascinatingly, two panel members endorsed Nixon's own view that Watergate was to blame for the demise of South Vietnam. When Lewis Sorley argued that Nixon's administration restored a sense of security to America, which felt "safe enough to obsess on this [the Watergate] *affair*," Parmet chimed in, deeming it a "luxury [for the United States] to be able to afford Watergate" and concluding with yet another conspiracy theory: "That *whole* generation going back to the 1940s despised Richard Nixon. They felt he was evil, and they were ready to defeat him."

After the question-and-answer session concluded, the panel and the audience adjourned for the inaugural event in the new Katherine B. Loker Center—a luncheon in the lobby of the library's new wing, which included, among other things, a full-size interior/exterior re-creation of the White House East Room. Always looking for the main chance, the Nixon Library used this new building as one more opportunity to tell its mythic story. Built on the spot where the library had maintained a small citrus grove in honor of the lemon trees that Frank Nixon had tried to grow in this soil about one hundred years earlier, the re-created East Room gives Nixon Library visitors a glimpse of the White House even as they pull into the parking lot. But the full symbolic significance of the new wing doesn't become clear until one enters the garden and visits the birthplace.

Turning to face the tiny wood-framed house in which Richard Nixon was born, one sees in the immediate left-hand background the familiar exterior of the White House. It's not quite a log cabin, but the juxtaposition of this humble first home with the ceremonial elegance of the president's mansion graphically represents Richard Nixon's life as a celebration of the myth that anyone can grow up to be president. Not visible in the photo, but behind the house and to the right, is Nixon's gravesite. Taken together, the points of this triangle map out the progression of Nixon's life, while telling the story that, for those willing to try, anything is possible. It's their story, and they're sticking to it.[71]

A man lies stiffly on a psychiatrist's couch, his jaw set, lips pouting, eyes fixed in a stare of deep existential anxiety. Seated nearby, his therapist matter-of-factly offers a cure: "It's *not* your imagination," he informs his worried patient. "You *are* seeing Nixon everywhere." The humor in this 1988 Stevenson cartoon from the *New Yorker* stems undoubtedly from Nixon's grim persistence in thrusting himself into the public spotlight. But the unsettling aspect of Stevenson's drawing cannot be explained simply in terms of Nixon's obsession with dictating his own place in history. The uneasy edge to the humor comes from the recognition that this man's obsession is our own. We are still unsettled by Richard Nixon, unsettled about the mythic America he represents, and therefore unsettled about our collective identity.

In a lithograph created after the former president's death, the artist Jeffrey Vallance had some fun with the interpretive uncertainty that surrounds Nixon. Playing in the limboland where the silly and the serious intermingle, "Nixon in Heaven with Washington" reproduced a piece from the period following Lincoln's assassination, with one alteration—Nixon's head is pasted on over the Great Emancipator's. For the Nixon-hater, Vallance's work was clearly tongue-in-cheek. The heavenly light shines down upon Nixon and the garlands of flowers are held over his head like a halo—these highly sentimental elements from the original now applied to Richard Nixon speak the language of parody. But for those who worshipped the man, there is no humor in this lithograph. In fact, Vallance advertised his handiwork in *Nixco News*, the newsletter of the Nixon Political Items Collectors Organization, aiming to turn a profit among those who took this comparison to one of America's greatest presidents without any trace of irony. In the case of Richard Nixon, we have lost the ability to distinguish satiric from sacred expressions of national values.

Visitors to the Nixon birthplace can see the familiar facade of 1600 Pennsylvania Avenue directly behind the little white frame house—a perfect visual summary of the cultural myth that anyone can grow up to become president. Photo by the author.

More significant, as this study of Nixon in contemporary culture has shown, the dominant formulation of cultural values has lost its broad, supporting consensus. Yet the debunking of our ideologies of success and mission has not brought with it any agreement on a new set of stories and beliefs. The confidence about a national self-definition that allowed Henry Luce to speak of an "American century" seems more than a little quaint now. What we have seen transpire in the years since the conclusion of World War II has done much to discredit the prevailing national myths. In this sixty-year span of time, Richard Nixon has never gone away, because, as we have seen, increasingly, political and cultural analysts and creative writers have found in Nixon a figure that allows them to explore the unresolved debate over what America is and should be.

On one level, Nixon's first two autobiographies, *Six Crises* and *RN*, encapsulate America's orthodox ideologies. In a self-representation that

"It's __not__ your imagination. You __are__ seeing Nixon everywhere."

is motivated by a disturbing mixture of real belief and cynical self-interest, Nixon patterned his life on the design of the self-made-man myth. His rise from his father's grocery store to the White House is as near a rags-to-riches narrative as modern politics has seen. Simultaneously, he tied his life to a vision of America's role in global politics straight out of the myth of national mission—the idea that Americans are a chosen people, entrusted with the preservation and growth of freedom. In this two-sided self-portrait, Nixon placed himself at the center of an ideological system that, at one time, enjoyed widespread support. As British journalist Godfrey Hodgson, looking at the period of the mid-1950s to the mid-1960s, observed, "It is impossible not to be struck by the degree to which the majority of Americans in those years accepted the same system of assumptions."[72]

To the Nixon critic, Jeffrey Vallance's lithograph "Nixon in Heaven with Washington" is a hilariously over-the-top parody. To the true believer, however, the lithograph appears entirely serious. © Jeffrey Vallance. Reprinted with permission. All rights reserved.

More than just a celebration of a way of life, however, Nixon's memoirs defended a mythology he perceived to be under attack. His forebodings of national decline, successfully assuaged in *Six Crises* and mournfully fulfilled in *RN*, responded to critiques of orthodoxy raised by voices from within and without the dominant culture. For instance, doubts about the goodness of the good life promised by the American myth of success spread even as affluence grew to record levels. The self-made-man label, which Nixon could legitimately claim, no longer carried unquestioning approbation. Thus, as Gore Vidal dramatized in *The Best Man*, the pragmatic, but ethically questionable, choices forced by our debased political system almost guaranteed that the truly best man never wins. Furthermore, Lawrence Ferlinghetti's *Tyrannus Nix?* argued that success in itself mattered less than the uses—"Fair or Foul"—to which the winners put their achievement. Yet, even taken as an end in itself, success came to be seen as a goal that offered paltry rewards. As the Nixon of *Secret Honor* realizes only after having bartered his soul for success, without some kind of "honor" to claim for himself, all the glory of his assorted political triumphs cannot sustain him in his exile.

Yet these dangers strike only those people in, or close to, the American mainstream, those for whom the work ethic is a meaningful concept. More and more during the years of Nixon's career, the nation recognized the limits of opportunity, saw that there was an "other America," an entire subculture of poverty from which people born to rags died in rags. In *Secret Honor*, Freed and Stone made an ironic comment on the failure of upward mobility in the United States, by juxtaposing Nixon's reenactment of his 1968 convention pledge to make the American dream come true for the "millions for whom it is an impossible dream today" with the status of the only minorities mentioned in the monologue: the "colored" waiters on the Sequoia and his Cuban servant, Roberto. Rejecting revisionist history pronouncing Nixon to be the last liberal president, African American artists like James Baldwin, the cartoonists of the *Black Panther* newspaper, Ishmael Reed, Gil Scott-Heron, and Amiri Baraka relate a different reality—one for which a devilishly evil Richard Nixon serves as a fitting symbol of a racist mainstream society determined to forever deny social, economic, and political equality to blacks. Furthermore, in *Don Quixote*, Kathy Acker envisions a culture that strips women of their identities and of their chance to participate in the national mythology—one cannot be self-made if one is not permitted to have a self. Each of these works gives voice to the charge that the ideology of success belongs only to those in the dominant culture: no underclass need apply.

Equally vulnerable to critique has been the other staple of American orthodoxy, the conception of national mission. Proud of its total victory in World War II, its mastery of the secret of the atomic bomb, and its altruism, as evidenced by the Marshall Plan, the United States too easily believed in its omnipotence, its virtue, and its rightful place as the divinely chosen leader of the Free World. But, as Coover illustrates devastatingly in *The Public Burning*, the underside of American mission is the zealot's hatred of self-created demons. Being American gets distilled into a simple litmus test of right belief: any deviation from orthodoxy is more than dangerous—it is an evil to be eradicated. However, after McCarthyism, a failed war in Korea, political assassinations, racial strife, and economic ills, it became harder to sustain the myth of American mission. As Hodgson noted, "In the age of Kennedy and Nixon [there] was something more than a mere acceleration in the pace of change. There was a real break in the continuity of the American experience."[73] Accustomed to perceiving ourselves as a country that always fought for the just cause, more and more people began to see the United States as fighting on the wrong side in Southeast Asia. W. D. Ehrhart, a seventeen-year-old eastern Pennsylvanian volunteer for Vietnam in the mid-1960s, told the makers of the PBS documentary *Vietnam: A Television History* (1983): "In grade school, we learned about Redcoats, the nasty British soldiers that tried to stifle our freedom. . . . [And while in Vietnam] I began increasingly to have the feeling that I was a Redcoat. . . . I wasn't a hero. . . . Somehow I had become everything I had learned to believe was evil."[74] Indeed, Philip Roth in *Our Gang*, Gore Vidal in *An Evening with Richard Nixon*, Ron Kovic in *Born on the Fourth of July*, and Jonathan Lowy in *Elvis and Nixon* each use Vietnam to depict the United States as engaging in a policy of senseless, and seemingly endless, violence based on murderous lies of national innocence. What's more, cynicism about America's motives had grown to the point that Freed and Stone could suggest in *Secret Honor* that the entire venture in Indochina had more to do with entrepreneurs' lust for foreign markets than for the preservation of democracy in a country that seemed neither to be a legitimate nation nor an authentic democracy.

Yet, if American orthodoxy has been compellingly demythologized during the Nixon era, its critics have rarely offered any sustainable public vision of community on which a new mythology can be founded. Hardly any more receptive to dialogue than their rivals, some ideological opponents of the hegemonic culture have stooped to the same name-calling polemics for which they rightly condemned their adversaries and have constructed a demonology of their own. In *Our Gang, An Evening with Richard Nixon*, and *Don Quixote*, we witness the indulgent tendency to ascribe to Nixon all imaginable sins and, hence, to denigrate the political and social philosophy of the opposition. Having made their rival into the living incarnation of evil, these liberals and radicals have relieved themselves of the necessity of listening and responding with respect to their fellow citizens.

Such contentiousness damages the nation's health because a country cannot function long without a mythology. In a 1982 *Foreign Affairs* article, "The Care and Repair of Public Myth," William H. McNeill argues that "a people without a full quiver of relevant agreed-upon statements, accepted in advance through education or less formalized acculturation, soon finds itself in deep trouble, for, in the absence of believable myths, coherent public action becomes very difficult to improvise or sustain."[75]

To fill the void, the American mainstream's orthodox system of beliefs, the ones Nixon so passionately defends in *Six Crises* and *RN*, resurged in the years following his resignation. The willingness of the majority of Americans to accept Nixon as an elder statesman and to discount the revelations of Watergate parallels a similar pretense in America's born-again orthodoxy—that the old myths were never discredited. In his 1980 book *Ambition*, Joseph Epstein defended his subject as a falsely maligned passion necessary for the achievement of excellence—as if the critiques of the American dream from *Death of a Salesman* and *The Organization Man* through *The Culture of Narcissism* never existed. In the absence of a compensatory mythology, the majority culture chose to reassert, despite evidence of downward mobility in American society and growing numbers of the homeless, that the *Wall Street Journal* was "the daily diary of the American dream" and that the Horatio Alger protagonist was still a folk hero.

During this seeming rejuvenation of orthodoxy, Nixon chose to concentrate his efforts on defending the myth of American mission. Whether appearing on *Meet the Press*, touring the Economic Clubs of the United States, or advising presidents, Nixon provided the rationale behind the assertion that Vietnam was a "noble cause." Reagan could bring a lump to the throat by uttering the assertion, but it took Nixon to explain the geopolitical theory behind such sentimentality. In this effort, he found unlikely allies in some liberal opponents willing to separate their judgment of his foreign policy achievements from the rest of his legacy. In this regard, the *Newsweek* "He's Back!" cover and the Goodman, Adams, and Sellars opera *Nixon in China*, with its characterization of Nixon as the earnest son of the middle class on a mission for world peace, could not have given him any better promotion. And, although his interest in salvaging his place in history did taint his efforts, he largely succeeded in becoming America's elder statesman, by promoting a revised standard version of American orthodoxy. His final memoir, *In the Arena*, as well as the museum at his presidential library, combined the idea that America has a special role to play on the world stage with a repackaged notion of success—that eventual vindication comes to the person who, like Nixon, never gives up. Like the parent who reassures the waking child that "it was all just a bad dream," the return to the orthodox mainstream worldview swept away any disturbing critiques, challenges, or self-doubts.

But because the discrediting of America's mainstream ideology was not an illusory nightmare, the unreflective reclamation of the values that Nixon represents is a dangerous act. Although Reagan himself seemed unaware of his deception, his assertion that it was "morning again in America" led the United States into a house of mirrors, encouraging a celebration of an uncomplicated version of the past. Most Americans still have not challenged this vision—and do not want to, because this revised standard orthodoxy cannot stand too strong a scrutiny. As Garry Wills explained in *Reagan's America*, the United States has settled "for a substitute past, an illusion of it . . . [and therefore] that fragile construct must be protected from the challenge of complex or contradictory evidence, from any test of evidence at all. . . . We cannot live with our real past. . . . We not only prefer but need a substitute."[76]

Unwilling, perhaps unable, to take its critics seriously, the dominant culture reasserted blindly the ideological world in which Reagan lived and that Nixon championed before Watergate. As a consequence, American politics has been diminished. We have decided not to learn from our blunders. We have decided, in fact, to deny we were wrong at all—a tactic that, as surely as the name-calling polemics of the Left, saps "our most fundamental strength, our ability as a democratic society to discuss and resolve our problems."[77]

Instead, we seemed fated to keep repeating the old mistakes, but with increasingly serious consequences. Much of conservative America still engages in idealized talk about individual initiative and responsibility. Dale Covey's *The Seven Habits of Highly Effective People* (1990), Spencer Johnson's *Who Moved My Cheese?* (1998), and other self-help books that echo the precepts of Dale Carnegie and Norman Vincent Peale continue to sell millions of copies. Meanwhile, Donald Trump's *The Apprentice, American Idol, Survivor,* and other reality television programs endlessly repeat the narrative of an individual rising above the crowd through talent, hard work, and savvy. Yet all these celebrations of the possibilities of self-made success are grounded in a nostalgic veneration of "supposedly halcyon times," without any recognition that these purported glory days "had been harsh, especially for racial and ethnic minorities, Catholics and Jews, the handicapped, senior citizens, the majority of women, and gay people." All the while, behind the fog of this nostalgia for a time that never really was, the gap between the wealthiest and the poorest Americans continues to grow to dangerous size.[78]

Meanwhile, a war in Iraq, ostensibly fought to free a people from tyranny and to save the world from terrorism, threatens, Vietnam-like, to bog down into a quagmire of sectarian violence, even as it radicalizes as yet unknowable numbers of young Muslims against the United States. In a series of very Nixonian acts, George W. Bush and his administration evoked national security as a means to chip away at civil liberties, increase the powers of government to spy on its own citizens, and erect a stone wall impeding congressional oversight and investigation. When news of domestic spying efforts broke in December 2005, both Oliphant and Tony Auth thought immediately of Nixon. Oliphant's sketch from December 19, has Nixon, Henry Higgins–like, praising George W. Bush's creation of an enemies list with a gleeful "I think he's got it!" The next day Auth had the ghost of Richard Nixon visit Bush, who had been caught spying, offering him a helpful, if familiar, denial: "You are not a Crook." But over a year later, it wasn't quite as clear who was the teacher and who was the student. Ben Sargent's March 27, 2007, cartoon shows George W. Bush walking down a White House hallway past a portrait of Richard Nixon, which displays the legend "Stonewaller." Passing the picture by, not even breaking stride, Bush dispatches his predecessor with a contemptuously dismissive judgment: "Amateur." American audiences during the summer 2007 Broadway run of *Frost/Nixon* laughed when Frank Langella offered Nixon's famous justification for abuse of executive power: "I'm saying that when the President does it, that means it's not illegal." But they laughed longer, and more revealingly, at the follow-up line: "But I realise that no one else shares that view," in wry recognition that yet another president not only believed such sentiments, but had been acting on them as well.[79]

Most contemporary editorial cartoonists have drawn Richard Nixon's ghost as a counselor for George W. Bush on how to run a cover-up. But by March 2007 Ben Sargent felt that Bush would have been able to teach Nixon a thing or two. SARGENT © 2007 Austin American-Statesman. Reprinted with permission of UNIVERSAL PRESS SYNDICATE. All rights reserved.

In 1975, British rock star David Bowie asked a generation of young Americans: "Do you remember your President Nixon?" Remember? As this cultural history of an American obsession has demonstrated, we can't even begin to forget him. And, what's more, in the wildly divergent reinventions of Richard Nixon, we get a tour of the culture war's front lines, a battle in which the winner gets to define the significance of such value-laden terms as "success," "honor," "patriotism"—even the meaning of America itself. In our responses to him, as to few other personalities, we find an angry failure to move into the future because we cannot agree on an interpretation of the past. *Cleveland Plain Dealer* columnist Dick Feagler's assessment, offered at the time of Nixon's death, still holds more than ten years later: "It's been twenty years since he was driven from office. And we have not been able to invent a new America to replace the

As its line of baby clothes suggests, the Nixon Library and Birthplace plans to pass on the struggle to control the reinventions of Richard Nixon to the next generation. Item from author's personal collection. Photo by John Herr Photography.

old one." Without recognizing the irony, Gore Vidal, in *An Evening with Richard Nixon*, fairly screams out at the pious hypocrisy of Nixon's inaugural address admonition: "We cannot learn from one another until we stop shouting at one another."[80] Indeed, public debate in America has descended into repeated platitudes and mudslinging, as a cursory glance at political talk shows like *Hardball*, Lou Dobbs, or most any Fox News Channel program tells us. Perhaps the emergence of new cultural myths may come from the humane, inclusive, and forgiving vision contained in *Nixon's Nixon*, Oliver Stone's film, *nixoncarver*, and "Nixon Under the Bodhi Tree." However, Nixon's die-hard critics refuse to forgive, and his loyalists acknowledge very little that needs pardoning. As groups, they both remain interested only in victory—and on their original terms. Consequently, now more than ever, Americans prefer shouting to listening, a preference that turns reinventing Richard Nixon into an act of war. And, as the Nixon Library and Birthplace's line of baby clothes—available in six-month, one, one-and-a-half, and two-year sizes—suggests, some of the combatants understand that the battle over Richard Nixon is a long-term battle for the nation's future.

NOTES

INTRODUCTION. RICHARD NIXON AND THE

MANY FACES OF A REPRESENTATIVE AMERICAN

1. George H. Gallup, *The Gallup Poll: Public Opinion, 1972–1977*, 1:325, 328, 335.

2. *NBC Nightly News*, 27 April 1994.

3. *State Funeral for Richard Nixon*, ABC, 27 April 1994. Subsequent references to ABC's coverage will appear in the text.

4. All the eulogies delivered at the funeral appear in a souvenir program sold by the Nixon Library Museum Store in the months following the former president's death. Dole's remarks appear in *Services for Richard Nixon, 37th President of the United States, Wednesday, April 27th, 1994*, 6, 8, 6 (hereafter cited in text as *Services*).

5. *State Funeral for Richard Nixon*, NBC, 27 April 1994. Subsequent references to NBC's coverage will appear in the text. For further discussion of Nixon's effect on Bill Clinton's failed 1974 congressional race, see Maraniss, *First in His Class*, 325–326; and Clinton, *My Life*, 222.

6. Remarkably, the context in which Graham places his biblical text is incorrect. David speaks his words in 2 Samuel 3 not at the death of Saul, which is related in 1 Samuel 31 and 2 Samuel 1, but upon hearing the news of Joab's murder by Abner.

7. Wright and Fuller, *Book of the Acts of God*, 117.

8. 1 Samuel 16:14 (Revised Standard Version).

9. Roth, *I Married a Communist*, 278, 279, 280 (page citations are to the Vintage International edition).

10. Greenfield, "My Generation Is Missing," 35.

11. For a list of some of the satires directed at the former president, see Whitfield, "Richard Nixon as a Comic Figure"; and Douglass, "Tricky Dick: Richard Nixon as a Literary Character." Aaron, "Nixon as Literary Artifact," places more emphasis on analysis than on catalog. Thomas Monsell has compiled a thorough annotated bibliography, in *Nixon on Stage and Screen*.

12. Billy Joel, "We Didn't Start the Fire," *Storm Front*, Sony Bo0000DCHL.

13. By my count, there are fifty-seven Nixon answers in the Baby Boomer Edition, compared to twenty-seven for John F. Kennedy. The remainder is divided in this way: Eisenhower, twenty-one; Lyndon B. Johnson, twenty; Jimmy Carter, twelve; Gerald Ford, ten; Ronald Reagan, eight; and Harry Truman, two. In addition, a quotation from Nixon's first book of memoirs, *Six Crises* ("Save yourself for the big decision.

Don't allow your mind to be cluttered with the trivia") appears on the Baby Boomer Edition's game card.

14. Dole's assertion, perhaps, is borrowed from political historian Herbert S. Parmet, who, in *Richard Nixon and His America*, labels recent U.S. history "the Age of Nixon" (ix).

15. Chambers, *Witness*, 5.

16. Defenders of the canon as it has been constructed include Allan Bloom, *Closing of the American Mind*; Hirsch, *Cultural Literacy*; DeSouza, *Illiberal Education*; William J. Bennett, *De-valuing of America*; and Harold Bloom, *Western Canon*. Critics of the status quo include Gates, *Loose Canons*; Gerald Graff, *Beyond the Culture Wars*; Robinson, *In the Canon's Mouth*; Jay, *American Literature and the Culture Wars*; and a variety of new readers for English composition classes, particularly those published by Bedford Books of St. Martin's Press.

17. Here I have in mind programs such as Pat Robertson's *The 700 Club*, radio talk show hosts like G. Gordon Liddy, Michael Savage, and Rush Limbaugh, and almost all of the television programming offered by the Fox News Channel.

18. Steele, *Content of Our Character*; West, *Race Matters*; Jordan, *Affirmative Acts: Political Essays*; McWhorter, *Losing the Race*; Dyson, *Is Bill Cosby Right: Or Has the Black Middle Class Lost Its Mind?*

19. In addition to the books by Bennett, Graff, and Gates, which are cited in note 16, the language of cultural conflict dominates books such as Hunter, *Culture Wars*; Bolton, *Culture Wars: Documents from the Recent Controversies in the Arts*; Robert Hughes, *Culture of Complaint*; Limbaugh, *The Way Things Ought to Be*; Limbaugh, *See, I Told You So*; Gitlin, *Twilight of Common Dreams*; Nolan, *American Culture Wars*; and Wilkinson, *One Nation Indivisible*.

20. Montrose, "Professing the Renaissance: The Poetics and Politics of Culture," 27.

21. Schudson, *Watergate in American Memory*, 3.

22. Greenberg, *Nixon's Shadow*, xix. Greenberg's study of Nixon in U.S. public culture covers terrain similar to that of this book. But Greenberg devotes less attention to literary and cinematic reinventions of Richard Nixon than I do, instead featuring especially perceptive and sure-footed readings of Nixon's treatment by journalists and historians.

23. Fish, "What Makes an Interpretation Acceptable?" in *Is There a Text in This Class?* 338. I am also influenced by the writings of Hayden White and William H. McNeill. See White, *Metahistory*; White, *Tropics of Discourse*; White, *Content of the Form*; and McNeill, *Mythistory and Other Essays*.

24. Mark Twain, "At the Funeral: From an Unfinished Burlesque of Books of Etiquette," in *Letters from the Earth*, ed. Bernard DeVoto (New York: Harper & Row, 1962), 193.

1. Ambrose, *Nixon: The Education of a Politician*, 636–638; "Nixon's Crises," *Newsweek*, 26 March 1962, 25.

2. "Best Seller List," *New York Times Book Review*, 8 April–2 September 1962. Positive reviews of *Six Crises* appeared in Maurice Dolbier, "Six Crises," *New York Herald Tribune*, 29 March 1962, 23; Willard Edwards, "Unique Political Memoir— Told with Rare Candor," *Chicago Tribune*, 8 April 1962, 4:1; Templeton Peck, "Step by Step through Six Crises of Nixon's Life," *San Francisco Sunday Chronicle: This World Magazine*, 1 April 1962, 28; William H. Stringer, "Self-Portrait of Nixon in the Campaign and Other 'Crises,'" *Christian Science Monitor*, 29 March 1962, 11; "Nixon's Crises," *Newsweek*, 26 March 1962, 25–26; and David Rees, "Tricks and Truth," *Spectator*, 5 October 1962, 520. Negative reviews can be found in William Costello, "Faceless Enemies, Waiting to Pounce," *New Republic*, 9 April 1962, 22–23; W. H. Allen, "President's Challenger," *Times Literary Supplement* (London), 5 October 1962, 771; and Richard Whalen, "Nixon: A Burnt Out Case," *National Review*, 22 May 1962, 372. Reviewers who confused the man with his book were Charles R. Foster, "Reinforced Image," *Christian Century*, 6 June 1962, 720; and Wicker, "Turning Points for a Man in the Running." Information on sales and royalty figures for *Six Crises* appears in Ambrose, *Nixon: Education of a Politician*, 640.

3. Georges Gusdorf, "Conditions and Limits of Autobiography," in *Autobiography: Essays Theoretical and Critical*, ed. James Olney (Princeton, NJ: Princeton University Press, 1980), 39.

4. Garry Wills claims that chapter 6 was the only section of *Six Crises* that Nixon wrote by himself. See Wills, *Nixon Agonistes*, 73–74. Ambrose notes that journalists Alvin Moscow and Stephen Hess helped Nixon with his memoirs but asserts that "it was such an intensely personal book that Nixon necessarily had to do most of the writing himself." See Ambrose, *Nixon: Education of a Politician*, 637.

5. Nixon, *Six Crises*, 1, 73 (hereafter cited in text as *SC*).

6. Quoted in Huber, *American Idea of Success*, 12 (page citations are to the Pushcart Press edition).

7. Ibid., 21.

8. Ibid., 23–24, 82.

9. Ibid., 215–216, 231, 517n1.

10. Ibid., 10.

11. Diggins, *The Proud Decades*; Patterson, *Grand Expectations*; O'Neill, *American High*.

12. Hine, *Populuxe*, 3.

13. These statistical figures come from Diggins, *The Proud Decades*, 186.

14. Patterson, *Grand Expectations*, 311.

15. From the 1940s mark of 19.4 births for every 1,000 persons, the birthrate in the United States leapt to 1957's rate of 25.3 (see O'Neill, *American High*, 40). The figure on Americans moving to the suburbs can be found in Diggins, *The Proud Decades*, 183.

16. Patterson, *Grand Expectations*, 311.

17. O'Neill, *American High*, 3, 7.

18. Franklin, *The Autobiography*, in *Autobiography, Poor Richard, and Later Writings*, 644–645. In addition to industry, frugality, and temperance, silence, order, resolution, sincerity, justice, moderation, cleanliness, tranquility, chastity, and humility make up Franklin's list of virtues.

19. Mott, *Golden Multitudes*, 158–159.

20. Alger, *Ragged Dick: Or, Street Life in New York with the Boot Blacks*, 77, 185.

21. This image is in the file for editorial cartoons from the year 1952, at the Richard Nixon Library and Birthplace, 52-2.

22. Von Hoffman, *Citizen Cohn*, 124 (page citation is to the Bantam Books edition).

23. De Toledano, *Nixon*, 14.

24. Peale, *The Power of Positive Thinking*, 263.

25. "Best Seller List," *New York Times Review of Books*, 19 July–25 October 1959.

26. Mazo, *Nixon: A Political and Personal Portrait*, 16, 25.

27. Quoted in Richard Weiss, *American Myth of Success*, 34.

28. De Toledano, *Nixon*, 13.

29. Kornitzer, *The Real Nixon*, 19.

30. Mazo, *Nixon: A Political and Personal Portrait*, 39.

31. De Toledano, *Nixon*, 13.

32. Kornitzer, *The Real Nixon*, 207.

33. For discussions of Nixon's prior knowledge of the content of Chambers's testimony to the FBI, see Weinstein, *Perjury*, 5–7; Ambrose, *Nixon: Education of a Politician*, 144–145; Wills, *Nixon Agonistes*, 34–37; Mazo, *Nixon: A Political and Personal Portrait*, 51; and Kornitzer, *The Real Nixon*, 174. Some sources dispute this point. See Parmet, *Richard Nixon and His America*, 167–168; Aitken, *Nixon*, 155; and Gellman, *Contender*, 222. Arguing that "it is inconceivable that the Nixon who was so zealous about exposing Communists to further his career" kept quiet about Hiss for over a year, Parmet claims that there is not "any direct evidence" that Nixon saw the reports in which Father Cronin quoted from Chambers's testimony to the FBI, except the "repeated assertions by the priest" that he gave them to Nixon (167). Two points must be made in response to Parmet. First, Nixon's silence is hardly "inconceivable." By 1947, the rumors about Hiss's communist sympathies had already eased him out of the State Department into the private sector. Second, Parmet's claim that "repeated

assertions" of one of the principal participants in an event do not constitute "direct evidence" is extraordinary—especially in light of his attempt to discredit Cronin by taking a single statement that might be read as a contradiction of the priest's much-repeated story as unequivocal evidence that he is mistaken.

34. Gellman, *Contender*, 222. Referring to a 1990 interview with Nixon biographer Jonathan Aitken in which Cronin changes his story, Gellman asserts a "recantation" of the priest's earlier position (498n88). But Gellman's conclusion overstates his evidence. In his own use of the interview, Aitken says only that Father Cronin's 1990 statement "gave *qualified* support to Nixon's claim [not to have heard of Hiss before August 1948]" (155, emphasis mine). Furthermore, neither Aitken nor Gellman explore the critical question—why should Cronin change his story now, after several decades of maintaining that he had met with Nixon and mentioned Hiss before Chambers's testimony? Nor do they explain why they should find this statement, made forty-two years after the fact, more credible than multiple statements made much closer to the actual events.

35. Aitken, *Nixon*, 155. Stripling is quoted in Morris, *Richard Milhous Nixon*, 508. Weinstein believes that Stripling was publicly expressing the belief, as early as 1962, that "Nixon [was] a liar about his role the [Hiss] Case." See Weinstein, *Perjury*, 531. For moments in which historical narratives suggest *Six Crises*'s downplaying of Stripling's vital role in the Hiss investigation, see Morris, *Richard Milhous Nixon*, 461; and Ambrose, *Education*, 189.

36. Julie Nixon Eisenhower, *Pat Nixon*, 17.

37. Jean Starobinski, "The Style of Autobiography," in *Autobiography: Essays Theoretical and Critical*, ed. James Olney (Princeton, NJ: Princeton University Press, 1980), 75.

38. For discussions of the American myth of divine mission, see Perry Miller, *Errand into the Wilderness*; Schlesinger, "The Theory of America: Experiment or Destiny?"; Tuveson, *Redeemer Nation*; Merk, *Manifest Destiny and Mission in American History*; Burns, *Idea of Mission in American History*; Baritz, *City on a Hill*; Bercovitch, *American Jeremiad*; Bercovitch, "'Nehemiah Americanus': Cotton Mather and the Concept of the Representative American"; Bercovitch, *Puritan Origins of the American Self*; and Richard T. Hughes, *Myths America Lives By*.

39. Bercovitch, *Puritan Origins of the American Self*, 87.

40. John Winthrop, "A Model of Christian Charity," in *Journal of John Winthrop, 1630–1649*, abridged edition, ed. Richard S. Dunn and Laetitia Yeandle (Cambridge, MA: Belknap Press of Harvard University Press, 1996), 10.

41. Abraham Lincoln, "Annual Message to Congress, December 1, 1862," in *Abraham Lincoln: Speeches and Writings, 1859–1865*, ed. Don E. Fehrenbacher (New York: Literary Classics of the United States, 1989), 415.

42. Herman Melville, *White-Jacket, or The World in a Man-of-War* (Evanston: Northwestern University Press; Chicago, Newberry Library, 1970), 151.

43. Quoted in Tuveson, *Redeemer Nation*, 211.

44. Luce is quoted in Diggins, *The Proud Decades*, 74.

45. Patterson, *Grand Expectations*, 88.

46. Data on attitudes about America's role in promoting self-determination for captive nations can be found in George H. Gallup, *The Gallup Poll: Public Opinion, 1935–1971*, 2:1410. The interview data on using teachers as goodwill ambassadors and on the Peace Corps can be found in ibid., 3:1679, 3:1791.

47. In fact, *Witness* sold more copies than any of them, appearing on the *New York Times Book Review*'s list of best sellers for twenty-six weeks in 1952 and ranking ninth in sales for nonfiction books for the entire year at 80,000 copies. For sales information on *Witness*, see "The Best Sellers," *New York Times Book Review*, 1 June 1952, 23 November 1952; Hackett, *70 Years of Best Sellers: 1895–1965*, 190–191.

48. Chambers, *Witness*, 799.

49. De Toledano, *Nixon*, 76.

50. Quoted in Kornitzer, *The Real Nixon*, 176.

51. Chambers, *Witness*, 33.

52. De Toledano, *Nixon*, 11–12.

53. Chambers, *Witness*, 793.

54. Wills, *Nixon Agonistes*, 99–100; Mazo, *Nixon: A Political and Personal Portrait*, 129.

55. See Brodie, *Richard Nixon*, 367 (page citation is to the Harvard University Press edition).

56. Jim Berryman, editorial cartoon, *Washington (DC) Star*, 16 May 1958, A20. The originals of the Hubenthal cartoons are in the collection at the Richard Nixon Library and Birthplace, 1959 Political Cartoon File, July.

57. De Toledano, *Nixon*, 222.

58. Chambers, *Witness*, 764; Kornitzer, *The Real Nixon*, 346; Friedman, *Capitalism and Freedom*, 1; Ayn Rand, "Doesn't Life Require Compromise?" in *The Virtue of Selfishness: A New Concept of Egoism* (New York: Signet, 1964), 79–80.

59. Patterson, *Grand Expectations*, 500.

60. Nixon's complaints that the media actively campaigned for Kennedy, trying to make his victory seem inevitable, conveniently fails to mention that the final October Gallup poll on the election held that the race was a dead heat and that CBS news made a computer projection of "an overwhelming Nixon victory" on election eve. See Diggins, *The Proud Decades*, 342–343.

61. George H. Gallup, *The Gallup Poll: Public Opinion, 1935–1971*, 3:1747, 3:1647.

62. Franklin, *The Autobiography*, in *Autobiography, Poor Richard, and Later Writings*, 626.

63. Gordon and Gordon, *American Chronicle*, 402.

64. Harrington, *The Other America*, 1 (page citations are to the Penguin edition).

65. Friedan, *Feminine Mystique*, 11, 7 (page citations are to the Dell edition).

CHAPTER TWO. JEREMIAH AT SAN CLEMENTE:
RICHARD NIXON AND THE DECLINE OF THE AMERICAN REPUBLIC

1. Quoted in Nixon, *RN: The Memoirs of Richard Nixon*, 641 (hereafter cited in text as *RN*).

2. Ambrose, *Nixon: Ruin and Recovery*, 484–485, 505, 512.

3. "Don't Buy Books by Crooks?" A22; Mitgang, "Dispute over Sale Precedes Release of Nixon Memoirs"; Mitgang, "Nixon Book Dispute Erupts at Meeting," A16; "Best Sellers," *New York Times Book Review*, 4 June–13 August 1978. One cannot put an exact number on the weeks that *RN* would have been on the best-seller list because, after 13 August 1978, a pressman's strike halted publication of the *New York Times* until 6 November 1978. At the time the work stoppage began, *RN* ranked number eight on the list, having dropped from number three the week before. When the *New York Times Book Review* reappeared, Nixon's memoirs had dropped from sight.

4. A clip from Nixon's appearance on the *Tonight* show with Jack Paar appears on *Nixon: The American Experience*, VHS, PBS Home Video, 1997.

5. Nixon rated tenth in 1963, seventh in 1965, ninth in 1966, moved back to seventh in 1967, and rose to fifth in 1968, before taking the top spot in 1969. See George H. Gallup, *The Gallup Poll: Public Opinion, 1935–1971*, 3:1856, 3:1981, 3:2043, 3:2100–2101, 3:2174–2175, 3:2231.

6. Mazo and Hess, *Nixon: A Political Portrait*, 3.

7. De Toledano, *One Man Alone*, 6.

8. Spalding, *The Nixon Nobody Knows*, 430, 435, 439.

9. Hoyt, *The Nixons*, 100, 4.

10. For my understanding of the jeremiad, I rely on Perry Miller, *Errand into the Wilderness*, 1–15; and Perry Miller, *The New England Mind*, 19–39; as well as Bercovitch, *American Jeremiad*, which extends and corrects Miller's analysis.

11. Bercovitch, *American Jeremiad*, 23, 17, 29.

12. "Dole Declares Nixon Is Not Rehabilitated," *New York Times*, 6 June 1977, 38; John Osborne, "White House Watch: R. Nixon, His Book," review of *RN: The Memoirs of Richard Nixon* by Richard Nixon, *New Republic*, 27 May 1978, 9; "This Week's Arrivals," review of *RN*, *Christian Century*, 13 September 1978, 836; Peter Goldman, "Nixon's Own Final Days," review of *RN*, *Newsweek*, 8 May 1978, 33; Daniel Schorr, "Nixon: Wrestling with Himself," review of *RN*, *Progressive*, August 1978, 41; John Kenneth Galbraith, "The Good Old Days," review of *RN*, *New York Review of Books*,

29 June 1978, 3. For more negative reviews, see Richard Rovere, "Richard the Bold," review of *RN*, *New Yorker*, 19 June 1978, 96–97; and Robert Sherrill, "The Sound of One Hand Clapping," review of *RN*, *Nation*, 8–15 July 1978, 53–57. Some of the reviewers tackled the issue of Nixon's ultimate persuasiveness head-on. Historian James MacGregor Burns, writing in the *New York Times Book Review*, pronounced that "the book's main importance lies in its potential usefulness to Nixon revisionists who will seek to restore him to the place that he feels he should adorn, the pantheon of great Presidents. Out of this bible . . . chapter and verse will be cited and adversaries denounced. For Richard M. Nixon and his band of followers it will be the ultimate Survivor's Kit." Christopher Lehmann-Haupt imagined a not "impossible scenario" in which some future audience finds Nixon's Watergate rationalizations convincing, resulting in Nixon's emergence "as the great President he believes history should finally judge him to have been." For this reason, Lehmann-Haupt finds *RN* a "fascinating performance" and recommends that those with "moral qualms about purchasing it, [should] borrow it from a friend or the library." By contrast, Garry Wills proposed making the book "required reading for any serious student of America," but only because he found Nixon's book persuasive in a way its author never intended: "Why should we lose the national self-knowledge to be gained from Nixon's self-deception?" See James MacGregor Burns, "A Final Appeal to History," review of *RN*, *New York Times Book Review*, 11 June 1987, 54; Christopher Lehmann-Haupt, "Books of the Times," review of *RN*, *New York Times*, 8 June 1978, C17; and Garry Wills, "Why All of Us Should Read Nixon's Memoirs," review of *RN*, *New York*, 3 July 1978, 59, 58.

13. *Nixon Interviews with David Frost: The Collector's Edition*, VHS, MCA Universal, 1992. All other references to the *Nixon Interviews* will be based on my transcriptions and will appear in the text.

14. In *RN*, Nixon hints at the extensive, and unnecessary, remodeling done to Kennedy's and Johnson's homes at taxpayer expense and assigns sinister connotations to the disappearance of the records of these expenditures (956).

15. None of these men, however, had submitted a backdated deed of gift of the papers and received a deduction on their income taxes to which they were not entitled.

16. "Sweet Home Alabama," Lynyrd Skynyrd, *Second Helping*, MCA B000002P74.

17. Carroll, *It Seemed Like Nothing Happened*, 168–169; Frum, *How We Got Here*, 49–50.

18. Frum, *How We Got Here*, 28–29.

19. Carroll, *It Seemed Like Nothing Happened*, 210.

20. Ibid., 213.

21. Sales information on Lasky, *It Didn't Start with Watergate*, appears in "Best Sellers of the Year," *New York Times Book Review*, 4 December 1977, 111.

22. On Nixon's use of de Toledano and Lasky, *Seeds of Treason*, in the 1950 campaign, see Mitchell, *Tricky Dick and the Pink Lady*, 136, 217. On Lasky's friendship with Nixon, see Ambrose, *Nixon: The Triumph of a Politician*, 29, 172, 251, 410.

23. Lasky, *It Didn't Start with Watergate*, 1.

24. See the Book-of-the-Month Club's advertisement in the *New York Times Book Review*, 29 January 1978, 6; and "A Selection of Noteworthy Titles: 1977," *New York Times Book Review*, 4 December 1977, 16.

25. Price, *With Nixon*, 254.

26. Lasky, *It Didn't Start with Watergate*, 5.

27. Price, *With Nixon*, 270.

28. Jeremiah 8:9 (Revised Standard Version).

29. Jeremiah 8:8 (Revised Standard Version).

30. Price, *With Nixon*, 180.

31. Aldebaran, *Nixon and the Foxes of Watergate*, 21.

32. Ibid., 41, 29.

33. Sabrepen, *I Quit*, 22, 33, 34.

34. Quoted in Frost, *I Gave Them a Sword*, 264.

35. Ibid., 316.

36. Jeremiah 7:8 (Revised Standard Version).

37. Carroll, *It Seemed Like Nothing Happened*, 127.

38. Arthur Burns's words appear in ibid., 134.

39. Ibid., 175; Patterson, *Restless Giant*, 39. The quotation from Ford's 1975 State of the Union address appears in Carroll, *It Seemed Like Nothing Happened*, 175.

40. The photo, taken on 2 April 1975 in Nha Trang, South Vietnam, appears in the photo insert section of Patterson, *Restless Giant*. In the Corbis online photo archive (http://pro.corbis.com), the photograph is cataloged under the image number BE 002465 (RM) © Bettmann/CORBIS.

41. The story of Boston's conflict over school busing can be found in Patterson, *Restless Giant*, 20–21.

42. Stanley J. Foreman won the Pulitzer Prize for this April 1976 photo. It also appears in the photo insert section of Patterson, *Restless Giant*.

43. Patterson, *Restless Giant*, 15.

44. Price, *With Nixon*, 352.

45. Franklin B. Smith, *Assassination of President Nixon*, 86, 86, 89.

46. Aldebaran, *Nixon and the Foxes of Watergate*, 37; Sabrepen, *I Quit*, 41, 88–93.

47. Aldebaran, *Nixon and the Foxes of Watergate*, 55.

48. Heschel, *The Prophets*, 124 (page citation is to the Harper Torchbook edition).

49. Price, *With Nixon*, 46, 34.

50. Aldebaran, *Nixon and the Foxes of Watergate*, 18, 21, 42. For the story about Nixon's pursuit of "liberal Jewish bureaucrats" conspiring against him, see Ambrose, *Triumph of a Politician*, 457.

51. Aldebaran, *Nixon and the Foxes of Watergate*, 10–11; Gary Allen, *Nixon*, 313, 330.

52. George Gallup Jr., "'Watergate' Twenty Years Later," in *The Gallup Poll: Public Opinion 1992*, 105.

53. Two examples illustrate this "crisis" interpretation. In *The Anxious Years*, historian Kim McQuaid calls Watergate one of the most severe tests of the American system of government, "during which America's constitutional system of checks and balances was faced with its most decisive and overt challenges since the Depression decade of the 1930s" (168–169). Legal scholar Stanley I. Kutler asserts, in *The Wars of Watergate*, that the scandal "has implications that go to the heart of our political and constitutional system" (xiii).

54. Frost, *I Gave Them a Sword*, 316.

55. In the years immediately following the publication of *RN*, many were far too sanguine about the casual assumption that Nixon would fail in his quest at rehabilitation. After having placed Nixon in a tradition of autobiographers who, like Cotton Mather, tell lies in the service of what they see to be a higher truth, John Seelye, in "The Clay Foot of the Social Climber: Richard M. Nixon in Perspective," unaccountably dismisses the former president: "Well, Nixon's idea has now passed into memory, fading fast as a bad dream" (133). As is certain now, however, Nixon did not disappear into oblivion, and one reason he did not is because of this complacent attitude among his opponents that he had been relegated to the dustbin of history.

56. See also Ronald Lee, "The Featuring of Will in History," 462. Lee asserts that Nixon's success as a best-selling author of foreign policy books and self-justifying memoirs served as "a symptom of the ailing health of public morality in liberal society."

57. Jeremiah 13:25 (Revised Standard Version).

58. Carroll, *It Seemed Like Nothing Happened*, 198, 200.

59. Ibid., 290–291.

60. Ibid., 292.

61. Peter Bonventre, with Thomas M. DeFrank and Hal Bruno, "Panama Canal: Reagan Speaks Out," *Newsweek*, 5 September 1977, 38.

62. Patterson, *Restless Giant*, 66, 133.

63. Carroll, *It Seemed Like Nothing Happened*, 324–325.

64. Rick Perlstein, *Before the Storm*, 505–506, 487. Perlstein's book *Nixonland: The Rise of a President and the Fracturing of America* is due to be published by Scribner in May 2008.

65. Patterson, *Restless Giant*, 131.

66. Quoted in Crawford, *Thunder on the Right*, 45–46.

67. Carroll, *It Seemed Like Nothing Happened*, 326–327.

68. Ibid., 328.

69. Patterson, *Restless Giant*, 152.

70. The Reagan quote appears in Tom Matthews, with Gerald C. Lubenow, "The Leading Man," *Newsweek*, 1 October 1979, 21; Nixon, *The Real War*, 3.

71. Carroll, *It Seemed Like Nothing Happened*, 343.

CHAPTER THREE. "ANYONE CAN BE THE PRESIDENT":
BEHIND THE MASK OF SUCCESS

1. John Cougar Mellencamp, "Pink Houses," *uh-huh*, Riva Records RVL 7504.

2. Costello, *The Facts about Nixon*, 17 (page citation is to the Viking edition).

3. "Have Gun, Will Unravel," *Family Ties: The Complete First Season*, DVD, 8 December 1982, CBS DVD, 2007.

4. *Secret Honor*, VHS, 1984, Vestron Video, 1987. All quotations from *Secret Honor* in this chapter are my transcriptions of the film's screenplay taken from the 1987 release of the film.

5. Ferlinghetti, *Tyrannus Nix?* 13.

6. Kaplan, *Gore Vidal*, 473; "Morosco Theatre," Internet Broadway Database, www .ibdb.com (accessed 5 July 2006). Eugene O'Neill's first full-length play produced on Broadway, the Pulitzer Prize–winning *Beyond the Horizon*, opened on 20 February 1920 at the Morosco. See Gelb and Gelb, *O'Neill*, 406.

7. Robert F. Kiernan, "Gore Vidal," *Dictionary of Literary Biography*, vol. 152, *American Novelists since World War II, Fourth Series* (Detroit: Gale Research, 1995), 235–236. Vidal's reputation was such that reportedly by 1960 his fee for a one-hour script was almost $5,000; see ibid., 236–237.

8. Kaplan, *Gore Vidal*, 460, 461.

9. Lewis Funke, "News and Gossip of the Rialto," *New York Times*, 28 February 1960, X1, X3; Stanley Levey, "Playwright with a Political Perspective," *New York Times*, 27 March 1960, X1; "Playwright Enters Race for House Seat Upstate," *New York Times*, 4 April 1960, 44.

10. "Theatre Directory," *New York Times*, 20 March 1960, X6, 1 April 1960, 39, 21 June 1961, 31.

11. Vidal, *The Essential Gore Vidal*, 57. Seeing *The Best Man* became almost a requirement for former and practicing politicians during New York visits. Harry

Truman, Indian prime minister Nehru, and president-elect Kennedy all took in the show during its run. See Arthur Gelb, "A Man Who Plays Ex-President Meets a Man Who Is One," *New York Times*, 21 April 1960, 23; Kaplan, *Gore Vidal*, 486; and "Nehru Is Applauded on Visit to Theatre," *New York Times*, 9 October 1960, 35.

12. "'Best Man' to Be Film," *New York Times*, 24 May 1960, 42; Kaplan, *Gore Vidal*, 534–536, 539.

13. Vidal, "Richard Nixon: Not *The Best Man*'s Best Man," in *United States: Essays, 1952–1992* (New York: Random House, 1993), 900.

14. Vidal, *The Best Man*, in *The Essential Gore Vidal*, 153 (hereafter cited in text as *Best*).

15. Quoted in Nixon, *RN*, 112.

16. Quoted in Nixon, *Six Crises*, 116.

17. Patterson, *Grand Expectations*, 338.

18. For a discussion of Galbraith's ideas, see Patterson, *Grand Expectations*, 340; Blum, *Years of Discord*, 8; and Lytle, *America's Uncivil Wars*, 53–55. See also Galbraith, *Affluent Society*, 5.

19. "Coaching Sen. Fuller," *A Face in the Crowd*, DVD, 1957, Warner Home Video, 2005.

20. Patterson, *Grand Expectations*, 351.

21. The Eisenhower administration–sponsored commission wrote *Goals for Americans* (1960); the Rockefeller Fund published reports between 1958 and 1960, collected in the 1961 publication *Prospect for America*; and Time, Inc. and the *New York Times* released *The National Purpose* in 1960. See Blum, *Years of Discord*, 12–13.

22. Vidal, "Note to 'A Note on *The Best Man*,'" in *Rocking the Boat* (Boston: Little, Brown, 1962), 299.

23. David Frye, "The Parable," *Richard Nixon Superstar*, Buddah Records BDS 5097.

24. Silesky, *Ferlinghetti*, 169; Larry Smith, *Lawrence Ferlinghetti: Poet-at-Large*, 43.

25. For details on Ferlinghetti's life and career, see Thomas McClanahan, "Lawrence Ferlinghetti," in *Dictionary of Literary Biography*, ed. Donald J. Greiner (Detroit: Gale Research Company, 1980), 5:248–255; and Larry Smith, "Lawrence Ferlinghetti," in *Dictionary of Literary Biography*, ed. Ann Charters (Detroit: Gale Research Company, 1983), 16:199–214.

26. Larry Smith, "Lawrence Ferlinghetti," 16:205, 16:207.

27. McClanahan, "Lawrence Ferlinghetti," 5:251, 5:253; Ferlinghetti, "Tentative Description of a Dinner to Promote the Impeachment of President Eisenhower" and "One Thousand Fearful Words for Fidel Castro," in *Starting from San Francisco* (New York: New Directions, 1967), 41–44, 48–52; Ferlinghetti, "Where Is Vietnam?" in *Open Eye, Open Heart* (New York: New Directions, 1973), 77–78.

28. Silesky, *Ferlinghetti*, 169; Ferlinghetti: *Tyrannus Nix? Assassination Raga, Big Sur Sun Sutra, Moscow in the Wilderness*, LP record, Fantasy Records 7014. As an indication of what *Tyrannus Nix?*'s sales figures suggest, note that in July 2006, *Newsweek*, in a story tracing the amazing success of the Disney Channel movie *High School Musical*, noted that the novelization had sold 350,000 copies. Keeping in mind that *Tyrannus Nix?* is a poem (which as a genre rarely makes the best-seller lists), that it is a topical poem at that, and that *High School Musical* is a cultural phenomenon (the sound track has topped Billboard's charts and the stars made an appearance on the *Today* show), one gets a sense of the success of Ferlinghetti's poem in reaching a good-sized portion of those Americans who read literature. (For sales figure on *High School Musical*'s novelization, see Marc Bain, "'Musical' Money Machine," *Newsweek*, 24 July 2006, 44.)

29. Ambrose, *Nixon: Triumph of a Politician*, 265, 275–276, 277.

30. Ibid., 303–306, 310, 311, 310.

31. Ferlinghetti, *Tyrannus Nix?* 6, 26, 26, 43, 4.

32. Ibid., 34.

33. *Millhouse: A White Comedy*, VHS, 1971, MPI Home Video; Ferlinghetti, *Tyrannus Nix?*, 35.

34. Allen Ginsberg, "Howl, Part II," in *The New American Poetry*, ed. Donald M. Allen (New York: Grove Press, 1960), 189.

35. In fact, in the case of the DuPont Company, Ferlinghetti has the process reversed. Initially a producer of gunpowder, only later did this family-run business diversify and turn to products made for home use.

36. Ferlinghetti, *Tyrannus Nix?* 29, 61.

37. David Frye, "The Election," *Richard Nixon Superstar*, Buddah Records BDS 5097.

38. *All in the Family: The Complete Second Season*, DVD, 1971, Columbia TriStar Home Entertainment, 2003; *All in the Family: The Complete Third Season*, DVD, 1972, Columbia TriStar Home Entertainment, 2004. Original airdates for *All in the Family* broadcasts can be found in McCrohan, *Archie & Edith, Mike & Gloria*, 228, 231.

39. Ferlinghetti, *Tyrannus Nix?* 53, 19, 73.

40. Ibid., 24, 68, 75–92.

41. Ibid., 69, 74. Larry Smith, in *Lawrence Ferlinghetti: Poet-at-Large*, expresses admiration at Ferlinghetti's ability to surprise "the reader who expects an easy personal attack . . . [with a] sincerity that goes beyond anger or insult" (173).

42. Ferlinghetti, *Tyrannus Nix?* 25.

43. Gitlin, *The Sixties*, 355.

44. Lytle, *America's Uncivil Wars*, 329–330; Gitlin, *The Sixties*, 353–359, 361.

45. Blum, *Years of Discord*, 357; Gitlin, *The Sixties*, 387–388.

46. Blum, *Years of Discord*, 357; Gitlin, *The Sixties*, 400–401.

47. Gitlin, *The Sixties*, 403.

48. Lytle, *America's Uncivil Wars*, 334–335; *Woodstock*, VHS, 1970, Warner Home Video, 1987.

49. Lytle, *America's Uncivil Wars*, 335; Blum, *Years of Discord*, 363, 361.

50. Blum, *Years of Discord*, 364.

51. There are harsher interpretations, of course. Celeste MacLeod doubts that a true counterculture existed at all. In *Horatio Alger, Farewell*, she draws an unflattering portrait of pampered young "rebels" who had the option of rejecting the American system while still living in comfort because of the continuing record expansion of the American economy. As former editors of the New Left magazine *Ramparts*, Peter Collier and David Horowitz have no doubt that a counterculture existed, but in *Destructive Generation* they argue that the movement in which they were participants was a negative force: "As one center of authority [of the American system] after another was discredited . . . we radicals claimed that we murdered to create. But while we wanted a revolution, we didn't have a plan" (15).

52. Ferlinghetti, "Watergate Rap," mini-sleeve to *Tyrannus Nix?*; John Lennon, "God," *Plastic Ono Band*, Capitol B00004WGEL.

53. On Freed's work on behalf of the Black Panthers, see Hilliard and Cole, *This Side of Glory*, 277, 285–288. For information about the Broadway run of Freed's play *Inquest*, see "Inquest," on the Internet Broadway Database.

54. Megan Rosenfeld, "Philip Hall's Quest for 'Secret Honor,'" *Washington Post*, 2 February 1986, Final Edition, K1.

55. Eleanor Blau, "Going Out Guide," *New York Times*, 1 November 1983, C15. The Provincetown Players staged early O'Neill plays like *The Emperor Jones* and *Desire under the Elms*. Edward Albee's first play, *The Zoo Story*, opened at the Provincetown Playhouse in 1960 and soon appeared as a double-bill with Beckett's *Krapp's Last Tape* (see "Provincetown Playhouse," Internet Broadway Database; "Provincetown Playhouse," Lortel Archives, Internet Off-Broadway Database, http://www.lortel.org/lla_archive/index.cfm [accessed 25 February 2008]).

56. "Secret Honor," Lortel Archives, Internet Off-Broadway Database (accessed 10 July 2006); Mel Gussow, "Stage: 'Secret Honor,' Nixon after the Pardon," *New York Times*, 11 November 1983, C4; W. Kim Heron, "Movie Set Moves to a College Dormitory," *Detroit Free Press*, 27 January 1984, NewsBank, http://www.newsbank.com (accessed 8 July 2006); Kevin Kelly, "Philip Baker Hall\A Blistering Portrayal of Nixon," *Boston Globe*, 19 February 1984, NewsBank.

57. Altman rented the Cannery Theater for one week to test audience response to *Secret Honor*. The test screening proved successful; after grossing nearly $9,000, the theater extended the film for an additional week. Jay Boyar, "Director Gambled, and

Beat the Odds," *Orlando (FL) Sentinel*, 14 September 1985, NewsBank; John Hartl, "The Seattle Film Festival Showing Strong after 10 Years," *Seattle Times*, 5 May 1985, NewsBank; Herb Michelson, "Robert Altman Takes on Nixon in 'Secret Honor,'" *Sacramento (CA) Bee*, 11 July 1984, NewsBank; "Altman Aiming for June 'Honor' Bow in San Francisco," *Variety*, 6 June 1984, 5, 26. For information on the Cannery Theater, see "Cannery Cinema," http://www.cinematreasures.org/theater/1946 (accessed 17 July 2006).

58. For *Secret Honor*'s inclusion on Siskel's and Ebert's best of 1984 lists, see Gail Shister, "On 'Cheers,' Motherhood Won't Come to Diane," *Philadelphia Inquirer*, 15 January 1985, NewsBank. *Secret Honor* appeared in such venues as the Orson Welles in Cambridge, Massachusetts, the Roxie in San Francisco, the Detroit Film Theatre, the Portland Film Festival, the Biograph in Washington, DC (after a premiere at the Smithsonian), the Ellis Cinema in Atlanta, and the Roxy in Philadelphia and had a one-month run at the Fine Arts Theatre in Chicago. For details, see Jay Carr, "Altman Humanizes Nixon," *Boston Globe*, 2 November 1984, NewsBank; Judy Stone, "'Engagement': A Look at Two Con Artists," *San Francisco Chronicle*, 7 February 1985, NewsBank; Michael Roberts, "Camera Eavesdrops on Richard Nixon," *Detroit Free Press*, 14 February 1985, NewsBank; "Portland Film Festival Announces List of Featured Films," *Seattle Times*, 24 February 1985, NewsBank; Eddie Cockrell, "Film Talk," *Washington Post*, 29 March 1985, Weekend, 21–22; Eddie Cockrell, "Film Talk," *Washington Post*, 10 May 1985, Weekend, 26; Scott Cain, "'Honor' Is Under-the-Skin Probe of Nixon," *Atlanta Journal and Atlanta Constitution*, 19 July 1985, NewsBank; Gene Siskel, "Friday," *Chicago Tribune*, 26 July, 2 August, 9 August, 16 August 1985, NewsBank; Joe Baltake, "'Secret' Portrait of a Destroyed Man," *Philadelphia Daily News*, 8 August 1985, NewsBank; Rick Lyman, "Film: Nixon All by Himself," *Philadelphia Inquirer*, 9 August 1985, NewsBank; and Jay Boyar, "Film Probes for Human beneath Nixon Facade," *Orlando (FL) Sentinel*, 18 September 1985, NewsBank.

59. Bill Cosford, "What Other Critics Picked," *Miami Herald*, 5 January 1986, NewsBank.

60. Jay Boyar, "Director Gambled, and Beat the Odds," *Orlando (FL) Sentinel*, 14 September 1985, NewsBank; Judy Stone, "Themes in Foreign Lands Highlights the Top Ten," *San Francisco Chronicle*, 29 December 1985, NewsBank; Jay Boyar, "The Best of 1985 Movies," *Orlando Sentinel*, 29 December 1985, NewsBank; "Secret Honor (1984), Awards," Internet Movie Database, imdb.com (accessed 30 June 2006); Megan Rosenfeld, "Philip Hall's Quest for 'Secret Honor,'" *Washington Post*, 2 February 1986, Final Edition, K4; Howard Thompson, "Critics' Choices; Cable TV," *New York Times*, 7 September 1986, 2:A2; *Secret Honor*, VHS, 1984, Vestron Video, 1987; *Secret Honor*, laserdisc, Criterion Collection, 1993; *Secret Honor*, DVD, Criterion Collection.

61. Jenkins, *Decade of Nightmares*, 183.

62. Patterson, *Restless Giant*, 157–158, 164; Jenkins, *Decade of Nightmares*, 182.

63. On Bohemian Grove, see Domhoff, *Bohemian Grove and Other Retreats*; and Philip Weiss, "Masters of the Universe Go to Camp: Inside the Bohemian Grove." For a conspiracy-minded critique of the Grove, its members, and their activities that is so far right wing as to be almost left wing, see Texas talk-radio personality Alex Jones's *Dark Secrets: Inside Bohemian Grove, Order of Death*, DVD (Austin, TX: www .infowars.com, 2005).

64. See Huber, *American Idea of Success*, 38.

65. David Mamet, *Glengarry Glen Ross* (1984; reprint, New York: Grove Weidenfeld, 1984), 30, 32.

66. Lewis, *Culture of Inequality*, 39 (citation is to the New American Library edition).

67. Elkin, *The Dick Gibson Show*, 400 (citation is to the E. P. Dutton edition); Novello, *The Lazlo Letters*.

68. Edward Pessen places Richard Nixon in the company of Millard Fillmore and James Garfield, as the small group of men who supposedly rose from the lower middle class to become president. Only Andrew Johnson actually ascended from the lower class. Edward Pessen, "The Families of the Presidents Compared," in *The Log Cabin Myth: The Social Backgrounds of the Presidents* (New Haven: Yale University Press, 1984), 55–73.

69. What struck many as the film's most outrageously fictional moment—the assertion that the Watergate scandal served as a smoke screen to hide the treason of having accepted "bribes to keep a fucking war going"—actually had a source. An *Atlantic Monthly* article by Renata Adler, who had served on the House Judiciary Committee's impeachment inquiry staff, argued that the conventional wisdom about Watergate failed to explain "why the Nixon presidency in particular had to end. . . . Unless Nixon did something beyond what is known about him, or his men, or any of his predecessors, his departure from office seems random, arbitrary, and even incomplete." See Adler, "Searching for the Real Nixon Scandal," 77, 80.

70. Lasch, *Culture of Narcissism*, 60.

71. Iain Johnstone, "Richard, the Confessor," review of *Secret Honor* (Sandcastle 5 Productions), *Sunday Times* (London), 10 February 1985, 8. Other reviewers who had difficulty in dealing with the fictionality of Freed and Stone's historical fiction include Stanley Kauffmann, "Poor Richard's Almanac and Others," review of *Secret Honor* (Sandcastle 5 Productions), *New Republic*, 15 July 1985, 32; Peter Waymark, "Casting Light on the Darkest Days of a President," review of *Secret Honor* (Sandcastle 5 Productions), *Times* (London), 2 February 1985, 16; and Pauline Kael, "Arf," review of *Secret Honor* (Sandcastle 5 Productions), *New Yorker*, 15 July 1985, 73. For a

more thoughtful response, see Geoff Brown, "Altman's Heroic Enterprise," review of *Secret Honor* (Sandcastle 5 Productions), *Times* (London), 8 February 1985, 12.

72. *Family Ties: The Second Season*, "Speed Trap," DVD, 11 November 1983, CBS, 2007. The quotation is based on my transcription of the episode's teleplay.

73. Bellah et al., *Habits of the Heart*, 65, 151 (citations are to the Harper & Row edition).

74. Troy, *Morning in America*, 134.

75. Haynes Johnson, *Sleepwalking through History*, 110, 111 (citations are to the Anchor Books edition).

76. Ibid., 115; Troy, *Morning in America*, 131–133.

77. Troy, *Morning in America*, 149; Patterson, *Restless Giant*, 205; Troy, *Morning in America*, 157, 155.

78. Troy, *Morning in America*, 161, 166, 163, 161.

79. Ambrose, *Nixon: Ruin and Recovery*, 549, 551, 560, 559.

80. Newman, *Declining Fortunes*, 212.

81. Ehrenreich, *Nickel and Dimed*, 199.

82. *NewsRadio: The Complete Third Season*, "Awards Show," DVD, 6 November 1996, Sony Pictures Home Entertainment, 2006. All quotations in the text are from my transcription of the episode's teleplay.

83. Huber, *American Idea of Success*, 457.

CHAPTER FOUR. THE SELF-MADE MONSTER:
AMERICA AND THE MYTH OF NATIONAL MISSION

1. "Peace Is at Hand, 1968–1973," *Vietnam: A Television History*, VHS, 1983, WGBH Educational Foundation and Sony Corporation of America, 1987.

2. Berman, *No Peace, No Honor*; and Kimball, *Nixon's Vietnam War*, 370. The cartoon appears in Feiffer, *Feiffer on Nixon: The Cartoon Presidency*.

3. Niebuhr, *The Irony of American History*, 25, 42.

4. Coover, *Whatever Happened to Gloomy Gus of the Chicago Bears? American Review* (New York: Simon and Schuster, 1975), 34–110.

5. Coover, *Whatever Happened to the Gloomy Gus of the Chicago Bears?* (New York: Simon and Schuster, 1987), 122.

6. My summary of *The Public Burning*'s composition and publication history is a composite of information derived from the following sources: Thomas Alden Bass, "An Encounter with Robert Coover," *Antioch Review* 40 (1982): 287–302; "Interview with Robert Coover," by Christopher Bigsby, in *The Radical Imagination and the Liberal Tradition: Interviews with English and American Novelists*, ed. Heide Ziegler and Christopher Bigsby (London: Junction Books, 1982), 79–92; "An Interview with Robert Coover," by

Kay Bonetti, May 1981, American Audio Prose Library AAPL 1052, audiotape recording; and Larry McCaffery, "Robert Coover," *Dictionary of Literary Biography: Volume 2, American Novelists since World War II* (Detroit: Gale Research Company, 1982).

7. "Best Sellers," *New York Times Book Review*, 2 October 1977, 12.

8. Coover, *The Public Burning*, 8.

9. Ibid., 8, 149, 6, 8, 149.

10. In fact, Coover believes that "if you read the trial record you pretty well have to conclude that the Rosenbergs were innocent of the charges against them. But they were either responsible for protecting some other secret, or believed themselves to be" (Thomas Alden Bass, "An Encounter with Robert Coover," *Antioch Review* 20 (1982): 297). Interestingly, Coover's secondary conclusion differs only slightly from the findings of Radosh and Milton in *The Rosenberg File*. Although they find no evidence of the wholesale fabrication of evidence against the Rosenbergs, which Coover had anticipated would come to light, Radosh and Milton would agree that the Rosenbergs were not guilty of stealing the secret of the atomic bomb, as the government had contended. However, they do contend that Julius Rosenberg was engaged in espionage (supplying secondary information on the Manhattan Project was one of his assignments), and this secret, along with the names of Julius's other contacts, was the secret the couple died to protect.

11. Coover, *The Public Burning*, 93, 123, 86, 531.

12. Ibid., 117.

13. Ibid., 131–132.

14. Ibid., 234.

15. Ibid., 362, 436, 363.

16. Ibid., 10, 41, 224.

17. Niebuhr, *The Irony of American History*, 126.

18. Greene, *The Quiet American*, 10, 155 (citations are to the Penguin edition).

19. Robert Stone, introduction to Greene, *The Quiet American*, xvi, xviii. On Nixon's support for American intervention to bail out the French forces at Dien Bien Phu, see Ambrose, *Nixon: Education of a Politician*, 342–347.

20. Lederer and Burdick, *The Ugly American*, 94 (citation is to the W. W. Norton edition).

21. The Nixon quotation comes from an April 1960 speech given at the University of San Francisco. It appears in Hellmann, *American Myth and the Legacy of Vietnam*, 18.

22. Fulbright, *Arrogance of Power*, 8, 3, 21 (citations are to the Vintage edition).

23. Baritz, *Backfire*, 18, 17 (citations are to the Ballantine edition). Sheehan, *A Bright Shining Lie*, 60; Hellmann, *American Myth and the Legacy of Vietnam*, 15. See also FitzGerald, *Fire in the Lake*.

24. *Millhouse: A White Comedy*, VHS, 1971, MPI Home Video.

25. "Life Is Cheap in the Orient," *Hearts and Minds*, DVD, 1974, Criterion Collection, 2002.

26. Caputo, *A Rumor of War*, xiv (citation is to the Henry Holt edition).

27. "Emotional Statements," *Coming Home*, DVD, 1978, MGM Home Entertainment, 2002.

28. "The Wedding," "Vietnam," "Russian Roulette," "The Life Left Behind," and "Playing the American," *The Deer Hunter*, DVD, 1978, Universal Studios Home Entertainment, 2005.

29. Information on the theatrical release dates for *Apocalypse Now* comes from the Internet Movie Database.

30. "Waiting in Saigon" and "Ending," *Apocalypse Now*, DVD, Paramount Home Video, 2006.

31. Ari L. Goldman, "Peace, with Honor," *New York Times*, 29 August 1976, Long Island Weekly, 2:1. As of 8 August 1976, *The Final Days* was number one on the *Times*' nonfiction best-seller list and had been on the list for sixteen weeks. Hellmann's *Scoundrel Time* was number three and had been on the list for thirteen weeks. Gore Vidal's novel *1876*, ranked at number seven, had been a best seller for over five months. See "Best Seller List," *New York Times Book Review*, 8 August 1976, 25.

32. The memoir was also excerpted in the July 1976 issue of *Playboy* and merited notice in the *New York Times Book Review*'s list of the most important books of the year. The characterization of *Born on the Fourth of July*'s reviews and the information about the book's appearance in *Playboy* can be found in Ari L. Goldman, "Peace, with Honor," *New York Times*, 29 August 1976, Long Island Weekly, 2:1, 20–21. For a sampling of the reviews, see C. B. D. [*sic*] Bryan, "Growing Up the Hard Way," review of *Born on the Fourth of July*, by Ron Kovic, *New York Times Book Review*, 15 August 1976, 1; Richard R. Lingeman, "Memorial Day on Wheels," review of *Born on the Fourth of July*, by Ron Kovic, *New York Times*, 17 August 1976, 29; Walter Clemons, "Hell on Wheels," review of *Born on the Fourth of July*, by Ron Kovic, *Newsweek*, 20 September 1976, 88; Josiah Bunting III, "Missing in Action," review of *Born on the Fourth of July*, by Ron Kovic, *Harper's*, September 1976, 80–82; John B. Breslin, "Vietnam Legacy," review of *Friendly Fire*, by C. D. B. Bryan, and of *Born on the Fourth of July*, by Ron Kovic, *America*, 25 September 1976, 173–174; and Phoebe-Lou Adams, review of *Born on the Fourth of July*, by Ron Kovic, *Atlantic Monthly*, September 1976, 99. The list of 1976's most significant books appeared in "1976: A Selection of Noteworthy Titles," *New York Times Book Review*, 5 December 1976, 59.

33. Kovic, *Born on the Fourth of July*, 50, 194–195, 218–219 (citations are to the Pocket Books edition).

34. Ibid., 165.

35. Ibid., 137, 154–155, 170, 171, 182–183.

36. Ibid., 167, 170, 171.

37. Wills, *Reagan's America*, 378, 383–384.

38. See Jenkins, *Decade of Nightmares*, 220–221; and Troy, *Morning in America*, 157.

39. See Jenkins, *Decade of Nightmares*, 232–233; and Troy, *Morning in America*, 246.

40. *First Blood*, DVD, Artisan Entertainment, 2002; "Hellhole," *Rambo: First Blood II*, DVD, 1985, Artisan Entertainment, 2002; *Rambo III*, DVD, 1988, Artisan Entertainment, 2002.

41. For information on Norris's film *Missing in Action*, on the 1985 prequel *Missing in Action 2: The Beginning*, and on the final film in the trilogy, see the Internet Movie Database.

42. *Heartbreak Ridge* grossed $42 million at the box office (see the Internet Movie Database). Figures for *Top Gun* can also be found on the Internet Movie Database.

43. A summary of the *A-Team* story line can be found on the Internet Movie Database.

44. Nixon, *The Real War*, 2, 10 (citations are to the Warner edition); Nixon, *No More Vietnams*, 9–10, 237.

45. George Gallup Jr., *The Gallup Poll: Public Opinion 1990*, 48, 49.

46. The Clash, "I'm So Bored with the U.S.A.," *The Clash*, Epic Records 367060.

47. Chapter 7, *Missing*, DVD, 1982, Universal Studios Home Entertainment, 2004.

48. Reagan's characterization of the contras appears in Patterson, *Restless Giant*, 209.

49. Ibid., 207–209.

50. Troy, *Morning in America*, 243; Jenkins, *Decade of Nightmares*, 216.

51. Troy, *Morning in America*, 243.

52. George Gallup Jr., *The Gallup Poll: Public Opinion 2000*, 381.

53. George Gallup Jr., *The Gallup Poll: Public Opinion 1990*, 49; George Gallup Jr., *The Gallup Poll: Public Opinion 1991*, 57.

54. "A Crusader," *Platoon*, DVD, 1986, Sony Pictures Home Entertainment, 2006. Not only did *Platoon* compete with Rambo at the box office, but it managed what Stallone's movies could never hope of doing—winning the Academy Award for Best Picture. *Platoon*'s revenues from U.S. rentals are three times those of *First Blood*, for example. *Rambo: First Blood II*, by far the most popular of Stallone's trilogy, only bests *Platoon* by $12.5 million in gross receipts in American theaters. (Significantly, it's outside of the United States where *Rambo* resoundingly outdraws *Platoon*—making ten times the money of Stone's movie.) *Rambo III*, although also wildly popular overseas, has taken in $84 million less than *Platoon* at the U.S. box office. Box office figures on these films can be found on the Internet Movie Database.

55. Ambrose, *Nixon: Ruin and Recovery*, 559.

56. Randy Roberts and David Welky, "A Sacred Mission: Oliver Stone and Vietnam," in Toplin, *Oliver Stone's USA*, 75; Jack E. Davis, "New Left, Revisionist, In-Your-Face History," in Toplin, *Oliver Stone's USA*, 136–137.

57. "The Yankee Doodle Boy (Main Titles)," "Donna's World," and "All for Nothing," *Born on the Fourth of July*, DVD, 1989, Universal Studios Home Video, 2004.

58. "The Rebel," ibid.

59. "Maybe We're Home," ibid. The Bryant Gumbel interviews with Stone can be found on "NBC News Archives: Back Story," Bonus Menu, ibid.; Randy Roberts and David Welky, "A Sacred Mission: Oliver Stone and Vietnam," in Toplin, *Oliver Stone's USA*, 90.

60. Bacevich, "New Rome, New Jerusalem," 98.

61. For an explanation of how Noriega moved from being an ally to a prisoner in a Miami jail, see Patterson, *Restless Giant*, 226–227. The quoted passage appears in Troy, *Morning in America*, 327. The release date of *Born on the Fourth of July* can be found on the Internet Movie Database.

62. Patterson, *Restless Giant*, 238.

63. Philip Freneau, "The Rising Glory of America," in *The Poems of Philip Freneau: Poet of the American Revolution*, vol. 1, ed. Fred Lewis Pattee (Princeton, NJ: University Library, 1902), 82; Bacevich, "New Rome, New Jerusalem," 95, 96.

64. Nixon, *1999: Victory without War*, 321; Nixon, *Seize the Moment*, 14; Nixon, *Beyond Peace*, 251.

65. *Kissinger and Nixon* aired three times that evening and was repeated five more times that month. Martie Zed, "Cable Links: HBO Airs Michael Jackson Concert," *Washington Post*, "TV World," 10 December 1995, 4; *Kissinger and Nixon*, VHS, Turner Broadcasting System, 1996. All quotations from *Kissinger and Nixon* in this chapter are my transcriptions of the screenplay taken from the 1996 VHS release of the film.

66. For Chetwynd's conversion to Reagan conservatism, see "A Conversation with Lionel Chetwynd," by Govindini Murty, on *Libertas: A Forum for Conservative Thought on Film*, produced by Liberty Film Festival, ed. Jason Apuzzo, www.libertyfilmfestival.com. Chetwynd's film credits can be found on the Internet Movie Database. For negative reactions to the film, see "Kissinger Blasts TV Docudrama," *Rocky Mountain News*, 4 December 1995, LexisNexis; "Kissinger Blasts Film," *Houston Chronicle*, 4 December 1995, LexisNexis; Alexander M. Haig Jr., letter to the editor, *New York Times*, Late Edition, Final, 15 December 1995, A42; William F. Buckley Jr., "Hate Kissinger," *National Review*, 31 December 1995, 54; and Bob Sokolsky, "TNT's 'Nixon' Is a Crook; TV Movie Rushed to Steal Oliver Stone's Film Thunder Is Tepid," *Press Enterprise* (Riverside, CA), 9 December 1995, LexisNexis. For reviews that mixed

criticism with praise, see Dusty Saunders, "'Kissinger and Nixon' Airs on Shaky Historical Ground," *Rocky Mountain News*, 7 December 1995, LexisNexis; Tom Feran, "TNT's 'Kissinger and Nixon,'" *Cleveland Plain Dealer*, 7 December 1995, LexisNexis; Pete Schulberg, "'Kissinger and Nixon' More Fantasy Than Fact," *Sunday (Portland) Oregonian*, Sunrise Edition, 10 December 1995, LexisNexis; and Mike McDaniel, "Kissinger, Nixon Appear in Poor Light on TNT," *Houston Chronicle*, 9 December 1995, LexisNexis. For positive reviews, see Alan Pergament, "Silver Is a Believable Kissinger," *Buffalo News*, City Edition, 7 December 1995, LexisNexis; Matt Roush, "A Cerebral 'Kissinger,'" *USA Today*, Final Edition, 8 December 1995, LexisNexis; Lon Grahnke, "Huge Egos Wage War and Peace in 'Nixon' Saga," *Chicago Sun-Times*, 8 December 1995, LexisNexis; Michael Blowen, "Machiavelli over the White House," *Boston Globe*, City Edition, 8 December 1995, LexisNexis; Drew Jubera, "Kissinger and Nixon," *Atlanta Journal and Constitution*, 8 December 1995, LexisNexis; Lloyd Grove, "'Kissinger and Nixon': A Powerful Drama," *Washington Post*, 9 December 1995, C1; Ed Bark, "This Nixon Is Not a Crook," *St. Petersburg (FL) Times*, 10 December 1995, LexisNexis; Helen Arthur, "Television: Kissinger and Nixon, Bye, Bye Birdie, the Haunting of Helen Walker," *Nation*, 11 December 1995, 763–764; and John Leonard, "The Devil and Dr. K.," *New York*, 11 December 1995, 83–84. *Kissinger and Nixon*'s award nominations can be found on the Internet Movie Database.

67. Despite Chetwynd's impeccable conservative credentials, his presidential portrait is a Nixon-hater's dream—perhaps indicating that his opinions about Nixon hardened during his days as a Democrat, surviving the crucible of his conversion to Reaganism unchanged.

68. For the publication date, see "Elvis and Nixon," review of *Elvis and Nixon* by Jonathan Lowy, *Kirkus Reviews*, 1 January 2001, LexisNexis (accessed 24 October 2002). For the favorable reviews, see Mary Jane Park, review of *Elvis and Nixon* by Jonathan Lowy, *St. Petersburg (FL) Times*, 20 May 2001, LexisNexis; Tom Walker, "Truth Stranger Than Fiction in Odd Meeting," review of *Elvis and Nixon* by Jonathan Lowy, *Denver Post*, 11 March 2001, LexisNexis; "Short Takes: Books People Are Talking About," review of *Elvis and Nixon* by Jonathan Lowy, *Sunday (Portland) Oregonian*, 8 April 2001, LexisNexis; Mark Rozzo, "Elvis and Nixon," review of *Elvis and Nixon* by Jonathan Lowy, *Los Angeles Times Book Review*, 18 March 2001, LexisNexis; Alanna Nash, "Milhous Rock," review of *Elvis and Nixon* by Jonathan Lowy, *New York Times Book Review*, 4 March 2001, 27; and "Picks and Pans, Pages, Worth a Look, Elvis and Nixon," review of *Elvis and Nixon* by Jonathan Lowy, *People*, 5 March 2001, 51. Lowy's novel did receive one negative review and one incendiary pan. For the former, see David Greenberg, "Photo Op," review of *Elvis and Nixon* by Jonathan Lowy, *Washington Post Book World*, 4 March 2001, 8. For the latter, see Alfred Alcorn,

"Cliches Get Fresh Airing," review of *Elvis and Nixon* by Jonathan Lowy, *Boston Herald*, 4 March 2001, 65.

69. Lowy, *Elvis and Nixon*, 2, 133.

70. Ibid., 117, 118.

71. Ibid., 18.

72. Ibid., 160, 277.

73. Niebuhr, *The Irony of American History*, 71; Bacevich, "New Rome, New Jerusalem," 96.

74. "Our Unity Is a Kinship of Grief," *Washington Post*, 15 September 2001, A13.

75. Woodward, *Bush at War*, 67.

76. Bush's words appear in Woodward, *Bush at War*, 339. Nixon's first inaugural address appears in Nixon, *RN*, 366. The quotations from Bush's speech before Congress are taken from *Our Mission and Our Moment: President George W. Bush's Address to the Nation before a Joint Session of Congress, September 20, 2001*, 21.

77. LeClair, *The Art of Excess*, 106–130.

78. Coover, *The Public Burning*, 532–533.

79. Ibid., 532.

80. Ibid., 531.

81. Lowy, *Elvis and Nixon*, 52: Coover, *The Public Burning*, 86; Lowy, *Elvis and Nixon*, 314, 166.

82. "Interview with Robert Coover," by Christopher Bigsby, in *The Radical Imagination and the Liberal Tradition: Interviews with English and American Novelists*, ed. Heide Ziegler and Christopher Bigsby (London: Junction Books, 1982), 86.

83. Lowy, *Elvis and Nixon*, 319.

84. John Ramage, "Myth and Monomyth in Coover's *The Public Burning*," *Critique* 23, no. 3 (1982): 53.

85. "Interview with Robert Coover," by Christopher Bigsby, in *The Radical Imagination and the Liberal Tradition: Interviews with English and American Novelists*, ed. Heide Ziegler and Christopher Bigsby (London: Junction Books, 1982), 86.

CHAPTER FIVE. RICHARD MEPHISTO NIXON:
FURTHER ADVENTURES IN AMERICAN POLITICAL DEMONOLOGY

1. Pynchon, *Gravity's Rainbow*, 754.

2. Frank Zappa and the Mothers of Invention, "Dickie's Such an Asshole," *You Can't Do That on Stage Anymore: Volume Three*, Zappa Records B0000009TP.

3. Vonnegut, *Jailbird*, 32.

4. Aquabox, "Dick Nixon and the Rover," *The Evolution Will Not Be Televised*, Aquabox 646158001010.

5. *Sleeper*, DVD, 1973, MGM/UA Home Video, 2000.

6. Muriel Spark, *Abbess of Crewe; Nasty Habits*, DVD, 1977, Jef Films, 2002.

7. Martin, *Born Standing Up: A Comic's Life*, 119; Steve Martin, *Let's Get Small*, Warner Brothers Records BSK 3090.

8. *The In-Laws*, VHS, 1979, Warner Home Video, 1995.

9. "Hold Up," *WKRP in Cincinnati*.

10. Groom, *Forrest Gump*, 155 (citation is to the Pocket Books edition). The film version of the novel shows Forrest, while meeting with Nixon after a tour of China with the U.S. ping-pong team, passively accept the president's lodging recommendation, an act that places him in the Watergate Hotel on the night of the break-in at Democratic National Headquarters. Noticing the burglars, Forrest, with his guileless innocence, calls the police and ends the Nixon presidency. See *Forrest Gump*, DVD, 1994, Paramount Pictures, 2001.

11. *Good Morning, Vietnam*, VHS, 1987, Touchstone Home Video, 1987.

12. Bad Examples, "She Smiles Like Richard Nixon," *Bad Is Beautiful*, Waterdog Records WD9101.

13. Depeche Mode, "Policy of Truth (Capitol Mix)," *Policy of Truth Compact Disc Maxi Single*, Sire Records 9 21534-2.

14. "Frankie and Ellie Get Lost," *The Critic: The Complete Series*, DVD, Columbia TriStar Home Entertainment, 2004.

15. John Lennon, "Give Me Some Truth," *Imagine*, Capitol Records SW 3379.

16. Tim O'Brien, *The Nuclear Age*, 214, 166, 165 (citations are to the Dell edition).

17. *Bob Roberts*, VHS, 1992, Live Home Video, 1993.

18. Crosby, Stills, Nash, and Young, "Ohio," *Four Way Street*, Atlantic Records SD 2-902.

19. Williams, "In the Heart of the Beast: May 1970."

20. The Nixon/Godzilla cartoon can be viewed in the Steadman collection in Steadman, *America*.

21. Rogin, *Ronald Reagan, the Movie*, xiii.

22. See Ambrose, *Nixon: Triumph of a Politician*, 428, 458–459, 446, 413.

23. Philip Roth, interview by Walter Clemons, *Newsweek*, 8 November 1971, 112; Roth, *Our Gang*, 36.

24. Henry Raymont, "Shy Roth Emerges: New Book and Play," *New York Times*, 26 October 1971, 48. For mixed and negative reviews, see "The Nixon Genre," *Time*, 25 October 1971, 10; "Our Gang by Philip Roth," anonymous review, *New Republic*, 6 November 1971, 29; "Nixon Wins!" review by Murray Kempton, *New York Review of Books*, 27 January 1972, 20–22; "The Limits of Roth's Satire," review by Christopher

Lehmann-Haupt, *New York Times*, 29 October 1971, 39; "Waxing Roth," review by Pearl K. Bell, *The New Leader*, 29 November 1971, 14–15; "Our Gang by Philip Roth," review by Arthur Cooper, *Saturday Review*, 6 November 1971, 53; "I Want to Make This Perfectly Clear," anonymous review, *Times Literary Supplement* (London), 26 November 1971, 1469; and "Sharp and Roth," review by Auberon Waugh, *Spectator*, 11 December 1971, 857. *Newsweek*'s Peter Prescott and Dwight MacDonald, writing in the *New York Times Book Review*, provided the few notable positive notices. See "Joking in the Square," review by Peter S. Prescott, *Newsweek*, 8 November 1971, 110; and "Our Gang," review by Dwight MacDonald, *New York Times Book Review*, 7 November 1971, 31–32. *Our Gang* appeared on the *New York Times* best-seller list on 21 November 1971 and made its last showing on 19 March 1972.

25. "One Man's Loss," *Newsweek*, 24 June 1974, 15.

26. Roth, *Our Gang*, 2.

27. Ibid., 87.

28. Ibid., 29–30.

29. Philip Roth, interview by Walter Clemons, *Newsweek*, 8 November 1971, 112; Roth, *Our Gang*, 185, 195, 193.

30. Roth, *Our Gang*, 32.

31. Ibid., 151.

32. Ibid., 201.

33. Yet Roth insists, with what Auberon Waugh, in "Sharp and Roth," review, *Spectator*, 11 December 1971, 857, called "a hysterical self-righteous note," that we see Tricky as responsible for the country's condition. Noting Roth's adoption of the demonology techniques of his ideological opponents, Waugh commented: "There is something rather pathetic about Americans who try to use humour in what they believe to be a good cause. The basic attitude is borrowed from right-wing mandarin humour which assumes a universally accepted orthodoxy from which any deviation can be judged as stupid or ridiculous or wrong, but it transplants badly because the self-assurance is not there."

34. Chicago, "Song for Richard and His Friends," *Chicago at Carnegie Hall*, Columbia C4X-30865. *Our Gang* fails because Roth avoids any comprehensive social commentary. In his *Newsweek* interview, Roth denied that *Our Gang* had any political effectivity, asserting instead that "my purpose is not to bring others around to my point of view, but rather to turn my own indignation and disgust from raw, useless emotion into comic art. . . . This is my way of letting off steam— this is *my* opinion" (Walter Clemons, *Newsweek*, 8 November 1971, 112). Such a motivation for writing may make for wonderful therapy but does not produce successful satire. Writing in the *New York Times*, Christopher Lehmann-Haupt pointed out that

because Roth demonizes Nixon, making him separate from the public, *Our Gang* "doesn't really touch the source of the folly that it is trying to ridicule" ("The Limits of Roth's Satire," review by Christopher Lehmann-Haupt, *New York Times*, 29 October 1971, 39). In the same vein, a *Times Literary Supplement* (London) review complained that to "[aggrandize Tricky] to diabolical proportions" misses the point, which "one had thought was that he was . . . perpetually replaceable by another Tricky, then another, for as long as Americans want to be tricked" ("I Want to Make This Perfectly Clear," anonymous review, *Times Literary Supplement* [London], 26 November 1971, 1469).

35. Myers, *The Tragedy of Richard II*; Bramwell, *The Tragedy of King Richard: Shakespearean Watergate*; Yale Repertory Theatre, *Watergate Classics*, *yale/theatre* 5 (Special Issue, Winter 1974).

36. Bob Dylan/The Band, *Before the Flood*, Asylum Records AB 201.

37. Production information on *All the President's Men* can be found on the Internet Movie Database.

38. Rossetto, *Take-Over*.

39. David Edgar, *Dick Deterred* (New York: Monthly Review Press, 1974), 9, 63.

40. Ibid., 109, 112.

41. "Death to Watergate," *Saturday Night Live*, originally aired on 25 March 1978 on NBC. Christopher Lee was the guest host.

42. Bishop, *The Secret Ascension: Philip K. Dick is Dead, Alas*, 316, 305.

43. Dick, *Radio Free Albemuth*, 14, 47, 22.

44. Donald Freed and Arnold M. Stone, *Secret Honor, the Last Testament of Richard M. Nixon: A Political Myth*, in *New Plays U.S.A. 2*, 31.

45. Heberlein, *Sixteen Reasons Why I Killed Richard M. Nixon*, 7, 2, 2.

46. Roth, *American Pastoral*, 299, 299–300 (citations are to the Vintage International edition).

47. Meat Puppets, "Lost," *Meat Puppets II*, Ryko RCD 10467; Pynchon, *Vineland*, 244, 204.

48. See Ambrose, *Nixon: Triumph of a Politician*, 493–524.

49. Ibid., 453, 478, 525–538, 539, 544–548.

50. "Shubert Theatre," Internet Broadway Database.

51. Vidal, *An Evening with Richard Nixon*, 6–7, 34, 34, 73.

52. Ibid., 115, 85, 85–86, 95.

53. Ibid., ix.

54. Compare ibid., 25, and de Toledano, *Nixon*, especially chapter 1, "A Measure of Decision."

55. William F. Buckley's *National Review* touched on exactly this weakness in its review of *An Evening with Richard Nixon* (Linda Bridges, "An Evening with

Vidal," review of *An Evening with Richard Nixon*, *National Review*, 9 June 1972, 652–653).

56. He displays what Henry Hewes described as the depressing presumption that "no force in the government or in the electorate [could be] capable of implementing the policy he favors" (Henry Hewes, "Distal and Proximal Bite," review of *An Evening with Richard Nixon*, *Saturday Review*, 20 May 1972, 62–63).

57. Vidal, *An Evening with Richard Nixon*, 91, 83.

58. Stanley Kauffmann, "Right Down the Middle," review of *An Evening with Richard Nixon*, *New Republic*, 27 May 1972, 34.

59. "Carlson for President," *WKRP in Cincinnati*.

60. *Dick* spent five weeks in theatrical release, earning $6 million (with an additional $16.9 million from video rentals through early March 2000). See Internet Movie Database. On the release of the 23 June 1972 tape, see Ambrose, *Nixon: Ruin and Recovery*, 412–417.

61. "Dick Resigns," *Dick*, DVD, 1999, Columbia TriStar Home Video, 1999.

62. Ehrlichman, *The Company*. *The Company* provided the basis for the 1977 mini-series, *Washington: Behind Closed Doors*, which featured the veteran actor Jason Robards as President Monckton. *Washington: Behind Closed Doors* originally aired on ABC from 6 to 12 September 1977.

63. Ehrlichman, *The Whole Truth*.

64. Condon, *Death of a Politician*; Condon, *The Vertical Smile*.

65. Hunter S. Thompson, *Fear and Loathing on the Campaign Trail '72*, 397 (citation is to the Warner edition); Hunter S. Thompson, *The Great Shark Hunt*, 213 (citation is to the Warner edition).

66. *Where the Buffalo Roam*, released on 25 April 1980, opened in 464 theaters nationwide and grossed $1,750,593 in its first three days, eventually earning over $6.5 million. See "The Numbers: Box Office Data, Movie Stars, Idle Speculation," Bruce Nash, 1997–2005, http://www.the-numbers.com/movies/1980/OWTBR.html (accessed 21 June 2006). For discussion of *The Real War*'s release, see Ambrose, *Nixon: Ruin and Recovery*, 530–532.

67. *Where the Buffalo Roam*, VHS, 1980, MCA Home Video, 1986. All quotations in this chapter are my transcriptions of the film's screenplay.

68. Leeming, *James Baldwin: A Biography*, 322.

69. King quoted in Branch, *Parting the Waters*, 219.

70. Lytle, *America's Uncivil Wars*, 98.

71. George H. Gallup, *The Gallup Poll: Public Opinion, 1935–1971*, 3:1694, 3:2164; George H. Gallup, *The Gallup Poll: Public Opinion, 1972–1977* (Wilmington, DE: Scholarly Resources, 1976), 1:76–77. In 1968, Gallup did not conduct an afterelection analysis. My approximation of Nixon's total of the African American vote

in 1968 is based on a poll taken in mid-September. For evidence suggesting that Nixon's support among blacks did not change significantly by election day, see Mayer, *Running on Race*, 94.

72. Colson, *Born Again*, 316.

73. For more on the Freedom Rides, see Blum, *Years of Discord*, 69–71; Patterson, *Grand Expectations*, 468–469; and Lytle, *America's Uncivil Wars*, 121–126. For more on Freedom summer, see Patterson, *Grand Expectations*, 553–557; Williams, *Eyes on the Prize*, 228–249; Branch, *Pillar of Fire*, 343–509; Hodgson, *America in Our Time*, 206–217; Lytle, *America's Uncivil Wars*, 152–160; and Hampton and Fayer, *Voices of Freedom*, 177–207.

74. See Lytle, *America's Uncivil Wars*, 227–228; and Patterson, *Grand Expectations*, 655–657. The Carmichael quotation defining black power appears in Lytle, *America's Uncivil Wars*, 228.

75. Lytle, *America's Uncivil Wars*, 236–237.

76. Reed, "D Hexorcism of Noxon D Awful."

77. "An Interview with Ishmael Reed," by John O'Brien, in *Conversations with Ishmael Reed*, ed. Bruce Dick and Amritjit Singh (Jackson: University Press of Mississippi, 1995), 16. Reed has insisted that he was the first to create a Nixon character. See Ishmael Reed, "Ishmael Reed—Self Interview," in *Shrovetide in Old New Orleans* (1978; reprint, New York: Avon Books, 1979), 155 (page citation is to the Avon Books edition). He was the first fiction writer to do so, but Gore Vidal's play *The Best Man* predates "Noxon" by at least nine years, and Ferlinghetti's poem *Tyrannus Nix?* appeared around the same time.

78. "An Interview with Ishmael Reed," by Peter Nazareth, in *Conversations with Ishmael Reed*, ed. Bruce Dick and Amritjit Singh (Jackson: University Press of Mississippi, 1995), 185; Reed, "D Hexorcism of Noxon D Awful," 165, 168.

79. Reed, "D Hexorcism of Noxon D Awful." In his poetry written during the Nixon presidency, Reed develops similar motifs. See Reed, "This Poetry Anthology I'm Reading," 74; and Reed, "Poem Delivered before Assembly of Colored People Held at Glide Memorial Church," 136–138.

80. Reed, "D Hexorcism of Noxon D Awful," 168, 170, 168, 180.

81. Ibid., 182.

82. See Hoff, *Nixon Reconsidered*; and Kotlowski, *Nixon's Civil Rights: Politics, Principle, and Policy*. The statistics on Nixon's record of desegregating public schools can be found in Hoff, *Nixon Reconsidered*, 89–90.

83. Ambrose, *Nixon: Triumph of a Politician*, 316–317.

84. O'Reilly, *Nixon's Piano*, 299–300.

85. Ambrose, *Nixon: Triumph of a Politician*, 364.

86. Ibid., 296, 330.

87. Ibid., 460–461.

88. O'Reilly, *Nixon's Piano*, 279. See also Mayer, *Running on Race*, 114–115.

89. Schell, *The Time of Illusion*, 44–47; O'Reilly, *Nixon's Piano*, 296. Even Nixon's successes in affirmative action served this scheme. The Philadelphia Plan, which worked to increase the number of blacks gaining unionized employment in the construction industry or the administration's program to give a predetermined number of federal contracts to businesses owned by minorities allowed Nixon to pit blacks against organized labor.

90. Scott-Heron, "No Knock," 60 (citation is to the Canongate edition).

91. Mel Watkins, "No Name in the Street," review of *No Name in the Street*, by James Baldwin, *New York Times Book Review*, 28 May 1972, 17.

92. Baldwin, *The Fire Next Time*, 141 (citation is to the Dell Laurel edition).

93. Baldwin, *No Name in the Street*, 92, 167.

94. Ibid., 168, 163, 88.

95. Advertisement for *No Name in the Street*, by James Baldwin, *New York Times*, 17 May 1972, 44.

96. "Best Seller List," *New York Times Book Review*, 28 May 1972, 25.

97. Leeming, *James Baldwin: A Biography*, 316.

98. For a description of, and the quoted passage from, Moynihan's 16 January 1970 memo, see Ambrose, *Nixon: Triumph of a Politician*, 331–332.

99. The statistics on unemployment rates can be found in Hacker, *Two Nations*, 103.

100. "Poverty: Historical Poverty Tables," U.S. Census Bureau, Housing and Household Economic Statistics Division http://www.census.gov/hhes/www/poverty/histpov/hstpov3.html (accessed 1 July 2006).

101. Hacker, *Two Nations*, 101.

102. Clarence "Gatemouth" Brown, "Please Mr. Nixon," *Gate's on the Heat*, Polygram Records 19730.

103. Thomas Shaw, "Richard Nixon's Welfare Blues," *Made in Texas*, Testament Records TCD 5027.

104. "Getting Up the Rent," "Black Jesus," "Michael Gets Suspended," *Good Times, Season One*.

105. Ratings information can be found at tv.com (accessed 27 June 2006).

106. "Getting Up the Rent," *Good Times, Season One*.

107. Hilliard and Cole, *This Side of Glory*, 26, 264, 265.

108. Carroll, *It Seemed Like Nothing Happened*, 49–51; Hampton and Fayer, *Voices of Freedom*, 512 (citations are to the Bantam Books edition).

109. Howlin' Wolf, "Watergate Blues," *The Back Door Wolf*, Chess Records CH50045. For information about the recording of *The Back Door Wolf*, see Segrest and Hoffman, *Moanin' at Midnight*, 294–297.

110. Baraka, "Afrikan Revolution," 244, 246, 247.

111. Baraka, "When We'll Worship Jesus," 252, 251.

112. The *Bakke* decision outlawed strict racial quotas, but at the same time the justices affirmed that race or ethnicity could be one factor of many considered in university admissions decisions. See Patterson, *Restless Giant*, 31.

113. Patterson, *Restless Giant*, 32.

114. Acker, *Don Quixote*, 102.

115. Ibid., 102–103, 109.

116. Ibid., 117, 112, 72, 73.

117. Ibid., 39, 109, 207; Ellen G. Friedman, "'Now Eat Your Mind': An Introduction to the Works of Kathy Acker," *Review of Contemporary American Fiction* 9 (1989): 41, 39.

118. Acker, *Don Quixote*, 20, 207.

119. Ellen G. Friedman, "'Now Eat Your Mind': An Introduction to the Works of Kathy Acker," *Review of Contemporary American Fiction* 9 (1989): 44.

120. Douglas Dix, "Kathy Acker's *Don Quixote:* Nomad Writing," *Review of Contemporary American Fiction* 9 (1989): 57.

121. "A Conversation with Kathy Acker," interview by Ellen G. Friedman, *Review of Contemporary American Fiction* 9 (1989): 18–19. Douglas Dix interprets this removal of oneself from a corrupt environment as a positive step; he lauds *Don Quixote* as an affirmation not of the power to "change the society itself in some final way . . . [but rather of the power to decide] to become a nomad," a disrupter of "the hegemonic control of the state apparatus" (Douglas Dix, "Kathy Acker's *Don Quixote:* Nomad Writing," *Review of Contemporary American Fiction* 9 [1989]: 61).

122. Lytle, *America's Uncivil Wars*, 272.

123. Ibid., 273–274.

124. Ibid., 276.

125. Ibid., 277.

126. Carroll, *It Seemed Like Nothing Happened*, 35; Patterson, *Grand Expectations*, 714–715.

127. Jenkins, *Decade of Nightmares*, 86.

128. Ibid., 110.

129. Lytle, *America's Uncivil Wars*, 281; the quoted passage appears in Jenkins, *Decade of Nightmares*, 86.

130. Faludi, *Backlash*, xxi; Limbaugh, *See, I Told You So*, 222 (citation is to the Pocket Star edition).

131. Faludi, *Backlash*, x–xi, 112–139.

132. Troy, *Morning in America*, 285; Fox-Genovese, *Feminism Is Not the Story of My Life*, 31–32; Wolf, *Fire with Fire*, xvi.

133. Simon, *Gramsci's Political Thought*, 28.

134. Raymond Williams quoted in Brantlinger, *Crusoe's Footprints*, ix. What makes Acker's inability to see a middle ground all the more poignant is that she recognizes the inherent limitations of separatism. As she acknowledged to Ellen Friedman, "You can't isolate yourself from the world . . . . [There is no] viable model of true separation. It's impossible" ("A Conversation with Kathy Acker," interview by Ellen G. Friedman, *Review of Contemporary American Fiction* 9 [1989]: 17). The pain in reading Acker's work comes from the combination of this strongly communicated sense of the inescapable degradation of American mainstream culture, coupled with the seeming impossibility of doing anything to alter the way of life that produces such depravity.

135. "Angst for the Memories," *Murphy Brown*, originally aired on 27 September 1993 on CBS.

136. "Treehouse of Horror IV," *The Simpsons: The Complete Fifth Season*; "Duffless," *The Simpsons: The Complete Fourth Season*.

137. "A Head in the Polls," *Futurama*, vol. 2; audio commentary to "Space Pilot 3000," *Futurama*, vol. 1.

138. The Funky Nixons, "(You Must Be) Stupid," *Still Not Crooks*, Berkeley/COMA Productions.

139. The Dick Nixons, "The Patriot Song," "The Answer," *Paint the White House Black*, Triple X Records 51088-2.

140. Nixon, *RN*, 774.

141. Ibid., 683.

CHAPTER SIX. "NEVER GIVE UP":
AMERICAN ORTHODOXY, REVISED STANDARD VERSION

1. Robyn Hitchcock, "1974," *A Star for Bram*, PAF.

2. Peter Morgan, *Frost/Nixon* (London: Faber and Faber, 2006), 82. *Frost/Nixon* opened at the Donmar Warehouse in London on 10 August 2006. After a standing-room-only run, it transferred to the Gielgud Theatre, a larger West End venue. In the spring of 2007, the play moved to Broadway, opening at the Bernard B. Jacobs Theatre on 22 April after one month of previews and running through 19 August, in the process winning a Tony award for Frank Langella's portrayal of Richard Nixon. After a film version, slated to be directed by Ron Howard, with British actor Michael Sheen and Langella reprising their stage roles and with a supporting cast that included Kevin Bacon, *Frost/Nixon* was expected to begin a national tour in the fall of

2008. See Ernio Hernandez and Andrew Gans, "Morgan's *Frost.Nixon* Earns Back Money on Broadway; Tour Slated for 2008," Playbill.com, 30 July 2007, http://www .playbill.com/news/article/109937.html (accessed 20 August 2007).

3. Keillor, *We Are Still Married*, xviii.

4. Schlesinger, *Running for President*, 393, 406, 383, 403.

5. Ambrose, *Nixon: Ruin and Recovery*, 560–561.

6. Martz et al., "The Road Back," 27, 29.

7. Ibid., 27, 32.

8. The quotation critical of *Newsweek* (and Nixon) appeared in a letter from Joan E. Dolamore of Cambridge, Massachusetts. The favorable assessment came in a letter from Kimberly T. Levine of Miami, Florida. The other letters, all highly negative in their reactions to the Nixon cover story, came from readers in Fort Collins, Colorado; Columbia, South Carolina; Ridgecrest, California; Astoria, New York; and Garden City, Kansas. See "My Turn," *Newsweek*, 9 June 1986, 11.

9. Nixon, *RN*, 559, 580.

10. Sulzberger, *World and Richard Nixon*, 75, xiii.

11. The first President Bush frequently used the phrase "only Nixon could go to China," suggesting their shared love of the masterly dramatic surprise. See Alter, "Bush Reaches Out," 26.

12. John Adams, *Nixon in China: An Opera in Three Acts*, Elektra/Nonesuch Digital 1979177-1. Because the idea for this opera originally came from director Peter Sellars, who participated in all phases of its coming to life, my analysis of the opera is based not only on the words of its libretto and its music but also on its staging during its premiere performance in Houston, in 1987. I owe my knowledge of Sellars's direction to PBS's *Great Performances*, which recorded the opera during its debut. For the Harvard connection to the opera, see Karen Monson, "The Making of 'Nixon in China,'" *Harvard Magazine*, January–February 1988, 24–32.

13. The *New York Times* critic Donal Henahan likened Nixon to a "confused Rotarian" abroad. "Opera: 'Nixon in China,'" review of opera *Nixon in China*, by John Adams, Houston Grand Opera, *New York Times*, 24 October 1987, 17.

14. The quotation from John Adams appears in Nancy Malitz, "Nixon in China," *Ovation*, October 1987, 18.

15. Alice Goodman, libretto of *Nixon in China*, Elektra/Nonesuch Digital 1979177-1, 32.

16. Ibid., 50, 51.

17. Ibid., 36–37, 32, 32.

18. The quotation from John Adams appears in Janos Gereben, "Nixon? Singing and Dancing?" review of the opera *Nixon in China*, by John Adams, *Marin (CA) Independent Journal*, 17 May 1987, D7.

19. Alice Goodman, "Towards *Nixon in China*," notes to libretto of *Nixon in China*, Elektra/Nonesuch Digital 1979177-1, 1987, 12.

20. The omission of any specific reference to Vietnam is particularly hard to justify, for Nixon believed that one of the primary short-term benefits of the opening of China would be a distancing of Beijing from the North Vietnamese government. By linking improvement in relations with the United States to Chinese help in convincing Hanoi to turn to peace, Nixon hoped to bring an end to the war in Vietnam.

21. Will Crutchfield, in his review of the audio recording of *Nixon in China*, noted this "dogged avoidance of comment on the whole Nixon" and complained about this "blinkered view of history" ("'Nixon' Opens New Chapter for Opera," *New York Times*, 3 April 1988, 2:31.

22. For more information on the Iran-contra scandal, see Patterson, *Restless Giant*, 210–211.

23. "The New York Times Book Review Best Sellers," *New York Times Book Review*, 13 May 1990, 36, and 14 October 1990, 54.

24. Nixon, *In the Arena*, audio adaptation read by the author.

25. Nixon, *In the Arena*, 25.

26. Ibid., 30.

27. Ibid., 44, 47, 76.

28. Ibid., 91, 98, 112–113.

29. Ibid., 156–157.

30. Ibid., 290.

31. Ibid., 305, 300, 326, 353, 355.

32. Ibid., 368, 368, 368, 369.

33. Ibid., 41.

34. Ibid., 40–43, 41; "The New York Times Book Review Best Sellers," *New York Times Book Review*, 8 July 1990, 26.

35. Mydans, "Nixon Library Set to Open, with Disputes Old and New," A1; *NBC Nightly News*, 19 July 1990. On the *CBS Evening News*, Lesley Stahl reported the cost of the library at $25 million. Both the NBC and the CBS coverage can be found at the Vanderbilt Television News Archives, Nashville, Tennessee. "Nixon Library Gets Delayed Kickoff"; "The Remaking of the President," 24. By 2000, the Nixon Library's annual budget had grown to $4.6 million, and the endowment had reached $13 million. (See Marquis, "Government Agrees to Pay Nixon Estate.")

36. King and Weaver, "Washington Talk; Briefing; Nixon Library's Request," B8.

37. Ibid., B8. The funding of presidential libraries, particularly the beggar's role it requires a former, even a sitting, president to play, has drawn increasing criticism. Lyndon Johnson twisted the Texas legislature's arm to fund a portion of his library. George H. W. Bush took one million dollars each from Saudi Arabia and Kuwait. Bill

Clinton gave a controversial pardon to the ex-husband of a major contributor to his library foundation. (See Matthew Cooper, "The Price Isn't Right," *Time*, 26 February 2001, 28; and Dallek, "Our Presidential Libraries.")

38. *NBC Nightly News*, 19 July 1990.

39. Hufbauer, *Presidential Temples*, 6, 24.

40. When I speak of the Nixon Library "in its original design," I refer to the museum's galleries, the displays, and the reader board texts that were part of the Nixon Museum when it was a privately run entity. In other words, this chapter analyzes the Nixon Library and Birthplace as it existed during the first fourteen years of its life. As I will discuss later, the Nixon Library has now entered the National Archives and Records Administration system of presidential libraries. And one of the promised changes will be in the museum's displays, particularly those dealing with the Watergate scandal.

41. My observations about and quotations taken from exhibits at the Nixon Library and Birthplace come from the notes of my thirteen visits to the library on 4, 14–16 August 1993, 5–9 May 2002, 13 June 2003, and 5, 6, 8 August 2004.

42. By contrast, on the day I toured the Gerald Ford Presidential Museum, I had to hunt for the theater and, finding it locked, had to request a showing of its film, "A Time to Heal." In the fall of 2004, the Jimmy Carter Presidential Library had shelved its orientation film entirely. I visited the Gerald R. Ford Presidential Museum in Grand Rapids, Michigan, on 11 June 2002 and the Jimmy Carter Library and Museum in Atlanta, Georgia, on 11 November 2004.

43. "Enshrined at Yorba Linda."

44. At the time of the dedication, the library claimed that the Watergate display was the second-largest in the museum. (See Devroy, "Nixon Library Dedicated as Three GOP Presidents Praise 'Architect of Peace.'") By 2002, however, some library publicity literature reportedly claimed that "the Watergate Gallery . . . [was] the largest exhibit dedicated to a single subject." (See Neil Swidey, "All the President's Spin," *Boston Globe*, 16 June 2002, LexisNexis (accessed 26 May 2007.)

45. When, during the dedication ceremonies, Nixon himself led the former Republican presidents in a tour of the museum, he ignored the display on the scandal. See Apple, "Another Nixon Summit, at His Library," A10.

46. "Briefly," *USA Today*, 23 June 1989, 2A.

47. "Nixon's Boyhood Home: A Personal Tour with Julie Nixon Eisenhower and Huell Howser," *California's Gold*, show no. 2007,VHS.

48. "Larry King and Julie Nixon Eisenhower Tour the Richard Nixon Library and Birthplace" originally aired on CNN's *Larry King Live* on 20 June 2001.

49. "Nixon's Boyhood Home: A Personal Tour with Julie Nixon Eisenhower and Huell Howser."

50. "Larry King and Julie Nixon Eisenhower Tour the Richard Nixon Library and Birthplace."

51. "Enshrined at Yorba Linda."

52. *Nixon at Andau* can be viewed on the Internet web page titled "Richard Nixon Library, Yorba Linda Pictures by Travel Photo Base," http://www.travelphotobase .com/s/CAARN.htm. According to the *New York Times*, Daday's massive painting measures ten feet by six feet. See Seth Mydans, "Yorba Linda Journal; Painting of Heroic Size Shows Nixon to Match," *New York Times*, 13 August 1992, http://query .nytimes.com/gst/fullpage.html?res=9E0CEFD6163CF930A2575BC0 A964958260 (accessed 15 March 2008).

53. The Travel Photo Base website also features a close-up shot of Daday's rendering of Nixon's face.

54. Hufbauer, *Presidential Temples*, 139; Elisa Crouch, "Patching a Legacy," *Arkansas (Little Rock) Democrat-Gazette*, 18 February 2001, 19A; "Clinton Library Open for Business," *BBC News* (UK Version), bbc.co.uk, 18 November 2004 (accessed 20 June 2007).

55. Ambrose, *Ruin and Recovery*, 420.

56. For a collection of photographs taken at Kent State University on 4 May 1970, see Davies and the Board of Church and Society, *The Truth about Kent State*, 52–137. A listing of the killed and wounded students and their distances from the National Guard can be found in ibid., 52–55. The museum had removed the badly misspelled reader boards on Kent State by the time of my June 2003 visit and had replaced them with a corrected version by August 2004.

57. Such torturous rationalizations seemingly must have exhausted the museum planners' patience with the Watergate tapes. At the dedication the library staff promised that two more Watergate tapes would be added to listening stations by September 1990. (In fact, the *New York Times* reported all three as being already available.) One year later that plan was abandoned in favor of creating a display of Pat Nixon's gowns. See Armstrong, "Opening of Nixon Library Attracts Detractors, Fans"; Apple, "Another Nixon Summit, at His Library," A10; Guilliatt, "The Life and Good Times of Richard and Ronnie; Old Presidents Never Die, They Just Open Museums," *Independent* (London), 22 October 1991, LexisNexis.

58. Groer, "The House of Milhous: At the Nixon Birthplace, the President Is Spinning from His Grave," E1, E5.

59. Richard Nixon Library and Birthplace, e-mail to RN e-news mailing list, 12 August 2004; Groer, "The House of Milhous: At the Nixon Birthplace, the President Is Spinning from His Grave," E5.

60. Hari, "Books, Lies, and Videotape," 31; Bourgoyne, "Nixon Library Booked for Tricia Fest"; Kamen, "Watergate," 33.

61. The attendance figures for the 5 May 2002 wedding show at the Nixon Library come from the library employee working the museum store's cash register on the morning of 6 May 2002. I take the Samuel Nixon quotation from Morris, *Richard Milhous Nixon*, 33.

62. Hufbauer, *Presidential Temples*, 194–195, 233n49.

63. Weikel, "Nixon Library Losing Money but Operators Not Fearful," *Houston Chronicle*, 19 December 1993, LexisNexis; John H. Taylor, letter to the editor, *Business Week*, 10 October 1994, 17; Justin, "Nixon Library's Exhibits Present a Pop-Culture President," *Star-Tribune* (Minneapolis), 28 January 1996, LexisNexis; Palmeri, 18; Kasdorf, "Family Fight Stains Efforts to Burnish Nixon's Legacy"; Werner, "Nixon Library Gets a Pardon: It Will Qualify as U.S. Archive"; "Presidential Libraries, Museums"; Garrett M. Graff, "I Like Ike, but Not Enough to Visit His Museum." Museums of the more recent presidents fare best among the presidential libraries. But the Nixon Library does better at attracting visitors than the George H. W. Bush Library. And of the libraries of Nixon's two immediate predecessors (Kennedy and Johnson) and of his two immediate successors (Ford and Carter), only the Johnson Library consistently outdraws the Nixon Library—but the LBJ Library is the only one to always provide free admission. (Johnson insisted that his library be open to all free of charge; see Hufbauer, *Presidential Temples*, 68–69.)

64. Weiser, "Nixon's Will Leaves Tapes to Family; Executors Told to Continue Battle against Public Access"; Marquis, "Government Agrees to Pay Nixon Estate"; Lardner, "Trial Likely to Derail Plans for U.S.-Run Nixon Library," *Chicago Sun-Times*, 25 January 1998, LexisNexis; "Nixon Estate Seeks Millions for Material Seized by Government."

65. Sterngold, "Nixon Daughters Battle over $19 Million Library Bequest"; Reid, "Nixon Daughters End Three-Year Feud over $20 M Gift to Their Father's Library," *Ottowa (Canada) Citizen*, 10 August 2002, LexisNexis; "Nixon's Daughters, Ford Team to Get Papers in Library."

66. "Matt [Construction Company] Building Nixon Library Addition," *California Construction Link*, August 2003, LexisNexis; Scott, "East Meets West; East Room Replica Added to Nixon Museum," *California Construction Link*, 1 November 2004, LexisNexis; Sarasohn, "Nixon Library Sounds Hill on His Records"; Werner, "Nixon Library Gets a Pardon: It Will Qualify as U.S. Archive"; Worsham, "Nixon's Library Now Part of NARA," 32, 34. But could its rescue through achieving National Archives and Records Administration status be a double-edged sword for the original Nixon Library and its Foundation? In March 2005, when the library cancelled an upcoming conference on the Vietnam War, one that was to establish the institution's academic credibility by, for the first time, bringing in historians critical of Nixon's handling of the conflict, the American Library Association joined with over a dozen

scholars in petitioning Congress to delay the transfer of Nixon's tapes and documents to the library until it established firmer legal guarantees of public access. (See Shane, "Nixon Library Stirs Anger by Canceling Conference.") This embarrassment opened the possibility that a NARA Nixon Library might become a better, more honest, place than its predecessor. Put on the defensive, the library promised to make changes to the museum's Watergate display and entered into an agreement with the new national archivist, Allen Weinstein, to secure the public release of the vast majority of Nixon's presidential materials. (See Scott Shane, "Director of Nixon Library Agrees to Make President's Tapes Public," *New York Times*, 18 March 2005, A16; and Albanese, "Nixon Library to Ease Access.") Naftali's plans for making the Nixon Library a center for study of U.S. history and culture during the Nixon era, perhaps even including visits from figures like Francis Ford Coppola and Joan Baez, and the first infusion of federal money into the Nixon Library budget, which meant that the library might cease its huckstering, offered some hopeful signs. (See Goffard, "First Federal Nixon Library Head Is Named"; Goldberg, "Sprucing Up Nixon"; and Christopher Lee, "Nixon Library Joins the Club: Operation by Archives Marks Transition from Private Sector.") Will things really change? When asked whether he anticipated trouble with ensuring access to the Nixon papers and tapes, Naftali gave an answer that, for now, should apply to the library/museum complex as a whole: "Check back with me in a year" (Goldberg, "Sprucing Up Nixon").

67. Patterson, *Restless Giant*, 230–233.

68. Ibid., 228, 229.

69. Ibid., 254–255.

70. Ibid., 251, 252.

71. *Rush Limbaugh: The American Dream*, VHS, Multimedia Entertainment in association with SKM Productions, distributed by New Video Group, 1996.

72. Patterson, *Restless Giant*, 341–342, 373.

73. Ibid., 374.

74. The Schwarzenegger quotations come from his speech at the 2004 Republican National Convention. See "Schwarzenegger: No Country More Welcoming Than the USA," 31 August 2004, http://www.cnn.com/2004/ALLPOLITICS/08/31/gop.schwarzenegger.transcript (accessed 20 July 2007). For the Nixon references from Schwarzenegger's 2003 gubernatorial campaign, see John Fund, "The New Nixon?" WSJ.com, Opinion Journal, from the Wall Street Journal editorial page, 5 September 2003, http://www.opinionjournal.com/diary/?id=110003967 (accessed 20 July 2007).

CHAPTER SEVEN. NIXON, NOW MORE THAN EVER

1. For the story of the funeral day airing of *Shining Time Station*, see John Carmody, "The TV Column," *Washington Post*, 28 April 1994, C4.

2. *Shining Time Station*, "The Mayor Runs For Re-election," 1993. All quotations in this chapter are based on my transcription of the program's teleplay.

3. John Carmody, "The TV Column," *Washington Post*, 28 April 1994, C4.

4. Russell Baker, "The Tiger with No Teeth"; Garry Trudeau, *Doonesbury*, in *Dallas Morning News*, 9 May 1994, A9. See also Quindlen, "Living Will"; and Lapham, "Morte de Nixon."

5. *ABC Evening News*, 23 April 1994, anchored by Judd Rose.

6. "Richard Nixon: President's Life Filled with Triumph, Adversity," editorial, *Dallas Morning News*, 23 April 1994, A30; Beck, "Memories of Nixon Should Transcend His 'Darker Side.'" The *Lancaster (PA) New Era* editorialized that "Nixon's successes on a global scale may, in the end, outweigh his failing" ("Richard Nixon: Successful Leader Undone by Watergate," 23 April 1994, A12). The *Cleveland Plain Dealer*, declaring that "the nation will miss him much more than he could have imagined 20 years ago," praised his creation of a "new persona more gracious and measured than any the public had seen from him before" and concluded that, although the shame of Watergate would never be expunged from the historical record, "if the record is complete, it will also reflect that he was much more than that" ("Richard M. Nixon," *Cleveland Plain Dealer*, 24 April 1994, C2). Longtime enemy Robert Scheer wrote that Nixon was a "true visionary" and demanded that we "be charitable . . . in the interest of accuracy" (Scheer, "A Major Leader, a Double Standard").

7. Witcover, "Richard Nixon Dies in Coma at 81."

8. Lurie's cartoon appeared in the *Washington Times* (26 April 1994, A16). Observers of varied political stripes competed to laud Nixon's foreign policy achievements. R. W. Apple Jr., in a retrospective piece headlined "About Nixon, Leaders Stress Triumphs, Not the Downfall," collected an anthology of praise for the former president's "epochal achievements." The title of Charles Dancey's 26 April 1994 editorial said everything before he began: "By Embracing China, Nixon Won the Cold War." James Hoagland wrote of Nixon's service to the nation through his foreign policy books and speeches. Seeing much more than a selfish attempt to salvage personal reputation, Hoagland credited Nixon with a public service of the highest measure: "Nixon's last great endeavor was to persuade his current successor and his countrymen that despite the end of the Cold War the need for American leadership in foreign affairs remains clear and constant. History, which must judge him harshly in so many other ways, will remember him kindly for that" (Hoagland, "His Last Great Endeavor"). The vice president for external affairs of the Vietnamese Community of Greater Dallas extolled Nixon "as a great leader, a true freedom fighter and a friend" (Phong D. Do, "Vietnamese Ally," letter to the editor, *Dallas Morning News*, 1 May 1994, J3). Another Dallas reader, noting that Nixon was one of a tiny fraction of people who get the chance to change the world for the better, concluded with the

benediction "Blessed are the peacemakers" (Robert I. Johnson, "Peacemaker," letter to the editor, *Dallas Morning News*, 8 May 1994, J4). Senator John McCain of Arizona, a prisoner during the Vietnam War, praised Nixon for an honorable end to the war and the safe return of the POWS, a sentiment echoed by the commander of Maxwell Air Force Base in Alabama, who led a "retreat" ceremony honoring the president on the day of his funeral. (Senator McCain was quoted in Weil and Randolph, "Richard M. Nixon, 37th President, Dies"; coverage of the Maxwell Air Force Base ceremony appeared in Frank Mastin Jr., "Retreat Ceremony Honors Nixon," *Montgomery [AL] Advertiser*, 28 April 1994, A4.)

9. George McGovern was quoted in "Nation Mourns Nixon; U.S., World Leaders Pay Tribute to a Friend, Foe."

10. "No Whining: Nixon Ended Career with Class"; Safire, "Mr. Comeback"; editorial cartoon, *Cleveland Plain Dealer*, 24 April 1994, C2. In the same vein, the *Christian Science Monitor* noted Nixon's "recovered prestige as a foreign policy adviser" (Chaddock, "US, World Leaders Pay Tribute to Richard Nixon"). The Knight-Ridder news service story on Nixon's funeral highlighted the much-touted theme of reconciliation: "That such warm sentiments could be expressed for a man who almost certainly would have been impeached—and possibly indicted—had he not resigned and been pardoned by his successor was itself a testament to the power of time to heal wounds and soften passions" ("A Final Tribute: Nixon's Funeral a Time of Healing"). "The faults of Richard Nixon are well documented," the *Lancaster (PA) New Era* asserted in an editorial the day following the funeral, "but even now, this early, the perspective of history is beginning to judge the man and his life, rather than his faults and mistakes" ("An 'Astonishing' Flow of Affection for Richard Nixon"). Tom Wicker, a *New York Times* reporter and Nixon biographer, warned that remembering Nixon only for Watergate was a dangerous oversimplification. "At his death," Wicker declared, "he had won his way painfully back from the Watergate scandal . . . to a relatively respected position" ("An Indomitable Man, an Incurable Loneliness"). David Broder marveled at how the funeral service "captured a spirit of national reconciliation which probably was not anticipated five days ago" ("A Farewell Not Only to a Man but Also to an Era of Deep Division"). Lyn Nofziger proclaimed Nixon "the classiest" of the five living former presidents, claiming that "before he died, . . . he had completely rehabilitated himself . . . [into] an international icon admired and respected by more people than when he was president and for better reasons than his detractors will ever understand" ("Remembering Richard Nixon"). Nackey Loeb, writing in the *Manchester (NH) Union Leader*, took the long view on judging Nixon's life and concluded that such a perspective will vindicate him: "When it is all played out, the value of his life will be judged on whether this is a better world for his having lived among us for 81 years. Taking it all together . . . we believe . . . the answer is yes" (editorial, 27

April 1994, 1). Paul Bedard, a reporter for the *Washington Times*, opened his story on the Nixon funeral by describing Nixon as a man "who won in death the respect and admiration he struggled for in life" ("A Journey Ends in Reconciliation," A1).

11. Estimates of the number of mourners at the Nixon Library and the description of the three-mile-line leading up to the Nixon Library appeared in Froomkin and Kriner, "Remembering Richard Nixon." The woman mourner was quoted in Associated Press, "Thousands Wait Hours to Pay Last Respects to Nixon."

12. See Apple, "Richard Nixon, 81, Dies; A Master of Politics Undone by Watergate," A1; and Olert, "Nixon Is Dead at Age 81."

13. Leubsdorf, "Richard M. Nixon Dies at Age 81: His Tumultuous Life Was Haunted by Controversy"; "The Angriest President," editorial; "Richard Nixon's Presidency," editorial, *Peoria (IL) Journal Star*, 27 April 1994, A4; Ohmann, editorial cartoon, *Portland Oregonian*, 24 April 1994, B2. On this topic, see also "Richard Nixon's Will," editorial, *Philadelphia Inquirer*, 24 April 1994, C6; and "The Richard Nixon Legacy," editorial, *Arizona Republic*, 24 April 1994, C4.

14. Rich, "Nixon, Big and Small"; Teepen, "Nixon's Dark Side Blots His Record"; Feagler, "Final Exit for an Obstinate Man." See also Schudson, "Watergate Will Always Be with Us"; Anderson and Binstein, "He Fought for Democracy Abroad but Undermined It at Home"; and Ellerbe, "Nixon Not Understood by Majority of Americans."

15. "On the Street: How Do You Think Richard M. Nixon Will Be Remembered"; Michael V. Nixon, letter to the editor, *Portland Oregonian*, 3 May 1994, B10; Bryan James, letter to the editor, *Atlanta Journal and Constitution*, 30 April 1994, A15. See also street polls conducted in Atlanta and Boise, Idaho ("Sound Off: What's Your Lasting Impression of Richard Nixon?"; and "What Was Said in Boise"). For a sampling of other letters to the editor that were critical of Nixon, see *Cleveland Plain Dealer*, 4 May 1994, B6; *Los Angeles Times*, 27 April 1994, B6; and *Philadelphia Inquirer*, 1 May 1994, C6. A reader of the *Portland Oregonian* suggested that, although we should sympathize with the Nixon family for its loss, "let us never forgive Nixon for trampling on the Constitution, and especially for the travesty of Watergate and the absolute and total disregard for our First amendment rights" (Gene Solomon, letter to the editor, 14 May 1994, D5). In Boston, one writer issued a correction to columnist Jeff Jacoby, declaring that "Watergate . . . did not 'mar' Nixon's career. Watergate was the inevitable culmination of his career" (Carlton Vogt, letter to the editor, *Boston Globe*, 29 April 1994, 18). A Philadelphian added that Richard Nixon "was divisive, mean-spirited, corrupt and calculating, and honoring such traits smacks of idiocy" (Elizabeth S. Hug, letter to the editor, *Philadelphia Inquirer*, 3 May 1994, A24).

16. Kaul, "Why the Federal Holiday Today?"

17. Novak, "Nixon and Hiss." For many of the same reasons, Ken Adelman, of the *Washington Times*, in "Taking a Measure of Nixon's Long Suits," objected to pronouncing Nixon a foreign policy genius, complaining rather that détente achieved nothing other than to legitimize communism and burden the United States with two very bad arms agreements, SALT I and the ABM Treaty. The opening of China, far from some diplomatic masterstroke, was inevitable, and his handling of the Vietnam War was consistently botched. K. E. Grubbs Jr., of the *Orange County (CA) Register*, bluntly recognizes that, from a libertarian standpoint, "Nixon's mistakes were egregious and many" ("The Transcendent Moment of Richard Nixon"). In fact, one of the negative assessments of Nixon's presidency from the *Manchester (NH) Union Leader*'s "On the Street" poll came from a man who pronounced Nixon as too liberal (Homer Cates, in "On the Street: How Do You Think Richard Nixon Will Be Remembered"). See also William A. Rushner, quoted in Phil McCombs, "The Man They Love to Hate," *Washington Post*, 25 April 1994, B8; and Kenny, "Remembering Nixon: Do We Have To?"

18. *Sunday Journal*, hosted by Connie Brod, guests Steve Bull and Hugh Sidey, C-SPAN, 24 April 1994; Bob Pool, "Forever a Hero: Classmates Voice Respect for Ailing Nixon," B4.

19. Rob Rogers, editorial cartoon, *Philadelphia Inquirer*, 11 May 1994, A18.

20. Dick Locher, editorial cartoon, *Chicago Tribune*, 26 April 1994, sec. 1, 20; Dana Summers, editorial cartoon, *Lancaster (PA) New Era*, 25 April 1994, A6.

21. John Trevor, editorial cartoon, *Colorado Springs (CO) Gazette Telegraph*, 3 May 1994, B5.

22. Jim Borgmann, editorial cartoon, *Los Angeles Times*, 26 April 1994, B7. See also a cartoon by Bill Deore of the *Dallas Morning News*, in which a curious Nixon inquires of St. Peter the identity of Deep Throat (editorial cartoon, *Dallas Morning News*, 28 April 1994, A30).

23. Bill Schorr, editorial cartoon, in *Peoria (IL) Journal Star*, 27 April 1994, A4, and in *Arizona Republic*, 29 April 1994, B7.

24. Tony Auth, editorial cartoon, *Philadelphia Inquirer*, 26 April 1994, A14.

25. Lorraine Rhoades, letter to the editor, *Peoria (IL) Journal Star*, 9 May 1994, A3.

26. Letters to the editor, *Idaho (Boise) Statesman*, 4 May 1994, A15; "Appalled at Bad Taste," letter to editor, *Idaho (Boise) Statesman*, 6 May 1994, A13.

27. The quoted passages are from Stanley W. Kandebo, letter to the editor, *Philadelphia Inquirer*, 28 April 1994, A14.

28. Jeff Koterba, editorial cartoon, *Omaha (NE) World-Herald*, 27 April 1994, A12.

29. William J. Bennett, *The Death of Outrage*, 138–154; Coulter, *High Crimes and Misdemeanors*, 105.

30. Baker, *The Breach*, 134–135, 343, 397, 121, 198 (page citations are to the Berkley edition).

31. "Fun with Real Audio," "TV Funhouse," *Saturday Night Live*, 26 September 1998, NBC.

32. Neil Young, "The Campaigner," *Decade*, Reprise Records REP 64 037.

33. For production information and a sampling of the reviews of *Nixon's Nixon*, see Ron Weiskind, "Tricky Night: Playwright Russell Lees Imagines the Night before the Resignation in 'Nixon's Nixon,'" *Pittsburgh Post-Gazette*, Weekend Section, 28 February 1997, 2; Damien Jaques, "Nixon's the One in Rep Show: Play Finds Humor in the Night before He Resigned," *Milwaukee Journal Sentinel*, 23 September 1997, LexisNexis (accessed 12 March 2005); Steven Winn, "'Nixon' Again Wins by a Landslide," *San Francisco Chronicle*, 21 October 1997, LexisNexis; Misha Berson, "Man of a Thousand Faces—Star of 'Nixon's Nixon' Is a Veteran Local Actor Known for Totally Immersing Himself in Characters," *Seattle Times*, 29 October 1998, LexisNexis; Lloyd Rose, "'Nixon,' In All His Glory," *Washington Post*, 7 April 1999, C1, C11; Alastair Macaulay, "Black and Funny Heart of History," *Financial Times* (London), 13 August 1999, LexisNexis; Benedict Nightingale and Jeremy Kingston, "Benedict Nightingale's Five Best West End Shows," *Times* (London) *Play*, 11 August 2001, 25; John Coulbourn, "A Vote for Nixon's Nixon: World Stage Presents Satire on Watergate Scandal," *Toronto Sun*, 21 April 2000, LexisNexis; Victoria Finlay, "Nixon's Nixon," *South China Morning Post* (Hong Kong), 13 February 2001, LexisNexis; Patrick McDonald, "Tricky with Dicky," *Advertiser* (Australia), 16 December 2002, LexisNexis; Kate Herbert, "Behind Closed Doors the Night Nixon Cried," *Herald Sun* (Melbourne, Australia), 14 February 2003, LexisNexis; Vincent Canby, "Of Nixon and Kissinger: What Might Have Been," *New York Times*, 13 March 1996, C13; and Charles Isherwood, "Some Nixonian Nostalgia: That Last Night with Henry," *New York Times*, 5 October 2006, E5.

34. Lawrence Van Gelder, "Nixon and Kissinger on Trial," *New York Times*, 14 October 1995, 1:15.

35. Russell Lees, *Nixon's Nixon* (New York: Dramatists Play Service, 1996), 9, 18.

36. Ibid., 29, 31.

37. Ibid., 45.

38. Ibid., 46, 47.

39. Ibid., 48, 29.

40. *Nixon*, DVD, 1995, Hollywood Pictures Home Video.

41. By contrast, Disney's hit movie during this period, Pixar's *Toy Story*, pulled in double that figure in one week. See "Domestic Box Office," *Variety*, 1–7 January 1996, 12; and "Domestic Box Office," *Variety*, 8–14 January 1996, 16. For the box

office figures on *Nixon*, see "Domestic Box Office," *Variety*, 1 January–18 February 1996.

42. For discussion of the production problems of *Nixon*, see Winnie Chung, "The Man They Love to Hate," *South China Morning Post* (Hong Kong), 21 February 1996, LexisNexis (accessed June 2005); Anita M. Busch, "Inside Movies: Tricky Bit of Casting," *Variety*, 23–29 January 1995, 9; Michael Fleming, "Buzz: Stone's View of Nixon . . . The New H'wood Hacks," *Variety*, 13–19 March 1995, 3; Anita M. Busch, "Inside Movies: Cinergi Nabs 'Nixon,'" *Variety*, 6–12 March 1995, 10.

43. Robert D. Novak, "Whoppers in the Nixon Movie," *Buffalo (NY) News*, 5 January 1996, LexisNexis. See also Mona Charen, "Oliver Stone Insults Public with 'Nixon,'" *Rocky Mountain News (Denver, CO)*, 28 December 1995, LexisNexis. Charen, calling Stone the "most pernicious liar at work in America today," indicting him for tampering with "the famous black-and-white Zapruder film," despite the impossibility of such a crime. Abraham Zapruder's famous movie was shot on color film.

44. Maureen Dowd, "Nix 'Nixon'—Tricky Pix: Stone and Nixon, Two of a Kind," *New York Times*, 21 December 1995, A29; and Howell Raines, "Oliver's World: The Good, the Bad, the Overly Competent," *New York Times*, 24 December 1995, E8. The *Times* did not save its vitriol for just the op-ed pages. See also Bernard Weinraub, "Professor Stone Resumes His Presidential Research," *New York Times*, 17 December 1995, H11, H26; Richard Reeves, "Nixon Revisited by Way of Creative Camera," *New York Times*, 17 December 1995, H1, H41; and Walter Goodman, "With Fact in Service to Drama," *New York Times*, 3 January 1996, C9, C15. For an example of attacks on Stone outside the *Times*, see "Stone Strikes Again, Alas," editorial, *Boston Herald*, 2 January 1996, LexisNexis.

45. *Nixon: An Oliver Stone Film* (New York: Hyperion, 1995), 113–114.

46. Roger Ebert, "Oliver Stone Finds the Humanity in 'Nixon,'" *Chicago Sun-Times*, 17 December 1995, B1, B8, B9. Many movie critics praised Stone's film in glowing terms. The *Boston Globe*'s Jay Carr rated the movie among the year's best: "'Nixon' is so far beyond any other Hollywood film this year in what it accomplishes—and how it accomplishes it—that I can't begin to think what might be second." Enthusiastic reviews appeared in such major newspapers as the *Christian Science Monitor*, the *New York Times* (in a break from its editorial and feature coverage), and the *Washington Post*. For these and other representative samples, see Jay Carr, "Baring the Heart of Nixon," *Boston Globe*, 20 December 1995, LexisNexis; Roger Ebert, "'Nixon' a Brilliant Study in Tragedy," *Chicago Sun-Times*, 20 December 1995, 45; David Sterritt, "'Nixon' Paints Dual Portrait," *Christian Science Monitor*, 20 December 1995, 14; Janet Maslin, "Stone's Embrace of a Despised President," *New York Times*, 20 December 1995, C11, C20; Hal Hinson, "'Nixon': A Heart of Stone; Superb Bio Is

the Tale of Two Tortured Men," *Washington Post,* 20 December 1995, C1, C11; Jeff Strickler, "'Nixon' Challenges Viewers' Opinions of Former President," *Star Tribune (Minneapolis),* 20 December 1995, LexisNexis; Howie Movshovitz, "Oliver Stone's Nixon Film Probes a Mind Full of Demons," *Denver Post,* 20 December 1995, Lexis-Nexis; Adam Mars-Jones, "Gargoyle in the White House," *Independent* (London), 14 March 1996, LexisNexis; and David Baron, "Stone Offers Gripping Look at Complex 'Nixon'; Psychological Portrait Shows Hopkins' Genius," *Times-Picayune (New Orleans),* 22 December 1995, LexisNexis.

47. *Nixon: An Oliver Stone Film,* 84, 127.

48. Ibid., 243.

49. Ibid., 109, 114.

50. Olds, "The Victims." In 2007, the *New York Times Magazine* published Megan Kelso's graphic novel *Watergate Sue,* another story dealing with Richard Nixon, families, and divorce. See Kelso, *Watergate Sue, New York Times Magazine,* 1 April–9 September 2007.

51. *Nixon: An Oliver Stone Film,* 307; "Closing Remarks/End Credits," *Nixon,* Collector's Edition Series DVD, 1995, Hollywood Pictures Home Video.

52. Kovacik, *Nixon and I;* Cahill, *A Nixon Man.*

53. Maxwell, *nixoncarver,* 1–2.

54. Ibid., 7.

55. Ibid., 153.

56. Ibid., 25.

57. Ibid., 3.

58. Ibid., 118, 119, 160.

59. Ibid., 130, 141, 137, 175.

60. Reilly, "Nixon under the Bodhi Tree," 494, 493.

61. Ibid., 494, 496–497, 497.

62. Ibid., 497.

63. Ibid., 498, 496, 500.

64. *The Final Days,* VHS, 1989, Republic Pictures, Republic Entertainment, 1996.

65. Phil Bosakowski, *Plays by Phil Bosakowski* (New York: Broadway Play Publishing, 2000), vii.

66. James Taylor, "Line 'Em Up," *Hourglass,* Columbia CK 67912.

67. Paul Oakenfold with Hunter S. Thompson, "Nixon's Spirit," *Bunkka,* Maverick B000067G5Y.

68. Carson, *Gilligan's Wake,* 67, 84.

69. "The Land of Plenty" and "Last Day," *The Assassination of Richard Nixon,* DVD, 2004, New Line Home Entertainment, 2005.

70. The Charles Logan character appears in the final nine episodes of Season Four, every episode of Season Five, and four episodes of Season Six. *24: Season Four*, DVD, 2004, 20th Century Fox Home Entertainment, 2005; *24: Season Five*, DVD, 2005, 20th Century Fox Home Entertainment, 2006; and *24: Season Six*, DVD, 2006, 20th Century Fox Home Entertainment, 2007.

71. Indeed, one of the most recent biographies—written by Nixon Center for Peace and Freedom trustee Lord Conrad Black—offered a reprise of this same basic theme song. Notice the familiar motifs: the first section of the book is titled "Meteoric Rise," and the first chapter is called "One of the Common People." Combined with these titles, the sentences of the book's initial paragraph provide a tidy summary of the mythic argument: "Richard Milhous Nixon was one of America's greatest political leaders, and probably its most controversial president. He was both brilliant and strangely awkward, but ultimately and uniquely indestructible. And in his perseverance he made many of his countrymen awkward also, throughout a very long career, and after. He would not go away, and lingers yet." See Black, *Richard M. Nixon: A Life in Full*, 3.

72. Hodgson, *America in Our Time*, 67 (page citations are to the Vintage edition).

73. Ibid., 14.

74. Ehrhart appears in the episode "America Takes Charge, 1965–1967," from *Vietnam: A Television History*, VHS, 1983, Sony Corporation and WGBH Educational Foundation, Video D0604, 1987.

75. McNeill, "The Care and Repair of Public Myth," 1.

76. Wills, *Reagan's America*, 386.

77. Keillor, *We Are Still Married*, 213.

78. Patterson, *Restless Giant*, 424.

79. Peter Morgan, *Frost/Nixon* (London: Faber and Faber, 2006), 74.

80. Feagler, "Nixon Took Us to Where We Are"; Vidal, *An Evening with Richard Nixon*, 93.

BIBLIOGRAPHY

BOOKS

Aitken, Jonathan. *Nixon: A Life*. Washington, DC: Regnery Publishing, 1993.

Alger, Horatio. *Ragged Dick: Or, Street Life in New York with the Boot Blacks*. Edited by Alan Trachtenberg. New York: Penguin, 1990.

Allen, Gary. *Nixon: The Man behind the Mask*. Belmont, MA: Western Islands, 1971.

Ambrose, Stephen E. *Nixon: The Education of a Politician, 1913–1962*. New York: Simon & Schuster, 1987.

———. *Nixon: The Triumph of a Politician, 1962–1972*. New York: Simon & Schuster, 1989.

———. *Nixon: Ruin and Recovery, 1973–1990*. New York: Simon & Schuster, 1991.

Anson, Robert Sam. *Exile: The Unquiet Oblivion of Richard M. Nixon*. New York: Simon & Schuster, 1984.

Baker, Peter. *The Breach: Inside the Impeachment and Trial of William Jefferson Clinton*. 2000. Reprint, New York: Berkley, 2001.

Baritz, Loren. *Backfire: A History of How American Culture Led Us into Vietnam and Made Us Fight the Way We Did*. 1985. Reprint, New York: Ballantine Books, 1986.

———. *City on a Hill: A History of Ideas and Myths in America*. New York: John Wiley, 1964.

Bellah, Robert N., Richard Madsen, William M. Sullivan, Ann Swindler, and Steven M. Tipton. *Habits of the Heart: Individualism and Commitment in American Life*. 1985. Reprint, New York: Harper & Row, 1986.

Bennett, William J. *The Death of Outrage: Bill Clinton and the Assault on American Ideals*. New York: Free Press, 1998.

———. *The De-valuing of America: The Fight for Our Culture and Our Children*. New York: Summit Books, 1992.

Bercovitch, Sacvan. *The American Jeremiad*. Madison: University of Wisconsin Press, 1978.

———. *The Puritan Origins of the American Self*. New Haven: Yale University Press, 1975.

Berman, Larry. *No Peace, No Honor: Nixon, Kissinger, and Betrayal in Vietnam*. New York: Free Press, 2001.

Black, Conrad. *Richard M. Nixon: A Life in Full*. New York: Public Affairs, 2007.

Bloom, Allan. *The Closing of the American Mind*. New York: Simon & Schuster, 1987.

Bloom, Harold. *The Western Canon: The Books and School of the Ages*. New York: Harcourt Brace, 1994.

Blum, John Morton. *Years of Discord: American Politics and Society, 1961–1974*. New York: W. W. Norton, 1991.

Bolton, Richard. *Culture Wars: Documents from the Recent Controversies in the Arts*. New York: New Press, 1992.

Branch, Taylor. *Parting the Waters: America in the King Years, 1954–1963*. New York: Simon & Schuster, 1988.

———. *Pillar of Fire: America in the King Years, 1963–1965*. New York: Simon & Schuster, 1998.

Brantlinger, Patrick. *Crusoe's Footprints: Cultural Studies in Britain and America*. New York: Routledge, 1990.

Brodie, Fawn M. *Richard Nixon: The Shaping of His Character*. 1981. Reprint, Cambridge, MA: Harvard University Press, 1983.

Burns, Edward McNall. *The Idea of Mission in American History*. New Brunswick, NJ: Rutgers University Press, 1957.

Caputo, Philip. *A Rumor of War*. 1977. Reprint, New York: Henry Holt, 1996.

Carroll, Peter N. *It Seemed Like Nothing Happened: The Tragedy and Promise of America in the 1970s*. New York: Holt, Rinehart & Winston, 1982.

Chambers, Whittaker. *Witness*. New York: Random House, 1952.

Clinton, Bill. *My Life*. New York: Alfred A. Knopf, 2004.

Collier, Peter, and David Horowitz. *Destructive Generation: Second Thoughts about the '6os*. New York: Summit Books, 1989.

Colodny, Len, and Robert Gettlin. *Silent Coup: The Removal of a President*. New York: St. Martin's, 1991.

Colson, Charles. *Born Again*. 1976. Reprint, Grand Rapids, MI: Fleming H. Revell, 1995.

Costello, William. *The Facts about Nixon*. 1960. Reprint, New York: Viking, 1974.

Coulter, Ann H. *High Crimes and Misdemeanors: The Case against Bill Clinton*. Washington, DC: Regnery, 1998.

Crawford, Alan. *Thunder on the Right: The "New Right" and the Politics of Resentment*. New York: Pantheon Books, 1980.

Davies, Peter, and the Board of Church and Society of the United Methodist Church. *The Truth about Kent State: A Challenge to the American Conscience*. New York: Farrar, Straus, Giroux, 1973.

DeSouza, Dinesh. *Illiberal Education: The Politics of Race and Sex on Campus*. New York: Free Press, 1991.

de Toledano, Ralph. *Nixon*. 2nd ed. New York: Duell, Sloan & Pearce, 1960.

———. *One Man Alone: Richard Nixon*. New York: Funk & Wagnalls, 1969.

————, and Victor Lasky. *Seeds of Treason: The True Story of the Hiss-Chambers Tragedy*. New York: Funk & Wagnalls, 1950.

Diggins, John Patrick. *The Proud Decades: America in War and Peace, 1941–1960*. New York: W. W. Norton, 1988.

Domhoff, G. William. *The Bohemian Grove and Other Retreats*. New York: Harper & Row, 1974.

Drew, Elizabeth. *Richard M. Nixon*. The American Presidents, edited by Arthur M. Schlesinger Jr. New York: Times Books, 2007.

Dyson, Eric Michael. *Is Bill Cosby Right: Or Has the Black Middle Class Lost Its Mind?* New York: Basic Civitas Books, 2005.

Ehrenreich, Barbara. *Nickel and Dimed: On (Not) Getting By in America*. New York: Henry Holt, 2001.

Ehrlichman, John. *Witness to Power: The Nixon Years*. New York: Simon & Schuster, 1986.

Eisenhower, Julie Nixon. *Pat Nixon: The Untold Story*. New York: Simon & Schuster, 1986.

Faludi, Susan. *Backlash: The Undeclared War against American Women*. New York: Crown Publishers, 1991.

Feeney, Mark. *Nixon at the Movies*. Chicago: University of Chicago Press, 2004.

Feiffer, Jules. *Feiffer on Nixon: The Cartoon Presidency*. New York: Random House, 1974.

Fish, Stanley. *Is There a Text in This Class? The Authority of Interpretive Communities*. Cambridge, MA: Harvard University Press, 1980.

FitzGerald, Frances. *Fire in the Lake: The Vietnamese and the Americans in Vietnam*. Boston: Little, Brown, 1972.

Fox-Genovese, Elizabeth. *"Feminism Is Not the Story of My Life": How Today's Feminist Elite Has Lost Touch with the Real Concerns of Women*. New York: Nan A. Talese, 1996.

Franklin, Benjamin. *The Autobiography*. In *Autobiography, Poor Richard, and Later Writings*. Edited by J. A. Leo Lemay. New York: Library of America, 1997.

Friedan, Betty. *The Feminine Mystique*. 1963. Reprint, New York: Dell, 1982.

Friedman, Milton. *Capitalism and Freedom*. Chicago: University of Chicago Press, 1962.

Frost, David. *I Gave Them a Sword*. New York: William Morrow, 1978.

————, with Bob Zelnick. *Frost/Nixon: Behind the Scenes of the Nixon Interviews*. New York: Harper Perennial, 2007.

Frum, David. *How We Got Here: The 70's, the Decade That Brought You Modern Life (For Better or Worse)*. New York: Basic Books, 2000.

Fulbright, J. William. *The Arrogance of Power*. 1966. Reprint, New York: Vintage, 1966.

Galbraith, John Kenneth. *The Affluent Society*. 1958. Reprint, Cambridge, MA: Riverside Press, 1960.

Gallup, George H. *The Gallup Poll: Public Opinion, 1935–1971*. 3 vols. New York: Random House, 1972.

———. *The Gallup Poll: Public Opinion, 1972–1977*. 2 vols. Wilmington, DE: Scholarly Resources, 1978.

Gallup, George, Jr. *The Gallup Poll: Public Opinion 1990*. Wilmington, DE: Scholarly Resources, 1991.

———. *The Gallup Poll: Public Opinion 1991*. Wilmington, DE: Scholarly Resources, 1992.

———. *The Gallup Poll: Public Opinion 1992*. Wilmington, DE: Scholarly Resources, 1993.

———. *The Gallup Poll: Public Opinion 2000*. Wilmington, DE: Scholarly Resources, 2001.

Gates, Henry Louis, Jr. *Loose Canons: Notes on the Culture Wars*. New York: Oxford University Press, 1992.

Gelb, Arthur, and Barbara Gelb. *O'Neill*. Enlarged edition with a new epilogue and introduction by Brooks Atkinson. New York: Harper & Row, 1960.

Gellman, Irwin F. *The Contender, Richard Nixon: The Congress Years, 1946–1952*. New York: Free Press, 1999.

Gitlin, Todd. *The Sixties: Years of Hope, Days of Rage*. New York: Bantam Books, 1987.

———. *The Twilight of Common Dreams: Why America Is Wracked by Culture Wars*. New York: Henry Holt, 1995.

Gordon, Lois, and Alan Gordon. *American Chronicle: Six Decades in American Life: 1920–1980*. New York: Atheneum, 1987.

Graff, Gerald. *Beyond the Culture Wars: How Teaching the Conflicts Can Revitalize American Education*. New York: W. W. Norton, 1992.

Greenberg, David. *Nixon's Shadow: The History of an Image*. New York: W. W. Norton, 2003.

Greene, Graham. *The Quiet American*. 1955. Reprint, New York: Penguin Books, 2004.

Hacker, Andrew. *Two Nations: Black and White, Separate, Hostile, Unequal*. New York: Charles Scribner's, 1992.

Hackett, Alice Payne. *70 Years of Best Sellers: 1895–1965*. New York: R. R. Bowker, 1967.

Hampton, Henry, and Steve Fayer, with Sarah Flynn. *Voices of Freedom: An Oral History of the Civil Rights Movement from the 1950s through the 1980s*. 1990. Reprint, New York: Bantam Books, 1991.

Harrington, Michael. *The Other America: Poverty in the United States*. 1962. Rev. ed., 1971. Reprint, with a new afterword, New York: Penguin, 1981.

Hellmann, John. *American Myth and the Legacy of Vietnam*. New York: Columbia University Press, 1986.

Heschel, Abraham J. *The Prophets: An Introduction, Volume I*. 1962. Reprint, New York: Harper Torchbook, 1969.

Hilliard, David, and Lewis Cole. *This Side of Glory: The Autobiography of David Hilliard and the Story of the Black Panther Party*. Boston: Little, Brown, 1993.

Hine, Thomas. *Populuxe*. New York: Alfred A. Knopf, 1987.

Hirsch, E. D. *Cultural Literacy: What Every American Needs to Know*. Boston: Houghton Mifflin, 1987.

Hodgson, Godfrey. *America in Our Time*. 1977. Reprint, New York: Vintage Books, 1978.

Hoff, Joan. *Nixon Reconsidered*. New York: Basic Books, 1994.

Hoyt, Edwin P. *The Nixons: An American Family*. New York: Random House, 1972.

Huber, Richard. *The American Idea of Success*. 1971. Reprint, Wainscott, NY: Pushcart Press, 1987.

Hufbauer, Benjamin. *Presidential Temples: How Memorials and Libraries Shape Public Memory*. Lawrence: University Press of Kansas, 2005.

Hughes, Richard T. *Myths America Lives By*. Urbana: University of Illinois Press, 2003.

Hughes, Robert. *Culture of Complaint: The Fraying of America*. New York: Oxford University Press, 1993.

Hunter, James Davison. *Culture Wars: The Struggle to Define America*. New York: Basic Books, 1991.

Jay, Gregory S. *American Literature and the Culture Wars*. Ithaca, NY: Cornell University Press, 1997.

Jenkins, Philip. *Decade of Nightmares: The End of the Sixties and the Making of Eighties America*. New York: Oxford University Press, 2006.

Johnson, Haynes. *Sleepwalking through History: America in the Reagan Years*. 1991. Reprint, New York: Anchor Books, 1992.

Kaplan, Fred. *Gore Vidal: A Biography*. New York: Doubleday, 1999.

Keillor, Garrison. *We Are Still Married: Stories and Letters*. New York: Viking, 1989.

Kimball, Jeffrey. *Nixon's Vietnam War*. Lawrence: University Press of Kansas, 1998.

Kornitzer, Bela. *The Real Nixon: An Intimate Biography*. New York: Rand McNally, 1960.

Kotlowski, Dean J. *Nixon's Civil Rights: Politics, Principle, and Policy*. Cambridge, MA: Harvard University Press, 2001.

Kutler, Stanley I. *The Wars of Watergate: The Last Crisis of Richard Nixon*. New York: Alfred A. Knopf, 1990.

Lasch, Christopher. *The Culture of Narcissism: American Life in an Age of Diminishing Expectations.* New York: W. W. Norton, 1978.

Lasky, Victor. *It Didn't Start with Watergate.* New York: Dial, 1977.

LeClair, Tom. *The Art of Excess: Mastery in Contemporary American Fiction.* Urbana: University of Illinois Press, 1989.

Lederer, William J., and Eugene Burdick. *The Ugly American.* 1958. Reprint, New York: W. W. Norton, 1999.

Leeming, David. *James Baldwin: A Biography.* New York: Alfred A. Knopf, 1994.

Lewis, Michael. *The Culture of Inequality.* 1978. Reprint, New York: New American Library, 1979.

Limbaugh, Rush H. *See, I Told You So.* 1993. Reprint, New York: Pocket Star Books, 1994.

———. *The Way Things Ought to Be.* New York: Pocket Books, 1992.

Lytle, Mark Hamilton. *America's Uncivil Wars: The Sixties Era from Elvis to the Fall of Richard Nixon.* New York: Oxford University Press, 2006.

MacLeod, Celeste. *Horatio Alger, Farewell: The End of the American Dream.* New York: Seaview Books, 1980.

Maraniss, David. *First in His Class: A Biography of Bill Clinton.* New York: Simon & Schuster, 1995.

Martin, Steve. *Born Standing Up: A Comic's Life.* New York: Scribner, 2007.

Mayer, Jeffrey. *Running on Race: Racial Politics in Presidential Campaigns, 1960–2000.* New York: Random House, 2002.

Mazlish, Bruce. *In Search of Nixon: A Psychohistorical Inquiry.* 1972. Reprint, Baltimore: Penguin, 1973.

Mazo, Earl. *Nixon: A Political and Personal Portrait.* New York: Harper, 1959.

———, and Stephen Hess. *Nixon: A Political Portrait.* New York: Harper & Row, 1968.

McCrohan, Donna. *Archie & Edith, Mike & Gloria: The Tumultuous History of All in the Family.* New York: Workman, 1987.

McNeill, William H. *Mythistory and Other Essays.* Chicago: University of Chicago Press, 1986.

McQuaid, Kim. *The Anxious Years: America in the Vietnam-Watergate Era.* New York: Basic Books, 1989.

McWhorter, John H. *Losing the Race: Self-Sabotage in Black America.* New York: Free Press, 2000.

Merk, Frederick. *Manifest Destiny and Mission in American History.* New York: Alfred A. Knopf, 1963.

Miller, Perry. *Errand into the Wilderness.* Cambridge, MA: Harvard University Press, 1956.

————. *The New England Mind: From Colony to Province*. Cambridge, MA: Harvard University Press, 1953.

Mitchell, Greg. *Tricky Dick and the Pink Lady: Richard Nixon vs. Helen Gahagan Douglas—Sexual Politics and the Red Scare, 1950*. New York: Random House, 1998.

Monsell, Thomas. *Nixon on Stage and Screen: The Thirty-seventh President as Depicted in Films, Television, Plays and Opera*. Jefferson, NC: McFarland, 1998.

Morris, Roger. *Richard Milhous Nixon: The Rise of an American Politician*. New York: Henry Holt, 1990.

Mott, Frank Luther. *Golden Multitudes: The Story of Best Sellers in the United States*. New York: Macmillan, 1947.

Newman, Katherine S. *Declining Fortunes: The Withering of the American Dream*. New York: Basic Books, 1993.

Niebuhr, Reinhold. *The Irony of American History*. New York: Charles Scribner's, 1952.

Nixon, Richard. *In the Arena: A Memoir of Victory, Defeat and Renewal*. New York: Simon & Schuster, 1990.

————. *In the Arena: A Memoir of Victory, Defeat and Renewal*. An audio adaptation read by the author. New York: Simon & Schuster Audioworks, 2 cassettes.

————. *Beyond Peace*. New York: Random House, 1994.

————. *1999: Victory without War*. New York: Simon & Schuster, 1988.

————. *No More Vietnams*. New York: Arbor House, 1984.

————. *The Real War*. 1980. Reprint, New York: Warner Paperbacks, 1981.

————. *RN: The Memoirs of Richard Nixon*. New York: Grosset and Dunlap, 1978.

————. *Seize the Moment: America's Challenge in a One-Superpower World*. New York: Simon & Schuster, 1992.

————. *Six Crises*. Garden City, NY: Doubleday, 1962.

Nolan, James L., Jr. *The American Culture Wars: Current Contests and Future Prospects*. Charlottesville: University Press of Virginia, 1996.

O'Neill, William L. *American High: The Years of Confidence, 1945–1960*. New York: Free Press, 1986.

O'Reilly, Kenneth. *Nixon's Piano: Presidents and Racial Politics from Washington to Clinton*. New York: Free Press, 1995.

Our Mission and Our Moment: President George W. Bush's Address to the Nation before a Joint Session of Congress, September 20, 2001. New York: Newmarket, 2001.

Parmet, Herbert S. *Richard Nixon and His America*. Boston: Little, Brown, 1990.

Patterson, James T. *Grand Expectations: The United States, 1945–1974*. Oxford History of the United States, edited by C. Vann Woodward. New York: Oxford University Press, 1996.

———. *Restless Giant: The United States from Watergate to Bush v. Gore*. Oxford History of the United States, edited by David M. Kennedy. New York: Oxford University Press, 2005.

Peale, Norman Vincent. *The Power of Positive Thinking*. 1952. Reprint, Englewood Cliffs, NJ: Prentice Hall, 1956.

Perlstein, Rick. *Before the Storm: Barry Goldwater and the Unmaking of the American Consensus*. New York: Hill & Wang, 2001.

———. *Nixonland: The Rise of a President and the Fracturing of America*. New York: Scribner, 2008.

Pessen, Edward. *The Log Cabin Myth: The Social Backgrounds of the Presidents*. New Haven, CT: Yale University Press, 1984.

Price, Ray. *With Nixon*. New York: Viking, 1977.

Radosh, Ronald, and Joyce Milton. *The Rosenberg File: A Search for the Truth*. 1983. Reprint, New York: Random House, 1984.

Reston, James, Jr. *The Conviction of Richard Nixon: The Untold Story of the Frost/Nixon Interviews*. New York: Harmony Books, 2007.

Robinson, Lillian S. *In the Canon's Mouth: Dispatches from the Culture Wars*. Bloomington: Indiana University Press, 1997.

Rogin, Michael. *Ronald Reagan, the Movie: And Other Episodes in Political Demonology*. Berkeley: University of California Press, 1987.

Schell, Jonathan. *The Time of Illusion*. New York: Alfred A. Knopf, 1975.

Schlesinger, Arthur M., Jr., ed. *Running for President: The Candidates and Their Images, Volume Two, 1900–1992*. New York: Simon & Schuster, 1994.

Schudson, Michael. *Watergate in American Memory: How We Remember, Forget, and Reconstruct the Past*. New York: Basic Books, 1992.

Segrest, James, and Mark Hoffman. *Moanin' at Midnight: The Life and Times of Howlin' Wolf*. New York: Pantheon Books, 2004.

Services for Richard Nixon, 37th President of the United States, Wednesday, April 27th, 1994. Yorba Linda, CA: Richard Nixon Library and Birthplace, 1994.

Sheehan, Neil. *A Bright Shining Lie: John Paul Vann and America in Vietnam*. New York: Random House, 1988.

Silesky, Barry. *Ferlinghetti: The Artist in His Time*. New York: Warner Books, 1990.

Simon, Roger. *Gramsci's Political Thought: An Introduction*. London: Lawrence & Wishart, 1982.

Small, Melvin. *The Presidency of Richard Nixon*. American Presidency Series, edited by Homer E. Socolofsky. Lawrence: University Press of Kansas, 1999.

Smith, Franklin B. *The Assassination of President Nixon*. Rutland, VT: Academy Books, 1976.

Smith, Larry. *Lawrence Ferlinghetti: Poet-at-Large*. Carbondale: Southern Illinois University Press, 1983.

Spalding, Henry D. *The Nixon Nobody Knows*. Middle Village, NY: Jonathan David, 1972.

Steadman, Ralph. *America*. San Francisco: Straight Arrow Books, 1974.

Steele, Shelby. *The Content of Our Character: A New Vision of Race in America*. New York: St. Martin's, 1990.

Sulzberger, C. L. *The World and Richard Nixon*. New York: Prentice-Hall, 1987.

Summers, Anthony, with Robbyn Swan. *The Arrogance of Power: The Secret World of Richard Nixon*. New York: Viking, 2000.

Toplin, Robert Brent, ed. *Oliver Stone's USA: Film, History, and Controversy*. Lawrence: University Press of Kansas, 2000.

Troy, Gil. *Morning in America: How Ronald Reagan Invented the 1980s*. Princeton, NJ: Princeton University Press, 2005.

Tuveson, Ernest Lee. *Redeemer Nation*. Chicago: University of Chicago Press, 1968.

Vidal, Gore. *The Essential Gore Vidal*. Edited by Fred Kaplan. New York: Random House, 1999.

von Hoffman, Nicholas. *Citizen Cohn: The Life and Times of Roy Cohn*. 1988. Reprint, New York: Bantam, 1988.

Weinstein, Allen. *Perjury: The Hiss-Chambers Case*. New York: Alfred A. Knopf, 1978.

Weiss, Richard. *The American Myth of Success: From Horatio Alger to Norman Vincent Peale*. New York: Basic Books, 1969.

West, Cornel. *Race Matters*. Boston: Beacon, 1993.

White, Hayden. *The Content of the Form: Narrative Discourse and Historical Representation*. Baltimore: Johns Hopkins University Press, 1987.

———. *Metahistory: The Historical Imagination in Nineteenth-Century Europe*. Baltimore: Johns Hopkins University Press, 1973.

———. *Tropics of Discourse: Essays in Cultural Criticism*. Baltimore: Johns Hopkins University Press, 1978.

Wicker, Tom. *One of Us: Richard Nixon and the American Dream*. New York: Random House, 1991.

Wilkinson, J. Harvie. *One Nation Indivisible: How Ethnic Separatism Threatens America*. Reading, MA: Addison-Wesley, 1997.

Williams, Juan. *Eyes on the Prize: America's Civil Rights Years, 1954–1965*. 1987. Reprint, New York: Penguin, 1988.

Wills, Garry. *Nixon Agonistes: The Crisis of the Self-Made Man*. Boston: Houghton Mifflin, 1970.

———. *Reagan's America: Innocents at Home.* Garden City, NY: Doubleday, 1987.

Witcover, Jules. *Very Strange Bedfellows: The Short and Unhappy Marriage of Richard Nixon and Spiro Agnew.* New York: Public Affairs, 2007.

Wolf, Naomi. *Fire with Fire: The New Female Power and How It Will Change the 21st Century.* New York: Random House, 1993.

Woodward, Bob. *Bush at War.* New York: Simon & Schuster, 2002.

Wright, G. Ernest, and Reginald H. Fuller. *The Book of the Acts of God: Contemporary Scholarship Interprets the Bible.* 1957. Reprint, Garden City, NY: Doubleday, 1960.

ARTICLES

Aaron, Daniel. "Nixon as Literary Artifact." *Raritan* 15 (1995): 83–96.

Adelman, Ken. "Taking a Measure of Nixon's Long Suits." *Washington Times*, 27 April 1994, A16.

Adler, Renata. "Searching for the Real Nixon Scandal: A Last Inference." *Atlantic Monthly*, December 1976, 76–95.

Albanese, Andrew. "Nixon Library to Ease Access." *Library Journal*, 15 April 2005, 18, 20.

Alter, Jonathan. "Bush Reaches Out." *Newsweek*, 30 January 1989, 22–26.

Ambrose, Stephen E. "Writing about Nixon." In *To America: Personal Reflections of an Historian*, 173–186. New York: Simon and Schuster, 2002.

Anderson, Jack, and Michael Binstein. "He Fought for Democracy Abroad but Undermined It at Home." *Portland Oregonian*, 29 April 1994, D7.

"The Angriest President." Editorial. *Baltimore Sun*, 24 April 1994, Perspective, E2.

Apple, R. W., Jr. "About Nixon, Leaders Stress Triumphs, Not the Downfall." *New York Times*, 24 April 1994, A1, A28.

———. "Another Nixon Summit, at His Library." *New York Times*, 20 July 1990, A1, A10.

———. "Richard Nixon, 81, Dies; A Master of Politics Undone by Watergate." *New York Times*, 23 April 1994, late edition, A1, A13.

Armstrong, Scott. "Opening of Nixon Library Attracts Detractors, Fans." *Christian Science Monitor*, 23 July 1990, 9.

Associated Press. "Thousands Wait Hours to Pay Last Respects to Nixon." *Lancaster (PA) New Era*, 27 April 1994, A1, A10.

"An 'Astonishing' Flow of Affection for Richard Nixon." Editorial. *Lancaster (PA) New Era*, 28 April 1994, A12.

Bacevich, Andrew J. "New Rome, New Jerusalem." In *The Imperial Tense: Prospects and Problems of American Empire*, edited by Andrew J. Bacevich, 93–101. Chicago: Ivan R. Dee, 2003.

Baker, Russell. "The Tiger with No Teeth." *New York Times*, 26 April 1994, A23.

Beck, Joan. "Memories of Nixon Should Transcend His 'Darker Side.'" *Chicago Tribune*, 28 April 1994, DuPage ed., 1:27.

Bedard, Paul. "A Journey Ends in Reconciliation: Richard Milhous Nixon Buried Where He Was Born." *Washington Times*, 28 April 1994, A1, A14.

Bercovitch, Sacvan. "'Nehemiah Americanus': Cotton Mather and the Concept of the Representative American." *Early American Literature* 8 (1974): 220–238.

Bourgoyne, J. E. "Nixon Library Booked for Tricia Fest." *New Orleans (LA) Times-Picayune*, 12 June 1996, Lexis-Nexis.

Broder, David. "A Farewell Not Only to a Man but Also to an Era of Deep Division." *Washington Post*, 28 April 1994, A13.

Chaddock, Russell. "US, World Leaders Pay Tribute to Richard Nixon." *Christian Science Monitor*, 25 April 1994, 9.

Dallek, Robert. "Our Presidential Libraries." *Nation*, 26 March 2001, 4–6.

Dancey, Charles. "By Embracing China, Nixon Won the Cold War." Editorial. *Peoria (IL) Journal Star*, 26 April 1994, A4.

Devroy, Ann. "Nixon Library Dedicated as Three GOP Presidents Praise 'Architect of Peace.'" *Washington Post*, 20 July 1990, A5.

Douglass, Wayne J. "Tricky Dick: Richard Nixon as a Literary Character." *Lamar Journal of the Humanities* 7, no. 2 (1981): 15–23.

Ellerbe, Linda. "Nixon Not Understood by Majority of Americans." *Portland Oregonian*, 23 April 1994, A20.

"Enshrined at Yorba Linda." *Economist*, 4 August 1990, 74.

Feagler, Dick. "Final Exit for an Obstinate Man." *Cleveland Plain Dealer*, 25 April 1994, A2.

———. "Nixon Took Us to Where We Are," *Cleveland Plain Dealer*, 27 April 1994, A2.

"A Final Tribute: Nixon's Funeral a Time of Healing." *Lancaster (PA) New Era*, 28 April 1994, A1, A6.

Froomkin, Dan, and Paula Kriner. "Remembering Richard Nixon: Saying a Last Goodbye." *Orange County (CA) Register*, 28 April 1994, A17.

Goffard, Christopher. "First Federal Nixon Library Head Is Named." *Los Angeles Times*, 11 April 2006, Lexis-Nexis.

Goldberg, Jeffrey. "Sprucing Up Nixon." *New Yorker*, 8 May 2006, 25.

Graff, Garrett M. "I Like Ike, but Not Enough to Visit His Museum." *Washingtonian*, April 2007, Lexis-Nexis.

Greenfield, Meg. "My Generation Is Missing." *Reporter*, 4 May 1967, 35–37.

Groer, Annie. "The House of Milhous: At the Nixon Birthplace, the President Is Spinning from His Grave." *Washington Post*, 10 August 1997, E1, E5.

Grubbs, K. E., Jr. "The Transcendent Moment of Richard Nixon." *Orange County (CA) Register*, 1 May 1994, J1.

Guilliatt, Richard. "The Life and Good Times of Richard and Ronnie; Old Presidents Never Die, They Just Open Museums." *Independent* (London), 22 October 1991, Lexis-Nexis.

Hari, Johann. "Books, Lies, and Videotape." *New Statesman*, 15 July 2002, 30–31.

Hoagland, James. "His Last Great Endeavor." *Washington Post*, 26 April 1994, A15.

Justin, Neal. "Nixon Library's Exhibits Present a Pop-Culture President." *Minneapolis Star-Tribune*, 28 January 1996, Lexis-Nexis.

Kamen, Al. "Watergate, 33." *Washington Post*, 13 June 2005, A17.

Kasdorf, Martin. "Family Fight Stains Efforts to Burnish Nixon's Legacy." *USA Today*, 30 April 2002, Lexis-Nexis.

Kaul, Donald. "Why the Federal Holiday Today?" *Lancaster (PA) Intelligencer Journal*, 27 April 1994, A14.

Kenny, Jack. "Remembering Nixon: Do We Have To?" *Manchester (NH) Union Leader*, 27 April 1994, 29.

King, Wayne, and Warren Weaver, Jr. "Washington Talk; Briefing; Nixon Library's Request." *New York Times*, 29 September 1986, B1, B8.

Lapham, Lewis H. "Morte de Nixon." *Harper's Magazine*, July 1994, 6.

Lardner, George, Jr. "Trial Likely to Derail Plans for U.S.-Run Nixon Library." *Chicago Sun-Times*, 25 January 1998, Lexis-Nexis.

Lee, Christopher. "Nixon Library Joins the Club: Operation by Archives Marks Transition from Private Sector." *Washington Post*, 20 March 2006, A13.

Lee, Ronald. "The Featuring of Will in History: Richard Nixon's Post-Presidential Writings." *Quarterly Journal of Speech* 75 (1989): 453–466.

Leubsdorf, Carl P. "Richard M. Nixon Dies at Age 81: His Tumultuous Life Was Haunted by Controversy." *Dallas Morning News*, 23 April 1994, A1, A28.

Loeb, Nackey. Editorial. *Manchester (NH) Union Leader*, 27 April 1994, 1.

Marquis, Christopher. "Government Agrees to Pay Nixon Estate." *New York Times*, 13 June 2000, A18.

Martz, Larry, with Thomas M. DeFrank, Howard Fineman, Martin Kasindorf, and Jonathan Alter. "The Road Back." *Newsweek*, 19 May 1986, 26–30.

McNeill, William H. "The Care and Repair of Public Myth." *Foreign Affairs* 61 (1982): 1–13.

Mitgang, Herbert. "Dispute over Sale Precedes Release of Nixon Memoirs." *New York Times*, 1 May 1978, A16.

———. "Nixon Book Dispute Erupts at Meeting." *New York Times*, 28 May 1978, 16.

Montrose, Louis A. "Professing the Renaissance: The Poetics and Politics of Culture." In *The New Historicism*, edited by H. Aram Veeser, 15–36. New York: Routledge, 1989.

Mydans, Seth. "Nixon Library Set to Open, with Disputes Old and New." *New York Times*, 16 July 1990, A1, A10.

"Nation Mourns Nixon; U.S., World Leaders Pay Tribute to a Friend, Foe." *Harrisburg (PA) Patriot News*, 25 April 1994, A1, A20.

"New Site Chosen for Nixon Library." *St. Petersburg (FL) Times*, 11 October 1987, Lexis-Nexis.

"Nixon Estate Seeks Millions for Material Seized by Government." *New York Times*, 2 December 1998, A25.

"The Nixon Genre." *Time*, 25 October 1971, 10.

"Nixon Library Gets Delayed Kickoff." *St. Petersburg (FL) Times*, 4 December 1989, Lexis-Nexis.

"Nixon's Daughters, Ford Team to Get Papers in Library." *Grand Rapids (MI) Press*, 2 January 2003, Lexis-Nexis.

Nofziger, Lyn. "Remembering Richard Nixon." *Washington Times*, 25 April 1994, A21.

Novak, Robert D. "Nixon and Hiss." *Washington Post*, 28 April 1994, A27.

"No Whining: Nixon Ended Career with Class." Editorial. *Montgomery (AL) Advertiser*, 25 April 1994, A10.

Olert, Chris. "Nixon Is Dead at Age 81." *Boston Globe*, 23 April 1994, A1, A3.

"On the Street: How Do You Think Richard M. Nixon Will Be Remembered." *Manchester (NH) Union Leader*, 26 April 1994, 6.

Pool, Bob. "Forever a Hero: Classmates Voice Respect for Ailing Nixon." *Los Angeles Times*, 26 April 1994, B1, B4.

"Presidential Libraries, Museums." *Grand Rapids (MI) Press*, 6 January 2007, Lexis-Nexis.

Quindlen, Anna. "Living Will." *New York Times*, 27 April 1994, A17.

Reid, Tim. "Nixon Daughters End Three-Year Feud over $20 M Gift to Their Father's Library." *Ottawa (Ontario) Citizen*, 10 August 2002, Lexis-Nexis.

"The Remaking of the President." *Newsweek*, 30 July 1990, 24.

Rich, Frank. "Nixon, Big and Small." *New York Times*, 24 April 1994, E17.

"Richard M. Nixon." Editorial. *Cleveland Plain Dealer*, 24 April 1994, C2.

"Richard Nixon: President's Life Filled with Triumph, Adversity." Editorial. *Dallas Morning News*, 23 April 1994, A30.

"Richard Nixon: Successful Leader Undone by Watergate." Editorial. *Lancaster (PA) New Era*, 23 April 1994, A12.

"The Richard Nixon Legacy." Editorial. *Arizona Republic*, 24 April 1994, C4.

"Richard Nixon's Presidency." Editorial. *Peoria (IL) Journal Star*, 27 April 1994, A4.

"Richard Nixon's Will." Editorial. *Philadelphia Inquirer*, 24 April 1994, C6.

Safire, William. "Mr. Comeback." *New York Times*, 25 April 1994, A15.

Sarasohn, Judy. "Nixon Library Sounds Hill on His Records." *Washington Post*, 23 October 2003, A29.

Scheer, Robert. "A Major Leader, a Double Standard." *Los Angeles Times*, 25 April 1994, B7.

Schlesinger, Arthur, Jr. "The Theory of America: Experiment or Destiny?" In *The Cycles of American History*, 3–22. Boston: Houghton Mifflin, 1986.

Schudson, Michael. "Watergate Will Always Be with Us." *Los Angeles Times*, 2 May 1994, B7.

Scott, Kathy Lee. "East Meets West; East Room Replica Added to Nixon Museum." *California Construction Link*, 1 November 2004, Lexis-Nexis.

Seelye, John. "The Clay Foot of the Social Climber: Richard M. Nixon in Perspective." In *Literary Romanticism in America*, edited by William L. Andrews, 109–134. Baton Rouge: Louisiana University Press, 1981.

Shane, Scott. "Director of Nixon Library Agrees to Make President's Political Tapes Public." *New York Times*, 18 March 2005, A16.

———. "Nixon Library Stirs Anger by Canceling Conference." *New York Times*, 11 March 2005, A16.

"Sound Off: What's Your Lasting Impression of Richard Nixon?" *Atlanta Journal-Constitution*, 28 April 1994, DeKalb extra, A6.

Sterngold, James. "Nixon Daughters Battle over $19 Million Library Bequest." *New York Times*, 16 March 2002, A10.

Swidey, Neil. "All the President's Spin." *Boston Globe*, 16 June 2002, Lexis-Nexis.

Teepen, Tom. "Nixon's Dark Side Blots His Record." *Atlanta Journal-Constitution*, 26 April 1994, A11.

Weikel, Dan. "Nixon Library Losing Money but Operators Not Fearful." *Houston Chronicle*, 19 December 1993, Lexis-Nexis.

Weil, Martin, and Eleanor Randolph. "Richard M. Nixon, 37th President, Dies." *Washington Post*, 23 April 1994, A1, A20.

Weiser, Benjamin. "Nixon's Will Leaves Tapes to Family; Executors Told to Continue Battle against Public Access." *Washington Post*, 18 May 1994, C1.

Weiss, Philip. "Masters of the Universe Go to Camp: Inside the Bohemian Grove." *Spy*, November 1989, 59–76.

Werner, Erica. "Nixon Library Gets a Pardon: It Will Qualify as U.S. Archive." *Newark (NJ) Star-Ledger*, 3 February 2005, 21.

"What Was Said in Boise." *(Boise) Idaho Statesman*, 28 April 1994, A2.

Whitfield, Stephen J. "Richard Nixon as a Comic Figure." *American Quarterly* 37 (1985): 114–132.

Wicker, Tom. "An Indomitable Man, an Incurable Loneliness." *New York Times*, 24 April 1994, E1.

———. "Turning Points for a Man in the Running." *New York Times Review of Books*, 1 April 1962, 22.

Wills, Garry. "Why All of Us Should Read Nixon's Memoirs." *New York*, 3 July 1978, 58–59.

Witcover, Jules. "Richard Nixon Dies in Coma at 81." *Baltimore Sun*, 23 April 1994, A1, A6.

Worsham, James. "Nixon's Library Now Part of NARA: California Facility Will Hold Documents and Tapes from a Half-Century Career in Politics." *Prologue: Quarterly of the National Archives and Records Administration* 39, no. 3 (2007): 30–41.

NIXON IN FICTION, GRAPHIC NOVEL, AND LITERARY NONFICTION

Acker, Kathy. *Don Quixote*. New York: Grove Press, 1986.

Adams, Alice. *Superior Women*. New York: Alfred A. Knopf, 1984.

Baldwin, James. *The Fire Next Time*. 1963. 3rd ed., New York: Dell Laurel Edition, 1988.

———. *No Name in the Street*. New York: Dial, 1972.

Bishop, Michael. *The Secret Ascension: Philip K. Dick Is Dead, Alas*. New York: Tom Doherty Associates, 1987.

Boyle, T. Coraghessan. *Budding Prospects: A Pastoral*. New York: Viking Penguin, 1984.

Cahill, Michael. *A Nixon Man*. New York: St. Martin's, 1998.

Carson, Tom. *Gilligan's Wake*. New York: Picador, 2003.

Condon, Richard. *Death of a Politician*. 1978. Reprint, New York: Ballantine Books, 1979.

———. *The Vertical Smile*. New York: Dial, 1971.

Coover, Robert. *The Public Burning*. New York: Viking, 1977.

———. *Whatever Happened to Gloomy Gus of the Chicago Bears?* New York: Simon & Schuster, 1987.

Dick, Philip K. *Radio Free Albemuth*. 1985. Reprint, New York: Vintage Books, 1998.

Ehrlichman, John. *The China Card*. New York: Simon & Schuster, 1986.

———. *The Company*. New York: Simon & Schuster, 1976.

———. *The Whole Truth*. New York: Simon & Schuster, 1979.

Elkin, Stanley. *The Dick Gibson Show*. 1971. Reprint, New York: E. P. Dutton, 1983.

Fincke, Gary. "The Nazi on the Phone." In *For Keepsies*, 1–23. Minneapolis: Coffee House Press, 1993.

Groom, Winston. *Forrest Gump*. 1986. Reprint, New York: Pocket Books, 1994.

Heberlein, L. A. *Sixteen Reasons Why I Killed Richard M. Nixon*. Livingston, LA: Livingston Press, 1996.

Hellman, Lillian. *Scoundrel Time*. Boston: Little, Brown, 1976.

Jordan, June. *Affirmative Acts: Political Essays*. New York: Anchor Books, 1998.

Kelso, Megan. *Watergate Sue*. *New York Times Magazine*, 1 April–9 September 2007.

Korda, Michael. *The Immortals*. New York: Poseidon Press, 1992.

Kovic, Ron. *Born on the Fourth of July*. 1976. Reprint, New York: Pocket Books, 1977.

Lowy, Jonathan. *Elvis and Nixon*. New York: Crown, 2001.

Mailer, Norman. *Miami and the Siege of Chicago: An Informal History of the Republican and Democratic Conventions of 1968*. New York: World, 1968.

———. *St. George and the Godfather*. New York: New American Library, 1972.

Maxwell, Mark. *nixoncarver*. New York: Buzz Books of St. Martin's Press, 1998.

Moody, Rick. *The Ice Storm*. Boston: Little, Brown, 1994.

Novello, Don. *The Lazlo Letters*. Rev. ed. New York: Workman, 1992.

Oates, Joyce Carol. *You Must Remember This*. New York: E. P. Dutton, 1987.

O'Brien, Tim. *The Nuclear Age*. 1985. Reprint, New York: Dell, 1989.

Pynchon, Thomas. *Gravity's Rainbow*. New York: Viking, 1973.

———. *Vineland*. Boston: Little, Brown, 1990.

Reed, Ishmael. "D Hexorcism of Noxon D Awful." In *Amistad 1*, edited by John A. Williams and Charles F. Harris, 165–182. New York: Vintage Books, 1970.

Reilly, Gerald. "Nixon under the Bodhi Tree." *Gettysburg Review* 11 (1998): 493–500.

Resnick, Mike, ed. *Alternate Presidents*. New York: Tom Doherty Associates, 1992.

Rossetto, Louis. *Take-Over*. Secaucus, NJ: Lyle Stuart, 1974.

Roth, Philip. *American Pastoral*. 1997. Reprint, New York: Vintage International, 1998.

———. *I Married a Communist*. 1998. Reprint, New York: Vintage International, 1999.

———. *Our Gang: (Starring Tricky and His Friends)*. New York: Random House, 1971.

Sabrepen. *I Quit! A Fable from the Dead Issue Scroll*. Nashville: Thomas Nelson, 1974.

Sayles, John. *Union Dues*. Boston: Little, Brown, 1977.

Seelye, John. *Dirty Tricks: Or, Nick Noxin's Natural Nobility*. New York: W. W. Norton, 1974.

Spark, Muriel. *The Abbess of Crewe: A Modern Morality Tale*. New York: Viking, 1974.

Tauber, Peter. *The Last Best Hope*. New York: Harcourt Brace Jovanovich, 1977.

Thompson, Hunter S. *Fear and Loathing on the Campaign Trail '72*. 1973. Reprint, New York: Warner Books, 1983.

———. *The Great Shark Hunt: Strange Tales from a Strange Time*. 1979. Reprint, New York: Warner Books, 1982.

Vallance, Jeffrey. *My Life with Dick*. Los Angeles: BükAmerica, 2005.

Vonnegut, Kurt. *Jailbird*. New York: Delacorte Press/Seymour Lawrence, 1979.

———. *Wampeters, Foma & Granfalloons (Opinions)*. 1974. Reprint, New York: Dell, 1999.

Aldebaran. *Nixon and the Foxes of Watergate.* Revised and enlarged. Whitestone, NY: Published for the Walter Bagehot Research Council by Griffon House Publications, 1980.

Baraka, Amiri. "Afrikan Revolution." In *The LeRoi Jones/Amiri Baraka Reader,* edited by William J. Harris, 243–247. New York: Thunder's Mouth Press, 1991.

———. "When We'll Worship Jesus." In *The LeRoi Jones/Amiri Baraka Reader,* edited by William J. Harris, 251–254. New York: Thunder's Mouth Press, 1991.

Berryman, John. "Dream Song 105." In *The Dream Songs,* 122. 1969. Reprint, New York: Farrar, Straus, Giroux, 2007.

Ferlinghetti, Lawrence. *Ferlinghetti: Tyrannus Nix? Assassination Raga, Big Sur Sun Sutra, Moscow in the Wilderness.* Fantasy Records 7014, 1969.

———. *Tyrannus Nix?* New York: New Directions, 1969.

Hayes, Ann. *Witness: "How All Occasions . . .": A Poem for the American Bicentennial.* Derry, PA: Rook Press, 1977.

Kovacik, Karen. *Nixon and I.* Wick Poetry Chapbook 2, no. 4. Kent, OH: Kent State University Press, 1998.

Levine, Philip. "Gin." In *What Work Is,* 31–33. New York: Alfred A. Knopf, 1992.

Lowell, Robert. "George III." In *The Faber Book of Political Verse,* edited by Tom Paulin, 404–406. London: Faber & Faber, 1986.

Merriam, Eve. *The Nixon Poems.* New York: Atheneum, 1970.

Neruda, Pablo. *A Call for the Destruction of Nixon and Praise for the Chilean Revolution.* Translated by Teresa Anderson. Cambridge, MA: West End Press, 1980.

Olds, Sharon. "The Victims." In *The Dead and the Living,* 34. New York: A. A. Knopf, 1984.

Powell, Elizabeth. "Pledge." In *The Republic of Self,* 16. Kalamazoo, MI: New Issues Poetry Press, 2001.

Reed, Ishmael. "Poem Delivered before Assembly of Colored People Held at Glide Memorial Church, Oct. 4, 1973, and Called to Protest Recent Events in the Sovereign Republic of Chile." In *New and Collected Poems,* 136–138. New York: Atheneum, 1988.

———. "This Poetry Anthology I'm Reading." In *New and Collected Poems,* 74. New York: Atheneum, 1988.

Scott-Heron, Gil. "No Knock." In *Now and Then: The Poems of Gil Scott-Heron,* 60. Edinburgh: Payback Press, 2000. Reprint, n.p.: Canongate/Brouhaha Books, 2003.

Walker, Alice. "talking to my grandmother who died poor (while hearing Richard Nixon declare 'I am not a crook.')." In *Her Blue Body Everything We Know: Earthling Poems, 1965–1990, Complete,* 300–301. New York: Harcourt Brace Jovanovich, 1991.

Williams, C. K. "In the Heart of the Beast: May 1970: Cambodia, Kent State, Jackson State." In *Poems: 1963–1983*, 116–121. New York: Farrar, Straus, Giroux, 1988.

NIXON IN MUSIC AND COMEDY

American Ambulance. "Hey! Richard Nixon." *Stray*. Rustic Records, 2003.

Aquabox. "Dick Nixon and the Rover." *The Evolution Will Not Be Televised*. Aquabox 646158001010, 2001.

Bad Examples. "She Smiles Like Richard Nixon." *Bad Is Beautiful*. Waterdog Records WD9101, 1991.

Bowie, David. "Young Americans." *Young Americans* Special Edition. 1975. Virgin Records US, 2007.

Brown, Clarence "Gatemouth." "Please Mr. Nixon." *Gate's on the Heat*. Polygram Records 19730, 1975.

Carlin, George. *Occupation: Foole*. Little David Records LD 1005, 1973.

Chicago. "Dialogue (Part One)." *Chicago V*. Columbia KC 31102, 1972.

———. "Song for Richard and His Friends." *Chicago at Carnegie Hall*. Columbia C4X-30865, 1971.

The Clash. "I'm So Bored with the U.S.A." *The Clash*, Epic Records 367060, 1978.

Crosby, Stills, Nash, and Young. "Ohio." *Four Way Street*. Atlantic Records SD 2-902, 1971.

Depeche Mode. "Policy of Truth (Capitol Mix)." *Policy of Truth Compact Disc Maxi Single*. Sire Records Company 9 21534-2, 1990.

The Dick Nixons. *Paint the White House Black*. Triple X Records 51088-2, 1992.

Dylan, Bob/The Band. "It's Alright, Ma (I'm Only Bleeding.)" *Before the Flood*. Asylum Records AB 201, 1974.

Fleck, Bela, and New Grass Revival. "Nuns for Nixon." *Deviation*. 1984. Rounder, 1995.

Frye, David. *I Am the President*. Elektra Records EKS 75006, 1969.

———. *Radio Free Nixon*. Elektra Records EKS 74085, 1971.

———. *Richard Nixon: A Fantasy*. Buddah Records 1600, 1973.

———. *Richard Nixon: Superstar*. Buddah Records BDS 5097, n.d..

Funky Nixons. "(You Must Be) Stupid." *Still Not Crooks*. Berkeley/COMA Productions, 1996.

Hal 9000. "Nixon Recites Mao Tse-Tung." *Is She Better in Bed Than I Was*. The Orchard, 2000.

Hiatt, John. "Gone." *Crossing Muddy Waters*. Vanguard Records 79576-2, 2000.

Hicks, Dan, and His Hot Licks. "Moody Richard (The Innocent Bystander)." *Striking it Rich*. 1972. Fontana MCA Nashville, 1990.

Hitchcock, Robyn. "1974." *A Star for Bram*. PAF, 2003.

Horwitz, Bill. "If I Had A Friend Like Rosemary Woods." *Lies, Lies, Lies*. Aphex Records, 1975.

Joel, Billy. "We Didn't Start the Fire." *Storm Front*. Sony B00000DCHL, 1989.

John, Elton. "Postcards from Richard Nixon." *The Captain and the Kid*. Interscope Records, 2006.

Klein, Robert. *Mind over Matter*. 1974. Rhino Records. R2 70768, n.d.

Lennon, John, and the Plastic Ono Band (with the Flux Fiddlers). "Give Me Some Truth." *Imagine*. Capitol Records SW3379, 1971.

Lynyrd Skynyrd. "Sweet Home Alabama." *Second Helping*. 1974. MCA Records B000002P74, 1997.

Martin, Steve. *Let's Get Small*. Warner Brothers Records BSK 3090, 1977.

Mason, Jackie. *The World according to Me*. White Star DVD, 2003.

Meat Puppets. "Lost." *Meat Puppets II*. 1984. Ryko RCD 10467, 1999.

Oakenfold, Paul, featuring Hunter S. Thompson. "Nixon's Spirit." *Bunkka*. Maverick, 2002.

Rundman, Jonathan. "Meeting Nixon." *Recital*. Salt Lady Records SL3, 1997.

Sahl, Mort. *Mort Sahl at the Hungry i*. 1960. Laugh.com. LGH 1122, 2002.

———. *Sing a Song of Watergate*. GNP Crescendo Records GNPS-2070, 1973.

Scott-Heron, Gil. "H2Ogate Blues." *Winter in America*. 1975. Rumal-Gia Records. Manufactured and distributed by TVT Records, 1998.

———. "No Knock." *Free Will*. 1972. RCA, 1995.

———. "The Revolution Will Not Be Televised." *Pieces of a Man*. 1971. RCA, 1995.

Shaw, Thomas. "Richard Nixon's Welfare Blues." *Born in Texas*. Testament, 1995.

Taylor, James. "Line 'Em Up." *Hourglass*. Columbia CK 67912, 1997.

Wolf, Howlin'. "The Watergate Blues." *The Back Door Wolf*. 1973. MCA Special Products, 1995.

Wonder, Stevie. "He's Misstra Know It All." *Innervisions*. 1973. Tamla, Motown Record Corporation 9052MD, n.d.

———. "You Haven't Done Nothing." *Fulfillingness' First Finale*. 1974. Tamla, Universal/Motown Records Group, 2000.

Young, Neil. "The Campaigner." *Decade*. Reprise Records REP 64 037, 1976.

Zappa, Frank, and the Mothers of Invention. "Dickie's Such an Asshole." *You Can't Do That on Stage Anymore: Volume Three*. Zappa Records B0000009TP, 1995.

NIXON IN FILM

All the President's Men. Special Edition DVD. Directed by Alan J. Pakula. Screenplay by William Goldman. With Robert Redford, Dustin Hoffman, and Jason Robards. 1976. Warner Brothers Entertainment, 2004.

Apollo 13. VHS. Directed by Ron Howard. With Tom Hanks. MCA Universal Home
   Video, 1995.

The Assassination of Richard Nixon. DVD. Directed by Niels Mueller. With Sean
   Penn. 2004. New Line Home Entertainment, 2005.

Atomic Café. DVD. Directed by Jayne Loader, Kevin Rafferty, and Pierce Rafferty.
   1982. New Video Group, 2002.

Beavis and Butt-Head Do America. DVD. Directed by Mike Judge. Screenplay by
   Mike Judge and Joe Stillman. 1996. Paramount Home Entertainment, 2006.

The Best Man. VHS. Directed by Franklin Schaffner. Screenplay by Gore Vidal.
   With Henry Fonda and Cliff Robertson. 1964. MGM/UA Home Video, 1990.

Bob Roberts. VHS. Directed by Tim Robbins. With Tim Robbins and Gore Vidal.
   1992. Live Home Video, 1993.

Born Again. VHS. Directed by Irving Rapper. With Dean Jones. 1978. Crown Video, 1998.

Born on the Fourth of July. Special Edition DVD. Directed by Oliver Stone. With
   Tom Cruise. 1989. Universal Studios Home Video, 2004.

Broadcast News. DVD. Directed and screenplay by James L. Brooks. With William
   Hurt, Holly Hunter, and Albert Brooks. 1987. Twentieth Century Fox, 1999.

The Candidate. VHS. Directed by Michael Ritchie. With Robert Redford, Melyvn
   Douglas, and Peter Boyle. 1972. Warner Home Video, 1992.

Citizen Cohn. DVD. Directed by Frank Pierson. With James Woods. 1992. HBO
   Home Video, 2001.

Clear and Present Danger. DVD. Directed by Philip Noyce. With Harrison Ford,
   Willem Dafoe, and Anne Archer. 1994. Paramount Home Video, 1998.

Dick. DVD. Directed by Andrew Fleming. With Dan Hedaya, Kirsten Dunst, and
   Michelle Williams. 1999. Columbia TriStar Home Video, 1999.

Elvis Meets Nixon. VHS. Directed by Alan Arkush. With Rick Peters and Bob
   Gunton. 1997. Avalanche, 2002.

A Face in the Crowd. DVD. Directed by Elia Kazan. Screenplay by Budd Schulberg.
   With Andy Griffith. 1957. Warner Home Video, 2005.

Fear and Loathing in Las Vegas. DVD. Directed by Terry Gilliam. Screenplay by Terry
   Gilliam, Tony Grisoni, Tod Davies, and Alex Cox. With Johnny Depp. 1998.
   Universal Home Video. 1998.

The Final Days. VHS. Directed by Richard Pearce. Written by Hugh Whitemore.
   With Lane Smith. 1989. Republic Pictures, Republic Entertainment, 1996.

Forrest Gump. Special Collector's Edition DVD. Directed by Robert Zemeckis.
   Screenplay by Eric Roth. Based on the novel by Winston Groom. With Tom
   Hanks. 1994. Paramount Pictures, 2001.

Good Morning, Vietnam. VHS. Directed by Barry Levinson. With Robin Williams.
   1987. Touchstone Home Video, 1987.

Hearts and Minds. DVD. Directed by Peter Davis. 1974. Criterion Collection, 2002.

Hiding Out. DVD. Directed by Bob Giraldi. With Jon Cryer, Annabeth Gish, and Keith Coogan. 1987. Anchor Bay Entertainment, 2001.

The Ice Storm. DVD. Directed by Ang Lee. With Kevin Kline, Joan Allen, and Sigourney Weaver. 1997. Twentieth Century Fox Home Entertainment, 2001.

In the Line of Fire. Special Edition DVD. Directed by Wolfgang Petersen. With Clint Eastwood, Rene Russo, and John Malkovich. 1993. Columbia TriStar, 2001.

The In-Laws. VHS. Directed by Arthur Hiller. Screenplay by Andrew Bergman. With Peter Falk and Alan Arkin. 1979. Warner Home Video, 1995.

Joe. VHS. Directed by John G. Avildsen. Screenplay by Norman Wexler. With Peter Boyle, Dennis Patrick, and Susan Sarandon. 1970. MGM Video and DVD, 2002.

Kissinger and Nixon. VHS. Directed by Daniel Petrie. Screenplay by Lionel Chetwynd. With Beau Bridges and Ron Silver. 1995. Turner Broadcasting System, 1996.

Men at Work. DVD. Directed and screenplay by Emilio Estevez. With Emilio Estevez and Charlie Sheen. 1990. MGM Video and DVD, 2002.

Millhouse: A White Comedy. VHS. Directed by Emile deAntonio. 1971. MPI Home Video, n.d.

Misery. DVD. Directed by Rob Reiner. Screenplay by William Goldman. With James Caan and Kathy Bates. 1990. MGM Video and DVD, 2000.

Missing. DVD. Directed by Costa-Gavras. With Jack Lemmon and Sissy Spacek. 1982. Universal Studios Home Entertainment, 2004.

Monty Python and the Holy Grail. Special Edition DVD. Directed by Terry Jones and Terry Gilliam. Writers and performers, Graham Chapman, John Cleese, Terry Gilliam, Eric Idle, Terry Jones, and Michael Palin. 1975. Sony Pictures Home Entertainment, 2001.

Moonlight Mile. DVD. Directed and screenplay by Brad Silberling. With Susan Sarandon, Dustin Hoffman, and Jake Gyllenhaal. 2002. Buena Vista Home Entertainment, 2003.

Mrs. Doubtfire. DVD. Directed by Chris Columbus. With Robin Williams. 1993. Twentieth Century Fox, 2006.

My Girl. DVD. Directed by Howard Zieff. Screenplay by Laurice Elehwany. 1991. Columbia TriStar Home Video, 1998.

My Girl 2. DVD. Directed by Howard Zieff. Screenplay by Janet Kovalcik. 1994. Sony Pictures, 2002.

Naked Gun 33 1/3: The Final Insult. DVD. Directed by Peter Segal. With Leslie Nielsen and Priscilla Presley. 1994. Paramount Home Video, 2000.

Nasty Habits. DVD. Directed by Michael Lindsay-Hogg. With Glenda Jackson. 1977. Jef Films, 2002.

National Lampoon's Animal House. DVD. Directed by John Landis. With John Belushi. 1978. Universal Studios, 2003.

1969. DVD. Directed and screenplay by Ernest Thompson. With Kiefer Sutherland, Winona Ryder, and Robert Downey Jr. 1988. MGM Video and DVD, 2002.

Nixon. Collector's Edition Series DVD. Directed by Oliver Stone. With Anthony Hopkins. 1995. Hollywood Pictures Home Video, n.d.

Nixon: An Oliver Stone Film. Screenplay by Stephen J. Rivele, Christopher Wilkinson, and Oliver Stone. New York: Hyperion, 1995.

Nixon: The American Experience. The Presidents Collection. VHS. Executive producer, Elizabeth Deane. 1990. PBS Home Video, 1997.

The Parallax View. DVD. Directed by Alan J. Pakula. With Warren Beatty. 1974. Paramount Pictures, 1999.

The Pelican Brief. DVD. Directed and screenplay by Alan J. Pakula. With Denzel Washington and Julia Roberts. 1993. Warner Home Video, 1997.

Point Break. DVD. Directed by Kathryn Bigelow. 1991. Twentieth Century Fox, 2006.

Quiz Show. DVD. Directed by Robert Redford. With Ralph Fiennes, Rob Morrow, John Tuturro, and Paul Scofield. 1994. Hollywood Pictures, 1999.

Running Mates. DVD. Directed by Michael Lindsay-Hogg. With Diane Keaton and Ed Harris. 1992. HBO Home Video, 2006.

Secret Honor. VHS. Directed by Robert Altman. Screenplay by Donald Freed and Arnold M. Stone. With Philip Baker Hall. 1984. Vestron Video, 1987. DVD, Criterion Collection, n.d.

Shampoo. DVD. Directed by Hal Ashby. Screenplay by Robert Towne and Warren Beatty. With Warren Beatty, Goldie Hawn, and Julie Christie. 1975. Columbia TriStar, 2003.

Sleeper. DVD. Directed by Woody Allen. Screenplay by Woody Allen and Marshall Brickman. With Woody Allen and Diane Keaton. 1973. MGM/UA Home Video, 2000.

The U.S. vs. John Lennon. DVD. Directed by David Leaf and John Scheinfeld. 2006. Lions Gate Entertainment, 2006.

Where the Buffalo Roam. VHS. Directed by Art Linson. With Bill Murray. 1980. MCA Home Video, 1986.

Wired. VHS. Directed by Larry Peerce. With Michael Chiklis. 1989. Avid Home Entertainment, 1991.

Woodstock. VHS. Directed by Michael Wadleigh. 1970. Warner Home Video, 1987.

NIXON ON TELEVISION

All in the Family: The Complete First Season. "Writing the President." Disc 1. DVD. Directed by John Rich. Written by Paul Harrison, Lennie Weinrib, and Norman Lear. Story by

Lee Erwin and Fred Freiberger. With Carroll O'Connor, Jean Stapleton, Rob Reiner, Sally Struthers. 19 January 1971. Columbia TriStar Home Entertainment, 2002.

All in the Family: The Complete Second Season. "Archie in the Lock-Up." Disc 1. DVD. Directed by John Rich. Written by Paul Wayne, Michael Ross, and Bernie West. 2 October 1971. Columbia TriStar Home Entertainment, 2003.

———. "Cousin Maude's Visit." Disc 2. DVD. Directed by John Rich. Written by Philip Mishkin, Michael Ross, and Bernie West. 11 December 1971. Columbia TriStar Home Entertainment, 2003.

———. "The Man in the Street." Disc 2. DVD. Directed by John Rich. Written by Don Nicholl, Paul Harrison, and Lennie Weinrib. Story by Paul Harrison and Lennie Weinrib. 4 December 1971. Columbia TriStar Home Entertainment, 2003.

All in the Family: The Complete Third Season. "Archie and the Editorial." Disc 1. DVD. Directed by Norman Campbell. Written by George Bloom and Don Nicholl. 16 September 1972. Columbia TriStar Home Entertainment, 2004.

———. "Archie Learns His Lesson." Disc 3. DVD. Directed by John Rich and Bob LaHendro. Written by Michael Ross and Bernie West. Story by John Christopher Strong III and Michael R. Stein. 10 March 1973. Columbia TriStar Home Entertainment, 2004.

———. "Archie's Fraud." Disc 1. DVD. Directed by Norman Campbell. Written by Michael Ross and Bernie West. 23 September 1972. Columbia TriStar Home Entertainment, 2004.

———. "Flashback: Mike and Gloria's Wedding, Part 1." Disc 2. DVD. Directed by John Rich and Bob LaHendro. Written by Rob Reiner and Philip Mishkin. 11 November 1972. Columbia TriStar Home Entertainment, 2004.

———. "Gloria, the Victim." Disc 3. DVD. Directed by John Rich and Bob LaHendro. Written by Austin and Irma Kalish and Don Nicholl. 17 March 1973. Columbia TriStar Home Entertainment, 2004.

———. "Gloria's Riddle." Disc 1. DVD. Directed by Bob LaHendro and Robert H. Livingston. Written by Don Nicholl. 7 October 1972. Columbia TriStar Home Entertainment, 2004.

———. "The Hot Watch." Disc 3. DVD. Directed by John Rich and Bob LaHendro. Written by Sam Locke and Olga Vallance. 17 February 1973. Columbia TriStar Home Entertainment, 2004.

———. "Mike Comes into Money." Disc 2. DVD. Directed by John Rich. Written by Michael Ross and Bernie West. 4 November 1972. Columbia TriStar Home Entertainment, 2004.

All in the Family: The Complete Fourth Season. "Archie and the Computer." Disc 1. DVD. Directed by John Rich and Bob LaHendro. Written by Lloyd Turner, Gordon Mitchell, and Don Nicholl. 27 October 1973. Sony Pictures Home Entertainment, 2005.

————. "Archie in the Cellar." Disc 2. DVD. Directed by John Rich and Bob LaHendro. Written by Don Nicholl. 17 November 1973. Sony Pictures Home Entertainment, 2005.

————. "Edith Finds an Old Man." Disc 1. DVD. Directed by John Rich and Bob LaHendro. Written by Michael Ross and Bernie West. Story by Susan Harris. 29 September 1973. Sony Pictures Home Entertainment, 2005.

————. "Et Tu, Archie." Disc 3. DVD. Directed by John Rich and Bob LaHendro. Written by Mickey Rose and Lila Garrett. 26 January 1974. Sony Pictures Home Entertainment, 2005.

————. "Henry's Farewell." Disc 1. DVD. Directed by John Rich and Bob LaHendro. Written by Don Nicholl. 20 October 1973. Sony Pictures Home Entertainment, 2005.

————. "The Taxi Caper." Disc 3. DVD. Directed by John Rich and Bob LaHendro. Written by Dennis Klein. 8 December 1973. Sony Pictures Home Entertainment, 2005.

————. "We're Having a Heatwave." Disc 1. DVD. Directed by John Rich and Bob LaHendro. Written by Don Nicholl. 15 September 1973. Sony Pictures Home Entertainment, 2005.

Blind Ambition. Directed by George Schaefer. Written by Taylor Branch, John Dean, Maureen Dean, and Stanley R. Greenberg. With Martin Sheen and Rip Torn. CBS, 20–23 May 1979.

Concealed Enemies. Directed by Jeff Bleckner. Written by Hugh Whitemore. With Peter Riegert, Edward Herrmann, and John Harkins. PBS, 1–3 April 1984.

The Critic: The Complete Series. "All the Duke's Men." Disc 3. DVD. Directed by Chuck Sheetz. Written by Patric M. Verrone. With Jon Lovitz. 23 April 1995. Columbia TriStar Home Entertainment, 2004.

————. "Dial 'M' for Mother." Disc 1. DVD. Directed by Brett Haaland. Written by Mike Reiss and Al Jean. Disc 1. DVD. 9 February 1994. Columbia TriStar Home Entertainment, 2004.

————. "Frankie and Ellie Get Lost." Disc 3. DVD. Directed by David Cutler. Written by Richard Doctorow. Story by Judd Apatow. 7 May, 1995. Columbia TriStar Home Entertainment, 2004.

————. "Marty's First Date." Disc 1. DVD. Directed by Alan Smart. Written by Tom Gammill and Max Pross. 2 February 1994. Columbia TriStar Home Entertainment, 2004.

D. C. Follies. Best of the D.C. Follies. VHS. Cannon Video, 1989.

Family Ties. "Beauty and the Bank." Directed by Asaad Kelada. Written by Steven J. Curwick. With Michael J. Fox, Meredith Baxter Birney, Michael Gross, Justine Bateman, and Tina Yothers. NBC, 30 October 1986.

———. "Cry Baby." Directed by Sam Weisman. Written by Bruce Helford and Bruce David. NBC, 7 February 1985.

———. "How Do You Sleep?" Directed by John Pasquin. Written by Marc Lawrence. NBC, 12 December 1985.

———. "Paper Chase." Directed by Sam Weisman. Written by Susan Borowitz. NBC, 8 May 1986.

———. "Til Her Daddy Takes Her T-Bird Away." Directed and written by Matthew Diamond. NBC, 26 February 1989.

———. "Where's Poppa?" Directed by Will Mackenzie. Written by Marc Lawrence and Susan Borowitz. NBC, 16 January 1986.

Family Ties: The Complete First Season. "A Christmas Story." Disc 2. DVD. Directed by Will Mackenzie. Written by Joanne Pagliano. 15 December 1982. CBS DVD and Paramount Home Entertainment, 2007.

———. "Have Gun, Will Unravel." Disc 2. DVD. Directed by Alan Bergmann. Written by Ruth Bennett. 8 December 1982. CBS DVD and Paramount Home Entertainment, 2007.

———. "I Got to Be Ming." Disc 4. DVD. Directed by Sam Weisman. Written by Douglas Wyman. 23 February 1983. CBS DVD and Paramount Home Entertainment, 2007.

———. "I Never Killed for My Father." Disc 1. DVD. Directed by Dick Martin. Written by Kimberly Hill. 3 November 1982. CBS DVD and Paramount Home Entertainment, 2007.

Family Ties: The Complete Second Season. "Speed Trap." Disc 1. DVD. Directed by Sam Weisman. Written by Michael J. Weithorn. 9 November 1983. CBS DVD and Paramount Home Entertainment, 2007.

Futurama: Volume One. "A Fishful of Dollars." Disc 2. DVD. Directed by Ron Hughart and Gregg Vanzo. Written by Patric M. Verrone. 27 April 1999. Twentieth Century Fox Home Entertainment, 2003.

———. "Space Pilot 3000." Disc 1. DVD. Directed by Rich Moore and Greg Vanzo. Written by Matt Groening and David X. Cohen. 28 March 1999. Twentieth Century Fox Home Entertainment, 2003.

———. "The Series Has Landed." Disc 1. DVD. Directed by Peter Avanzino. Written by Ken Keeler. 28 March 1999. Twentieth Century Fox Home Entertainment, 2003.

Futurama: Volume Two. "A Head in the Polls." Disc 1. DVD. Directed by Bret Haaland. Written by J. Stewart Burns. 12 December 1999. Twentieth Century Fox Home Entertainment, 2003.

———. "War Is the H-Word." Disc 4. DVD. Directed by Ron Hughart. Written by Eric Horsted. 26 November 2000. Twentieth Century Fox Home Entertainment, 2003.

Futurama: Volume Three. "Insane in the Mainframe." Disc 2. DVD. Directed by Peter Avanzino. Written by Bill Odenkirk. 8 April 2001. Twentieth Century Fox Home Entertainment, 2003.

Futurama: Volume Four. "A Taste of Freedom." Disc 1. DVD. Directed by James Purdum. Written by Eric Horsted. 22 December 2002. Twentieth Century Fox Home Entertainment, 2004.

————. "Crimes of the Hot." Disc 2. DVD. Directed by Peter Avanzino. Written by Aaron Ehasz. 10 November 2002. Twentieth Century Fox Home Entertainment, 2004.

————. "The Devil's Hands Are Idle Playthings." Disc 4. DVD. Directed by Rich Moore. Written by Ken Keeler. 10 August 2003. Twentieth Century Fox Home Entertainment, 2004.

Futurama: Bender's Big Score. DVD. Twentieth Century Fox Home Entertainment, 2007.

Good Times: The Complete First Season. "Black Jesus." Disc 1. DVD. Directed by John Rich and Bob LaHendro. Written by John Donley and Kurt Taylor. With Esther Rolle, John Amos, and Jimmie Walker. 15 February 1974. Columbia TriStar Home Entertainment, 2003.

————. "Getting Up the Rent." Disc 1. DVD. Directed by Donald McKayle and Perry Rosemond. Written by Eric Monte. 22 February 1974. Columbia TriStar Home Entertainment, 2003.

————. "Michael Gets Suspended." Disc. 1. DVD. Directed by Herbert Kenwith. Written by Eric Monte. 8 March 1974. Columbia TriStar Home Entertainment, 2003.

Kent State. Directed by James Goldstone. NBC, 8 February 1981.

"Larry King and Julie Nixon Eisenhower Tour the Richard Nixon Library and Birthplace." VHS. The Richard Nixon Library and Birthplace and Cable News Network LP, LLLP, An AOL Time Warner Company, 2001.

Laugh-In. "Episode #15." *The Best of Rowan and Martin's Laugh-In.* Disc 2. DVD. Produced by George Schlatter. With Dan Rowan, Dick Martin, and Richard Nixon. 15 September 1968. Rhino Home Video/SFM Entertainment, 2003.

Law & Order: Special Victims Unit, The First Year. "Limitations." Disc 4. DVD. Directed by Constantine Makris. Written by Michael R. Perry. With Christopher Meloni and Mariska Hargitay. 11 February 2000. Universal, 2002.

Maude: The Complete First Season. "Doctor, Doctor." Disc 1. DVD. Directed by Bill Hobin. Written by Budd Grossman. With Beatrice Arthur and Bill Macy. 19 September 1972. Sony Pictures Home Entertainment, 2007.

————. "Flashback." Disc 1. DVD. Directed by Bill Hobin. Written by Alan J. Levitt. 31 October 1972. Sony Pictures Home Entertainment, 2007.

Murphy Brown. "Angst for the Memories." Directed by Peter Bonerz. Written by
    Rob Bragin. With Candace Bergen. CBS, 27 September 1993.
———. "Bummer of 42." Directed by Barnet Kellman. Written by Diane English
    and Tom Palmer. CBS, 26 November 1990.
———. "Devil with the Blue Dress On." Directed by Barnet Kellman. Written by
    Korby Siamis. CBS, 21 November 1988.
———. "Frank's Appendectomy." Directed by Barnet Kellman. Written by Tom
    Seeley and Norm Gunzenhauser. CBS, 9 April 1990.
———. "I Would Have Danced All Night." Directed by Barnet Kellman. Written by
    Steven Peterman and Gary Dontzig. CBS, 9 January 1989.
———. "Murphy's Pony." Directed by Barnet Kellman. Written by Diane English.
    CBS, 11 December 1988.
———. "Signed, Sealed, Delivered." Directed by Barnet Kellman. Written by Diane
    English. CBS, 5 December 1988.
NewsRadio: The Complete Third Season. "Awards Show." Disc 1. DVD. Directed by
    Tom Cherones. Written by Drake Sather. 6 November 1996. Sony Pictures
    Home Entertainment, 2006.
The Nixon Interviews with David Frost: The Collector's Edition. Produced by John Birt
    and David Frost. Directed by Jorn Winthur. 1977. MCA Universal, 1992.
"Nixon's Boyhood Home: A Personal Tour with Julie Nixon Eisenhower and Huell
    Howser." VHS. *California's Gold*, Show #2007, n.d.
The Pentagon Papers. Directed by Rod Holcomb. With James Spader. fX Network, 9
    March 2003.
Saturday Night Live. "Ask President Carter." Directed by Dave Wilson. With Dan
    Ackroyd and Bill Murray. NBC, 12 March 1977.
———. "Blonde Ambition." Directed by Dave Wilson. With Dan Ackroyd and Dick
    Cavett. NBC, 13 November 1976.
———. "Death to Watergate." Directed by Dave Wilson. With Christopher Lee,
    Dan Ackroyd, John Belushi, and Jane Curtin. NBC, 25 March 1978.
———. "The Final Days." Directed by Dave Wilson. With Dan Ackroyd, Madeline Kahn,
    Chevy Chase, Gilda Radner, Garret Morris, and John Belushi. NBC, 8 May 1976.
———. "The Huston Plan." Directed by Dave Wilson. With Dan Ackroyd and
    Broderick Crawford. NBC, 19 March 1977.
———. "It's a Wonderful Newt." With John Turturro and Chris Farley. NBC, 19
    November 1994.
———. "The New Dick." Directed by Dave Wilson. With Dan Ackroyd. NBC, 2
    December 1978.
———. "The Nixon Interviews." Directed by Dave Wilson. With Dan Ackroyd, Eric
    Idle, Gilda Radner, and Jane Curtin. NBC, 23 April 1977.

———. "The Nixon Mansion." With Tony Rosato and Robert Conrad. NBC, 23
January 1982.

———. "Nixon's Book." Directed by Dave Wilson. With Dan Ackroyd. NBC, 20
May 1978.

———. "Remembrance of Things Past." Directed by Dave Wilson. With Dan
Ackroyd and Jane Curtin. NBC, 14 February 1976.

———. "Saturday TV Funhouse." "Fun with Real Audio." "Presidential Address
Outtakes." Directed by J. J. Sedelmaier. Written by Robert Smigel. NBC, 26
September 1998.

———. "Saturday TV Funhouse." "The X-Presidents." NBC, 12 April 1997.

———. "60 Minutes." With Joe Piscopo and Tim Kazurinsky. NBC, 14 April 1984.

———. "Watergate Was a Joke." Directed by Dave Wilson. With Dan Ackroyd and
Buck Henry. NBC, 26 May 1979.

Seinfeld: Season 7. "The Cadillac, Parts 1 and 2." Disc 3. DVD. Directed by Andy
Ackerman. Written by Larry David and Jerry Seinfeld. 25 January and 8
February 1996. Sony Pictures Home Entertainment, 2006.

Shining Time Station. "The Mayor Runs for Re-election." Directed by Wayne Moss.
Written by Ellis Weiner. 1993. Thirteen/WNET. Produced in association with
YTV Canada, 24 April 1994.

The Simpsons. "Worst Episode Ever." Directed by Matthew Nastuk. Written by Larry
Doyle. With Dan Castellaneta, Julie Kavner, Yeardley Smith, Nancy Cartwright,
Hank Azaria, and Harry Shearer. Fox, 4 February 2001.

———. "The Dad Who Knew Too Little." Directed by Mark Kirkland. Written by
Matt Selman. Fox, 12 January 2003.

The Simpsons: The Complete First Season. "Simpsons Roasting on an Open
Fire." Disc 1. DVD. Directed by David Silberman. Written by Mimi Pond. 17
December 1989. Twentieth Century Fox Home Entertainment, 2001.

The Simpsons: The Complete Third Season. "Mr. Lisa Goes to Washington." Disc 1.
DVD. Directed by Wes Archer. Written by George Meyer. 26 September 1991.
Twentieth Century Fox Home Entertainment, 2003.

———. "Burns Verkaufen der Kraftwerk." Disc 2. DVD. Directed by Mark
Kirkland. Written by Jon Vitti. 5 December 1991. Twentieth Century Fox Home
Entertainment, 2003.

———. "Dog of Death." Disc 3. DVD. Directed by Jim Reardon. Written by John
Swartzwelder. 12 March 1992. Twentieth Century Fox Home Entertainment,
2003.

The Simpsons: The Complete Fourth Season. "Duffless." Disc 3. DVD. Directed by Jim
Reardon. Written by David M. Stern. 18 February 1993. Twentieth Century Fox
Home Entertainment, 2004.

———. "Whacking Day." Disc 4. DVD. Directed by Jeff Lynch. Written by John Swartzwelder. 29 April 1993. Twentieth Century Fox Home Entertainment, 2004.

The Simpsons: The Complete Fifth Season. "Homer Goes to College." Disc 1. DVD. Directed by Jim Reardon. Written by Conan O'Brien. 14 October 1993. Twentieth Century Fox Home Entertainment, 2004.

———. "Rosebud." Disc 1. DVD. Directed by Wes Archer. Written by John Swartzwelder. 21 October 1993. Twentieth Century Fox Home Entertainment, 2004.

———. "Treehouse of Horror IV." Disc 1. DVD. Directed by David "Dry Bones" Silberman. 28 October 1993. Twentieth Century Fox Home Entertainment, 2004.

———. "Deep Space Homer." Disc 3. DVD. Directed by Carlos Baeza. Written by David Mirkin. 24 February 1994. Twentieth Century Fox Home Entertainment, 2004.

———. "The Boy Who Knew Too Much." Disc 3. DVD. Directed by Jeffrey Lynch. Written by John Swartzwelder. 4 May 1994. Twentieth Century Fox Home Entertainment, 2004.

The Simpsons: The Complete Seventh Season. "Who Shot Mr. Burns? (Part Two)." Disc 1. DVD. Directed by Wes Archer. Written by Bill Oakley and Josh Weinstein. 17 September 1995. Twentieth Century Fox Home Entertainment, 2005.

———. "Scenes in the Class Struggle in Springfield." Disc 3. DVD. Directed by Susie Dietter. Written by Jennifer Crittenden. 4 February 1996. Twentieth Century Fox Home Entertainment, 2005.

The Simpsons: The Complete Eighth Season. "Homer's Enemy." Disc 4. DVD. Directed by Jim Reardon. Written by John Swartzwelder. 4 May 1997. Twentieth Century Fox Home Entertainment, 2006.

That '70s Show: Season One. "Eric's Burger Job." Disc 1. DVD. Directed by David Trainer. Written by Mark Brazill. With Topher Grace, Mila Kunis, Ashton Kutcher, Danny Masterson, Laura Prepon, Wilmer Valderrama, Debra Jo Rupp, and Kurtwood Smith. 20 September 1998. Twentieth Century Fox Home Entertainment, 2004.

———. "Punk Chick." Disc 4. DVD. Directed by David Trainer. Written by David Schiff. 21 June 1999. Twentieth Century Fox Home Entertainment, 2004.

———. "Streaking." Disc 1. DVD. Directed by David Trainer. Written by Eric Gilliland. 6 September 1998. Twentieth Century Fox Home Entertainment, 2004.

———. "Thanksgiving." Disc 2. DVD. Directed by David Trainer. Written by Jeff Filgo and Jackie Behan. 22 November 1998. Twentieth Century Fox Home Entertainment, 2004.

24: Season Four. 9 episodes: "10:00 PM-11:00 PM"–"6:00 AM-7:00 AM." Discs
4–6. DVD. Directed by Bryan Spicer, Jon Cassar, and Kevin Hooks. With Kiefer
Sutherland and Greg Itzin. 4 April–23 May 2005. Twentieth Century Fox Home
Entertainment, 2005.

24: Season Five. 24 episodes. "7:00 AM-8:00 AM"–"6:00 AM-7:00 AM." Discs 1–6.
DVD. Directed by Jon Cassar, Brad Turner, Dwight Little, Tim Iacofano, and
Sam Montgomery. With Kiefer Sutherland and Greg Itzin. 15 January–22 May
2006. Twentieth Century Fox Home Entertainment, 2006.

24: Season Six. 4 episodes. "3:00 PM-4:00 PM–6:00 PM-7:00 PM." Discs 3–4.
DVD. Directed by Brad Turner, Tim Iacofano, and Jon Cassar. With Kiefer
Sutherland and Greg Itzin. 19 February–12 March 2007. Twentieth Century Fox
Home Entertainment, 2007.

Washington: Behind Closed Doors. Directed by Gary Nelson. With Jason Robards.
ABC, 6–12 September 1977.

Will. Directed by Robert Lieberman. Written by John Abatemarco. With Robert
Conrad. NBC, 10 January 1982.

WKRP in Cincinnati. "Carlson for President." Directed by Will Mackenzie. Written
by Jim Paddock. With Gordon Jump, Gary Sandy, Loni Anderson, Frank Bonner,
Howard Hesseman, Tim Reid, Richard Sanders, and Jan Smithers. CBS, 5
November 1979.

———. "Hold Up." Directed by Asaad Kelada. Written by Tom Chehak. CBS, 16
October 1978.

———. "The Americanization of Ivan." Directed by Hugh Wilson. Written by Dan
Guntzelman and Steve Marshall. Story by Hugh Wilson. CBS, 28 January 1980.

———. "Filthy Pictures, Part One and Part Two." Directed by Rod Daniel. Written
by Steve Marshall and Dan Guntzelman. Story by Hugh Wilson. CBS, 18
February, 3 March 1980.

———. "Circumstantial Evidence." Directed by Frank Bonner. Written by Tim Reid
and Peter Torokvei. CBS, 24 February 1982.

The X-Files. "Deep Throat." Directed by Daniel Sackheim. Written by Chris Carter. With
David Duchovny, Gillian Anderson, and Jerry Hardin. Fox, 17 September 1993.

———. "E.B.E." Directed by William Graham. Written by Glen Morgan and James
Wong. Fox, 18 February 1994.

———. "The Erlenmeyer Flask." Directed by R. W. Goodwin. Written by Chris
Carter. Fox, 13 May 1994.

———. "Eve." Directed by Fred Gerber. Written by Kenneth Bilber and Chris
Brancato. Fox, 10 December 1993.

———. "Fallen Angel." Directed by Larry Shaw. Written by Alex Gansa and
Howard Gordon. Fox, 19 November 1993.

———. "Ghost in the Machine." Directed by Jerrold Freedman. Written by Alex Gansa and Howard Gordon. Fox, 29 October 1993.

———. "Young at Heart." Directed by Michael Lange. Written by Scott Kaufer and Chris Carter. Fox, 11 February 1994.

NIXON IN THEATER AND OPERA

Adams, John. *Nixon in China: An Opera in Three Acts.* Libretto by Alice Goodman. Orchestra of St. Luke's, conducted by Edo De Waart. Elektra/Nonesuch Digital 1979177-1.

Bosakowski, Phil. *Nixon Apologizes to the Nation.* In *Plays by Phil Bosakowski*, 89–144. New York: Broadway Play Publishing, 2000.

Bramwell, Dana G. *The Tragedy of King Richard: Shakespearean Watergate.* Salina, KS: Survey Publishers, 1974.

Edgar, David. *Dick Deterred.* New York: Monthly Review Press, 1974.

Freed, Donald, and Arnold M. Stone. *Secret Honor, the Last Testament of Richard M. Nixon: A Political Myth.* In *New Plays U.S.A. 2*, edited by Elizabeth Osborn and Gillian Richards, 1–31. New York: Theatre Communications Group, 1984.

Gray, Spalding. *Swimming to Cambodia.* New York: Theatre Communications Group, 1985.

Lees, Russell. *Nixon's Nixon.* New York: Dramatists Play Service, 1996.

Morgan, Peter. *Frost/Nixon.* London: Faber and Faber, 2006.

Myers, Robert J. *The Tragedy of Richard II.* Washington, DC: Acropolis Books, 1973.

Reddin, Keith. *Rum and Coke.* New York: Broadway Play Publishers, 1986.

Vidal, Gore. *The Best Man.* In *The Essential Gore Vidal*, edited by Fred Kaplan, 57–177. New York: Random House, 1999.

———. *An Evening with Richard Nixon.* New York: Random House, 1972.

Yale Repertory Theatre. *Watergate Classics.* In *yale/theatre* 5 (Special Issue, Winter 1974).

INDEX

Williams, Raymond, 167

Wills, Garry, 35, 118, 234, 246n12

Wilson, Pete, 43

Wilson, Sloan, 83

Wilson, Woodrow, 33

Winthrop, John, 32, 75

Witcover, Jules, 85, 205

With Nixon (Price), 60, 63

Witness (Chambers), 8, 34, 38, 244n47

WKRP in Cincinnati (TV show), 134, 147, 148

Wolf, Naomi, 167

Wolfowitz, Paul, 199

Women's International Terrorist Conspiracy from Hell (WITCH), 165

women's movement, 44, 165–67. *See also* abortion issues

Woodstock Music and Art Fair, 91, 92

Woodward, Bob, 62, 63, 116, 130, 141–42, 148, 223

Wright, Ernest, 4

Yom Kippur crisis, 60

Yorba Linda, Cal., 2, 182–83, 197–98

Young, Neil, 214

Zappa, Frank, 133

Zinga, Zinga, Za! (Fischetti), 12